Open Borders

SUNY series in Contemporary Italian Philosophy

Silvia Benso and Brian Schroeder, editors

Open Borders

Encounters between Italian Philosophy and Continental Thought

Edited by

Silvia Benso and Antonio Calcagno

Cover image: Royal Collection Trust / © Her Majesty Queen Elizabeth II 2020.

Published by State University of New York Press, Albany

© 2021 State University of New York

All rights reserved

Printed in the United States of America

No part of this book may be used or reproduced in any manner whatsoever without written permission. No part of this book may be stored in a retrieval system or transmitted in any form or by any means including electronic, electrostatic, magnetic tape, mechanical, photocopying, recording, or otherwise without the prior permission in writing of the publisher.

For information, contact State University of New York Press, Albany, NY
www.sunypress.edu

Library of Congress Cataloging-in-Publication Data

Names: Benso, Silvia, editor. | Calcagno, Antonio, 1969– editor.
Title: Open borders : encounters between Italian philosophy and continental thought / Silvia Benso and Antonio Calcagno.
Description: Albany : State University of New York Press, 2021. | Series: SUNY series in contemporary Italian philosophy | Includes bibliographical references and index.
Identifiers: LCCN 2020019391 | ISBN 9781438482194 (hardcover : alk. paper) | ISBN 9781438482200 (pbk. : alk. paper) | ISBN 9781438482217 (ebook)
Subjects: LCSH: Philosophy, Italian. | Continental philosophy.
Classification: LCC B3551 .O64 2021 | DDC 195—dc23
LC record available at https://lccn.loc.gov/2020019391

10 9 8 7 6 5 4 3 2 1

Contents

Acknowledgments ix

Open Borders: Introduction 1
   Silvia Benso and Antonio Calcagno

Part One: Being, Beings, Nothingness

1. Luigi Pareyson's Ontology of Freedom: Encounters with
Martin Heidegger and F. W. J. Schelling 21
   Silvia Benso

2. Emanuele Severino versus Western Nihilism (A Guide for
the Perplexed) 45
   Alessandro Carrera

3. Increase or *Kenosis*: Hermeneutic Ontology between
Hans-Georg Gadamer and Gianni Vattimo 65
   Gaetano Chiurazzi

Part Two: Temporality, Subjectivities, Performances

4. Lingering Gifts of Time: Ugo Perone, Edith Stein, and
Martin Heidegger's Philosophical Legacy 83
   Antonio Calcagno

5. Failing to Imagine the Lives of Others: Remo Bodei and
Jean-Luc Nancy on Citizenship and Sancho Panza 99
   Alexander U. Bertland

6. A Political Gesture: The Performance of Carlo Sini and
   Michel Foucault   117
   Enrico Redaelli

Part Three: Thinking, Estrangement, Ideologies

7. What Does It Mean to Think? Antonio Gramsci and
   Gilles Deleuze   137
   Richard A. Lee Jr.

8. Herbert Marcuse in Italy   159
   Michael E. Gardiner

9. Engaging Contemporary Ideology with Mario Perniola,
   Slavoj Žižek, and Robert Pfaller   177
   Erik M. Vogt

Part Four: Community, Apocalypse, the Political

10. Between the Inoperative and the Coming Community:
    Jean-Luc Nancy and Giorgio Agamben on the
    Task of Ontology   199
    María del Rosario Acosta López

11. Who Can Hold the Apocalypse? Massimo Cacciari,
    Carl Schmitt, and the *Katechon*   219
    Pietro Pirani

12. Movements or Events? Antonio Negri versus Alain Badiou
    on Politics   231
    Christian Lotz

Part Five: Voices of Difference

13. A Critique of the Forms of Political Action: Carla Lonzi
    and G. W. F. Hegel   255
    Maria Luisa Boccia

14. C'è Altro: Luisa Muraro on the Symbolic of Sexual
    Difference along and beyond Luce Irigaray — 275
    Elvira Roncalli

15. Adriana Cavarero and Hannah Arendt: Singular Voices
    and Horrifying Narratives — 301
    Peg Birmingham

Part Six: Topology, New Realism, Biopolitics

16. Topology at Play: Vincenzo Vitiello and the Word of
    Philosophy — 325
    Giulio Goria

17. On the Question of the Face of Reality: Addressing the
    "Myths" of the New Realism and Postmodernity — 341
    Rita Šerpytytė

18. Deconstruction or Biopolitics — 353
    Roberto Esposito

Contributors — 365

Index — 371

Acknowledgments

Over many months, in various places of the world and in different ways, numerous individuals have given us great motivation, encouragement, and support, which have helped lead to the publication of this volume. Partners, children, other family members, friends, colleagues, students, and occasional interlocutors have gifted us many times with the generosity of an inspirational word, a kind gesture, a joyful smile, a reassuring comment, or even a critical but insightful remark. There are too many of these individuals for us to list all their names here, but we trust that they know who they are. And they should also know that our indebtedness to them is great and our gratitude is sincere and deep.

We are especially thankful to Andrew Kenyon, James Peltz, Michael Rinella, and the staff at SUNY Press, not only for their editorial competence, good-humored attitude, and enthusiastic backing of this volume but also for their constant support of the SUNY series in Contemporary Italian Philosophy in which this book appears.

We wish to thank the anonymous reviewers who took the time to read the initial version of the manuscript thoroughly and carefully and who offered important insights to help us make the volume a better work.

We wish to thank Karen Lawson and the Royal Collection Trust/ © Her Majesty Queen Elizabeth II 2020 for kind permission to use the image by Leonardo da Vinci, "A Sprig of Blackberries," on the front cover of the volume.

And last but not least, we extend our sincerest and deepest appreciation and thanks to the contributors to this volume for their prompt responsiveness, ongoing collaboration, and unending patience. Without them and their thinking, there would be no volume, the intersections of various aspects of Italian and continental philosophy would be less practiced, and the borders of thought would remain less open.

Silvia Benso and Antonio Calcagno

Open Borders

Introduction

Silvia Benso and Antonio Calcagno

Roberto Esposito opens his work *Living Thought: The Origins and Actuality of Italian Thought* by noting that there has been a great resurgence of interest in Italian philosophy. As he remarks,

> After a long period of retreat (or at least of stalling), the times appear to be favorable again for Italian philosophy. The signs heralding this shift, in a way that suggests something more than mere coincidence, are many. I am not just referring to the international success of certain living authors, among the most translated and discussed writers in the world, from the United States to Latin America and Japan to Australia, leading to a resurgence of interest in Europe as well. There have been other cases of this sort in the past, but they have involved individuals instead of a horizon: a group that in spite of its diversity of issues and intentions somehow remains recognizable by its common tone. This is precisely what has been taking shape in recent years, however, with an intensity that recalls the still recent landing of "French theory" on the coasts and campuses of North America.[1]

Esposito pointedly draws a connection between Italian thought and its many interlocutors in North and South America, Asia, and Europe. As Remo Bodei remarks, the *forte* of Italian philosophy in the world today is that it "responds to a widespread need for concreteness and reality (*realtà*) after the finicky inquiries of the analytic philosophers and the (apparent) conceptual acrobatics of French Theory," which has dominated continental philosophy in the last decades.[2] A peculiarity of Italian philosophy, according to Bodei, is that its interlocutors have never been a specialized audience (scholars, clerics, university students), but rather have been a wider public ultimately made of the majority of the human beings, the "non-philosophers," as Benedetto Croce used to call them. Hence, the questions that Italian philosophy addresses are largely themes of broad concern to human beings in general, whose characteristics are those of being "not only rational animals but also desiring and projecting animals, whose thoughts, actions, and expectations escape predetermined argumentative rules or rigorously defined methods."[3]

Mindful of the dialectical, dialogical nature of Italian philosophy as Bodei presents it—a dialectics that emerges from the discrepancy between thought and lived life—the present volume explores one important strand of the ongoing dialogue to which Esposito alludes, namely, the provocative, if not sometimes troubling, relationship between Italian philosophy and continental European thought. This relationship has existed ever since the beginning of what was not yet entirely identifiable either as Italian or as continental thinking. The aims of this collection, which explicitly addresses a relationship that is constitutive of Italian thought broadly understood, are threefold. First, we wish to show the intimate relationship between contemporary Italian philosophy and continental thinking, not only in terms of its more recent framework, as articulated by Esposito, but from late modernity to the present. We do this to highlight the depth and expanse of the dialogue that is taking place. Second, we focus on the philosophical fruits of this encounter of minds. Questions about the nature and scope of politics, life, being, women, literature, sociality, power, aesthetics, hermeneutics, and technology are taken up to expose new or underinvestigated aspects, which are both meaningful for and relevant to our rapidly changing world. Finally, we see the dialogue as a means for bringing to the fore figures of Italian thought who, though well known in the Italian and European contexts, may not be equally familiar to Anglophone readers. For example, and just to name a few, we consider Carla Lonzi, Luisa Muraro, Ugo Perone, Mario Perniola, and Vincenzo Vitiello. Regrettably and due to various editorial constraints, this foregrounding requires leaving in the background some figures and movements (such as Mario Tronti, Paolo Virno, and other thinkers in the workerist tradition, as well as theorists such as Laura Bazzicalupo, Norberto Bobbio, Silvana Borruti, Giacomo Marramao, Salvatore Natoli, Elena Pulcini, and Salvatore Veca, to name just a few). These figures and movements are either less prominent in the current Italian philosophical debate than they are abroad, already somewhat accessible and known outside

Italy, or, in some other, truly unfortunate cases, so little known outside Italy that it was hard to find contributors available to take them up.

It would be limiting to perceive the dialogue we are staging in this volume as unfolding in a unilateral direction, that is, with an emphasis purely on the Italian side of the discussion. Each chapter in the volume also engages with figures and issues that lie at the heart of continental philosophy. Italian thought must not be regarded as a mere supplement to or extension of the continental tradition; rather, it seriously challenges many of its recent developments: Esposito and Agamben challenge the biopolitical paradigm that Foucault introduced into philosophy, the social sciences, and activist circles; Sini and Vattimo rethink the legacy of hermeneutics; Lonzi and Muraro critique dominant forms of liberal and French feminisms that stress both equality and difference; Severino and Vitiello rethink what it means to do metaphysics; and Pareyson forces us to reevaluate the legacy of German Idealist and existentialist understandings of freedom.

When one employs geographical descriptors (Italian as well as French, German, Anglo-American, Japanese, etc.) to characterize, delimit, and thereby possibly restrict the universality of the philosophical quest, the risks of drifting into narrow-minded forms of nationalism, sovereignism, and the closures of identity politics are never completely absent. By focusing on the multilateral dialogues and the mutual contributions and engagements that unfold (and have unfolded) between Italian philosophy and various authors from the continental tradition, this volume aims at dispelling all such suspicions and ghosts of a past that is unfortunately still too ready to let itself be renewed. Despite the challenges, contributions, additions, revisions, expansions, and criticisms that Italian philosophy brings to the continental discussion, the intention of this volume is neither to extol the superiority of Italian thinkers nor to underline the inadequacies of other, non-Italian ways of doing philosophy. On the contrary, by featuring dialogues and conversations that involve a plurality of participants from across various borders, we aim to create a space where echoes, resonances, vibrancies, refractions, diffractions, and reverberations function to highlight points of richness and fecundity of each and every position. By presenting aspects of the perennial dialectics between particularity and universality, identity and difference, same and others that make up all true dialogues and conversations, this volume shows that if there are borders in place, they are in fact, and ought to be kept, *open* borders: borders that are there only to be crossed and to provide enrichment on all sides through the generosity offered by the act of crossing itself.

At the moment, there exists no volume that engages both Italian philosophy and the continental tradition in the (modes of) conversations that we present here. The contributions in the collection cover many authors from a variety of backgrounds on various topics. Because of the range and, at times, even the indefinability of the geographical, national, ethnic, institutional, conceptual, or simply cultural backgrounds of the continental interlocutors, the Italian thinkers, and the contributors featured in this collection, we have avoided identifying and gathering the essays around "regions" of belonging (French, German, existentialist, phenomenological, feminist, metaphysics, epistemology, aesthetics, and so on). Although there may be borders of various kinds, our authors (as well as the thinkers on whom they reflect) immediately cross them in a variety of directions, and the content of the volume itself becomes a powerful representation of what the title suggests: an activity of passing, trespassing, and ultimately opening up all predetermined territorializations in order to generate new, kaleidoscopic configurations and collaborations. While there is an undeniable overlap of figures, issues, interests, concerns, approaches, and methodologies, we have decided to group the essays around themes of crossing, including being, time, subjectivity, biopolitics, and realism, to name a few. Since the act of crossing is a constitutive constant of the conversations we stage, none of the groupings is stable or final and other groupings could be imagined. One of the ambitions of the volume is actually to encourage the reader to conjure up other gatherings, other conversations, other border crossings.

A quick glance at the table of contents will certainly convey to the reader not only the multiplicity of thinkers collected here but also the wide spectrum of questions and issues that are examined. In *Living Thought*, Esposito typifies the uniqueness of Italian thought as being marked by a plurality of voices that tackle many of life's most pressing questions and problems, from the problem of the vast power of states to control biological and political life to the environment and the migrant and refugee crisis. He also historically traces Italian thought as rising out of a break from medieval thought by Renaissance thinkers, who sought refuge in thought as a form of resistance and of thinking otherwise, for example, Pico della Mirandola, Giordano Bruno, Niccolò Machiavelli, and Giambattista Vico. Yet as Bodei reminds us and Esposito would concur, what makes Italian philosophy different is its heavy emphasis on the human condition, especially the suffering and misery of the human situation.

Rootedness in the concreteness of the embodied human situation means that Italian thinkers never truly speculate in the abstract or theorize in isolation from what occurs in the broader philosophical—international but especially Italian—debate. Many of the positions of the Italian theorists who populate this volume in fact develop and unfold in response to one another, in concrete conversation, exchanges, and at times even altercations and polemics whose moments and passages would regrettably be too long and complex to contextualize here.[4] As quick examples of the ongoing reciprocal resonances that spur and nourish Italian philosophy, we note that Gianni Vattimo's weak thought is, at least in part, a response both to the metaphysical residues of his teacher, Luigi Pareyson, and to the call to a more militant philosophy endorsed by a young Antonio Negri and other workerist theorists. Analogously, it is impossible to understand the deep motivations of Massimo Cacciari's negative dialectics in separation from his initial proximity and later distance from the philosophical and political positions of Antonio Negri or Mario Tronti. As for Emanuele Severino, his neo-Parmenidism and emphasis on the necessity of being can be better appreciated against the background of the postmetaphysical speculation found in Vattimo's weak thought and other theories of difference, becoming, and possibility understood as the core of Being, as found in Cacciari's or Vitiello's thought. As for Carla Lonzi, Luisa Muraro, and Adriana Cavarero, here too, their internally quite distinct emphasis on sexual difference, which in the 1980s generates the thought of sexual difference, unfolds as a radical objection to the alleged neutrality of what is, in fact, the male subject and his patriarchal way of thinking as exemplified by many prominent Italian theorists (who, in most cases, are men). In all these cases, Italian philosophy proves to be the outcome of—and hence the testimony to—the fruitfulness and creativity of the intersection of ideas, the circulation of thoughts, the exchange of experiences, and the interrelationality of all life dimensions. Italian philosophy is, ultimately, a matter of the open borders and border crossing characterizing the philosophical elaborations of its participants.

Each of the scholars who contributed a critical chapter to this volume works on Italian philosophy and is a specialist in continental thinking. Their affinities, scholarly interests, and specializations are diversified and enriched through their provenance from such varied geographical, cultural, and institutional environments as Canada, Colombia, Lithuania, Austria, Germany, Italy, and the United States. From this privileged scholarly position, each of the contributors stages an encounter and a conversation between two (or more) thinkers on fundamental aspects of the human condition, which are explored here in six sections.

The volume opens with a section devoted to some of the most classical, orthodox themes of philosophical speculation, namely, the notions of being, beings, and nothingness. Luigi Pareyson, Martin Heidegger, and Friedrich Wilhelm Joseph Schelling are the thinkers taken up in the first chapter of this section, "Luigi Pareyson's Ontology of Freedom: Encounters with Martin Heidegger and F. W. J. Schelling," by Silvia Benso. The philosophy of Luigi Pareyson (1918–1991), a Turinese thinker brought up in the personalist school of Augusto Guzzo, begins as a reflection on existentialist themes and especially on Jaspers, whom Pareyson introduced into the Italian philosophical debate in the 1950s. Through a subsequent meditation on art and aesthetics focused on the notion of "formativity," that is, of a "forming form" that guides artistic realizations both in terms of the artwork and of the artist's production, Pareyson arrives at a hermeneutic philosophy in which the truth appears as the inexhaustible source of interpretations that are, at the same time, both particular—because they are always the outcome of a personal choice—and universal—because they are a disclosure of the truth. The truth, for Pareyson, presents itself not in the form of a rational account, but rather in the form of *mythos*, mythology or narrations, as understood in the Greek sense. Pareyson's philosophical development concludes with an ontology of freedom, or tragic thought, in which freedom as the potentiality for goodness and evil is retraced to the core of the very notion of being. In Benso's essay, Pareyson's philosophy is disclosed as a radicalization of Heidegger, yet also one that moves beyond Heidegger and, in some ways, remedies one of Heidegger's greatest shortcomings, namely, the inability to address the issue of evil in a satisfactory way, especially in light of the event of the Shoah. Whereas Heidegger understands freedom as human freedom in relation to being (but not to nothing) and thus is incapable of accounting for the evilness of nothingness, through his confrontation with Schelling, Pareyson understands being in relation to freedom as originary freedom, that is, freedom as both originary beginning and choice. This difference between the two thinkers accounts for the possibility, on Pareyson's side, of presenting the evilness of nothingness as one of the alternatives among which originary freedom is free to choose when it comes to being and nothing. In other words, Pareyson's position is capable of accounting for the power of the ontological destructiveness of nothingness (*Vernichtigung*), whereas Heidegger can only account for ontological nothingness as negativity (*Verneinung*). This is the deepest sense, Benso argues, of Pareyson's ontology of freedom.

Emanuele Severino (1929–2020), another thinker about beings, being, and nothingness, is at the center of the following chapter by Alessandro Carrera, "Emanuele Severino versus Western Nihilism (A Guide for the Perplexed)." Severino's philosophical position, which unfolds through numerous works devoted to the themes of nihilism, *techne*, Western philosophy, faith and religion, destiny, the will, power, and democracy, among others, can be understood as a form of neo-Parmenidism that denies the Greek notion of becoming in favor of being understood as unchanging. Carrera begins with Emanuele Severino's apparently simple and straightforward definition of nihilism as the belief that something can come out of nothing and something can become nothing. As Carrera points out, what follows from this simple proposition is that creation, change, possibility, agency, and the very notion of becoming are put to the test. With his much-debated return to Parmenides (Being is and non-Being is not), Severino takes an anti-Nietzschean and anti-Heideggerian stance that rejects the submission of Being to time or historicization. To Severino, Carrera explains, entities are eternal, the horizon where the entity appears is eternal, and the order whereby they hide or show themselves within the horizon of appearing is eternal too. Everything exists forever. Severino's philosophy is a shock to common sense, but it does not lack a logical foundation and it cannot be easily dismissed. Regardless of whether one accepts his premises, Severino is one of the strongest thinkers of total immanence, Carrera argues. That everything exists forever and everything is eternal does not mean that the empirical you and I are immortal; rather, at each moment, every slice of reality *is* and, therefore, is forever, since whatever is cannot come into being or cease to be. According to Carrera, Severino's antimetaphysical metaphysics, therefore, needs to be discussed in the context of post-Heideggerian metaphysics, Deleuzian immanence, Badiou's notion of the event, Meillassoux's speculative realism, the anticorrelationist trends, the currents of eternalism dating back to John McTaggart, the logic of possible worlds, and the theology of the death of God.

Gaetano Chiurazzi's chapter, which concludes the first section, is devoted to the ideas of Gianni Vattimo (1936) and Hans-Georg Gadamer. A student of Pareyson in Turin and of Gadamer in Heidelberg, Vattimo is most famous for his hermeneutic readings of Nietzsche and Heidegger, which lead to the original standpoint of "weak thought" or an "ontology of actuality" in which the strong ontological structures of classical metaphysics are weakened in order to correspond to the needs of our postmetaphysical times. In "Increase or *Kenosis*: Hermeneutic Ontology between Hans-Georg Gadamer and Gianni Vattimo," Chiurazzi argues that despite sharing a common Heideggerian heritage in terms of their understanding of being as time and the horizon of meaning, Gadamer and Vattimo are also very different because of the role that Nietzsche's thought plays in each of their philosophies. Chiurazzi sums up the difference between Gadamer and Vattimo in the opposition between increase, which characterizes Gadamer's ontology, and *kenosis*, which is central to Vattimo's position. Through an analysis of these two notions, Chiurazzi explores how the difference leads to two very specific understandings of the concept of interpretation.

With a departure prepared by the chapter on Vattimo's reflection on weak thought and interpretation, the second section in the volume turns the reader's attention from metaphysical and ontological themes toward spheres of existence that are more mundane and modest yet not less significant, while engaging with topics of temporality, subjectivities, and performance. Ugo Perone, Edith Stein, and Martin Heidegger are the thinkers addressed in the first chapter in this section, which was written by Antonio Calcagno and is titled "Lingering Gifts of Time: Ugo Perone, Edith Stein, and Martin Heidegger's Philosophical Legacy." Perone (1945–), who, like Vattimo, was a student of Pareyson in Turin, is a philosopher operating in the hermeneutic tradition with a strong attention and loyalty to the notion of the human being and its finitude. Perone's principal themes for reflection are the attempt at defining modernity, the issue of secularization, the question of the subject, and the themes of time, public space, and the relations between reason and feelings, philosophy and theology, and secular thought and religious inspiration. Calcagno draws on Martin Heidegger's revolutionary way of thinking about time and its relation to being and examines the impact of Heidegger's legacy on the positions of Perone and the German phenomenologist Edith Stein. Lingering and security emerge as an individual's two fundamental comportments toward being, as revealed by both Stein's and Perone's analyses of the temporal dimension. Accepting both Stein's and Perone's conclusions about time, Calcagno engages the two thinkers, which leads him to argue for the possibility of an intimate relationship between lingering and security. Lingering requires a deep ontic sense of security in order for it to manifest itself, but lingering, in turn, conditions the intensity with which we feel the very security offered to us by being. Calcagno argues for a dialectical relationship between lingering and security that ultimately gives rise to a more meaningful relationship of one's own being to itself, others, and the world.

The following chapter focuses on Remo Bodei and Jean-Luc Nancy, who are addressed by Alexander Bertland in "Failing to Imagine the Lives of Others: Remo Bodei and Jean-Luc Nancy on Citizenship and Sancho Panza." Bodei (1938–2019) was a philosopher and historian of ideas who especially devoted himself to the study of the modern forms of individuality, the theory of passions and their political use, the genesis of the modern individual, the paradoxes of time and memory, forms of knowledge, aesthetics, the genesis of machine culture, and the possibility of a planetary ethics based on a minimal number of shared ethical norms. In his contribution, Bertland retraces Bodei's discussion of the postmodern notion of the subject as singular in relation to a similar notion of singularity proposed by Nancy. For Nancy, the singular must be understood as a unique entity that lacks a definite connection to its past and thus is always open to the future. Bodei does not deny the openness of the singular; however, he asserts that the singular must acknowledge that alongside openness, there is an underlying stratum of coherence. The singular should mediate these two aspects of itself. Thus, for Bodei, individuals need to learn by imagining the lives of others and must do so in a way that reflects practical reality. Bertland argues, then, that Bodei brings a sense of practical urgency to Nancy's ontology.

Carlo Sini and Michel Foucault are at the center of the following chapter by Enrico Redaelli, "A Political Gesture: The Performance of Carlo Sini and Michel Foucault," which concludes the second section. Sini (1933–) is a Milanese philosopher who studied with Enzo Paci—one of the most original Italian Marxist existentialists—and who, in the course of his long professional career, has been especially concerned with phenomenological thinking (from Hegel to Husserl and Heidegger), the hermeneutic problem, and the horizon of linguistic and semiotic thought. Most notably, Sini has devoted himself to reflection, inspired partly by Peirce, on the intertwining of practices and, more specifically, on the practice of writing and the ethics that such a practice generates. In his contribution, Redaelli shows how Sini's philosophy is to be understood as a political gesture, which is in many respects analogous to, but also radically different from, the thought of Michel Foucault. Like French poststructuralists, Sini too considers the subject to be the result of practices. As subjects, we are instituted and blinded by historically determined practices, which Foucault calls *dispositifs* (apparatuses) and Deleuze terms *machines*. These practices have shaped and transformed us, orienting our ways of life, thinking, and acting. The interweaving of practices, with their inherent or constitutive mistakes, constantly toys with us, ultimately designing precise, but always contingent, power relations. According to Redaelli, Sini's philosophy can be viewed as a political gesture that abolishes the aforementioned mistakes: "the mistakes of the sign," to borrow an expression from Sini himself. Sini's philosophy must be understood as a critical practice that is genealogical or constructive and that acts to problematize all that appears true, obvious, and natural or institutionally accepted or guaranteed. In the end, Sini's philosophy has one goal, namely, to bring the subject to the edge of itself in order to show such a subject the interweaving of habits, techniques, and truths that constitute and subjectivate him or her, ultimately generating different ways of being a subject.

Thinking, estrangement, and ideologies are the themes that organize the following section, which opens with a chapter by Richard A. Lee Jr. devoted to Antonio Gramsci and Gilles Deleuze. Gramsci (1891–1937) was a Marxist philosopher and politician, perhaps most famous for his reflections on the role of the intellectual in society and for his attempt at breaking away from the determinism found in much traditional Marxist thought. In "What Does It Mean to Think? Antonio Gramsci and Gilles

Deleuze," Lee brings Gramsci and Deleuze into a conversation about the general question of "how to think the real." Lee views "the real" not just as that which actually exists, but also as that which is effective. Therefore, structures are real because they are effective. In this way, the real is not constituted by identity, but rather by effectivity. The essay brings Gramsci and Deleuze into dialogue by focusing on how each deals with creativity, assembly, and reality. The conversation that Lee unfolds, however, is not a mere "compare and contrast" exercise; rather, it is productive in that it may enable us to discover why these issues are crucial for us. In the end, Lee argues that Gramsci may be in a better position than Deleuze to analyze the effectivity of structures, an analysis that is crucial for our times.

The section continues with a chapter on Franco "Bifo" Berardi and Herbert Marcuse, who are at the center of the essay by Michael E. Gardiner, "Herbert Marcuse in Italy." Gardiner examines key themes in Marcuse's work through the lens of Italian autonomist thinker "Bifo" Berardi (1949–). Berardi, who studied aesthetic theory under the guidance of Luciano Anceschi in Bologna and there met Antonio Negri, has been a prominent actor in the Italian autonomist, extraparliamentary, workerist movement in the 1960s and 1970s. He has devoted much of his philosophical production to an analysis of the role of the media and information technology in the postindustrial capitalist world while focusing his attention on the role that emotions, desires, and embodied communication play in the production of the consumption patterns that sustain the market economy. As Gardiner highlights, Berardi is critical of what he takes to be the Hegelian and Freudian residues in Marcuse's thought. Specifically, he asserts that the concept of alienation must now be abandoned. Similarly, with regard to Marcuse's thesis of instinctual renunciation, according to Berardi, liberation cannot be vouchsafed by the elimination of "surplus repression." Yet Gardiner argues that at the same time, Berardi glosses over certain anticipations of autonomist ideas in Marcuse's writings, especially when the latter draws on Marx's *Grundrisse* in order to evoke what autonomists later referred to as the "general intellect." Similarly, Marcuse foresees and theorizes the subsumption of desire in work and consumption, which is a key autonomist insight, through what he calls "repressive desublimation."

Concluding the section is a chapter by Erik M. Vogt devoted to Mario Perniola in dialogue with Slavoj Žižek and Robert Pfaller. After studying aesthetic theory in Turin with Pareyson, Perniola (1941–2018) came in contact with the Situationist International founded by Guy Debord in Paris and developed his own philosophical position, which was focused on the concept of simulacra as opposed to the traditionally metaphysical distinction of being and appearing. His philosophy has always been open to the most problematic, alienating, allegedly negative sides of the contemporary situation. Among the topics he studied were sexuality, embodiment, and the world, but also communication media and, most recently, the worlds of religion and politics, yet without neglecting more synthetic overviews of the role of art in modern times. In "Engaging Contemporary Ideology with Mario Perniola, Slavoj Žižek, and Robert Pfaller," Vogt examines how, according to Perniola, the notion of experience that lies at the center of contemporary Western society is to be grasped in terms of an inversion between humans and things, the organic and the inorganic. This inversion has not only affected knowledge, belief, and action but also, and above all, feeling, in that feeling has been subjected to a profound process of reification. This transformation of feeling has to be related to the emergence of a collective and socialized sensory horizon before which all modes of feeling seem to take on the guise of something already-felt. Perniola defines the quasi-transcendental-schematic status of the already-felt as *sensology*. Sensology not only entertains complex relations with the notions of ideology, *mediocracy*, and *specularism*, but it has also differentiated into multiple cultures or styles of the already-felt that, in concert with mass communication, exhibit a striving for totality that seems to render impossible lines of flight from contemporary totalistic society. Vogt highlights how Perniola manages to unearth impersonal and anonymous modes of feeling, harboring the potential for displacing the grip of sensology in that they suggest nonmetaphysical relationships between feeling and thinking as well as feeling and acting. Moreover, Vogt argues, Perniola's elaboration of a historical anthropology of externalized and ritualized feeling exhibits affinities with the notion of interpassivity elaborated by Slavoj Žižek and Robert Pfaller. Vogt presents some of these affinities in light of the urgent task of reaffirming the necessity of a public-symbolic realm of appearances.

The theme of the political, which constitutes a major focus of the preceding section, continues in part four, which is devoted to community, apocalypse, and the political. The section begins with a chapter on Giorgio Agamben and Jean-Luc Nancy by María del Rosario Acosta López. In recent years, and possibly more abroad than in Italy, Agamben (1942–) has become a well-known voice in the political-philosophical debates that are focused on the notions of community, sovereign power, the state of exception, forms of life, *homo sacer*, and biopolitics. In "Between the Inoperative and the Coming Community: Jean-Luc Nancy and Giorgio Agamben on the Task of Ontology," Acosta López engages in a dialogue with Nancy's and Agamben's works on community, and her essay emphasizes the role that the concept of community plays in the move of both thinkers from politics to ontology. According to Acosta López, in the work of both Nancy and Agamben, the question of being in common is linked not only to a critique of ontology but also to a new critical ontology and even to an *ontology as critique*.

Pietro Pirani's chapter, "Who Can Hold the Apocalypse? Massimo Cacciari, Carl Schmitt, and the *Katechon*," identifies a central aspect of the contemporary debate in political theory in the relationship between theology and politics. Pirani addresses Massimo Cacciari's more recent work, *Il potere che frena* (*The Withholding Power*), and his reflections on the concept of political theology. Cacciari (1944), who is both an academic philosopher trained in art and aesthetic theory and a public figure who has devoted much of his life to active politics, has produced scholarly works that span over narrowly defined disciplines and extend to architecture, literature, political theory, theology, and philosophy through a strong reevaluation of nondialectical thought. In his essay, Pirani compares Cacciari's understanding of the *katechon* (the withholding power) to Carl Schmitt's classical interpretation. Whereas for Schmitt the restraining power of the *katechon* is a stabilizing force that aims at repelling the external foe, for Cacciari the *katechon* is an expression of the Christian eschatological view. The *katechon*, then, is inherently characterized by a tension between *potestas* (power) and *auctoritas* (authority) that jeopardizes the stability of the *polis* (the city or community) from within. According to Pirani, by reading Cacciari's latest works we become able to address one of the major weaknesses of contemporary theories of secularization: their incapacity to detect the implicit secularizing movement already present and at work in Christian theological categories.

The concluding chapter in the section stages a confrontation between Antonio Negri and Alain Badiou. A political theorist and militant activist in the workerist and autonomist movements, where he came in contact with Cacciari and Berardi, in addition to Mario Tronti, Negri (1933–) has become world renowned in recent years because of his analysis of globalization, the neoliberal economy, the idea of multitude as the set of social subjects enslaved to global capitalism, the concept of permanent global conflict and emergency understood as mechanisms to control productive and financial forces, and the delineation of social subjects that are capable of building an alternative global democracy. In "Movements or Events? Antonio Negri versus Alain Badiou on Politics," Christian Lotz argues that although Negri (and Hardt) are usually identified as a "nondogmatic" version of post-Marxism, their position can be identified with the attempt to offer a contemporary vision of Marxist thought that, at least to some extent, remains true to its basis, namely, the connection between Marxist social theory and political philosophy. Accordingly, for them political thought can only be understood in connection with a theory of subjectivity and labor defined by recent developments in global capitalism. In contradistinction, and seen from the problem of how to combine social theory, political economy, and political thought, Badiou appears as furthest away from a Marxian social base (broadly defined). The reason for this distance lies in the fact that one of his central claims is that politics needs to be rethought as a "true" politics, which he conceives of as independent from questions of social form and social-economic structure. Lotz argues that Negri's concept of the political in connection with the social is far superior to Badiou's regressive concept of communist politics. Siding with Negri, Lotz suggests that Badiou's political thinking should be rejected due to its empty abstractions, and instead, Negri's model of thinking about the political in connection with the social should be favored.

The fifth section is devoted to voices of difference: women philosophers whose activities originated and intersected in the feminist movements of the 1970s and 1980s, principally in Milan, Rome, and Verona, and produced distinct theoretical positions of broad philosophical latitude that can nevertheless perhaps be gathered under the shared descriptor, "thinking of sexual difference." The section opens with a chapter by Maria Luisa Boccia on Carla Lonzi (1931–1982), an early feminist theoretician belonging to the Roman group Rivolta Femminile (Women's Rebellion). In the early 1970s, when the notion of sexual difference was not widely entertained and the complications of that concept brought about by queer theory and intersectionality were still entirely untheorized and perhaps even unimaginable, Lonzi declared the need for women to start from their differences and inequalities with respect to men and use those differences as standpoints from which to elaborate and vindicate political goals that respond to the specificity of women's concrete needs and desires. In "A Critique of the Forms of Political Action: Carla Lonzi and G. W. F. Hegel," Boccia examines Carla Lonzi's treatment of the differentiation of sexes in relation to Hegel's concepts of individuality, struggle, power, domination, and the political sphere. Lonzi maintains that these notions, as they are elaborated by Hegel, work at erasing sexual difference precisely by neutralizing it through its subsumption into the universal. The goal of Lonzi's critique of the (Hegelian) notion of the political sphere is to claim that sexual difference pertains to the human being, understood both as an individual and as a species. Lonzi is interested in grasping the manifestation of a woman's "I," who finds within herself the principle and sense of her own being, understood as a sexed being. This leads Lonzi to formulate the concept of an "I" that is turned to the world in order to redefine its codes, forms, and relations. According to Boccia, Lonzi remains loyal to this thematic core and does so in forms and ways that are rarely found in other feminist thinkers. There is, for Lonzi, no "woman problem" as such; rather, there exists the problem that belongs to this and/or that specific woman of thinking of herself as "a woman Self" and positing herself as such in the world. Lonzi's thought, as well as her practice, which is inseparable from her thinking, are faithful to the demand to elaborate forms in which the woman subject can speak and posit herself as an "I." Herein lies the power of her critique of the abstract and universal forms of politics.

Luisa Muraro and Luce Irigaray are at the center of Elvira Roncalli's "C'è Altro: Luisa Muraro on the Symbolic of Sexual Difference along and beyond Luce Irigaray." Muraro (1940–) has been one of the animating voices behind the Milan-based Libreria delle Donne (Women's Bookstore), a women's bookstore collective devoted to the theoretical elaboration of the thought of sexual difference. Specifically, Muraro theorizes the figure of the mother—once it is liberated of the symbolisms assigned to it by the patriarchal tradition—as the place where a women's genealogy, as based on the nonconflictual mother-daughter relationship, can be created. In her contribution, Roncalli begins by acknowledging that Muraro's thinking has been deeply inspired and informed by Irigaray's thought on sexual difference and by the need for a female genealogy. A fundamental place and practice to which Muraro is also deeply indebted is the Libreria delle Donne in Milan, which was a stronghold of feminine experience and learning where the politics of women relationships was practiced in a concrete way. Roncalli explores both these roots in Muraro's work and examines how they lead to what Muraro calls the need for a "symbolic revolution," that is, a radical transformation of the order of thought and language. It becomes apparent that while both Muraro and Irigaray see the recovery and reinvention of the mother-daughter relationship as necessary for such a transformation to happen, they do not necessarily agree on the way in which this is to come about.

The section concludes with a chapter on the philosophical positions of Adriana Cavarero and Hannah Arendt. After participating, in the 1980s, in the Verona-based philosophical group Diotima, which focused on the elaboration of a theory of sexual difference that was strongly influenced by the French feminism of Luce Irigaray and Julia Kristeva, Cavarero (1947–) shifted her attention to the themes of language, narration, and storytelling as ways to give direct, broad philosophical expression, at least in part, to women's voices otherwise suppressed by the male-dominated discursive horizon. In "Adriana Cavarero and Hannah Arendt: Singular Voices and Horrifying Narratives," Peg Birmingham examines the ways in which Cavarero's relational ontology relies upon and departs from Arendt's thinking of the in-between by specifically focusing on Cavarero's insistence on the primacy of voice, her thinking of vulnerability and violence, and her reading of Arendt's notion of superfluousness. Birmingham also raises the question of Cavarero's engagement with the Italian Marxist tradition, given Arendt's debt to Marx, especially in her analysis of the economic conditions understood as constitutive elements of the origins of totalitarianism. Birmingham concludes by addressing the concern with care and horror as fundamental affects in Cavarero's relational ontology while interrogating their contribution to Arendt's own analysis of horror as the affect that today provokes thinking.

The concluding section of the volume is devoted to specific examinations of the themes of topology, the new realism, and biopolitics—these being some of the conceptual formulations through which Italian philosophers have confronted and contrasted the perceived shortcomings of the metaphysical, modern tradition with original, novel concepts and positions. Giulio Goria's opening chapter, "Topology at Play: Vincenzo Vitiello and the Word of Philosophy," takes up Vincenzo Vitiello (1935) and his relationship to Immanuel Kant and Martin Heidegger. Vitiello's thought has focused on the themes of nihilism, modernity, the concept of space, and the notion of possibility understood as both the possibility of the impossible *and* the enabling possibility—an "and" that, for Vitiello, constitutes the contradiction that thought cannot think (and, hence, that also represents its limit). In his contribution, Goria addresses Vitiello's most original philosophical proposal, namely topology, starting from Vitiello's main areas of theoretical concern, that is, philosophy, art, and religion. Within these areas, Vitiello's thought unfolds in the direction of a unique goal: topology understood as a philosophical machine aimed at detecting the indeterminate "X" that underlies Western thought. In Kant's *Critique of Pure Reason*, the indeterminate is the *noumenon*; in Heidegger's works, it is indeterminate potency; and in the main directions pursued by twentieth-century pictorial art and poetical experiences, it is the expression of the material power of colors and sounds, of bodily tension and gestures. Goria examines Vitiello's account of these historical and philosophical turning points and suggests that topology, a key notion in Vitiello's thought, arises from a radicalization of the anti-Aristotelian operation of Heidegger's *Being and Time*, in which possibility is primary over reality. Like Heidegger, Vitiello is focused on preserving the indeterminacy of possibility. Topology encounters ontology and, in particular, contradiction. As Goria maintains, speaking the contradiction encapsulates the sense of Vitiello's overall program of research and, at the same time, the ethical attitude of his philosophy.

The section continues with an examination of Italian postmodernism as represented by Gianni Vattimo's weak thought, which we contextualized previously in this essay, and Maurizio Ferraris's recent proposal of new realism as a way to combat postmodernism. Ferraris (1956–), a student of Vattimo who was initially educated in the hermeneutic and deconstructionist tradition, subsequently embraced a form of realistic objectivism that is rooted in the analytic tradition and based on the recognition of a sphere of reality that is independent of interpretations. Ferraris's "new realism," as he has named it, presents itself as an antidote to postmodern, deconstructionist alleged degenerations and is inspired by the interaction of three concepts: ontology, critique, and enlightenment. The two philosophical currents of Vattimo's weak thought and Ferraris's new realism are at the center of the chapter by Rita Šerpytytė, titled "On the Question of the Face of Reality: Addressing the 'Myths' of the New Realism and Postmodernity." In this chapter, Šerpytytė starts from the conviction that the controversy between the two positions and their mutual critique is based on the criterion of *reality* that each of them posits. Yet the criterion of *reality*, which raises the question of the end of postmodernity, is in itself quite problematic. As an important landmark standing between postmodernism and new realisms, such a criterion leads Šerpytytė to ask, What kind of reality are we talking about? She shows that Vattimo understands reality in terms of *"effettualità* (effectiveness)" or *"attualità* (actuality)" (*Wirklichkeit*). That is, from its very beginning, "weak thought" is taken and treated (from the point of view of reality) as a performative philosophy, with an orientation to reality as actuality. Meanwhile, the "game" of the new realism, the "recovery" of *reality* for which Ferraris's thought is an introduction, is focused on the restoration of the ontological significance of perception. Šerpytytė's question then becomes whether postmodernism and the new realism address the same reality. The new realism, which is clearly affected by what Šerpytytė refers to as Nietzschean neurosis, attempts to grasp reality, insofar as it provides a new *interpretation* of perception. Conversely, Vattimo focuses on the issue of the relationship between the move toward so-called second-degree reality and reality. According to Šerpytytė, the question continues to spiral within the realm of the distinction between *Realität* and *Wirklichkeit* that is drawn by Kant and Hegel. Šerpytytė argues that Vattimo alone, being encouraged by Nietzsche and Heidegger, attempts to take a step forward, whereas Ferraris's "new" realism takes us back to the old dispute between Jacobi and his contemporaries.

The volume concludes with a chapter by Roberto Esposito (1950–), whose words have been cited at the beginning of this introduction, thus bringing this collection full circle. In "Deconstruction or Biopolitics," Esposito addresses the Italian paradigm of biopolitics in relation to Jacques Derrida and Michel Foucault. He focuses on two interrelated questions: the relationship of the Derridean paradigm of deconstruction to the Foucaultian model of biopolitics, and the relationship between French Theory and Italian Thought, a recent theoretical paradigm focused on notions of *bios* (life), biopolitics, conflict, the common, processes of governmentality and subjectivation, among others. Contrary to the widely held thesis maintaining that both relations are contiguous or continuous, Esposito argues that to understand the specificity of the paradigms of deconstruction and biopolitics, one must return them to the originary tension that differentiates them. This move does not amount to privileging one paradigm over the other, nor should it be seen, with respect to Derrida and Foucault specifically, as undermining the recognition due to two of the great philosophical masters of the twentieth century. One must remain faithful, Esposito claims, to a heterogeneity that neither thinker has ever hidden; it is only by examining this heterogeneity that it becomes possible to recognize the tense relationship between French Theory and Italian Thought. Despite all its undeniable debts and lexical contaminations, Italian Thought is born not from the development of French Theory, but from the crisis within it: a crisis that Italian Thought intensifies.

It is our hope as editors that, through this collection of essays, our readers will not only expand their knowledge and thinking about figures and issues explored in this volume, but will also be moved by what they encounter and read so that they may in turn critique, develop, and even initiate new ways of questioning and thinking, hopefully for the betterment of the human condition that the essays in the collection address. We all operate within our own borders in that every age and culture gathers and reworks received philosophies, for better or for worse. Yet our borders need not be constraining boundaries. We believe that the dialogue we have brought forward in this collection not only makes a contribution to our understanding of a lively and dynamic philosophical movement in Italy but can also bear fruit and help improve the world we dwell in together and in common, resulting in more open borders.

Notes

1. Roberto Esposito, *Living Thought: The Origins and Actuality of Italian Thought*, trans. Zakiya Hanafi (Stanford, CA: Stanford University Press, 2012), 1.

2. Remo Bodei, "Dall'Italia," in *La filosofia nel Novecento (e oltre)* (Milan: Feltrinelli, 2006), 210.

3. Bodei, 211.

4. For a first-person account of the philosophical positions and developments of many of the Italian thinkers addressed in this volume, see Silvia Benso, *Viva Voce: Conversations with Italian Philosophers* (Albany: State University of New York Press, 2017), and the bibliographical information contained therein.

Part One

Being, Beings, Nothingness

I

Luigi Pareyson's Ontology of Freedom

Encounters with Martin Heidegger
and F. W. J. Schelling

Silvia Benso

Pareyson's Philosophical Project

In Italy, Spain, South America, and, to a lesser extent, France and Germany, Luigi Pareyson (1918–1991) is counted among the most notable Italian philosophers of the post–World War II period.[1] If students' success can be considered testimony to the inspirational impact and conceptual legacy of their teachers, among Pareyson's students one could name such figures as Gianni Vattimo, Umberto Eco, Mario Perniola, Sergio Givone, and Ugo Perone, many of whose works are accessible and quite familiar to Anglophone readers as well. Despite the reputation of Pareyson's students in the English-speaking philosophical community, it was only in 2013 that one of Pareyson's major works, *Truth and Interpretation*, was translated into English.[2] In it, Pareyson's hermeneutic theory fully unfolds in its theoretical vibrancy.[3]

Unlike Heidegger who, to Pareyson's mind, walks down the "dead end" of an ontology of the ineffable or "negative ontology,"[4] Pareyson understands truth as something not unfathomable (that is, to be addressed through concepts such as cypher, symbol, allegory, the inadequate, partiality, elusiveness, allusion, the symbolic) but rather inexhaustible (*inesauribile*); that is, as "fertile reserve of an inexhaustible secret," "unending and diffuse abundance of the implicit," "ulteriority of truth-bearing thought."[5] Inexhaustibility, whose original inspiration Pareyson finds in Schelling's 1821 *Erlangen Lectures*, is arguably Pareyson's most relevant contribution to hermeneutic theory and to the contemporary philosophical debate in general. It marks truth's residence in language rather than in silence and mystery (which possibly are "a simple overturning of the rationalistic cult of the explicit while preserving all nostalgia for it"), and this also accounts for the primacy Pareyson consistently assigns to philosophical rather than poetic discourse. Yet the residence of truth in language is an inhabitation that does not fully identify with the word that is spoken, with the said, because "no revelation worthy of the name exhausts" truth.[6] This is why truth cannot be understood as object but rather as source, spring, and origin of philosophy. Quoting Pareyson's most significant claim, "Of the truth there can only be interpretations; and all interpretations can only be of the truth."[7] Pareyson's position, with its emphasis on the philosophical need for dialogue among various interpretations of the truth, is especially significant in the extremely globalized world in which we live, where differences and multiplicities have become both the norm to which we are constantly exposed and an ethical task to be embraced against the recurrent dangers of the totalitarianism embodied in various nativist, sovereignist, and identitarian temptations that are presently resurging in many world countries.[8] Because of its inexhaustibility, truth constantly invites new interpretations, that is, new relations to itself—in its unity, truth acts as the source (not the object or goal),[9] spurring and originating multiplicities that are both related and *un*related to the origin itself.

Yet not all interpretations are equally sustainable, in Pareyson's view, and the difference between truth (or revelatory thought, which has the truth as its source and of which philosophy is "the guardian") and ideology (or merely expressive thought, which considers truth a subject and which philosophy must resist becoming) remains.[10] What prevents philosophy's slippage into ideology is philosophy's commitment to being, its fundamentally ontological engagement, which requires the solidarity of truth (universality, eternity, and so on) and person (particularity, historicity, and so on), whereas ideology is merely historical and pragmatic and thus ends up being a technicization of reason and thinking. As Pareyson writes, "Revelatory thought demands an originary commitment, through which one complies with being rather than rejecting it, and one agrees to bear witness to it rather than sacrifice it to history."[11] Because of the fundamental commitment (which is always a personal commitment) to the inexhaustibility of being and truth, "only in philosophy is it possible to acknowledge other philosophies while adopting one of them, and thus truly open up those perspectives to dialogue."[12]

Pareyson's important philosophical contributions are limited neither to the field of hermeneutics, as these opening remarks may suggest, nor to the realm of aesthetics, in which he first becomes known, in the 1950s, through his proposal of a theory of art as formativity in sharp opposition to Croce's aesthetic theory of expression.[13] In his own description, Pareyson's philosophical itinerary unfolds on a three-step path: from existentialism[14] to hermeneutics to ontology (of freedom).[15] In this development, Pareyson, as the excellent connoisseur of the history of philosophy that he is, is in constant conversation with major thinkers in the Western tradition: Pascal, Kant, Fichte, Schelling, Hegel, Kierkegaard, Dostoevsky, and Jaspers, but also Plotinus and, especially, Heidegger. On being invited to give a lecture on Heidegger, Pareyson confesses, "After having spoken for an entire life *with* Heidegger, it is now almost impossible for me to speak *of* or *about* Heidegger."[16]

In light of this self-avowed lifelong proximity between Pareyson and Heidegger, it is in relation to Heidegger that this chapter will engage Pareyson's thought. Pareyson is by no means a historian or a scholar of Heidegger's thinking; rather, with respect to Heidegger, he is "a truly theoretical interlocutor."[17] Without either entering a close textual reading of Heidegger's works, which Pareyson himself approaches in a rather liberal way, or venturing a critical assessment of the accuracy of Pareyson's interpretation of the thought of the German philosopher, which would require a somewhat complex and sophisticated philological analysis, the goal of this chapter is to provide an exploration, which at times remains expository in nature, of aspects of a conversation that leads Pareyson to speak with, but also, ultimately, *beyond* Heidegger. In the end, this conversation between Pareyson and Heidegger discloses two different, intermingled yet distinct, variations of a single relation, namely, the hermeneutic relation between truth and being, or truth and its manifestation(s). As will become clear in the course of this essay, whereas Heidegger's project ultimately moves within the limits of an ontology, that is, a philosophical consideration tied to the notion of being (whether the being of *Dasein* or being as *Ereignis* or event), through his post-Heideggerian confrontation with Schelling's notion of freedom—a third author who will also be addressed in this chapter— Pareyson is capable of infusing his own ontological, hermeneutic project, which he shares with Heidegger, with a distinctly ethical *motif* that finds its roots in being and renders his philosophy well equipped to confront and account for reality in its multiplicities and differences, including evil ones. As Pareyson writes, the originary bond between freedom and nothingness "seems to be the fundamental problem of our days" (*OL* 466). This was as true in 1988, when Pareyson pronounced these words, as it is today (and as it was in 1933), I would argue, because, as he remarks, "It is through freedom that the good arises and affirms itself, yet it is also through freedom that evil is born and spreads" (*OL* 472).[18]

Pareyson and Heidegger

More or less sustained references to Heidegger are to be found throughout the *corpus* of Pareyson's work. One of the primary sites of Pareyson's direct and most developed confrontation with Heidegger's thought is the lecture titled "*Il nulla e la libertà come inizio* (Nothing and Freedom as Beginning)." The lecture was delivered by Pareyson in Naples on March 13, 1989, on occasion of the International Philosophy Seminar dedicated to celebrating the centennial of Heidegger's birth, and it constituted the inaugural speech for the event. The theme of the seminar, which saw the participation of Emmanuel Levinas, Felix Duque, Gianni Vattimo, Emanuele Severino, and Carlo Sini among others,[19] was "Heidegger and the Destiny of Philosophy." Pareyson's lecture, which was also reprinted in the *Annuario Filosofico* (the yearly journal directed by Pareyson and, later, his students) with the slightly revised title, "*Heidegger: La libertà e il nulla* (Heidegger: Freedom and Nothingness),"[20] addresses Heidegger's thought with explicit relation to the topic of freedom.

The essay begins autobiographically: Pareyson recalls reading Heidegger's "*Was ist Metaphysik?* (What Is Metaphysics?)" during his own sojourn in Germany in 1936–1937. Pareyson remembers his encounter with Heidegger, which was the culminating point of his stay, at his home on September 21, 1937. It was "an absolutely memorable day for [a] not yet twenty-year-old," he recollects. Already voices were circulating regarding the "new path" of Heidegger's thinking as presented in the 1935 lectures published as *Einfuhrung in die Metaphysik* (*Introduction to Metaphysics*) and in the conference, "*Die Ursprung des Kunstwerks* (The Origin of the Work of Art)," Pareyson recalls.[21] When, later, it became clear that Heidegger's thought was "refractory to all anthropological interpretations" and that what dominated in it was "not human beings (*l'uomo*) but being (*l'essere*)," Pareyson felt "completely open to Heidegger's fecund suggestions." What draws Pareyson to Heidegger both during his youth and later in life is neither the idea of the history of being and of metaphysics as oblivion of being—that is, Heidegger's hermeneutic relation to the metaphysical tradition—nor the tendency to a negative ontology—that is, Heidegger's alleged religious-mystical inclinations. Rather, it is "the primacy of being, the ontological difference, commemorating thinking, the origin and the originary, the unsaid, the unthought, disclosure and undisclosure, the secret, the gift, the unsayable and the immemorial, the abyss, the ground that is not ground, and so on," Pareyson confesses (*OL* 441) in a statement that is also the formulation, almost a manifesto, of Heidegger's philosophical program, as understood and accepted by Pareyson.

Amid the multiplicity of inspirational themes he finds in Heidegger, from the outset ambiguity appears to Pareyson as the essential core of Heidegger's thought, and possibly what attracts him the most: "All fundamental antitheses are found in it," Pareyson comments. Yet, Pareyson immediately qualifies his statement by noting the limits of Heidegger's thought and its capacity to encompass ambiguities, which Heidegger embraces "except for ethical ambiguity," Pareyson remarks (*OL* 452). This absence constitutes the ultimate ground of Pareyson's own self-distancing from the German thinker. The ethical ambiguity is thus the source of Pareyson's critical relation with Heidegger, insofar as it allows Pareyson both to align himself with Heidegger (regarding ambiguity) and to move beyond the German thinker whom he so admires (regarding ethics). Whereas Pareyson's criticism of Heidegger on the grounds of Heidegger's ethical failure is nothing new at this point in terms of Heidegger scholarship, what is interesting instead is the way in which Pareyson works at bypassing this inadequacy on a terrain that still remains delimited by a general affinity with Heidegger.

The greatest ambiguity Heidegger formulates is, in Pareyson's reading, the ambiguity that lies in the notion of the two beginnings and the related overcoming of metaphysics. According to these concepts—two beginnings and the overcoming of the metaphysics, which appear to be closely connected—by exhausting the first beginning, by walking its path down to its end, one can open up the "other beginning," which recovers the first in its unsaid, unthought-of aspects (*OL* 453); this recovery allows for an overcoming of metaphysics.[22] Heidegger's move toward the other beginning is not the enactment of "a secret dialectic" (*OL* 453) of, perhaps, a Hegelian nature, Pareyson specifies, thereby countering the interpretation of some scholars who nevertheless remain unnamed.[23] Opening up the other beginning means encountering what, for Pareyson, is the greatest, unsolvable ambiguity that lies at the core of reality, namely, the ambiguity of being and nothingness, with which Western philosophy has always found itself uneasy. This ambiguity is of the uttermost interest to Pareyson, and Heidegger constitutes a formidable companion for its exploration.

With respect to the question of nothingness, Pareyson considers Heidegger's perspective to be groundbreaking. Heidegger addresses the problem of nothingness under the rubric of the fundamental question or *Grundfrage*: a radical reformulation of Leibniz's august question of the "*ratio cur aliquid potius existat quam nihil* (the reason why something rather than nothing exists)" or "*pourqoui il y a plutôt quelque chose que rien* (why is there something rather than nothing)?" In his formulation of the question, still framed within the question of the relation of the will and the intellect, Leibniz's understanding of nothingness is in terms of possibility, Pareyson remarks. That is, for Leibniz, creation is a question of the passage not from nonbeing to being, but from possibility to existence. As Pareyson notes, "Caught between the greater simplicity of nothingness and the greater perfection of existence, [Leibniz] remained at the strictly metaphysical level with the invention of the principle of sufficient reason" (OL 464). It is at this juncture that the novelty of Heidegger's interpretation becomes evident, Pareyson remarks. The urgency of the *Grundfrage* as articulated by Heidegger moves beyond Leibniz's merely metaphysical formulation, Pareyson maintains.[24] Heidegger moves further than Leibniz because, according to Pareyson, he unifies the metaphysical standpoint and the existential *pathos* in a way that produces a new perspective that is neither metaphysical nor existentialist.[25] In this sense, the *Grundfrage* as posed by Heidegger could be crystallized in the pure, sharp, diamantine interrogative "Why?"—as Nietzsche in fact does (OL 354)—that is at the root of all existential anxiety.[26]

In the 1929 *Antrittvorlesung* "*Was ist Metaphysik?*," which the very enthusiastic young Pareyson read in 1936–1937 during his sojourn in Germany, the *Grundfrage* is expressed by Heidegger as the question, "*Warum ist überhaupt Seiendes und nicht vielmehr Nichts* (why are there beings at all instead of nothing)?" (OL 362).[27] The question sounds similar to Leibniz's own formulation of it, but the difference is, for Pareyson, profound. Heidegger's question is, in fact, no longer about *a* being or some thing (*aliquid* or *quelque chose*) but about beings in general or what is (*Seiendes*), Pareyson emphasizes. His commentary then goes to the core of the difference between the two German thinkers, a difference that confines Leibniz still within the realm of traditional metaphysics, whereas Heidegger moves to the plane of an ontological exploration of reality. In Pareyson's own words, which are worth quoting at length because of their theoretical density,

> Leibniz's intent is to find the supreme being, that is, the first and originary cause of all that is; his question is asked in a metaphysical mode, geared toward understanding a causal nexus; his thought is representational thinking, whose object is beings and which considers also the fundamental ground of beings as a being, distinct only because of its higher level. . . . Heidegger's intent is fundamentally different. For him, the fundamental question challenges the entirety of beings so that the issue is not finding the supreme being but rather thinking of being; not reconstructing metaphysics but penetrating its ontological core. (OL 366)

Whereas Leibniz remains at the level of ontotheology, Heidegger moves to the plane of a purely ontological consideration of the being of being as such and its ambiguous relation to nothingness, whose relevance has been disclosed through the notion of *Angst* purified of its merely existentialist undertones. A few lines below the passage we just quoted, Pareyson adds: "By capitalizing the word *Nichts*, [Heidegger] asserts that being is less (rather than more) distinct from nothingness than it is from beings, with the consequence that there is no ontology without meontology. In one single stroke, Heidegger has problematized the relation between being and beings and that between being and nothingness, and has shown that this knot can be loosened up not by representational metaphysical thinking but only by commemorative ontological thinking, which alone is aware of the *inseparability of the three terms*" (OL 366, emphasis added). Pareyson will remain loyal to Heidegger's fundamental intuition of the inseparability of being, beings, and nothingness by taking up Heidegger's commemorative thinking in his own way, that is, in the form of a hermeneutics of novels (mainly Dostoevsky), myths, and religious experience.[28]

In Pareyson's reading, what constitutes Heidegger's greatness and prevents him from falling victim to traditional metaphysics (which mistakes being for beings) as well as to nihilism (here understood in the intense and negative sense of despair in all possible meaningfulness of existence) is the thematization of the inseparability of being, beings, and nothingness. Being cannot be mistaken for *a* being. Likewise, nothingness cannot be simply mistaken for "negative nothingness" (*nichtiges Nichts*), for sheer negativity (*das bloss Nichtige*), nullity, void, or emptiness, because nothingness possesses as much actual being or existence (*essenza*) as being does—"there is" being as much as "there is" nothingness. Heidegger claims that human beings are the shepherds of being, Pareyson recalls. Likewise, Pareyson remarks that in "*Was Ist Metaphysik?*" Heidegger also asserts that human beings are the placeholders of nothing. There is inseparability, coincidence, or affinity of being and nothingness. It is their "ambiguity or two-headedness," Pareyson concludes, that gives meaning to—and takes up meaning in relation to—beings (OL 369). The ontological difference is not simply between being and beings, but also between beings and nothingness, which is the other side of being, that which prevents being from amounting to one more instance of *a* being (neglecting the ontological difference) or from being simply *a* being (falling prey to ontotheology). Being, beings, and nothingness stand (and fall) together: this is, for Pareyson, the great conceptual realization of Heidegger's thinking.

For Heidegger, then, nothing constitutes the reserve of being thanks to which being may not be reduced to beings. Pareyson also notes, however, that Heidegger's nothingness is indeed negativity, but it is not devastating negativity like the negativity of evil, which is actual destructiveness and the real, active, effective power of annihilation. Pareyson is primarily concerned with the capacity for destruction, devastation, and extermination that evil possesses and displays (OL 460). In Pareyson's view, Heidegger's thought is very powerful and successfully thinks of nothingness as negation (*Verneinung*), but not as annihilation and destruction (*Vernichtung*). What is needed for this other kind of thinking that is capable of addressing the destructiveness of negativity and understanding nothingness as power of evil is a way of reasoning that thinks of the ambiguity of negation *alongside* the categories of ethical ambiguity (good and evil). Here lies, for Pareyson, Heidegger's miscarriage and failure, his inability to open up to the darkest aspects of reality, which are given not as negation, but as evil.

Heidegger does not address evil, and this is a major problem for Pareyson (and not only for him). In Heidegger's thinking, the ontological ambiguity of being and beings, an ambiguity that is kept open by the bordering of being and nothing, by their mutual leaning out onto each other, does not have a source capable of accounting for the ambiguity itself. According to Pareyson, to retrace being's ambiguity back to the "ambiguity/exchangeability of being-nothing risks relocating being at the level of metaphysics" (OL 461), which is the level of beings. In Heidegger, being and nothing border on each other, but without an account of the dynamism that may turn one into the other. This dynamic force, this outburst or impulse, would be the real ambiguity, Pareyson thinks, which however remains unthought in Heidegger because in order to think of it in terms that escape metaphysics, one would have to move to a different level of analysis than Heidegger's ontological plane. Such a level, however, is not available to Heidegger because of his refusal to leave the plane of being, to which his analysis remains committed, whether he inquires into the being of *Dasein* or into being as *Ereignis*. Hence, in Heidegger, being and nothing end up being simply two opposite forms of the disclosure of being. In the end, what reigns in Heidegger is being itself, in its fullness and splendor, which shines also where nothing is involved. Silence, stillness, homelessness, the earth into which meaning withdraws: these are not destructive elements, but rather are protective for Heidegger. As the shrine of nothing, for him even death harbors within itself the presencing of being. The primacy of being prevents Heidegger from understanding the radicality of nothingness understood as evil, that is, as absolute devastation and annihilation.[29]

The passage from one term of the ambiguity to the other, the convertibility of the opposites (from being to nothing as well as from speech to silence, from presence to absence, from *Grund* to *Abgrund*) occurs in Heidegger very easily, even too easily, without any serious and deep problematization, and the two sides—wonder and fear, surprise and anxiety, forgetfulness and memory, oblivion and remembrance, recovery and refusal,

Lichtung and *Verbergung*—risk being mixed up and confused one for the other, Pareyson laments. More fundamentally, despite the originary character of the ontological ambiguity of being and nothingness, Heidegger fails to thematize the very origin of that ambiguity, that is, ambiguity in its very origin. Therefore, for Pareyson, Heidegger's thinking is radical in the sense that it does not rest either on being or on nothingness alone and rather operates in terms of their ambiguity, which does not absolutize either. Yet such a thinking is ultimately consigned to being a "blocked radicalism" (*OL* 454), that is, a radicalism that is not radical enough in the sense that it does not go to its own roots; it does not apply to its own source, its own origin, and instead stops short of the ultimate ambiguity—that which only would be able to account for the existence of ambiguity itself. As Pareyson remarks, this is not meant to be a criticism of Heidegger as much as the call for a radicalization of Heidegger's thought so as to "grasp the principle of ambiguity that can only be freedom, from which the entire reality depends" (*OL* 454) and on which it is suspended.

The radicalization has thus to do, to Pareyson's mind, with elevating freedom from an anthropological plane (to which existentialist thinkers still confine it) to the position of "originary freedom," that is, of pure, unlimited, abysmal freedom at the heart of reality. It has to do with acknowledging that one and the same energy that leads to being also moves toward nothingness. Such energy is, for Pareyson, freedom itself, which for him becomes the main ontological principle and ground of reality in its ambiguity of being and nothingness. To anticipate what we will say later: it is not nothingness that renders being possible (nor vice versa); it is freedom—neither as *Grund* nor as *Abgrund* but rather as *Ur-grund*—that makes possible the distinction between being and nothingness, between good and evil, claims Pareyson. Nothingness is that which enables (in a way that is nevertheless not transcendental) not being per se, but rather the *choice for* being and goodness.

Heidegger and Freedom

Heidegger too, of course, is not alien to considering the topic of freedom. Pareyson acknowledges Heidegger's treatment of freedom as occurring within three contexts. First, Heidegger addresses freedom within the context of truth: human beings are owned by freedom, and not vice versa, and it is such freedom (in *Being and Time*, for example, attained through one's own resoluteness toward death) that enables the path to the truth;[30] additionally and along similar lines, the theme of *Gelassenheit* appears as the freeing of beings toward their own being, which is also their truth. Second, Heidegger engages freedom within the context of being: *Ereignis* is thematized as the appropriating event that frees beings toward being. Third, Heidegger confronts freedom within the context of the notions of destiny/destination (*Geschick*), as in *The Question Concerning Technology*, in which human beings are placed in relation to something more than human, something beyond the relation between human beings and being. Here human beings are said to become free only insofar as they belong to destiny/destination, which, however, does not render humans slaves but rather listeners.[31]

We reach here the point at which Pareyson most distances himself from Heidegger. For Pareyson, the task becomes, in fact, pushing freedom—which appears in Heidegger but in a blocked form, still in relation to being and truth, not to nothing—beyond the *relation* of human beings-being or freedom-truth, freedom-destiny, or freedom-necessity. These alternatives are where modern philosophy has taken freedom before Heidegger and from where Heidegger has been, in turn, incapable of recovering it. For Pareyson, though, the task is to retrace freedom within being itself. The task that Heidegger's thought mandates, albeit unwittingly, is therefore that of subverting the primacy of being, which he still endorses despite his confrontation with nothingness, and of replacing the centrality of being with the centrality of freedom. This move, which amounts to radicalizing Heidegger's ontology, is exactly what Pareyson sets himself up to do with the development of his own ontology, which will precisely take the form of an ontology neither of being nor of nothing(ness), but of *freedom*: understood as an ontological, and not an existential, principle.

Pareyson and Schelling

Along the path of radicalizing Heidegger, Pareyson encountered Schelling.[32] Heidegger, too, had encountered Schelling, most notably in a 1936 summer lecture course devoted precisely to Schelling's treatment of freedom.[33] Yet according to Pareyson (and his statement is, of course, arguable), toward Schelling, Heidegger "did not exhibit that depth and penetration that he displayed toward other thinkers" (*OL* 458). Additionally, and this is a more fundamental, conceptual criticism for Pareyson, among the primary ambiguities that constellate his own philosophy, Heidegger did not incorporate the antithesis between good and evil, "which is on the contrary especially stressed by Schelling, who situates the problem of evil in an entirely prominent place and thinks of freedom exactly as the faculty of good and evil" (*OL* 458).

What Pareyson intends to pursue, therefore, is to radicalize freedom in Heidegger through an encounter, which is "in some ways wanted by things themselves" (*OL* 458), between Heidegger and Schelling, so that "Heidegger's being as nothing and Schelling's freedom as faculty of good and evil cross-fertilize each other" (*OL* 458). In its attempt at bringing together Schelling and Heidegger, or being, nothingness, and freedom, Pareyson's philosophy is thus a radicalization of Heidegger, yet one that moves beyond Heidegger and in some ways remedies one of Heidegger's greatest shortcomings, namely, the inability to address the issue of evil in a satisfactory way, especially in light of the event of the Shoah (but other events as well). Whereas it is not at all clear what "the things themselves" Pareyson mentions as mandating the necessity of the encounter between Heidegger and Schelling might be, it is not inappropriate to read the statement as a reference to the Shoah, given Pareyson's overall sensibility toward the theme of "innocent suffering" narrated by Dostoevsky and to which the Shoah bears witness.[34]

How does Pareyson operate the cross-fertilization of the two German thinkers he invokes? By "liberating Schelling from the constraints with which the notion of necessity has burdened his thought and [by freeing] Heidegger from the cumbersome and blocking issue of the relations between being and beings." What will be gained from such a double emancipation will be a terrain where Schelling and Heidegger "will be able to suggest the idea of freedom and the concept of nothing respectively, in their purity and authenticity" (*OL* 457).

Schelling and Freedom

Having devoted careful studies and lecture courses to a variety of thinkers involved in the theme of freedom, from Kierkegaard to Fichte to existentialists such as Jaspers and Lavelle, why does Pareyson select Schelling rather than, for example, Sartre or some other existentialist thinker to set in motion the confrontation with Heidegger on the theme of freedom? Because through his philosophy of freedom, Pareyson argues, Schelling challenges the modern tradition which, starting with Descartes, in both its mechanistic and rationalistic variations thinks of freedom in terms of necessity as *libera necessitas*, or free necessity, that is, as necessity that is free of all external bonds and constraints; as autonomy, self-legislation, and self-sovereignty.

According to Pareyson's interpretation, the culmination of this necessity-based trend of thought is, not surprisingly, Hegel's system, in which absolute freedom amounts to the Spirit's self-realization of being the principle of all necessity. After initially participating in the formation of the Hegelian system, Schelling, however, contributes to its dissolution precisely through his own intent of developing a philosophy of freedom at the core of reality, Pareyson remarks (*OL* 9). In this sense, according to Pareyson, Schelling brings to completion "on the one hand, Plotinus (for his conception of the freedom of the One), and on the other, Pascal (for his notion of the ecstasy of reason)" (*OL* 9).

And yet, despite Schelling's merits in terms of his dealing with the notion of freedom as opposed to Hegel's, Pareyson also recognizes the necessitarian trap in which the problem of freedom is still cast in Schelling who, among the three categories of modality (reality, possibility, and necessity), still chooses to connect freedom to necessity. Yet Schelling's placement of freedom at the core of reality opens the way for the recognition that the ontology of freedom, and not of being, is what enables us to remain faithful to the nature of reality in its ambiguity.

Pareyson declaredly reads Schelling not simply as a post-Hegelian but also, and more radically, as a post-Heideggerian, and he does so perhaps without much hermeneutic loyalty or fairness to Schelling's own position. Analogously, he deliberately and unapologetically reads Heidegger selectively. As he confesses in his inaugural Naples lecture on Heidegger, "My conversation [with Heidegger] has been strongly interpretative and choosy: entire regions traversed by him remain little familiar to me because I crossed them without searching or exploring them deeply, and I am almost incapable of guaranteeing with firmness and consistency the loyalty of my interpretations" (*OL* 441). If this may be an issue for the commentator who wishes to adjudicate the accuracy or correctness of Pareyson's interpretation (that is, for someone who moves within a still representational theory of truth), it is however not a problem on the grounds of Pareyson's own hermeneutic principle. As he says, "each chooses his or her authors. . . . And each reads and meditates on such authors very selectively, according to what Pascal claims: 'It is not in Montaigne but in me that I find all that I see in him.'" Thus, in relation to his own reading of Schelling, Pareyson remarks: "I wish to acknowledge my indubitable debt to Schelling, but also the not entirely Schellingian way in which I unfold him" (*OL* 9). In the context of his reflections on art and aesthetics and, later, on truth and interpretation, Pareyson names "congeniality" or "kindredness" (*congenialità*), that is, cocreating, the interpretative relation that creates and innovates by inevitably somehow betraying the original from which it receives its inspiration and whose core it recovers through a personalized interpretation: an original of which the interpretation wishes to be more than a mere copy, emulation, and repetition.[35]

How does Pareyson's congenial reading of Schelling on freedom unfold? And how does Pareyson deploy Heidegger in this congenial reading of Schelling? The answer lies in the intertwining Pareyson sets in place between freedom, being, and nothingness; in other words, Pareyson reads freedom in relation to the nothingness that always nourishes reality but also haunts it.[36]

Pareyson, Heidegger, and Schelling: or, An Ontology of Freedom

"*In cammino verso la libertà* (On the Way to Freedom)" is the title of a lecture course given by Pareyson in Naples on April 26–30, 1988, that is, three years before his death. Pareyson is at the end of his academic career: his last lecture, titled "Philosophy of Freedom," was to be delivered at the Università di Torino at the end of October (the 27th) of that same year, 1988. To the phenomenologically and hermeneutically trained reader, the title of the Naples lecture course is a clear evocation of Heidegger. Yet the reference, which leaves the German thinker unnamed, twists Heidegger's path in a different direction: Pareyson's path of thinking is on the way, not toward language, but toward freedom. As a matter of fact, the lectures contain Pareyson's most developed version of that ontology of freedom, which becomes the legacy of his thought after (albeit in continuity with) his hermeneutic project in *Truth and Interpretation*.

From the outset of the lectures, Pareyson acknowledges the vestiges of existentialism in choosing freedom as a central theme. He also remarks, however, that the most appropriate terrain on which to confront freedom is neither anthropology nor morality, as has been the case for existentialism, but rather ontology. "The plane of morality lies at a lower level than the one at which one can inquire—in a much higher, more radical, and originary way—into the concept of freedom" (*OL* 9). To understand freedom from a plane so high that it also allows for a greater, abysmal depth, one must situate this concept in its primary relation with being. When freedom is understood as self-subsistent activity, as relinquished to itself and absolute, according to the model set forth by Sartre and much existentialist thought, freedom runs the risk of becoming pure practice, capriciousness, arbitrariness, abuse, and possibly even self-destruction and condemnation. For Pareyson, as was already the case for Rousseau, Kant, and a host of other thinkers, freedom cannot be freedom without some limits, which are the limits constituted by being itself.

> Freedom is spurred by being in the very act in which being gives and entrusts itself to freedom. Even better said, the fact that being entrusts itself to freedom reveals that freedom is launched

by being. . . . That being is entrusted to freedom means that through its own practice, freedom testimonies the originary presence which, in giving itself to freedom, spurs freedom; the originary presence which rules freedom insofar as it demands to be freedom's first object. It means that freedom is so tied to being that it asserts it even when it denies or betrays it . . . freedom's betrayal of being is a self-betrayal. (*OL* 18–19)

What ensues is not a metaphysics of being, where being is discovered as the ultimate horizon of reality, but rather an ontology of freedom, where freedom is disclosed in its *inseparability* from being. "Freedom can be exercised only in the presence of being" (*OL* 19). The inseparability turns out to be also the *convertibility*, which is neither confusion nor mixture, of being and freedom. Freedom and being are not two separate entities, as if freedom were to find being already there as a self-subsistent entity. On the contrary, "being is freedom and freedom is being," Pareyson explicitly claims (*OL* 21). Pareyson calls the convertibility of the two concepts "a vertiginous opening onto the abysmal ground of freedom, of its inexhaustibility" (*OL* 21). The fact that being is freedom means that "being is a free appeal to choose in the sense that what is at stake in choosing are both freedom and being—the two aspects are the same" (*OL* 21). This leads to what Pareyson names the "double abyss" of freedom, which is without limits (except for those given by itself) but also without ground (except for that which it itself is). Only freedom precedes freedom, and only freedom follows freedom (*OL* 22). In that sense, it is always a matter of *pure* freedom. The thematization of the inseparability and convertibility of freedom and being leading to the notion of pure freedom emerges out of Pareyson's encounter with Heidegger and Schelling: a radicalized Heidegger, as we have seen, but also a post-Heideggerian Schelling.

In what sense can one speak here of a post-Heideggerian Schelling? This is in the sense that, as already mentioned, Schelling's notion of freedom as hermeneutic principle of explanation of reality is purified of its necessitarian limitations through the deployment of Heidegger's concept of nothingness. In other words, Heidegger's idea of nothingness disables the deterministic framework within which Schelling's notion of freedom is still cast, according to Pareyson.

Pareyson starts with reality and retraces freedom there, at and as the core of reality, as "the heart itself of reality and its unfathomable depth" (*EP* 27). Of the three categories of modality already mentioned (reality, possibility, and necessity), reality is, for Pareyson, the most important as well as the most inexplicable and mysterious. Reality as such is completely gratuitous and ungrounded. About reality, one "can say neither that it is because it *could* be nor that is because it *could but* [that is, *had to*] be" (*OL* 465). Reality is grounded neither on possibility, which is rather "the shadow of reality, detached from it and transposed backward," nor on necessity, which is "a reality so heavy and stubborn that it clings to nothing but itself" (*OL* 465). As Angelus Silesius's rose, which blooms because it blooms, reality simply is because it is; it is neither announced by possibility nor grounded on necessity. As both gratuitous and ungrounded, it may appear, on the one hand, as a surplus, a gift of generosity, pure excess that becomes an object of wonder and admiration; on the other hand, though, it may also appear in its darkest aspect of groundlessness as condemnation, punishment, the source of sorrow and unhappiness for one's own existence, regret for being, and desire for nonbeing instead: as witnessed by the cry "better not to be born" raised by the Silenus, by the Greek tragic poets, up to Shakespeare and Leopardi. By itself, reality provokes simultaneously "amazement and horror, anxiety and wonder: its essential feature is ambiguity. The other side of being is nothingness; ontology is always accompanied by meontology" (*OL* 466).

Saying that reality is gratuitous and ungrounded means saying that reality depends on nothing: it has neither reason nor ground for its own being real. All events are both unforeseeable and irrevocable. Unforeseeability means that events are an absolute beginning: unexpected, surprising, unpredictable, sudden; "like the telephone ring, the alarm clock, a gunshot, or a lightening in the dark" (*OL* 30). Irrevocability implies that what was not there at a previous moment now is and cannot but be. But this irrevocability, the fact that reality is as is and cannot be changed, is only "a seeming necessity," Pareyson explains, "a hypothetical necessity, tied to a condition, namely, the condition that there be an 'if,' which is itself the very act of freedom" (*OL* 32). This, for Pareyson, amounts to saying that "reality *hangs on freedom*; it is, as it were, vertiginously suspended over the abyss of freedom" (*EP* 20). This constitutes, for Pareyson, Schelling's (and Plotinus's) major lesson, namely, retracing freedom at the heart of reality. Events are preceded by nothing, nothing is their necessary cause, and this constitutes their freedom; even better said, this *is* freedom. In fact, as Pareyson remarks, "The characteristic of freedom is precisely this, namely, that nothing precedes it. Freedom is preceded only by freedom itself. . . . Freedom that is nothing but freedom is freedom that has nothingness, the void, nothing at its outset. Freedom is postulated by freedom itself. The act that affirms freedom is itself already an act of freedom" (*OL* 31).

Freedom is thus originary; it is the ground and origin of reality. This ground is, however, not a ground; it is an abyss. If the beginning of freedom is freedom itself, freedom is both beginning and choice: choice that finds no ground except, once again, its own act of being by choosing.[37] This is what Pareyson names "the nothingness of freedom," its abysmal character, the fact that freedom begins in and from nothingness, there is nothing that grants its existence except freedom itself. Freedom is "in a relation with *negativity* precisely at the moment when it asserts itself" (OL 458). This is the point where the relation with nothingness, on which Heidegger has meditated brilliantly, finds the most appropriate place; that is, the idea that meontology is as fundamental to reality as ontology is.

Nothingness acquires its ontologically powerful status precisely in the presence of freedom alone, Pareyson claims. As he writes,

> It is not being that is in contact with nothingness; the truly originary contact lies between nothingness and freedom. Where there is nothingness, there is also freedom, and vice versa. Freedom can be positive only if it has experienced and defeated negation by asserting itself as victory over nothingness and evil. In a metaphysics or philosophy of being, the alternative inherent in freedom as choice is missing; thus, there is only compact positivity, which leaves no room for nothingness and thereby reduces evil to non-being, lack, and privation. . . . On the contrary, in a philosophy of freedom, nothingness is central and profound: the term 'positive' is deserved only by that which could have been negative; "good" [can be said] only of that which has risked being evil. The two terms only subsist in mutual reference—not by logical-dialectical necessity but rather by the power of freedom. . . . It is by freedom that the good arises and asserts itself, but it is also by freedom that evil is born and spreads. (OL 459–460)

Being is an appeal to freedom because it is only in the act of freedom that being is brought to be, yet freedom always chooses within an alternative, between being and nothingness. The interval that is generated between freedom, being, and nothingness is what enables the move from ontological nothing (the nothing of meontology) to the ethical nothingness of destructiveness and annihilation (the nothing of evil). Nothingness is, per se, neither better nor worse than being. When freedom *chooses* nonbeing, that is, when freedom actualizes nonbeing, evil emerges and nothingness becomes destructive. What is good is, for Pareyson, not being but chosen being, being that has been chosen as such. Analogously, what is evil is not nothingness but the choice, the free act that chooses in favor of nothingness and nonbeing, and enacting the choice also activates the destructiveness of nothingness as evil. Good and evil do not preexist freedom's choice. This is true, for Pareyson, to the point of claiming that a chosen evil is preferable to an imposed good (OL 468). A good that has been imposed, a good that lacks its origin in freedom, is not in fact a good but a constraint, a lack of freedom; on the contrary, an evil that has been chosen is an evil that can always be remedied and undone through a choice in favor of being. Pareyson also frames this positivity and negativity in terms of faithfulness to or betrayal of being, respectively. Being and nonbeing are an appeal to choice, not an appeal by that which precedes choice, but rather an appeal to be (or not to be) through the choice. By responding to the appeal, freedom also initiates that to which it responds, which does not exist beforehand. Ontology and freedom are inextricably joined (and with them, one could add responsibility, which is thus also as originary and absolute as freedom).[38]

The conclusion of Pareyson's line of reasoning is that ambiguity not only affects reality, as Heidegger had already recognized, but that freedom too is ambiguous, as a post-Heideggerian reading of Schelling brings one to realize. Freedom is what energizes reality; it *is* reality. Freedom is the one, the unity that generates the two, the duplicity (and then the multiplicity) that arises not by internal scission or by self-duplication, but rather by choosing within an alternative that, itself, originates in the very act of choosing; and what is generated is itself double (being and nothing). There are not two freedoms—positive freedom or negative freedom—any more than there are two realities, Pareyson repeats. Freedom is only one, it is unique, but it is ambiguous, duplicitous; it is both positive *and* negative freedom at once, a choice between assertion and a denial of being, possibility of initiative but also of termination, choice of being (the being of freedom) or choice of nothing (the nothing of freedom). Unlimited because otherwise it is not freedom, freedom "ignores all limits, laws, or norms except the ones that it has freely accepted" (EP 27).

What Pareyson gives his readers in these lectures—which are arduous, complex, and demanding to read and understand, both linguistically and conceptually because of an essentiality that may appear as cursory—is not a phenomenology of human freedom, as he repeats often;[39] nor (and for some of the same reasons) does he offer an existentialist account of freedom focused on morality or on the notion of the will. Rather, his legacy is that of an ontology of originary freedom in the sense that freedom is at the core of reality and is the beginning of, but also the choice for, existence. Between human freedom and originary freedom there is inseparability; they differ yet they are homogeneous. It is only on the background of an ontological understanding of freedom as the core of reality that human freedom can reverberate in its ontological meaning. "Being and nothingness, good and evil, joy and suffering are present not only within human existence and historical reality . . . but also at the heart itself of the real, at the highest level of freedom" (*EP* 33).

Whereas Heidegger understands freedom as human freedom in relation to being (but not to nothing) and thus is incapable of accounting for the evil of nothingness, Pareyson understands being in relation to freedom as originary freedom, that is, freedom as both beginning (origin) and choice. This difference between the two thinkers accounts for the possibility, on Pareyson's side, of presenting the evil of nothingness as one of the alternatives among which originary freedom is free to choose when it comes to being and nothingness. In other words, Pareyson accounts for destructive evil, for nothingness as annihilation (*Vernichtigung*), whereas Heidegger can only account for ontological nothing, for nothing as nonbeing (*Verneinung*).

Why can Heidegger not descend into the abyss of freedom despite the acuteness of his speculation on reality? What prevents Heidegger from descending deeply down the path suggested, at least in part, by Schelling? For Pareyson, the reason lies in Heidegger's anti-Christian or (more neutrally stated, since Heidegger never engages in an explicit criticism of Christianity) non-Christian sentiment—more specifically, in his commitment to Greek thought. The Greeks only understood freedom in epistemological-political terms as *eleutheria*, as power of free deliberation within (or even without or outside) the *polis*. Conversely, the notion of freedom as choice is, according to Pareyson, one of Christianity's main contributions to the history of Western thought.

Is Pareyson trying to Christianize Heidegger? Pareyson's answer is a resounding "No."[40] The task, for Pareyson, is rather that of retrieving, at the core of Christianity, the tragic dimension that locates the origin of both good and evil at the heart of the ontological principle and thus acknowledges nothingness in all its ontological power of destruction. This is the "daring" effort of retracing the root of evil (as well as of goodness) *in* and *as* the principle of reality. This principle of reality is what the religious experience, which is however in need of the critical activity of philosophical hermeneutics, names "God." Pareyson's ultimate project, which remains incomplete because of his passing, is thus one of retracing evil in God: an outrageous, "temerarious" proposal, as he is very much ready to acknowledge, and a proposal we cannot follow here.[41]

We will conclude this discussion of Pareyson's encounter with Heidegger and Schelling with a suggestion, which is, in fact, a provocation. Pareyson's unfinished, audacious, undaunted and possibly even heroic project of positioning freedom as the ultimate ambiguity at the source of reality is perhaps also an attempt at going beyond the path—which Heidegger, in his alleged nihilism, partly follows—trodden by an author who is not among Pareyson's favorites, namely, Nietzsche. As is well known, "Dionysus versus the Crucified" are the words Nietzsche places as the conclusion of *Ecce Homo*; the choice is here between two exclusive modes of approaching reality, being, and nothingness; namely, the Greek attitude and the Christian. Against Heidegger's interpretation of Nietzsche as the last metaphysician, Pareyson reads Nietzsche as a tragic philosopher, as a philosopher of tragedy. But is tragedy not that which also, ultimately and fundamentally, characterizes Pareyson's own thought of the ambiguity of freedom, thereby possibly bringing Pareyson close to Nietzsche at least in terms of a shared belief in the tragic core of reality? The question is complex, but if we follow (as the same time as we radicalize) Pareyson with Schelling beyond Heidegger, might it not be that Nietzsche's sentence could, or perhaps even should, be read alternatively as Dionysus *and* the Crucified? This union that is also a unity might be Pareyson's last, undeclared, unconfessable, and perhaps even abhorred legacy, given his lack of enthusiasm for Nietzsche. It would certainly be an explosive legacy, as Nietzsche would say, yet it could also contain a hopeful promise: one that would freely celebrate the ambiguity of life in all its aspects, joyful and good (Dionysus) as well as tragic and even evil (the Crucified). Could it be that Pareyson has found a way to move beyond Heidegger also through his own recovery of the tragic spirit of the Greeks while at the same time not becoming anti-Christian? Perhaps this is another legacy that Pareyson's philosophy might leave us as a topic for free exploration and border crossing.

Notes

1. As Paolo Diego Bubbio writes, "Three philosophers will be remembered as the greatest thinkers in the first generation of the theorists of Hermeneutics after Heidegger. The first is the German philosopher Hans-Georg Gadamer. The second is the French philosopher Paul Ricoeur. The third is the Italian philosopher Luigi Pareyson"; see Paolo Diego Bubbio, "Introduction: Luigi Pareyson: The Third Way to Hermeneutics," in *Luigi Pareyson: Existence, Interpretation, Freedom* (Aurora, CO: Davies Group, 2009), 1.

2. Luigi Pareyson, *Truth and Interpretation*, trans. Robert T. Valgenti (Albany: State University of New York Press, 2013). For an overview of the reception of Pareyson's philosophy and the status of Pareyson studies in the English-speaking countries, see Silvia Benso, "Lost in Translation. Luigi Pareyson e gli studi pareysoniani in ambito anglosassone [*Lost in Translation*: Luigi Pareyson and Pareyson Scholarship in the Anglophone World]," *Annuario Filosofico* 33 (2017): 195–207.

3. For an early essay in English on Pareyson's hermeneutic theory, see Peter Carravetta, "An Introduction to the Hermeneutics of Luigi Pareyson," *Differentia: Review of Italian Thought* 3–4, 3 (1989): 217–241. Among the many works on Pareyson's overall philosophy, which is extensively studied in Italy, see Francesco Russo, *Esistenza e libertà* (Rome: Armando, 1993); Marianna Gensabella Furnari, *I sentieri della libertà* (Milan: Guerini, 1994); Francesco Paolo Ciglia, *Ermeneutica e libertà* (Rome: Bulzoni, 1995); Francesco Tomatis, *Ontologia del male* (Rome: Città Nuova, 1995); Claudio Ciancio, *Pareyson e l'esistenzialismo* (Milan: Mursia, 1998); and Rosaria Longo, *L'abisso della libertà* (Milan: Angeli, 2000).

4. On this, see, among others, John D. Caputo, *The Mystical Elements of Heidegger's Thought* (Fordham, NY: Fordham University Press, 1986), and also Iain D. Thompson, *Heidegger, Art and Postmodernity* (New York: Cambridge University Press, 2011), 20n22.

5. Pareyson, 142.

6. Pareyson, 23.

7. Luigi Pareyson, *Verità e interpretazione* (Milan: Mursia, 1971), 53. Unless the English edition is esplicitly referenced in the notes, references in this essay are to this Italian edition, in which case translations into English are my own.

8. On Pareyson's proposition concerning a philosophy of the inexhaustible, see Silvia Benso and Brian Schroeder, eds., *Thinking the Inexhaustible: Art, Interpretation, and Freedom in the Philosophy of Luigi Pareyson* (Albany: State University of New York Press, 2018), and Justin L. Harmon, "Interpretation from the Ground Up: Luigi Pareyson's Hermeneutics of Inexhaustibility and Its Implications for Moral Ontology," *Trópos: Journal of Hermeneutics and Philosophical Criticism* 10, 1 (2017): 69–90.

9. On this theme, see Lauren Swayne Barthold, "Truth as the Origin (Rather than Goal) of Inquiry," in Benso and Schroeder, eds., *Thinking the Inexhaustible*, 123–138.

10. See the chapter devoted to "Truth and Ideology" in Pareyson, *Truth and Interpretation*," 79–165.

11. Pareyson, 106.

12. Pareyson, 107.

13. On the topic of Pareyson's contributions to aesthetic theory, see many of the essays contained in Benso and Schroeder, eds., *Thinking the Inexhaustible*, and especially Paolo D'Angelo, "Pareyson's Role in Twentieth-Century Italian Aesthetics," in Benso and Schroeder, eds., *Thinking the Inexhaustible*, 43–60, and Umberto Eco, "Pareyson vs. Croce: The Novelties of Pareyson's 1954 *Estetica*," in Benso and Schroeder, eds., *Thinking the Inexhaustible*, 61–80. See also, in a special journal issue devoted to Italian critical theory, Justin Harmon, "Adventures of Form: Italian Aesthetics from Neo-Idealism to Pareyson," *Annali d'Italianistica* 29 (2011): 363–379.

14. On Pareyson's existentialist stage, see the pages (some of the very few in English) devoted to this by Edward Baring in "Existential Journey: 1930–1940," in *Converts to the Real: Catholicism and the Making of Continental Philosophy* (Cambridge,

MA: Harvard University Press, 2019), 180–181. See also Claudio Ciancio, "Pareyson e l'esistenzialismo," *Annuario filosofico* 13 (1997–1998): 449–462.

15. Luigi Pareyson, *Esistenza e persona* (Genoa: Il Melangolo, 1985); hereafter referred to as *EP*. All quotations will be from the fourth edition, which contains as an addition the important autobiographical essay, "Dal personalismo esistenziale all'ontologia della libertà [From Existential Personalism to the Ontology of Freedom]."

16. Luigi Pareyson, *Ontologia della libertà. Il male e la sofferenza* [*Ontology of Freedom: Evil and Suffering*] (Turin: Einaudi, 1995), 441; hereafter referred to as *OL*. Pareyson's first essay on Heidegger appeared in 1938 as part of his "Note sulla filosofia dell'esistenza," *Giornale critico della filosofia italiana* 6 (1938): 406–438, and was then republished as "Esistenziale ed esistentivo nel pensiero di M. Heidegger e K. Jaspers," in Luigi Pareyson, *Studi sull'esistenzialismo* (Milan: Mursia, 2001), 141–173. The first edition of this book was published in 1943 and the essay appears in chapter 5 of part 2 of the volume. On Pareyson's relation to Heidegger's thought and the development of that relationship, see Salvatore Rindone, "Una filosofia 'incompiuta.' Pareyson interprete di Heidegger," *Dialegesthai. Rivista telematica di filosofia* 20 (2018), https://mondodomani.org/dialegesthai/sr01.htm#rif7. In this essay, Rindone organizes the unfolding of such a relation according to six subsequent descriptions through which Pareyson qualifies Heidegger: (1) existentialist philosopher; (2) atheist and humanist philosopher; (3) philosopher of finitude; (4) philosopher of being; (5) philosopher of "blocked radicalism"; and (6) anti-Christian philosopher.

17. See Francesco Paolo Ciglia, "Heidegger e l'interrogazione religiosa. Un intreccio esegetico e speculativo," *Idee. Rivista di filosofia* 31–32 (1996): 191. On Pareyson's relation to Heidegger, see, among others, Ugo Maria Ugazio, "Pareyson interprete di Heidegger," *Archivio di filosofia* 57, 1–3 (1989): 93–102.

18. What is here translated as "through" freedom could also be rendered as "due to" freedom; the Italian proposition is *per*, which can in fact mean both "through" and "due to" as well as "because of."

19. For discussions of some specific aspects of the philosophies of Severino, Vattimo, and Sini, see chapters 2, 3, and 6 in this volume.

20. The essay also appears in *Ontologia della libertà* as "Il nulla e la libertà come inizio [Nothingness and Freedom as Beginning]."

21. On the so-called *Kehre* in Heidegger's thought, see, among the many available works, James Risser, ed., *Heidegger toward the Turn: Essays on the Work of the 1930s* (Albany: State University of New York Press, 1999); Thomas Sheehan, "The Turn and *Ereignis*: A Prolegomenon to *Introduction to Metaphysics*," in *The Companion to Heidegger's Introduction to Metaphysics*, ed. Richard Polt and Gregory Fried (New Haven: Yale University Press, 2004); Richard Capobianco, *Engaging Heidegger* (Toronto: Toronto University Press, 2011); and Bret W. Davis, "Returning the World to Nature: Heidegger's Turn from a Transcendental-Horizonal Projection of World to an Indwelling Releasement to the Open-region," *Continental Philosophy Review* 47, 3–4 (2014): 373–397.

22. On the "second beginning," see especially Martin Heidegger, *Contributions to Philosophy: On the Event*, trans. Richard Rojcewicz and Daniela Vallega-Neu

(Bloomington: Indiana University Press, 2012). Pareyson makes frequent reference to the *Beiträge* in the course of his lecture, especially in the section devoted to Heidegger's anti-Christian sentiments and his discussion of the notion of God; see OL 442–449.

23. On Pareyson's not entirely sympathetic position toward Hegel, see Maurizio Pagano, "Presenza di Hegel nel pensiero di Luigi Pareyson," *Archivio di Filosofia* 85, 1 (2017): 121–134. See also Maria Cristina Di Nino, *La dialettica della libertà nell'ermeneutica di Luigi Pareyson. Un dialogo con Hegel* (Vercelli: Mercurio, 2007).

24. On the urgency of the *Grundfrage* for Pareyson, see Massimo Cacciari, "Pareyson e la domanda fondamentale," *Atti dell'Accademia delle Scienze di Torino* 128, 2 (1994): 16–24.

25. On Heidegger's relation to Leibniz, see, for example, Hans Ruin, "Leibniz and Heidegger on Sufficient Reason," *Studia Leibnitiana* 30, 1 (1998): 49–67, and Daniel Selcer, "Heidegger's Leibniz and Abyssal Identity," *Continental Philosophy Review* 36, 3 (2003): 303–324.

26. Nietzsche, 1887–88, Fragments (no. 27), where he writes: "Nihilism: the goal is missing; the answer to 'why?' is missing." Pareyson also extensively quotes Dostoevsky's *Demons* as well as Giacomo Leopardi's *Canto Notturno*.

27. On Heidegger and nothing in the context of his *Introduction to Metaphysics*, see Richard Polt, "The Question of Nothing," in *A Companion to Heidegger's Introduction to Metaphysics*, ed. R. Polt and G. Fried (New Haven: Yale University Press, 2001), 57–82.

28. On this topic, see Sergio Givone, "Philosophy and Novel in the Later Pareyson," in Benso and Schroeder, ed., *Thinking the Inexhaustible*, 185–200. See also Giuseppe Riconda, "Ermeneutica dell'esperienza religiosa e ontologia," *Archivio di filosofia* 64, 1–3 (1996): 355–366.

29. A similar claim is made also, in ways that cannot be analyzed here, by Jean-Luc Nancy, *The Experience of Freedom*, trans. Bridget McDonald (Stanford, CA: Stanford University Press, 1993).

30. On the place and role of freedom especially in *Being and Time*, see Charles Guignon, "Heidegger's Concept of Freedom, 1927–1930," in *Interpreting Heidegger: Critical Essays*, ed. Daniel Dahlstrom (Cambridge: Cambridge University Press, 2011), 79–105. See also Simon Critchley, "The Null Basis-Being of a Nullity, or between Two Nothings," in *Phenomenologies of the Stranger: Between Hostility and Hospitality*, ed. R. Kearney and K. Semonovitch (New York: Fordham University Press, 2011), 145–154.

31. On Heidegger and freedom, see the essay by Hans Ruin, "The Destiny of Freedom: In Heidegger," *Continental Philosophy Review* 41, 3 (2008): 277–299.

32. For Pareyson's indebtedness to Schelling on various fronts and for his assessment of the fecundity of Schelling's thought for contemporary philosophy, see Pareyson, *Truth and Interpretation*, 142–144.

33. See Martin Heidegger, *Schelling's Treatise on the Essence of Human Freedom*, trans. Joan Stambaugh (Columbus: Ohio State University Press, 1985). On Heidegger's treatment of Schelling, see, among many, Parvis Emad, "Heidegger on

Schelling's Concept of Freedom," *Man and World* 8 (1975): 157–174, and Sonia Sikka, "Heidegger's Appropriation of Schelling," *Southern Journal of Philosophy* 32 (1994): 412–448.

34. On the topic of Pareyson's attitude toward suffering and evil, see Claudio Ciancio, "Il male e la sofferenza in Pareyson. Un'interpretazione filosofica di Dostoevskij," in *Giobbe. Il problema del male nel pensiero contemporaneo*, ed. A. Pieretti (Assisi: Cittadella Editrice, 1996), 109–135.

35. See Pareyson, *Truth and Interpretation*, 34–35 and 41–42; see also Robert T. Valgenti, "The Unfamiliarity of Kindredness: Towards a Hermeneutics of Community," in Benso and Schroeder, eds., *Thinking the Inexhaustible*, 105–122.

36. On the itinerary that brings Pareyson from Schelling to the development and proposal of his own ontology of freedom, see Claudio Ciancio, "De Schelling a la ontología de la libertad," *Contrastes. Revista Internacional de Filosofía* 20, 1 (2015): 67–82.

37. On this, see Luca Ghisleri, *Inizio e scelta. Il problema della libertà nel pensiero di Luigi Pareyson* (Turin: Trauben, 2003).

38. On this, one could retrace possible similarities between Pareyson and Levinas.

39. See also Francesco Tomatis, "Luigi Pareyson, Good, Evil, Free Will," *Annali d'Italianistica* 29, 1 (2011): 131–140.

40. On this topic, with some reference to Pareyson, see William Franke, "Existentialism: An Atheistic or a Christian Philosophy?" in *Analecta Husserliana: The Yearbook of Phenomenological Research Volume CIII: Phenomenology and Existentialism Book One: New Waves of Philosophical Inspiration* (Dordrecht: Springer Science and Business Media, 2009), 371–394.

41. On this, see Martin G. Weiss, "Evil in God: Pareyson's Ontology of Freedom," in Benso and Schroeder, *Thinking the Inexhaustible*," 169–184. See also Paolo Galli, "Libertà e male in Dio. Pareyson a confronto con Schelling," *Rivista di filosofia neoscolastica* 92, 1 (2000): 26–58, and Antonio Stevenazzi, *Il "male in Dio." Rivelazione e ragione nell'ultimo Pareyson* (Verona: Fede e Cultura, 2006).

2

Emanuele Severino versus Western Nihilism

(A Guide for the Perplexed)

Alessandro Carrera

Time Is *Not* of the Essence

As much as journalistic statements amount to something, in Italy very few people would dispute that Emanuele Severino (born in Brescia, Italy, in 1929 and died in 2020) has been one of "the greatest Italian philosophers." Even his critics admit that in his teaching and eighty-something books he has erected a formidable wall of thought—and of words. Severino has fashioned a philosophical system that works like a magical castle—it is easy to get in and hard to get out. The fundamental lines of his system, which were anticipated in *La struttura originaria* (*The Original Structure*, 1958, 1981), are brought into the light in *The Essence of Nihilism* (1972, 1982), which is the focus of this chapter.[1] More accessible to the common reader than *La struttura originaria*, *The Essence of Nihilism* is the key to the castle's main entrance. The reader must be warned, though: it will take some time to explore the whole building. You get in, lose yourself in its hallways and rooms, and even if you do not agree with the architecture, which is perhaps too solid for your postmodern sensibility, you do not want to leave. The next turn will open up an unexpected view on the interior; the sudden shift of a window curtain will allow you to cast a glimpse outside the impregnable walls. From a distance, you will be able to look at what today's world has become. See from this bulwark the sad fate of religion dissecting God to bits and pieces for ungodly purposes; witness from a balcony the inevitable decline of all totalitarian systems, including planetary capitalism; get a chill from the next window down the corridor while you watch the army parade of destructive technology passing by. You may think that as long as you stay inside those thick walls you will be safe. Outside, everything is transient and destined to decay. Inside, everything is incontrovertible, eternal, joyous, and glorious.

Then Severino himself, like the gentle host he is, will come to tell you that you are mistaken. There is no safe haven from the pervasive nihilism of a civilization embracing the unquestioned belief that "all things must pass." You should welcome the opposite notion instead, that nothing passes and everything is eternal inside and outside the castle. To be more accurate: everything goes *beyond* your perception; everything crosses the threshold of what appears, fading away into the invisible land of what does not appear. What no longer appears, however, stays; and it stays forever, because there is no place where what has been, is, or will be can cease to exist. You object that the wisdom of the world says the opposite. It says that there is no place where what does not appear could reside. But Severino will give you no quarter. Can anything that exists, can Being, turn into nothingness? Can nothingness really turn into Being? Do you really believe *that*?

Nietzsche was elated and terrified at the intimation of the eternal return. Heidegger despaired over the inadequacy of language to conceptualize the Event that changes the history of Being. On his part, Severino suggests that the terror at the idea that nothing goes away, or the cry over the impossibility of rationalizing the logic of becoming, must be superseded by the realization that our transience and our pains are already comprehended in the joy and glory of All-Being, never submitted to the tyranny of time. In his vision, the ultimate nihilism of our civilization must be blamed on the reduction of Being to a product of time. Let us be careful, though; the anti-Platonic edifice that Severino has built is not meant to demonstrate that the everyday world is just an appearance and that we live in the Matrix. On the contrary, Severino's point is that every appearance *is*, no matter how deceiving it looks, for if it is something (and even appearances are something), it could not reside outside Being. That everything exists forever and everything is eternal does not mean that the empirical you and I are immortal in time (eternity is not immortality), but that each moment, every slice of reality *is*, and therefore is forever, since whatever is cannot come into being or cease to be.

Initially billed as "neo-Parmenidism," Severino's philosophy is an all-encompassing critique of the "wrong path" taken by post-Parmenidean metaphysics, namely, the assumption that time and becoming are self-evident, need no demonstration, and consequently, in the words of the *Sophist*'s Stranger (and in blatant violation of Parmenides's sharp distinction between Being and nonbeing), it is acceptable to think that beings come into being or emerge from nothing only to disappear into nothingness after their time has run its course. Severino has taken a different route. Paraphrasing King Lear, he wants you to understand that "nothing will come of nothing." Beings cannot "come into being"; either they are or they are not. Not only that: beings cannot be created. The very act of creation implies that things can emerge from nothing by virtue of an external agency and, as long as they have been brought into the world, can be annihilated too. Creationism is nihilism under another name.

Back in the 1960s, Severino's criticism of the nihilistic core of creation led him to a long and painful dispute with the Vatican hierarchy and the Catholic University in Milan, where he was an associate professor. The controversy culminated in 1969 with a verdict of heresy from the Supreme Sacred Congregation of the Holy Office (now Congregation for the Doctrine of the Faith) and the termination of his appointment. No one else has been officially sentenced for heresy since.

The label of Last Heretic is a distinction that Severino has carried over the years with an unusual grace. After being removed from the Catholic University, during his tenure at the University of Venice and later on at the University San Raffaele in Milan, he has greatly expanded the logical, historical, and cultural implications of his anti-Platonic and anti-Aristotelian approach. The assumption that beings come into being and return into nothingness, either by creation or by production, brings about the notion that the world can be produced or destroyed as it pleases God or humans. Yet if all beings exist eternally (in a sense that has nothing to do with the religious notion of eternal life or eternity imagined as time stretching into infinity), they cannot be annihilated. Equally critical of Catholic creationism and Heidegger's emphasis on time and ontological difference at the expense of Being; equally critical of communism and capitalism (both based on a nihilistic faith in the infinity of production), Severino's philosophical enterprise has commanded respect, not to mention fascination, even among thinkers who could not disagree more with him. Does it sound surprising that he now has a following among Catholic academicians? They cannot share his philosophy, yet they cannot stop conversing with him. As a matter of fact, Severino enjoys a cultish following in different strata of Italy's intellectual *milieu*, from high school teachers to independent scholars, and from professional philosophers to scientists. The recently founded Associazione Studi Emanuele Severino (ASES) has already held two large Severino conferences. One could say jokingly that if Italians were not prevented from creating new religions by the overwhelming presence of the Catholic Church, Severino could be the originator of a new creed.

The Essence of Nihilism in Detail

The Essence of Nihilism is Severino's first book to be translated into English.[2] The introductory chapter, "The Structure of Western History and the Supersession of the Alienated Critique of Alienation," which was written in 1978 and later revised, defines the structure of Western civilization according to the "essential unconscious of the West," that is, the will that things be nothing. The inhabitants of the West are the inhabitants of "time" to the extent that Europe's scientific knowledge and technological domination, now extended to the rest of the world, are in fact the product and triumph of Being's submission to time, change, and nothingness. In Severino's view, Heidegger's critique of technology did not go far enough; in fact, it did not find a way out (Severino wrote his massive dissertation on Heidegger long before Heidegger's name was on everyone's lips in Italy).[3] Nihilism and technology are related because they are both based on the assumption that beings can be brought into Being or erased from Being.

No European or Western ideology has ever rejected this unholy union of nihilism and technology, which regards each thing (every being, every entity) as "isolated" from Being and therefore subject to endless manipulation. In fact, nihilism sees the entire world as a "thing" that can be produced or destroyed like any other. Nihilism therefore goes deeper than the forgetfulness of Being lamented by Heidegger. Since the beginning of Western history, what has been forgotten or better suppressed was not the ontological difference between Being and beings, but the much more radical difference between Being and nothingness.

This repression/suppression has brought about the unquestioned faith in becoming and in beings that can appear or disappear without leaving a trace. An atomic bomb destroys Hiroshima and as a result, common sense accepts that Hiroshima has become "nothing." But if Hiroshima was *not* "nothing," then it cannot "become" nothing. In the dimension of Being, inaccessible to metaphysics (to nihilism), Hiroshima is always-already saved insofar as every instant of its reality has been, is, and will always be nowhere else than in Being, from which it will never exit (admittedly, this is a highly controversial statement, one of the most difficult to accept in Severino's entire system yet not the easiest one to refute, despite being incompatible with common sense).[4]

The reduction of Being to "presence" has greatly contributed to the oblivion of the opposition between Being and nothingness. Aristotle is the main culprit here, since his principle of noncontradiction (*Metaphysics*, Book IV) accepts that identity is not absolute, and it is subject to time (A=A *as long as* A is A). The fundamental distortion of declaring Being perishable and therefore equal to nonbeing is already ingrained in the very formula designed to avoid it. But all Being is immutable, and the ontological difference does not take place between a supreme, unperishable Being and the perishable beings. Yet becoming is not an illusion either; rather, it is part of Being's Appearing.

Therefore, we return to Parmenides. "Ritornare a Parmenide (Returning to Parmenides)" is the 1964 article (thoroughly revised in *The Essence of Nihilism*) that established Severino as a strong philosophical voice (in his library, Heidegger had a copy both of "Ritornare a Parmenide" and of Severino's dissertation on him, possibly thanks to Gadamer). A return to Parmenides means a radical reconsideration of the path that was lost when philosophy chose (but it was destiny rather than choice) becoming over Being. The relationship between the One and the Many does not find a resolution in the assumption that beings can "become." The plurality of modes of existence, which is undisputable, can only be a plurality of modes of not-being-nothing, not a plurality of different shades of nothingness. The plurality of modes is neither proof that beings cease to be nor that Being becomes different from itself. Even the ontological argument for the existence of God, which affirms that full and immutable existence belongs only to a being elevated to the status of perfect Being, sacrifices the concrete world of beings to nothingness and is therefore nihilistic to the core. We have to admit instead that all beings are ontologically "perfect." Otherwise, they simply would not be.

Existence is not a predicate of essence; it is a consequential necessity. Each thing that exists, exists necessarily. Becoming exists too (it is not nothing), but its existence does not prove that things subjected to becoming exit from Being. In fact, Parmenides too is responsible for the difficulty of holding on to the opposition of Being and nothingness. Having introduced the problematic distinction between truth and opinion in a way that resembles the difference between Being and nonbeing, Parmenides too has unwillingly contributed to the "destiny" that ultimately led to the nihilistic turn of Western philosophy (for opinion is not nothing either). The ultimate *aporia* that thinking is compelled to resolve is that nothingness, no matter the theoretical subtlety with which it is introduced, has always been posited as something.[5]

In the chapter called "The Path of Day," Severino claims that the history of the West is that of a metaphysical experiment that has progressed from theology (the production of God) to technology (the production of things). As we have seen, the defining moment occurred when Plato, in *Sophist*, introduced a middle ground (participation, *metaxy*) between Being and nothingness, which led to the inevitable "parricide" of Parmenides.

Severino points out that Plato's philosophy is not a "description" of the world; Plato literally "created" the world. Plato's "participation" of Being and nothingness is what constitutes the very notion of "world" that we still share. The world as becoming, the world as made of "things," and, ultimately, the world as the result of a creating activity—"our" world here and now, is the middle ground between Being and nothingness that Plato envisioned.

> Plato founded not a theory of the "world," but the "world" itself. Before Plato there was neither "world" nor production and destruction: they had been waiting, in concealment, to be called into the light. For the "world" (the *metaxy* between Being and Nothing) to come to light, Being and Nothing had first to be called forth from concealment. But this is not to say that they *emerge* from a total concealment—since Being and Nothing always already appear: rather, "calling forth" expresses the need to bear witness to that which eternally appears. Parmenides was this witness. Thus only the West was to call the "world" into the light; yet in evoking the "world," at the same time it [the West] abandoned the truth of Being dawning in the testimony. The "world," as a middle ground between Being and Nothing, appeared on the horizon only because of the attention paid to Being and Nothing; but with the supervention of the "world," the *truth* of Being and Nothing was abandoned.[6]

To answer the most obvious objection, yes, there was a world before Plato, but Homer's world was a world of deeds and passions entirely acted out, a world where the just man was just without depending on the idea of justice. And what about the East? The East has not encountered "the world" the same way the West did. The East has inhabited the Earth and has looked up at the sky, but it has not occupied, singled out, and conceptualized its dwelling place as a composite world made of many isolated pieces.

As Severino has argued, the so-called parricide was not entirely successful.[7] At any rate, it could not be avoided. It was a matter of destiny, not personal decision. Here we might as well paraphrase Winston Churchill's famous quip ("Democracy is the worst form of government, except for all the other forms that have been tried from time to time"). Platonism was the worst of all metaphysical systems, except that all other available systems were even worse (Sophism anyone?). The parricide allowed the determinations to leave the realm of pure Being, come forward, and occupy "the world" as a concrete totality. Yet the equivalence of Being and nothingness, the possibility of one becoming the other, soon translated into the West's obsession with creation ex nihilo that culminated in Nietzsche's overman as the "new" creator who would replace God's creating power. In this sense, we might say that the "death of God" inscribed in the destiny of the West was nothing but the prelude to the "death of Man," as both have claimed the role of creators and destroyers.

The West is incapable of receiving the Sacred (the sacredness of Being, independent from creation). The Book of Genesis is already a destruction because the creator could have decided not to create and still could decide to destroy. The nihilism of Western metaphysics cannot be separated from the nihilism of religion. "Salvation" will come from neither of them.[8]

The Sacred (Western style) must relearn how to speak the language of what Parmenides called "the path of day," where the opposition between Being and nothingness is still maintained. Being must appear in the light of the day or Appearing would be nothing. But appearing is part of Being's destiny, and of our being and destiny as well. What must be saved is not an individual soul that God's will can raise up to eternal bliss or abandon to damnation. Salvation comes from truth, and the Appearing of truth is the only event that always takes place for those who want to see it.

The objection against the eternity of beings (based on the obvious fact that things are made and living beings are born and then die) does not touch the core of Severino's thought. Such objection is based on the notion that reality is indeed the "participation" of Being and nothingness that Plato transmitted to us (it is, therefore, a critique subjected to the logical fallacy of circular reasoning). Under this respect, hermeneutics fares no better. First, interpretation already sets thinking on the way of production. Second, what can be interpreted is only the single entity (the Earth, "the world") in its isolation from the totality of Being, not Being itself. Yet Earth is also "safe" from the violence of interpretation because in the end no modification can undermine the totality of Being. We are not free from the dangers of isolation (all our pains come from it), but truth does not depend on our interpretations of the "isolated Earth."

In the chapter *"Aletheia"* and in the final section ("Concluding Remark") of the book, Severino asks his readers to reconsider the Greek word for "truth" (which Heidegger interpreted as *a-letheia*, non-*lethe*, removal of latency) in accordance to the wisdom of "the path of day." The belief that things can oscillate between Being and nothingness is the "preconscious" of the West, merely surfing over reality. Nihilism, on the other hand, is the West's "unconscious," the structure that remains hidden (a comparison with Freud's death drive could be made, although Severino does not venture that far). As we have already said, when Aristotle affirms that Being is Being as long as it is Being, he drives this nihilistic oscillation into the very structure of Being—an oscillation that has found its way in every major thinker of the West up to Heidegger and beyond.

The overcoming of nihilistic alienation can be shown only in the light of necessity. Again, it is not a matter of choice or some sort of early-Heideggerian, existential decision toward authenticity. Far from being the dominion of frozen possibilities, necessity is the only region of Being that is always open outside the confines of nihilism. The key issue here is a reconsideration of freedom in nonnihilistic terms. There is no freedom within the boundaries of nihilism. Freedom can be spoken of, paradoxically, only from the location of necessity. As long as action, praxis, choice, possibility, and decision remain within the "unconscious destiny" of nihilism, they are problematic notions.

Freedom belongs to truth, and we can positively speak of freedom only in the language of truth. Severino is aware, however, that freedom and necessity are connected just as truth is connected to error (there would be no emergence of truth without the presence of error and the same can be said about freedom and necessity). Necessity, freedom, destiny, truth, and error make a tight knot, but freedom has nothing to do with the liberty to create and destroy. The path of night (the road to error), correctly understood, is the first step toward the path of day (the road to salvation). In the end, however, every path is sent by destiny. The assumption that necessity undermines human freedom stems from the nihilistic presupposition that freedom is something that we can have at our command and dispose of. Freedom, on the contrary, only germinates from the structure of necessity. The final pages of *The Essence of Nihilism* anticipate Severino's inquiry on destiny and necessity, which was eventually published in 1980.[9]

Philosophies of the Past

Let us now focus on one particular issue, namely, Severino's refusal of hermeneutics. How does such refusal stand vis-à-vis the vital necessity to interpret the passing of time (which is an appearance, but not nothing)? A non-Severinian premise will be necessary in dealing with this issue.

The past and the future share the peculiar status of happening nowhere else but in the interpretation that captures and sets them in terms of "past time" and "future time." As objects of thought, the time they refer to begins to exist as "past" or "future" only when we define it as such. Time's nature is what makes both past and future two-faced, like the moon always hiding one of its sides. The moment it happened, the past was not actually past, therefore, it lacked the hallmark—of being past—that the present lays on it retrospectively. Equally, the moment the future realizes its premises, it is no longer future, and it lacks the hallmark—of being in the future—that is laid on it in the present and by our present judgment.

The French Revolution was the present for whoever lived it out, but no one at that time was in the position to conceptualize it as the totalization of events that we place in the past and describe as "the French Revolution." In fact, what we call "the French Revolution" is an incomplete totalization of an innumerable accumulation of events whose full understanding is constantly delayed into the future, for no historical interpretation happening in our present will ever be definitive. Furthermore, by conceptualizing the French Revolution as past and by turning it into available data for our present and future research, we are deprived of what the men and women of that age experienced as a wide spread of events that still bore no name (no one storming the Bastille was thinking, "Hey, I am making the French Revolution here"). The past we speak of and compile is based on a (then) "unpastness" that cannot be assigned exact space and time limits and whose experiential essence will always be missed by whoever comes later. Such intrinsic and contradictory feature (the elusive unpastness of the past, that is) constitutes the ontological, inner difference of the past, its internal split, within the past itself.

The past never returns the way it was and never altogether because there is no place from which and where it could return. A time machine will never be invented because the past does not exist as an unconnected entity; it is not a "place" you can go back to. What has never passed, though it remains "missing" and not at hand, is precisely the unpastness of the past, the past's *always-present event*, which is entirely hidden from us for the simple reason that we cannot but interpret as "past" the signs it sends us in the present. Because such a conceptualization happens in our present, the past only exists here and now, for us who think of it. The same line of reasoning applies to the future.

This conclusion is not novel at all. In the twentieth century, a wide choice of disparate thinkers, from Walter Benjamin to Claude Lévi-Strauss, has suggested it. Emanuele Severino's claim, however, is of a more radical nature. Although Severino does not deny that the present time is the only place where the past shows its own signs, he intends to prove that the past never stops existing and, if anything, it goes on lingering as past, without ever entering the nothingness of not-being or—which for Severino is the same—of not-being-anymore.

It is hard to decide whether Severino's argument for the eternal permanence of the past (and the eternal presence of the future, as we shall see) is at odds with what we have called the "unpastness" of the past. As an event present to itself but not to us, the unpastness of the past constitutes the never exhaustible foundation of the past as an object of thought. Severino, however, affirms that the attempt to "master" the past by means of endless interpretations, albeit unavoidable, amounts to a sheer display of aggressive will-to-power toward the having-been-ness of the past—a wish to "possess" what has been (but, in fact, still is) in order to change it and make it more suitable to our present goals.

One way to make sense of such claim would connect Severino's criticism of historical hermeneutics to Walter Benjamin's "Theses on the Philosophy of History" and the latter's grim observation that not even the dead are safe from the enemy if he wins.[10] A different approach would regard historiography and the hermeneutics of history as a mere necessity to which we submit in order to get our bearings through those signs of the past that we acknowledge in our present. It is likely that Severino would have none of both. We might come closer to his stance, however, if we say that the unpastness of the past lingers on because every occurrence "is" (stays) in its event, that is, in the relations it establishes while happening. Because such relations institute the temporality of the event itself, they cannot become past. The most scrupulous historical research will never "save" the network of infinite *facta* that make up a day in anyone's life. The connections among those facts are not past; they are (or were) not present either. They are transcendental, and therefore "eternal."

This would be a relatively easy, safe way to approach Severino's critique of the hermeneutics of time. However, as soon as we conclude that such network of impalpable events (albeit transcendental) is *nothing* for us, insofar as it represents the threshold of interpretation that we cannot cross, we have departed from Severino, who is asking us to make a much bigger leap of (deductive) faith.

In the "philosophy of the past" that we have stated so far, the event in the moment of its happening is not the happening itself but just—as we said—its transcendental (neither a thing nor a being, which to Severino is an inacceptable definition). Moreover, in order to give a meaning to the network of relations established in an occurrence that is past for us, we position ourselves in a present that judges those relations, not in their own present (the present that is now "nothing" to us), but rather in their effect on our present. In Severino's stance, however, to say that the relations among past occurrences are lost to us and therefore have become "nothing" is tantamount to embracing nihilism: namely, the belief that "something" (the event in its happening) can indeed become "nothing."

Here we measure how much Severino has distanced himself from the classics of modernity. Nietzsche and Heidegger have both dealt with the past's ambivalent nature. The former did so in order to conceive a superior morality "wanting the past" exactly the way it has been (as it has been then, that is, in its "unpastness") with no resentments or desire for revenge—but in actuality, as Severino points out, submitting the past to the present's demands, and thus laying claim so as to make it fully conquerable. The latter did so in order to undermine the traditional metaphysical hierarchy that has constructed Being as untouched by time and immutable with respect to becoming.

Yet Nietzsche did not formulate his theory of the eternal return of the same to scrap the difference between (on the one hand) the unpastness of a then-present and (on the other hand) the interpretation that happens in the now and makes it past. On the contrary, he intended to revivify such a dissimilarity, to turn it into a cognitive, ethical, and social force. By acknowledging that there persists a difference, a split, a gap made of "nothing" between the unpastness and the interpretation that makes it past, Nietzsche built up the theoretical power of the eternal return, which would otherwise be read in a purely allegorical and allusive vein or, more fleetingly, as a consoling ideology.

On his part, Heidegger wondered whether time might be defined as the horizon within which Being's various epochs (Being's past) would disclose themselves not as an imposition or a revelation, but as an impersonal "gift" surfacing from the very structure of the event. That new direction of thought was supposed to free him from the *aporias* of metaphysics: for which the pastness is a mere object of thought rather than a gift. Later on, however, such new direction led him to further *aporias* and to the conclusion that the descriptive pattern of metaphysics cannot be transcended with the objectifying language available to the philosopher.

A decidedly anti-Heideggerian and anti-Nietzschean thinker, Severino firmly opposes whatever submission of Being to time, to becoming or occurring. To Severino, the decision to subordinate Being to any type of historicization amounts to asserting that entities become nothingness every time they draw back into the past, which would be like giving ourselves up, unarmed, to the most destructive nihilism. Aiming to counter this "Western folly," as the philosopher himself has repeatedly called it, Severino has therefore outlined his controversial statement of a triple eternity: *one*, eternity of the entity; *two*; eternity of the horizon where the entity appears; and *three*, eternity of the order whereby the entities hide or show themselves on the horizon of the appearing (otherwise said, the unpastness of their then-present, laying hidden and replaced by their present pastness). In Severino's final, provocative statement, *everything exists forever*. The past neither vanishes merely because it is past, nor restricts itself to leaving a meager trace for the present interpretation. The city of Hiroshima exists forever (not "still" but "forever") at any of its instants—before, during, and after the explosion of the A-bomb that destroyed it, as all instants exist forever, though they have left the horizon where they appear to us.

> Everything is eternal. Not in the traditional sense, whereby the world as a whole is eternal or the matter's constitutive elements are eternal, or the law of reality, or reality as it is known by a divine mind, or God as separated from the world's temporality. Not in this sense. "Everything is eternal" means that each moment of reality is—that is, it does not get out and does not return into nothingness; it means that even the humblest and most intangible things and events deserve the triumph we usually intend for God.[11]

Severino was an intellectual figure very much courted by Italy's media scene, yet the core of his thought remains impervious to the world of communication that elevated him to the role of *maître à penser*. More than anyone of his colleagues, Severino embodies the Kantian characterization of the philosopher who knows "everything and nothing else." The statement is not meant to be constricting, let alone ironical. Severino has always addressed topical subjects, from Catholicism to communism, from Christianity to the stem cell controversy, and from capitalism to Islam, but in a world where everyone runs around for something, Severino really takes care of Everything and, in the end, of Everything only. And, in his key work on destiny and necessity, he maintains that "as it goes beyond the totality of the contradiction of finitude, Everything is Joy."[12]

The appearance of such a word, "Joy," which is certainly Augustinian and Hölderlinian as much as it is Schillerian, is more than a *coup de théâtre*. By maintaining that Everything equates with Joy, Severino lays out an undialectical resolution of the entity's contradictions—not only those between past, present, and future, or time and eternity, but also those between pain and release from pain, or alienation and restoration.

We may wonder, however, whether such a salvific appearance, repeated and expanded twenty years later, is fully philosophical or whether it has a theological and even poetic *coloratura* (coloring).[13] The presence of a strongly eschatological streak, which is increasingly evident in Severino's works after 1980, makes us surmise that the institution of philosophy cannot, ultimately, either say or prove what Severino would like to get it to say or prove. The becoming is unprovable, Severino remarks. He has relentlessly reproached Western philosophy for having always taken becoming for granted, without ever seeking a strict deduction for it. Even the eternal permanence of the past, however, might be unprovable with the philosophy's tools, even those as sharp as Severino's.

And what about the future, whose structure in Severino's system appears as paradoxical as that of the past? The future is not simply what is not yet. Just as the present cannot cease to be when it becomes past, so the present cannot have nothingness ahead through which it advances. Thus, the future is not there, but then again it is already all there, because were it not already there, it could not gain access to being. The term "future," Severino admits, is inadequate for describing what to all intents and purposes is a fate that is already spread out in its entirety on the nontemporal horizon of Being. This fate is precisely "Joy," and its manifestation is "Glory"—a ground where only a "future philosophy," which is not a philosophy of the future, can venture.

Perhaps, in the guise of a philosophical body of work now extended over seventy years, Severino has been giving us majestic heavenly poems, where the insuperable theoretical horizons of Being and time, appearance and truth, facts and interpretations are overcome through the *imposition* of poetic words. This leap of faith allows the emergence of theological-mystical names such as "Joy" and "Glory," in which past, present, and future find redemption at last. These are *imposed* names, to be sure, like the names of the beloved ladies in medieval poems, for they are the proper nouns, Severino says, "of the mortals' deepest unconscious."[14] They are names, however, that are not intended to be an explanation of our unconscious. They are more like a converging of total meaning, not metaphors or metonymies but rather (one might say) absolute and mystical *symbola*—etymologically, a token that, once reunited to its ringer, restores totality.

The World and the Real

The greatest challenge that Severino's philosophy poses is the problematic connection between destiny and agency (that is, between the implied absence of possibilities on the part of human agents and the chance of overcoming a destiny that is stronger than any personal or historical power). Coming from a phenomenological-hermeneutic background, I too feel challenged by Severino's criticism of interpretation, possibility, *praxis*, and decision. Not only that: Is everything an entity, an *ens* in the medieval sense of the word, just because it is not nothing? Is language an entity? And, if the answer is yes, is every utterance, either silent or spoken, an entity as well? Does that mean every actual utterance or just an utterance that would be possible within a given language? (Were the answer to this last question to be in the affirmative, then David Lewis and his theory of the reality of all possible worlds would be an ideal counterpart to Severino). The real issue, however, is how can the eternal "save" the determined being *while leaving it determined*, without annihilating its determination within the infinite totality of Being (without *negating* it). It is no wonder that so many Catholics feel a strong affinity with Severino. He is a heretic, yet his philosophy is still a philosophy of individual salvation; not of every soul, but of every *ens*. It still obeys the sin-fall-redemption strategy (Plato's parricide of Parmenides, nihilism, and the overcoming of nihilism by means of returning to Parmenides—or returning to the Father).

Having said that, it is also true that Severino asks questions that cannot be easily dismissed, and he does so with an extraordinary stylistic consistency. The long-overdue translation of *The Essence of Nihilism* makes it clear that Severino needs to be discussed in the context of post-Heideggerian metaphysics, Deleuzian immanence, Badiou's notion of event, Meillassoux's speculative realism, the anticorrelationist trends, John McTaggart's eternalism, David Lewis's logic of possible worlds, and J. J. Altizer's theology of the death of God. Both *La struttura originaria* and *The Essence of Nihilism* would give analytic philosophers plenty of food for thought. Rudolf Carnap is in fact one of the few contemporary philosophers in whom Severino has shown a constant interest. In 1966, he translated and edited Carnap's *The Logical Structure of the World and Pseudoproblems in Philosophy*, and in 1979 he published a short but remarkable essay on Carnap.[15]

Severino makes us rethink the modern idolatry of the "event" as a defining moment that is supposed to change the very essence of Being. The secularization of Christianity generated the false belief that history harbors a destiny that will ultimately subjugate eternity itself. In Severino's view, however, the history of Christianity is the history of how nihilism subjugated Christianity itself. And the fundamental flaw of Aristotle's principle of noncontradiction (A = A *as long as* A = A, A = A *insofar as* A = A) has led to the threefold dogma of historical-ideological nihilism: X is nothing because it is not Y, X is nothing unless it is Y, X is nothing until it becomes Y. Consequently, we live in the time of reverse Incarnation: instead of the Eternal (the Son of God) becoming history, modernity is plagued by history aiming to become eternal (an obsession that applies to all the modern totalitarian systems, but also to the foolish post-1989 assumption that "history is over" and that the triumph of neoliberalism is the realization of the Absolute Spirit).

And who could deny that Severino's account of Plato's creation of "the world" bears a striking similarity to the emergence of the signifier in Lacan's *Seminar*, Book VII? ("The primordial Real . . . suffers from the signifier").[16] If Plato's parricide of Parmenides truly opened up the world of appearances and ideas (the world where we constantly negotiate between the imaginary and the symbolic), then Plato's world was the signified of the signifier that summons the fullness of Being into the light of Appearance—the light of the world of phenomena.[17] The price paid, however, was the nullification of Being's Oneness. Plato reduced the absolute Real of Parmenides's Being, where there was no place for the nuances of possibility, to the disposable remainder of predialectic times. In other words, Plato made Parmenides irretrievable. By rejecting Parmenides, Plato rejected the unbearable weight of Being and offered us the option to roam the middle ground (*metaxy*) between Being and nonbeing. Once the hierarchy of Platonic ideas was established, the Parmenidean identity of Thought and Being (*noein te kai einai*) was broken, and the Real was excluded from the language of philosophy. Platonic and Aristotelian reality (our reality) is the result of the prephilosophical, "primordial Real" being banned from the symbolic order.

Severino has taken on himself the Herculean task of bringing back the Real of Being, knowing very well that his "discourse in the Real [*dans le reel*] of Being" cannot but look paradoxical and untenable to the "discourse of philosophy," which has established itself precisely on the dismissal of that Real. In the end, when Severino says that every entity (every totality of appearance) is eternal, what, exactly, is he saying?

Let us put it this way. If we could take a picture of the whole universe in a specific instant and if we could discern in that picture each thing that is actually happening (not unlike the vision haunting the narrator in Borges's *The Aleph*),[18] we would not see "the world," because the world (the Platonic world) is made of visible and invisible things, of beings and ideas, of the past that is no more and the future that is not yet.[19] What would we see instead? We would see a slice of the Real, of "the" Being without the reassuring barriers of the symbolic order. An adequate approximation of Severino's Being would be a synchronic picture of every totality of appearances that has disappeared from the horizon of appearances and of every totality of appearances that will appear within the horizon of appearances, including the totality of appearances that appears in the moment the picture is taken plus the picture itself, whoever or whatever is taking the picture and whoever is seeing it. Possibly, it would be something akin to the synchronic vision of Rome that appeared to Freud at the beginning of *Civilization and Its Discontent*.[20]

Bergson, the philosopher of creation and becoming, is quite remote from Severino, yet when Bergson writes that reality is a series of images, he says precisely that reality can be perceived only as a slice, a temporal cut in the fabric of the world.[21] In other words, reality is a picture, because it is likely that Bergson was thinking of photography. And a picture is not a Platonic idea; it is absolute yet casual, undisputable yet apparently contingent—but it is, in fact, imbued with necessity, because the networks of relations among the elements of the taken image are now absolute in their "unpastness." A picture is not a picture of "the world" because a picture does not portray ideas. It is a fragment of the Real. Every picture is real; and every picture is eternal. The temporal cut it has captured will never change. True, Bergson would still say that a picture is a compromised experience as it "cuts away" becoming, the *durée* (but Severino would not be touched by such objection). True, a picture may be interpreted in different ways, but interpretation belongs in the discourse of the world, not in the silence of the Real. A visual equivalent of this temporal cut can be found in the "library scene" in the film *Interstellar* (Christopher Nolan, 2014). Every moment that Murphy Cooper has spent in her room is forever "present" in the space-time continuum her father "visits." In Severino's universe, however, Joseph Cooper (the father) would not be able to move freely back and forth in time—from a position outside the continuum—to instruct his daughter to stay in the room and wait for his messages to come. The father too would be in his own continuum, parallel to his daughter's continuum but not able to interact with it (not free to "interpret" it and change its course).[22]

Severino's long-standing concern about the *aporias* of nothingness is the necessary integration to his discourse on Being.[23] Nothingness does not belong in reality, but it fully belongs in the discourse of the Real. In fact, Severino's massive output is proof that an entire life of study may not be enough to probe the depths of the nullity of nothingness.[24] The issue at stake is that by getting rid of Parmenides's Being, philosophy has outlined a void, a lack, a "little nothing," a hole in the middle of a white canvas around which philosophers have built their language, rhetoric, and credibility. Severino intends to show his fellow philosophers that that little nothing from which things supposedly emerge and in which they disappear is indeed nothing; it is not there, it is not. Yet if philosophers do not acknowledge the nothingness of nothing, then that little nothing, that little black square inside the large white picture of Western philosophy, will grow wider and wider until it eats up the whole canvas—which is, in fact, what has happened to metaphysics, always too self-assured that it could keep the power of nothingness at bay. The true horror, in other words, is that such little nothing quickly turns into "a thing," or actually into the Thing, the formless substance that, having no reality of its own, grows limitlessly, occupying all space and time.

What therapy does Severino prescribe to those who have such a bad case of the virus of nihilism? To admit that there is nothing but Being, nothing but the Real of Being, is the first step that the Nihilists Anonymous ought to take toward recovery from their addiction to nothingness. Are they willing to take it? Do they need to be dragged in kicking and screaming? Are they afraid that by accepting Severino's argument, no language but Severino's will be left to them? (This is a serious question, as anyone who fell under his spell should know).

In Severino's philosophy, the salvific message is paired with the obsessive compulsion to say "the same thing" again and again in eighty-something books. It is a salvation without God, but not without Gnosis, and Gnosis requires initiation. I sense Gnostic overtones in Severino's use of theologically charged terms such as *Joy* and *Glory*. His desire to endlessly repeat that becoming is not nothing (because nothing is nothing), but rather just a state in the horizon of appearance that is already-always overcome by eternity and that all the evil in the world is an appearance already-always surpassed by the eternal Joy, is akin to a Gnostic claim.

To be sure, Severino's Gnosis includes neither a clumsy Demiurge (unless, in an ironic reversal of Plato's *Timaeus*, the Demiurge is Plato himself) nor a renunciation of the world of the flesh. Yet there are many paths to Gnosis, and one of them is the exaltation of the "divine spark" preceding, or in fact replacing, creation, which is present in every soul and exempt from decay and annihilation because it coexists with God. It is the "dew of light" in Isaiah 26:19 and the "eternal shine" mentioned in the *Corpus Hermeticum*. If you replace God with the Destiny of Necessity contemplating itself, you may get the essence of Severino's Gnosticism. Was it perhaps the old specter of Gnosis that scared the Holy Office into declaring him a heretic?

Our task, we who are not the Holy Office, is to understand the place from where Severino's *philosophical* discourse emanates. In his writings as well as his voice, we get a glimpse of how thinking must have been before Socratic questions and answers, Platonic dialectic, and Aristotelian logic took over. It is the authority that once came from assessing one's position in such a way that the opponents were bound to contradict themselves even before they voiced their objections. Severino is always willing to discuss his theories, other people's theories, and everything going on in the world. He is a philosopher, not a guru. In the heart of his philosophy, however, there is no provision for mundane discussion just as there is no fundamentalist dogma. Fundamentalism is always intent on defending itself. Severino does not really think he has to defend himself, not even when he meticulously rebukes his critics. His discourse speaks from a place that has nothing to do with individual authority. It is not that he never leaves his magical castle. Rather, his magical castle grows around him everywhere he goes. It is the place of the "impossible" full speech, the all-encompassing fullness of meaning that leaves no room for the imaginary speeches of my, your, or everybody's ego, including his. Listening to that voice is more rewarding than agreeing with it or not. It is the homophony of the ancient choir before the drama of individuation began to unfold, the perfect unison of the music of identity before the harmonics of difference cut a crack in it.[25]

Notes

1. Emanuele Severino, *La struttura originaria* (Brescia: La Scuola, 1958; new and expanded edition: Milan: Adelphi, 1981); Emanuele Severino, *The Essence of Nihilism: The Nihilistic Basis of Western Thought*, ed. Ines Testoni and Alessandro Carrera, trans. Giacomo Donis (London: Verso Books, 2016).

2. Emanuele Severino, *Nihilism and Destiny*, ed. Nicoletta Cusano, trans. Kevin William Molìn (Milan: Mimesis Internationals, 2016), an Italian publication aimed at the international market, was in print concurrently with *The Essence of Nihilism*. Without detracting at all from the Mimesis book (which is an introductory anthology), *The Essence of Nihilism* is the first non-Italian edition of a Severino book. See also Emanuele Severino, "On Virtue," in *Contemporary Italian Philosophy: Crossing the Borders of Ethics, Politics, and Religion*, ed. Silvia Benso and Brian Schroeder (Albany: State University of New York Press, 2007), 227–243; "Technics, Nihilism, Truth," in *Italian Critical Theory*, ed. Alessandro Carrera, monographic issue of *Annali d'Italianistica* 29 (2011): 107–122; and "Phenomenology, Freedom, Causality, and the Origin of Western Civilization," in Fabio Scardigli, Gerard 't Hooft, Emanuele Severino, and Piero Coda, *Determinism and Free Will: New Insights from Physics, Philosophy, and Theology* (Cham, Switzerland: Springer-Nature, 2019), 49–77. *The Essence of Nihilism* has also been translated into German as *Vom Wesen des Nihilismus* (Stuttgart: Klett-Cotta, 1998).

3. Emanuele Severino, *Heidegger e la metafisica* (1950; expanded edition, Milan: Adelphi, 1994).

4. I have discussed the theoretical and ethical implications of the "Hiroshima argument" in Alessandro Carrera, *La consistenza del passato. Heidegger Nietzsche Severino* (Milan: Medusa, 2007), 45–70.

5. For a further discussion on this crucial point, see Massimo Donà, "The Original Betrayal: Nihilism and Nullification of the Negative," in *Italian Critical Theory*, ed. Alessandro Carrera, monographic issue of *Annali d'Italianistica* 29 (2011): 69–89.

6. Severino, *The Essence of Nihilism*, 151–152.
7. Emanuele Severino, *Il parricidio mancato* (Milan: Adelphi, 1985).
8. Whether Being is ruled by necessity alone or must preserve its freedom "to be or not to be" is a point that Massimo Cacciari has endlessly argued with Severino. See Massimo Cacciari, *Dell'inizio* (Milan: Adelphi, 1990, 2001) and *Della cosa ultima* (Milan: Adelphi, 2004, 2019).
9. Emanuele Severino, *Destino della necessità. Katà tò chreón* (Milan: Adelphi, 1980).
10. Walter Benjamin, "Theses on the Philosophy of History," in *Illuminations*, ed. Hannah Arendt, trans. Harry Zohn (New York: Schocken Books, 2007), 253–264.
11. Emanuele Severino, *La filosofia futura* (Milan: Rizzoli, 1989), 280. My thanks to Santo Pettinato for his help in the translation of this quote.
12. Severino, *Destino della necessità*, 594.
13. Emanuele Severino, *La Gloria. óssa ouk élpontai: Risoluzione di "Destino della necessità"* (Milan: Adelphi, 2001).
14. Severino, *Destino della necessità*, 592.
15. Rudolf Carnap, *La costruzione logica del mondo—Pseudoproblemi della filosofia*, ed. and trans. Emanuele Severino (Milan: Fabbri, 1966; reprint, Turin: UTET, 2017); Emanuele Severino, *Legge e caso* (Milan: Adelphi, 1979).
16. Jacques Lacan, *The Seminar of Jacques Lacan Book VII: The Ethics of Psychoanalysis 1959–1960*, ed. Jacques-Alain Miller, trans. Dennis Porter (New York: Norton. 1992), 118.
17. Severino and Lacan might also agree that the belief in creation "from nothing" is the surest path from religion to atheism: "The frontiers represented by 'starting from zero,' *ex nihilo*, is, as I indicated at the beginning of my comments this year, the place where a strictly atheist thought necessarily situates itself. A strictly atheist thought adopts no other perspective than that of 'creationism'"; see Lacan, *The Seminar of Jacques Lacan Book VII*, 260–261.
18. See Jorge Luis Borges, *The Aleph and Other Stories 1933–1969*, ed. and trans. Norman Thomas Di Giovanni in collaboration with Jorge Luis Borges (New York: Dutton, 1979), 3–17.
19. To quote loosely from Hilary Putnam's stance on internal realism, "the world" is made of the world and of our views of the world—which means (in Severino's parlance) that the cyclical attempts on the part of well-intentioned philosophers to move back to absolute metaphysical realism are doomed to fail insofar as they do not break the Platonic mold. See Hilary Putnam, *Realism with a Human Face*, ed. James Conant (Cambridge, MA: Harvard University Press, 1990).
20. See Sigmund Freud, *Civilization and Its Discontents*, ed. Todd Dufresne, trans. Gregory C. Richter (Peterborough, Canada: Broadview Press, 2016).
21. See Henry Bergson, *Matter and Memory*, trans. Nancy Margaret Paul and W. Scott Palmer (London: Allen & Unwin, 1911), chap. 1.
22. Rocco Ronchi has highlighted the similarities and differences in Bergson's and Severino's critique of contingency in *Il canone minore. Verso una filosofia della natura* (Milan: Feltrinelli, 2017), 75–93.

23. Emanuele Severino, *Intorno al senso del nulla* (Milan: Adelphi, 2013).

24. See also my first assessment of the theme of nothingness in Severino and Carlo Sini in Alessandro Carrera, *L'esperienza dell'istante. Metafisica, tempo, scrittura* (Milan: Lanfranchi, 1995), 99–113.

25. As far as I know, and aside from this article, no secondary literature on Severino exists at the moment in the English language. In Italy, on the contrary, the bibliography on Severino is growing by the minute. The following selection is necessarily incomplete: Cornelio Fabro, *L'alienazione dell'Occidente. Osservazione sul pensiero di Emanuele Severino* (Genoa: Quadrivium, 1981); Leonardo Messinese, *Essere e divenire nel pensiero di Emanuele Severino. Nichilismo tecnologico e domanda metafisica* (Rome: Città Nuova, 1985); Andrea Antonelli, *Verità, nichilismo, prassi. Saggio sul pensiero di Emanuele Severino* (Rome: Armando, 2003); Arnaldo Petterlini, Giorgio Brianese, and Giulio Goggi, eds., *Le parole dell'Essere. Per Emanuele Severino* (Milan: Bruno Mondadori, 2005); Massimo Donà, *La libertà oltre il male. Discussione con Piero Coda ed Emanuele Severino* (Rome: Città Nuova, 2006); Giorgio E. Crapanzano, *L'immutabilità del diveniente. Saggio sul pensiero di Emanuele Severino* (Rome: Il Filo, 2008); Andrea Dal Sasso, *Dal divenire all'oltrepassare. La differenza ontologica nel pensiero di Emanuele Severino* (Rome: Aracne, 2009); Marco De Paoli, *Furor logicus. L'eternità nel pensiero di Emanuele Severino* (Milan: Franco Angeli, 2009); Leonardo Messinese, *Il paradiso della verità. Incontro con il pensiero di Emanuele Severino* (Pisa: ETS, 2010); Nicoletta Cusano, *Emanuele Severino. Oltre il nichilismo* (Brescia: Morcelliana, 2011); Paolo Poma, *Necessità del divenire. Una critica a Emanuele Severino* (Pisa: ETS, 2011); Giulio Goggi, *Al cuore del destino. Scritti sul pensiero di Emanuele Severino* (Milan: Mimesis, 2014); Giulio Goggi, *Emanuele Severino* (Rome: Lateran University Press, 2015); Andrea Dal Sasso, *Creatio ex nihilo. Le origini del pensiero di Severino tra attualismo e metafisica* (Milan: Mimesis, 2015); Luca Mauceri, *La hybris originaria. Massimo Cacciari ed Emanuele Severino* (Naples: Orthotes, 2017).

3

Increase or *Kenosis*

Hermeneutic Ontology between Hans-Georg Gadamer and Gianni Vattimo

Gaetano Chiurazzi

Preface

Gianni Vattimo's conception of hermeneutics has had lasting influences on Italian philosophical debates and has given a very peculiar characterization, which is internationally known as "weak thought," to the Italian hermeneutic tradition. Vattimo's translation of Hans-Georg Gadamer's *Truth and Method*, the first translation anywhere in the world of this work by Gadamer, appeared in Italy in 1972. The translation sealed Vattimo's relationship with Gadamer, who was Vattimo's second major teacher after Luigi Pareyson and can be viewed as the great theoretician of contemporary philosophical hermeneutics. Vattimo and Gadamer certainly share an interest in the ontological aspects of hermeneutics, which Vattimo, however, understands in a very different manner. Whereas, according to Habermas's expression, Gadamer carries out an "urbanization of the Heideggerian province," Vattimo would effect a displacement of such province toward the Latin countries, or a "Latinization of hermeneutics," as Grondin writes.[1] This displacement signals the postmodern character that hermeneutics takes up in such countries, especially France and Italy.[2] Although this geographical characterization may not be entirely appropriate, it certainly grasps a phenomenon that has specifically affected the aforementioned Latin countries, the so-called Nietzsche-Renaissance, which has played a central role in the variegated postmodern galaxy. Nietzsche is the author who constitutes the real watershed between Gadamer and Vattimo. In Gadamer's reconstruction of the history of hermeneutics in *Truth and Method*, Nietzsche is never quoted. Conversely, Nietzsche plays a fundamental, even preponderant, part in Vattimo's historical and theoretical reconstruction of the same phenomenon. Despite their shared ontological interest, whose common denominator is perhaps represented by Heidegger, Gadamer and Vattimo part ways when it comes to Nietzsche. In the following pages, I will provide an account of their affinity and separation, first by showing the sense in which the reference to Heidegger constitutes a common denominator for Gadamer's and Vattimo's philosophical proposals, and then by showing the differences that result precisely from the role Nietzsche plays in their respective philosophies.

Being Is Meaning; That Is, Possibility

Contemporary philosophical hermeneutics is born under the sign of ontology. Heidegger's publication of *Being and Time* in 1927 inaugurated a new way of understanding ontology that directly influences Gadamer's and, in Italy, Vattimo's subsequent elaborations. Gadamer develops an ontology of the work of art and language that is in open contrast with the subjectivism of modern philosophy and, for some, even has realist outcomes (at least in the sense that it attributes an objective independence to spiritual productions).[3] Vattimo develops instead a hermeneutic ontology that is radically rooted in Nietzsche's philosophy and thus unfolds in antirealist and nihilistic directions.

In order to understand Gadamer's and Vattimo's common background, one must refer to Heidegger. In *Being and Time*, Heidegger brings about a deep transformation of the way of understanding ontology. As is well known, the question that inspires *Being and Time* is the question of the meaning of being in general.[4] This means that being is mainly an event of understanding. This is the main transformation to which Heidegger subjects Husserl's phenomenology. The move is obviously not without consequences at the ontological level. For Husserl, the fundamental way of accessing the world is intuition or perception; being is thus presence insofar as presence is the temporal determination of perception, whose object can only be that which is present. The primacy of understanding, on the contrary, affords a widening of the temporal dimension so as to include also that which is not present, is absent, or will never be present. Understanding means going beyond presence.

As object of understanding, the meaning of being acquires an implicit temporal connotation. More than something actual, being expresses a possibility, a potentiality that may or may not become actual. Understanding opens a new ontological dimension unknown to perception, namely, the dimension of possibility. Meaning is defined by Heidegger as *können*, as a not entirely determined modality of the object that is further defined only through the interpretative process, which actualizes possibility. Unlike what is generally thought by the hermeneutic tradition, for Heidegger we do not interpret so that we can understand; rather, we understand so that we can interpret. Interpretation is derivative of understanding; it is the unfolding of possibilities that are projected in understanding,[5] that is, in its actualizing determination.

This has important ontological implications as the outcome of an ontological path whose itinerary is provided in the quotation that opens *Being and Time*. As is well known, the quotation comes from Plato's *Sophist*. The passage refers to the moment when Socrates reveals his total perplexity with respect to the meaning of the word "being," which seemed to be made clear and evident by Parmenides's ontology.[6] The *Sophist* plays a fundamental role in the elaboration of *Being and Time*, as testified by the lectures devoted to it by Heidegger in Marburg during the 1924–1925 winter semester.[7] In the dialogue, against the two opposing fronts of the "children of the earth" (the materialists) and the "friends of the ideas" (the idealists, and perhaps Plato's own philosophy), Plato proposes a third solution, which is entirely innovative and destined to be very successful, especially within the Neoplatonic tradition: being is primarily neither *soma* (body) nor *eidos* (form) but rather *dunamis* (possibility). This definition is thus presented as an alternative to both materialism and idealism, that is, two forms of "static" realism that find their conceptual correspondents in Parmenides's logic and metaphysics. Plato seems cautious, however, when advancing this definition. To my mind, though, the definition is the outcome of a wide and extremely sophisticated reflection, implying the most radical ontological-conceptual crisis of ancient thought, namely, the crisis of the incommensurables (the echo of which is to be perceived even in contemporary formulations of philosophical hermeneutics).[8]

Heidegger follows up on this definition of being as *dunamis*; the consequence is the accentuation of the dynamic, temporal, and historical dimension of existence, of its mobility (*Bewegtheit*)[9] to the point of thinking of being as itself time and event. We can therefore say that, in general, the ontology of philosophical hermeneutics is the ontology not of reality (if by this term we mean the field of existing things present in their essential and atemporal determination), but rather of possibility. Simply put, this entails a *different* concept of reality: certainly not the one belonging to "metaphysical realism" as understood in Hilary Putnam's definition,[10] but rather the one, we could say, proper to history and physics, that is, a dynamic reality, in movement and transformation.

Understanding meaning in terms of possibility, on the one hand, and the close connection between being and time, on the other, are two entirely related outcomes of the way in which Heidegger has structured the ontological question, namely, as a question about the meaning of being. Such "ontology of the possible" constitutes the background of twentieth-century theorizations of philosophical hermeneutics and needs to be considered also with respect to the lively debate on the "new realism" that has recently animated the Italian philosophical scene and has targeted Gianni Vattimo as its polemical referent. The debate is spirited by one of Vattimo's former students, Maurizio Ferraris, who had been among the first supporters of weak thought.[11]

Gadamer: An Ontology of Historical Happening

In *Truth and Method*, Gadamer develops the ontology of *Being and Time* in a hermeneutic sense. This development entails three moments that correspond to the three sections in which the work is divided. First, one finds the elaboration, through the notion of play, of an ontology of the work of art as exemplifying the ontological dimension of "happening," that is, that event that is not subject to, but rather guides, the wills of the participants through the acceptance of minimal rules, but also, more simply, as the event in which they partake, thereby being affected by it. Second, there is the definition of historical reality, understood as the totality of effects by which one is determined, that is, the *Wirkungsgeschichte*. Third is the reproposal of Plato's notion of dialogue as a moment of interaction in which, once again, individual singularities are "transcended" by a movement that they never completely control. In this section, I will consider the first two aspects, and in the following section, I will come back to the third.

The concept of play becomes ontologically important because, in Gadamer's consideration, it highlights the radically accidental character of historical happening. The original title of *Truth and Method*, which was changed on the publisher's request, was *Geschehen und Verstehen*, that is, *Happening and Understanding*. Unlike the pair "truth and method," which created various misunderstandings because it was erroneously understood as oppositional and, therefore, functional in an antiscientific polemic, the expression *Geschehen und Verstehen* couples a specifically defined ontological phenomenon (happening) with a consequent cognitive modality (understanding). What is underlined and what constitutes the real core of

Gadamer's ontology is the event-like character of experience, an accidental feature whose contingency is not only experiential but also refers to an ontological dimension; that is, it concerns being as such insofar as it is time and history. Such an ontological dimension cannot be grasped through the experimental method of science, which presupposes the repeatability and idealization of phenomena. Its radical feature emerges in what Heidegger calls "the fundamental metaphysical question," namely, "why is there being rather than nothing?" The very fact of asking such a question indicates a particular ontological understanding, which induces us to think that the real may be entirely contingent, that it may have not been (as is well known, in *Being and Time* such an understanding is aroused by the consciousness of death). That possibility precedes the real and thereby renders it entirely contingent ("Higher than reality is possibility," Heidegger writes, quoting Husserl)[12] is an axiom inverting the axiom of Aristotle's metaphysics according to which substance (that which endures) precedes accident (that which passes, happens, and disappears).[13]

The ontology of the accidental, which is worked out through the concept of play (which constitutes a form of interaction that is not ruled a priori and thus is nonmethodic), prepares the way for the considerations carried out in the second part of *Truth and Method* that are devoted to the problem of historical reality. We can find here the real concept of reality characterizing philosophical hermeneutics. Historical reality is reality, yet in the sense not of *Realität* but rather of *Wirklichkeit*. These two notions appear in Kant's table of categories under the rubric Quality and Modality, respectively, so as to underline the fact that the former concerns the qualitative attributes of a thing (*realitas* in scholasticism), its metaphysical definition, whereas the latter refers to its physical dimension (its *actualitas*), its possible givenness for consciousness. Unlike *Realität*, *Wirklichkeit* is reality that we can experience, and not reality escaping all experience by its very nature. As Kant writes, it is the reality of existence as it is given to us, an existence that can in no way be construed.[14] The contemporary debate on realism and antirealism oscillates between a conception of reality in terms of *realitas* (that is, thingly content, essence) and one in terms of *actualitas* (existence). Both Kant and Heidegger (and most philosophical hermeneutics) can be qualified as "antirealist" only with reference to the first sense of reality, though, since they think that the "what" of an object is somehow construed, interpreted, the outcome of a process of synthesis or attribution of meaning. Yet they are not at all antirealists with respect to the second sense of reality. In this latter case, the charge of antirealism even takes up a rather paradoxical character, given that no other philosophical movement has more greatly asserted the antecedence of existence to any essential definition. Existence is an absolute a priori—both the existence of *Dasein* and the existence of beings, since they are all *given* in the sense of *es gibt*.

The crucial element in the distinction between *Realität* and *Wirchlichkeit* is that the difference enables the elaboration of a notion of reality that is no longer metaphysical but rather experiential and, thus, physical. It is not by accident that such a definition can be found within the context of the foundation of modern physics. Modern science is born precisely at the moment when the metaphysical conception of reality is abandoned and another one is elaborated; that is, modern science is born at the moment when things are no longer conceived of in terms of objects but rather of causes. In sum, the thing is not *res* but *causa*. This concept is not alien to seventeenth- and eighteenth-century empiricism either. Locke's criticism of the notion of substance presupposes that what we can know of things is simply the effects of their interactions; this is possible, as Locke writes, because the ground of reality is power, that is, *dunamis*.[15] Objects are thus nothing else but the outcome of an intertwining of powers, actions and reactions, and points of balance that are found at various intersections.

The conception of reality as *Wirklichkeit* implies that reality becomes a modality, as attested by Kant's insertion of this concept within his table of categories: unlike *Realität*, *Wirklichkeit* expresses the dynamic dimension of the real, its possible transformation, its potential contingency. This is appropriately captured in Gadamer's notion of *Wirkungsgeschichte*, the "history of the effects" of a work.[16] According to its usual meaning in literary history, such a notion indicates the history of the work's reception and success; but, as Jean Grondin remarks, it more properly indicates the *work* of history, its action ahead of all subjective assumption of control.[17] There is no substantial identity of the work outside the history of its effects; or, more precisely, identity can be accessed only on the basis of such effects and can only be conceived of as *dunamis*, as something that affects its spectator. Historical reality (aesthetic experience here being an emblematic case) is a fabric of effects, at the same time their outcome (*historia rerum gestarum*, the history of things done) and their self-production (*res gestae*, the things done).

History thus appears as a *field of forces*, the effects of which operate on us even unwittingly and which, as a matter of fact, always remain somewhat unknown, precisely because they are *historical*, that is, not controllable by any methodic consciousness. Consciousness of historical determination (*wirkungsgeschichtliches Bewusstsein*) is consciousness of this effectivity that acts on us and, above all, on individual subjectivity. This is analogous to the way in which play stands above the individuality of the specific players, since play is the real subject of that which is represented through the players. "Consciousness" of historical determination therefore finds its own limit as consciousness, that is, as reflection, in the fact that it is always in some way the outcome of historical effectiveness: *"to be historically means that knowledge of oneself (Sichwissen) can never be complete."*[18] *Wirkungsgeschichte* is what subtracts consciousness from absolute control over both itself and reality. It is not only the history of the effects that a given work has produced; it is the overall idea that history is a pile of effects, and its reality (*Wirklichkeit*) lies in this pile. For this reason, we can then consider *Wirkungsgeschichte* as something more than the pure pile of more or less classical interpretations; we can understand it not only as a merely philological but also as a critical concept, precisely because it allows us to regard textual productions as effects whose motivations and causes (that is, the formative process) are as important for understanding as they are for meaning (the outcome).

Vattimo: A Nihilist Ontology of Actuality

Gianni Vattimo was a student of Luigi Pareyson (1918–1991),[19] who was among the first to introduce into Italy ideas proper to existentialism and contemporary philosophical hermeneutics. In Vattimo, ontological hermeneutics undergoes a decisive transformation in a nihilistic direction. This was affected by a strong Nietzschean influence, which bent Gadamer's ontology of language as developed in the third part of *Truth and Method* in a derealizing direction.

More than any other philosopher in the hermeneutic tradition, Vattimo has sought to link Heidegger's ontology and Nietzsche's nihilism. This nexus becomes explicit especially in works from the 1980s such as *The Adventures of Difference*[20] and *The End of Modernity*,[21] which elevate Vattimo to become one of the main theoreticians of philosophical postmodernism. The title of the latter work reveals another essential component of Vattimo's thought, namely, the idea that one of the main tasks of philosophy (which is hermeneutic precisely for this reason, namely, because of its effort to actualize meaning) is that of defining our "situation" within the contemporary world. This means that ontology can only be "ontology of actuality."[22] The expression comes from Foucault who, in "What Is Enlightenment?," distinguishes between the analytics of truth (the inquiry into the conditions of knowledge) and the ontology of actuality (the genealogical inquiry into what we are and how we have become what we are).[23] Ontology is possible, for Vattimo, only in these terms: not as "science of being as being" or even of being in general, but as attempt at understanding the meaning of our current, actual (*attuale*) being. As was already the case for Foucault, this implies shifting the attention from the eternal structures of being to those that are *contingent*, changing, and historical. Actuality is not the sheer condition of being present; it is presence understood, in a Hegelian mode, in relation to its becoming. In his philosophical project, Vattimo carries out the transformation, which occurs in Heidegger especially after the "turn," of the ontological approach from "transcendental" inquiry into the meaning of being in general to an inquiry into the history of the meaning of being, its receptions, and its transformations. Vattimo also couples such a transformation with a genealogical inquiry à la Nietzsche, an inquiry aimed at grasping the "human, all too human" roots of metaphysical constructs.

The fact that, at the ontological level, being comes to coincide with the history of its meanings, as they have been handed down to us, is understood by Vattimo as a "weakening" of the strong structures of metaphysics. This is the term that qualifies his philosophical project, which is known as "weak thought." With this appellation (which refers to the title of a 1983 volume coedited with Pier Aldo Rovatti),[24] Vattimo indicates the condition of postmetaphysical thought, that is, of thought that has experienced the death of God. In the contemporary epoch, being, or God, no longer gives itself as privileged object of thought; rather, it appears as what is absent, and thus only as the object of recollection (in the sense of Heidegger's *Andenken*) insofar as it is deposited historically in our language and culture.[25] By now, this is the form of its presence within the contemporary world: a *weakened* presence understood as historical manifestation and, thus, as interpretation.

It is within this context that we should view the peculiar nihilistic inflection that Vattimo impresses on the linguistic ontology of the third part of Gadamer's *Truth and Method*. In this section, Gadamer tries to elaborate a theory of language that understands language as the place of universal mediation, the meeting point where the fusion of horizons among the dialogical interlocutors is realized. The meeting point is not, for Gadamer, under the control of the interlocutors themselves. Like a play, dialogue is not guided by the interlocutors, who are guided by the dialogue itself or, better, by the "cause/thing" (*Sache*), by that of which they speak, as in Plato's dialogues where the interlocutors seek agreement on "the thing itself." The element of linguistic objectivity, viewed in terms of the model of Hegel's objective spirit—an element understood by some authors as a realist feature of Gadamer's ontology—constitutes the point of condensation of the dialectical process of interpretation that produces the historical accumulation concretized in "the classical." That is, it produces those works that remain as a substantial and general, universal substrate lying at the bottom of all processes of historical transmission. This process is understood by Gadamer as an "increase in being," as a way through which reality comes to its truth, that is, is "transmuted" along the lines of the concept of the "transmutation of form" (*Verwandlung ins Gebilde*) that, once again, is simply a reformulation of Hegel's notion of *Aufhebung*, or sublation.

The nihilistic inflection Vattimo places on philosophical hermeneutics can be clearly grasped in his interpretation of Gadamer's sentence, which expresses Gadamer's speculative conception of language: "*Being that can be understood is language.*"[26] For Gadamer, this sentence would mean that in language, being acquires the particular transmutation that makes it understandable and thus capable of manifestation. Vattimo understands the claim in a restrictive manner, though: as the total identification of being and language; being is exactly what comes to language, and it gives itself nowhere else except in language.[27] This idea entails the exclusion of all metaphysical or objective situations external to language; hermeneutics becomes the philosophy that best expresses such a self-deletion of all realist residues through interpretation. At the basis of this idea, which also implies a specific reading of the history of hermeneutics starting with the Reformation, is a philosophy of history understood as the progressive lightening up (*alleggerimento*) of all peremptoriness and immediacy, as the disappearing of a strong sense of the real in favor of a freeing of interpretations, which thus become the only true "substance." The claim Vattimo is fond of repeating, which refers to Nietzsche, is that "there are no facts, only interpretations, and this too is an interpretation."[28] This claim constitutes a real challenge to positivism and is but another way of expressing the same concept, namely, the dissolution of the real (of being) in its interpretations (in language).

This ontological thesis implies a series of factors and processes that are internal to Western civilization and that, for Vattimo, are strictly dependent on Christianity[29] and, hence, on the history of hermeneutics, namely, secularization and nihilism. The coming of Jesus is, for Vattimo, the beginning of both these processes because it is the sign of *kenosis*, that is, a process of "emptying out" and weakening of the cogency and peremptoriness of the Old Testament God. As we read in the Letter to the Philippians, Jesus "has emptied himself out [*heautòn ekénosen*]" (Phil. 2:7). The link between *kenosis* and nihilist ontology is essential. "Nihilism is too much 'like' *kenosis* for one to see this likeness simply as a coincidence, an association of ideas," Vattimo writes.[30]

In an essay titled "History of Salvation, History of Interpretation," Vattimo ties this aforementioned ontological conception to the history of salvation and, hence, to hermeneutics.[31] Interpretation characterizes the culture of the Book, that is, the Bible. As "history of liberation from dogmas," as Dilthey writes, the history of the interpretation of the Sacred Scripture becomes the paradigm not only for the history of salvation, but also for the history of interpretation in general. The historical event of the incarnation, the *kenosis* that is also the fundamental event of salvation, also constitutes the fundamental scheme for the history of the interpretation of the Scriptures. The *kenosis* is a hermeneutic event. Even the resurrection and the descent of the Holy Spirit are inscribed in this process: "The meaning of scripture in the age opened by the descent of the Holy Spirit becomes increasingly 'spiritual' and thereby less bound to the rigour of dogmatic definitions and strict disciplinarian observance," Vattimo writes.[32] Salvation—that is, the goal of Christianity, of nihilism, and of hermeneutics—consists in the reduction of the dogmatic, imposing, authoritarian, and "metaphysical" elements in favor of a more free and variegated relation with the content itself of revelation, that is, with "truth."

As one can tell from the foregoing considerations, what motivates Vattimo's nihilistic ontology and hermeneutics is not a metaphysical or cognitive interest, but rather a fundamentally ethical concern. His project is, in fact, functional to the development of emancipation not as the attainment of a more real, authentic, or true dimension of reality, following a broadly interpreted Platonic model, but rather as the multiplication of perspectives, as the Babelic and even chaotic proliferation of differences. Contemporary society becomes more emancipated not insofar as it is more transparent (that is, closer to the ideal of self-transparency represented by Hegel's absolute spirit, which according to Vattimo remains the ideal *telos* of Habermas's communicative action), but rather insofar as it is more complex, opaque, and diversified: "Only on this condition can hermeneutics present itself as philosophy of the society of generalized communication. This is its only possibility to argue for itself as somewhat 'true' theory."[33] This constitutes the core of Vattimo's conception of postmodernism.

The assertion of the interpretative (which, for Vattimo, means "derealizing") character of the very notions of reality and truth is the consequence not only of the history of salvation, understood as history of interpretation; rather, it is also the outcome of the history of metaphysics, which, fulfilling itself in the world of contemporary technology, comes to its own nihilistic dissolution and becomes "fable."[34] One of the most interesting and perhaps most original aspects of Vattimo's thought (insofar as it marks an important distinction with respect to Heidegger) is the role he reserves for technology, and especially for the new electronic and communicative technologies. Far from proposing an oppressive world of mechanical and homogenizing relations (as it was in Ford's era of the assembly lines, an alienating world wonderfully described in Charlie Chaplin's *Modern Times*), electronic and information technologies represent a positive chance for emancipation because they multiply rather than compress the possibilities of relations; they grant access to communication, and thereby give us more and different possible interpretations and perspectives on the world. For Vattimo, new information technologies are precisely to be credited for the derealizing turn in ontology that has contributed to promoting a new "sense of being" beyond the metaphysics of presence. Hermeneutics is the philosophy of this stage of European culture. It can only "follow to its extreme the 'derealizing' drift glimpsed at by Nietzsche,"[35] that is, the transformation of the world into a fable. Derealization is the awareness that the world is "a play of interpretations and nothing more."[36]

The sense of derealization is the fabulation of the world; interpretation contributes to this through the elaboration of fictional, "unreal" constructs that neither have truth nor claim to be true. One can thus also understand the sense of Nietzsche's claim that perhaps best catches the sense of Vattimo's philosophy: "There are no facts, only interpretations." From a formal viewpoint, the thesis that "there are no facts, only interpretations" lends itself to many objections resembling the kind of confutation to which Plato subjects Gorgias's thesis that "all speeches are false." If everything is interpretation, this applies also to this very statement, which therefore cannot claim to be true. Far from being perturbed by such a logical conclusion, Vattimo insists in specifying that the meaning of this claim is ethical-emancipatory precisely because its effect is the dissolution of the very concept of truth, its violent peremptoriness, and its resolution into interpretation.[37] "There are no facts, only interpretations, and this too is an interpretation" is not an ontological thesis as much as a historical and ethical claim.

On the one hand, the claim simply manifests the necessarily circular, recursive structure of historical existence, that is, of the hermeneutic circle. If, from a formal viewpoint, the circularity may appear as a defect, from the standpoint of philosophical hermeneutics it is simply the inevitable logical form of that which is the object of any hermeneutics, namely, life. Life unfolds by itself and generates, as Dilthey says, a series of sense formations that are simultaneously the presupposition for further development and a product of life's creativity. Precisely through its logical difficulty, the claim that "there are no facts, only interpretations, and this too is an interpretation" lets us think about the circular structure of life, a structure that we can find in hermeneutics as the relations between comprehension and interpretation, between possibility and actuality, and between being and language. Hegel has expressed this circularity in general as the relation between subject (that is, consciousness) and object (that is, historical objectification), for itself and in itself. This consideration refers us once again to the kind of ontology that is implied in philosophical hermeneutics and in the Kantian and Hegelian traditions that it recalls.

On the other hand, as Vattimo clarifies in various essays, and especially in his writings from the 1990s, the force of the meaning of the claim that "there are no facts, only interpretations, and this too is an interpretation" is mainly ethical.[38] To interpret means never being able to consider any fact as final. It means to consider facts as outcomes of interpretations that are in turn interpretable, that is, transformable. Moreover, the need to not collapse interpretations onto facts seems, to Vattimo, a way of defending the very meaning of the ontological difference, which once again is not understood as an ontological structure as much as an ethical exigency, "a 'duty' that one never completes."[39] It is the exigency always to keep open an ulteriority, an opening that prevents the blockage of conversation in front of the peremptoriness of facts.

Conclusion

The different curvature that Gadamer, on the one hand, and Vattimo, on the other hand, impose on hermeneutics thus clearly appears. Although both thinkers share the background of Heidegger's dynamic ontology, they move in two completely opposite directions. Gadamer is, ultimately, a more loyal follower of Hegel's ontology, and so the real is a constant augmentation, an accumulation of meanings that sediment, and thus constitute, the substantial ground supporting and nourishing the life of spirit. Even images, which for Plato were some kind of nonbeing, a diminution of the ontological fullness of the ideas, are for Gadamer a form of increase in being, a surplus, an addition that expresses truth. Truth is linked to the real by a relation not of equivalence or conformity, but of increase. "With regard to knowledge of the true, the being of the representation is more than the being of the thing represented, Homer's Achilles more than the original."[40] This idea is plainly expressed in a passage that, through the use of the term *Aufhebung*, clearly highlights the Hegelian reference we mentioned: "Thus the concept of transmutation characterizes the independent and superior mode of being of what we called form. From this viewpoint 'reality' is defined as what is untransmuted, and art as the raising up (*Aufhebung*) of this reality into its truth."[41] Art reveals the feature characterizing all truths, including the truth of the natural sciences, namely, the fact that all truth entails a formal transformation through which reality is elevated to a superior level, becoming more intense and true; only through this transformation does art become, as Hegel would have it, more *concrete*, that is, it grows on itself.

Images (as well as all representations, whether pictorial, literary, theatrical, or something similar) are not an *other* reality; rather, they are reality in a different formal constitution that has become truth; that is, truth *for* someone: a consciousness, a subject, or a spectator. As a general relation to such a further dimension of the real, that is, as a relation to a world of meanings, interpretation simply contributes to the continuous increment of reality.

Vattimo's perspective goes in precisely the opposite direction. For Vattimo, interpretation does not increase reality; rather, it empties it out, weakens it, and erodes it. Its function is the derealization or fabulation of the world. The fact that Vattimo sees in this an emancipatory power constitutes one of the most original aspects of his theoretical proposal, which can be understood only in connection with Nietzsche and his critique of metaphysics as violence.[42] Interpretation, art, language are not "increments in being"; rather, they function in a kenotic way, as reducing the peremptoriness of being. In some ways, understanding the incarnation (that is, the self-materialization of spirit) as derealization appears indeed problematic. It entails a theological problem that is not irrelevant; one could, in fact, say that, on the contrary, it is the resurrection (that is, the idealization, the becoming spirit) that constitutes the true moment when reality dematerializes itself and loses its substantial cogency. As a matter of fact, what is at stake here is a radical interpretation of Christianity, which becomes central in Vattimo's reflections, especially after the religious turn constituted by the publication in 1996 of *Belief*.[43] For Vattimo, the truly significant moment of Christianity is not the resurrection but the incarnation, not the *parousia* (the second coming) but the *kenosis*, not the elevation of the real to the ideal but its nihilistic dissolution.[44]

Their different conceptions of the function of interpretation also affect the different interests that Gadamer and Vattimo manifest for art. Gadamer is undoubtedly more tied to a classical conception of art, which brings him to distance himself from contemporary movements such as deconstruction[45] and, in general, postmodernism. The distance is motivated by the fact that, following Kant, the task of art remains that of creating a horizon of sharing, of universality, of *sensus communis*, which is an essential condition for dialogue. Conversely, for Vattimo, who remains closer to Heidegger and his essay "On the Origin of the Work of Art," art functions as break, as a shock, such as what we find in contemporary art.[46] This corrosive function is the correlate of philosophical criticism, and in some ways it is even more effective. This is another way to underline how, after Nietzsche, the paths of emancipation are no longer, or not mainly, those of philosophy, but rather those of art and aesthetic existence.

Translated by Silvia Benso

Notes

1. Jean Grondin, "Vattimo's Latinization of Hermeneutics: Why Did Gadamer Resist Postmodernism?" in *Weakening Philosophy: Essays in Honour of Giann Vattimo*, ed. S. Zabala (Montreal: McGill-Queen's University Press, 2007), 203–216.

2. Giovanna Borradori, "'Weak Thought' and Postmodernism: The Italian Departure from Deconstruction," *Social Text* 18 (Winter 1987–1988): 39–49.

3. Grondin, 209ff.

4. Martin Heidegger, *Being and Time*, trans. Joan Stambaugh (Albany: State University of New York Press, 1996), sec. 1.

5. Heidegger, 139.

6. Plato, *Sophist*, 247e.

7. See Martin Heidegger, *Plato's Sophist*, trans. Richard Rojcewicz and André Schuwer (Bloomington: Indiana University Press, 2003).

8. I have tried to explain such a thesis in Gaetano Chiurazzi, "Being as Diagonal and the Possibility of Truth: A Reading of Plato's *Theaetetus*," in *Truth and Experience*, ed. D. Jørgensen, G. Chiurazzi, and S. Tinning (Cambridge: Cambridge Scholar, 2015), 31–43.

9. Martin Heidegger, *Phenomenological Interpretations of Aristotle: Initiation into Phenomenological Research*, trans. Richard Rojcewicz (Bloomington: Indiana University Press, 2008).

10. Hilary Putnam, *Reason, Truth and History* (Cambridge: Cambridge University Press, 1981), 49.

11. See especially Maurizio Ferraris, *Manifesto of New Realism*, trans. Sarah De Sanctis (Albany: State University of New York Press, 2014); and Maurizio Ferraris and Mario De Caro, *Bentornata realtà. Il nuovo realismo in discussione* (Turin: Einaudi, 2012).

12. Heidegger, *Being and Time*, 33.

13. Aristotle, *Meta.* 9: 8.

14. It is not by chance that this distinction can be grasped if one considers Kant's example of the one hundred dollars, which appears in the confutation of the ontological proof. For Kant, "Existence is not a real predicate [*kein reales Prädikat*]"; see Immanuel Kant, *Kritik der reinen Vernunft* (Hamburg: Meiner, 1983), A 598/B 626. This expression means that existence does not belong to the *Realität* of a concept: one hundred possible dollars and one hundred real (*wirklich*) dollars have the very same *Realität*, yet they are distinct in their mode of being.

15. "Most of the simple ideas that make up our complex ideas of substances, when truly considered, are only powers, however we are apt to take them for positive qualities"; see John Locke, *An Essay Concerning Human Understanding*, ed. P. H. Nidditch (Oxford: Oxford University Press, 1975), bk. 2, chap. 33, 37.

16. Hans-Georg Gadamer, *Truth and Method*, trans. J. Weinsheimer and Donald G. Marshall (London: Continuum, 2006), 298ff.

17. See Jean Grondin, *Introduction à Hans-Georg Gadamer* (Paris: Les Editions du Cerf, 1999), 136–139. The French translation that Grondin proposes for the term "*Wirkungsgeschichte*," namely, "*travail de l'histoire*," at first would seem incongruent,

since it inverts the genitive present in Gadamer's expression, which literally means *histoire du travail*. Yet it translates the meaning very aptly: *Wirkungsgeschichte* is the work of history, in both the subjective and objective sense; it is its operation, its ability to produce even new meanings and horizons of sense as well as its works, the outcomes it attains.

18. Gadamer, 301.

19. On the relation between Pareyson and Vattimo, see Gaetano Chiurazzi, "Pareyson and Vattimo: From Truth to Nihilism," in *Companion to Hermeneutics*, ed. Jeff Malpas and Hans-Helmut Gander (New York: Routledge, 2015), 179–190.

20. See Gianni Vattimo, *The Adventure of Difference: Philosophy after Nietzsche and Heidegger*, trans. C. P. Blamires and T. Harrison (Baltimore: Johns Hopkins University Press, 1993).

21. See Gianni Vattimo, *The End of Modernity: Nihilism and Hermeneutics in Postmodern Culture*, trans. J. R. Snyder (Baltimore: Johns Hopkins University Press, 1988).

22. Gianni Vattimo, "Ontology of Actuality," in *Contemporary Italian Philosophy*, ed. Silvia Benso and Brian Schroeder (Albany: State University of New York Press, 2007), 89–107; and "Dalla fenomenologia a un'ontologia dell'attualità," in *Pensare l'attualità, cambiare il mondo*, ed. Gaetano Chiurazzi (Milan: Pearson PBM, 2008), 173–179.

23. Michel Foucault, "Qu'est-ce que les Lumières?" in *Dits et écrits II, 1976–1988* (Paris: Gallimard, 2001), 261.

24. See Pier Aldo Rovatti and Gianni Vattimo, *Weak Thought*, trans. Peter Carravetta (Albany: State University of New York Press, 2012).

25. Vattimo, *The Adventure of Difference*, 110–136.

26. Gadamer, 470.

27. Gadamer, 470.

28. This concept can be found in many texts by Nietzsche, for example Friedrich Nietzsche, *Nachgelassene Fragmente 1885–1887*, ed. G. Colli and M. Montinari (Berlin: de Gruyter, 1988), 7; and also *Beyond Good and Evil: Prelude to a Philosophy of the Future*, trans. W. Kaufmann (New York: Vintage, 1989), sec. 22, 30.

29. Gianni Vattimo, "The West or Christianity," in *After Christianity*, trans. Luca D'Isanto (New York: Columbia University Press, 2002), 69–82.

30. Gianni Vattimo, *Beyond Interpretation*, trans. David Webb (London: Polity Press, 1997), 52.

31. Gianni Vattimo, "History of Salvation, History of Interpretation," in *After Christianity*, 63–64.

32. Vattimo, *Beyond Interpretation*, 50.

33. Gianni Vattimo, *La società trasparente* (Milan: Garzanti, 2000), 107. (Translator's note: The final chapter, "The Limits of Derealization," 101–121, is available only in the Italian edition.)

34. Friedrich Nietzsche, "How the 'True World' Finally Became a Fable," in *Twilight of the Idols and the Anti-Christ*, trans. R. J. Hollingdale (New York: Penguin Books, 2003).

35. Vattimo, *La società trasparente*, 107.

36. Vattimo, *La società trasparente*, 109.

37. For a presentation of the nexus between nihilism and emancipation in Vattimo, see Silvia Benso and Brian Schroeder, ed., *Between Nihilism and Politics: The Hermeneutics of Gianni Vattimo* (Albany: State University of New York Press, 2010).

38. See Gianni Vattimo, "The Ethical Dissolution of Reality," in *Of Reality: The Purposes of Philosophy*, trans. Robert T. Valgenti (New York: Columbia University Press, 2016), 113–118.

39. Vattimo, "The Ethical Dissolution of Reality, 117.

40. Gadamer, 114.

41. Gadamer, 112 (translation modified).

42. Gianni Vattimo, "Metaphysics, Violence, Secularisation," trans. B. Spackman, in *Recoding Metaphysics: The New Italian Philosophy*, ed. Giovanna Borradori (Evanston, IL: Northwestern University Press, 1988), 45–61; and Vattimo, "Metaphysics and Violence: A Question of Method," in *Of Reality*, 121–146.

43. Gianni Vattimo, *Belief*, trans. L. D'Isanto and D. Webb (Cambridge: Polity Press, 1999).

44. Vattimo, *Belief*.

45. Hans-Georg Gadamer, "Text und Interpretation," in *Hermeneutik II: Wahrheit und Methode* (Tübingen: Mohr, 1993), 330–360; "Destruktion und Dekonstruktion," in *Hermeneutik II*, 361–372.

46. Vattimo, "Art of Oscillation," in *The Transparent Society*, trans. David Webb (Baltimore: Johns Hopkins University Press, 1992), 45–61. Oscillation is perhaps the best notion properly to characterize Vattimo's attitude toward some hermeneutic presuppositions such as the one we mentioned, that is, *sensus communis* as a necessary condition of dialogue. On the one hand, Vattimo in fact insists on the need, which is of Rortyan descent, not to stop the conversation ("as long as conversation continues"); on the other, even the minimal condition that enables such occurrence (a minimal agreement) is seen as an excess of violence, a sort of imposition that makes conflict preferable; see Gianni Vattimo, "Dal dialogo al conflitto," in *Tropos. Rivista di ermeneutica e critica filosofica* 1 (2009): 9–17.

Part Two

Temporality, Subjectivities, Performances

4

Lingering Gifts of Time

Ugo Perone, Edith Stein, and Martin Heidegger's Philosophical Legacy

Antonio Calcagno

Martin Heidegger's *Being and Time* revolutionized the twentieth-century way of thinking about time and its relation to being. Heidegger's careful analysis of care and temporality exposes a new fundamental way of being for *Dasein* as it questions its being in the world. Heidegger's insights had a deep and meaningful impact on the thinking of the Italian philosopher Ugo Perone and the German phenomenologist Edith Stein. In his work *The Possible Present*, Perone argues for a conception of the present, always occurring within the dynamic of the flow of and within the "ecstases" of time, that facilitates the very possibility of lingering in being and thought.[1] Edith Stein, especially in her *magnum opus*, *Finite and Eternal Being*, argues that the flow of time reveals that the living present is experienced as being-held-in-being, a security of being that arises from the expectation that being will continue to be given to us as one moment passes into the next.[2]

Lingering and security, then, are the two fundamental comportments toward being revealed by both Stein's and Perone's analyses of the present. I accept both Stein's and Perone's conclusions about time, but I wish to argue for the possibility of an intimate relation between lingering and security. Lingering requires a deep ontic sense of security in order for it to manifest itself, but lingering, in turn, conditions the intensity with which we feel the very security offered to us by being. In short, I wish to establish a dialectical relation between lingering and security: while the security in being is a fundamental condition for the possibility of the manifestation of lingering, it is lingering in being that can intensify the quality and very lived experience of security, ultimately giving rise to a more meaningful relation of one's own being to itself, others, and the world in the lived present.

The Possible Present: A Threshold

In his deeply insightful work *The Possible Present*, Ugo Perone argues that time is experienced in two unique ways. First, there is physical time, the time of nature, which moves chronologically forward. This time can be measured or anticipated in three primary modes: the past, the present, and the future. This is the time of the sciences. For example, one can measure a heart rate per second, time a race, and so forth. Second, drawing from Husserl and Heidegger as well as Bergson, there is the time we live, which is replete with meanings, a time that flows with its own rhythms and cadences. It is the time of what phenomenology calls lived experience (*Erlebnis*) or inner time consciousness. Here, the emphasis is on how time is lived, for us, in conscious experience. Rather than measurements of instants of the past, present, and future, we have, Husserl teaches us, retention of the past or having been, the living present of the now, and anticipation or expectation of a future. Heidegger phenomenologically recasts temporality as the deep structure of care, which reveals how Dasein's being unfolds in the world.

Drawing from but also distancing himself from Heidegger, Perone argues that Heidegger's predilection for the future or anticipatory structure of lived time is problematic. "Heidegger's attempt goes in the direction of rooting temporality in the finitude of Dasein. To avoid all risks of ontological essentialization, he chooses the primacy of the purely anticipatory modality of the future. *Zeitlichkeit zeitig sich ursprünglich aus der Zukunft*: Temporality temporalizes itself primordially out of the future. The consequence is that in order to escape the inauthentic temporality of the now, which is reflected in the ontology of *Vorhandenheit*, one consigns oneself to the primacy of the not-yet, of the instant [*Augenblick*] as manifestation of the time that passes [*vergeht*]" (PP 9). In describing time as passing instants, Heidegger maintains that it is impossible to authentically seize what it is for Dasein to be, for it has no access to that which has passed. Dasein's inauthentically tries to make present that which is impossibly so. Dasein can anticipate a future, but this future is not-yet. In the temporality of the instants of the past, present, and future, there is a nothing: the nothing of the having been of the past, the nothing of the fleeting instant of the present, and the nothing of the not-yet of the future. This nothing reveals

Dasein as profoundly finite, incapable of transcending the time to which it is subject. Perone notes,

> The extreme attempt at situating oneself on the side of finite temporality is accompanied by the anticipating consummation of time. In this context Dasein itself appears as inexorably inclined toward the direction of the not, so much so that it can find its authenticity only through the anticipation of non-being, that is, of death. What emerges is a temporality inexorably attracted toward the ending of finitude, and unable to grasp the initialness [*inizialità*] of time. What also derives is a life that is thought within the transcendental horizon of death and an ontology that is marked by an immanent nihilistic outcome. (PP 10)

Heidegger's failure to account for the initialness of time, so Perone claims, serves as the launching pad for Perone's own discussion of the present, understood as a possible present and as a threshold. Perone admits, however, that Heidegger lays down an important challenge: how can we not reduce the present to presence, a presence that can never fully be, a presence that philosophy has traditionally sought to make clear and distinct (PP 14). Perone notes that we must reconceive the present outside traditional philosophical categories, including the eternal, the instant, and the now (PP 10). If the present is eternal, then no extension of time is possible, nor are any discrete moments in time possible. If time is eternal, then how and why do we come to experience the loss or passing of time? Furthermore, if the present is simply a now that can be supposedly shared in common with other subjects, the problem arises of how to account for the unique, individual experience of subjective time outside this communal now. Finally, if the present is understood simply to be an instant, though the instant may account for the loss or passing of time or its fall into nothingness, the category of the instant cannot account, by definition, for its integration into the flow of time in general; that is, the becoming of another instant that somehow is connected to and follows from the previous instant.

For Perone, the present is a beginning in the sense that it is a kind of "discriminating" limit that divides it from two other modes of the human experience (that is, past and future) of time and natural temporality in general.

> The present is that which discriminates, the passing that withholds, the hand that closes up so as to support itself and others. . . . Such a divide can be so short, unexpected, and

> extraneous that it holds only for an instant, which is nevertheless decisive because it divides time and ploughs through history by virtue of interruptions. [The divide] also designs the now to which we belong reciprocally and that crosses shared paths with us. Somehow [the divide] can also be the eternal, and it can constitute an image of it in its having secured forever something that could no longer be and that was drawn to being and saved through it. (PP 14–15)

The divide is then described as an existence (PP 15). In the lived experience of the flow of time, a present begins: it surges against, and is consciously and meaningfully differentiated from, a past and a future. The present is not constituted simply as a Bergsonian duration or intensity, but rather as divisionary beginning. Yet we do not possess this beginning, for it can never be made present in the form of a presentification or eternalization.

> Time is essentially and originally that which I do not have. Such not-having that traces and marks me is nevertheless the unbalance on which I build my life daily. The present is the threshold where the not-having of time (subjective genitive) intersects existence. It is the fleeting intersecting of an encounter. Life is always the recommencing attempt at expanding such a small opening and controlling time by seconding it without merely suffering from its offenses. All this, in truth, eliminates presence, because in the form of objectification presence confronts one with the contradictoriness of having and not-having. Here having is instead a seconding, where activity and passivity are equally legitimized, and moreover, where the subject of having is from the beginning confronted with the alterity of something that escapes not because it is other (intolerable positivism or transcendence). Rather, [the subject is] confronted with the alterity of a time that is essentially fleetingness and that therefore confronts the subject with alterity (from which it would nevertheless like to protect itself). (PP 15)

The subject who lives the threshold is confronted with a having and not-having of time. The not-having given by the fleeting of time reveals an alterity that is not the subject, a not-me. And it is this experience of the not-me that makes visible or felt the presence of a subjectivity, one who undergoes and lives the threshold experience of the possible present. The threshold is a horizon, a limit that opens and closes a space in which the subject is given to herself, but not fully. The limit of the threshold also manifests that which is not the subject.³ The threshold of the present is truly a possibility in the sense that it stands between having and not-having, being and not-being. It lies within the freedom and the power of the subject to dilate the possible present in order to help build a world as well as a narrative account and interpretations of oneself and the world in which one dwells. The possibility of the present is a beginning but also an initiative. This double sense of the *inizialità*, understood as both beginning and subjective initiative, stems from the work of Ugo Perone's teacher, Luigi Pareyson, who saw in persons a unique capacity for initiative that helped build a world and personhood, but also helped build an ethics of responsibility.⁴

Perone claims that the threshold that is the present manifests certain features. He notes that we must not think of the threshold as a line; rather, it is a zone (*PP* 16). Furthermore, "this zone can be recognized only *a posteriori*, insofar as one has crossed it or has anticipated its crossing in the form of imagination. Also, it cannot be inhabited, but only crossed over. Finally, the one who perceives the threshold simultaneously dilates and deepens it" (*PP* 16). Drawing on the work of Walter Benjamin, Perone describes the threshold as a space of copresencing that is both familiar and disquieting (*PP* 16). The threshold of the present is marked by fleetingness where one is present, but never fully so. The present is never fully my own: "In this sense and from this perspective, despite the spatial origin of the metaphor, [the threshold] seems capable of expressing an essential element of time: its structural feature of fleetingness, its essential never-being-mine, and the cipher of negativity that belongs to it" (*PP* 17). Perone follows Heidegger, affirming a negation that manifests itself in the experience of the present, but he also wishes to affirm the present's presencing: the present manifests content.

If the present is fleeting reality and it is not mine, this means that it belongs to no one. It is only for "someone" (*PP* 17), yet not for any particular individual person.

> The threshold is the not-mine that nevertheless is for me. It is the place and time of the crossing; the path that is proposed to me, the memory of what has been crossed, the waiting for a pass. It is not, however, the place of dwelling. The threshold turns [things] upside down because it transforms the over-here into an over-there, the inside into the outside, and the mine into the other's. It affects the I that crosses it, which becomes alienated. The threshold installs itself in the I, and not the I in

the threshold. The time that the I covers indeed traverses the I, and turns it upside down. (*PP* 17)

For Perone, the present is never fully present, it is not a Bergsonian intensity or *élan* or duration, nor is it simply fleeting and ungraspable: it is an in-between. From a phenomenological perspective, he claims, presencing, retention, and anticipation are all moments of the present, a position that is in line with most readings of Husserlian phenomenology. Memory can retain aspects of the present while anticipating an opening of time through the dilation of time by the subject: "The threshold that has been overcome is not eliminated; rather, it is withheld in memory. The threshold is even the protrusion of the memory of that to which we no longer belong. The threshold is severe because it destabilizes; it is severe because it never lets one go. It protrudes into the I, who thought itself able to dominate it, and brings to the I the not-having-time, which is the time that one has in the present" (*PP* 18).

What is unique about Perone's discussion of the threshold are the positions of the subject and affectivity. The threshold has a deep and marking structure, which shapes the life of the subject but also allows the subject to dilate the present in order to create a world and a sense of self, both of which are seized in retrospective apprehension.[5] It should come as no surprise that Perone places an emphasis on both subjectivity and affectivity as these two themes are highly privileged in his work.[6] In a deep sense, time gives the I to itself, but this is not the I of identity, the ego of modern philosophy. What is given is a sense of selfhood, of appropriation: if the threshold is a beginning marked by possibility, a subject is a possibility that can come to be here within this space. By dilating and even compressing the present, a subject opens up senses of herself, senses that mark the life of a subject, an individual who bears the affects of the time of the present. The subject can linger in the present, thereby experientially lengthening it.[7] For Perone, the present becomes a remainder that cannot be taken away from us.[8]

The Time of Being-Held-in-Being and the Giving of Time: Edith Stein

Undoubtedly, both Ugo Perone and Edith Stein would agree with Heidegger that the present is both fleeting and, therefore, negating. But whereas Perone views the present as a possible beginning where the finite subject feels itself and comes to be, Stein views the present as something given, not of our own making: the present is a becoming of being, which calls us to fuller personhood, both human and divine. In *Finite and Eternal Being*, Stein argues that, like Descartes and Husserl, one of the most evident things we can say about ourselves is that we exist (FEB 35–36). But our existence is also most certainly marked by a passing. What is flows away into nonexistence. We live our lives between these two poles of existing and not existing. The move from being to nonbeing is a change and it marks the flow of time. Stein notes,

> When I turn toward being as it is in itself, it reveals to me a dual aspect: that of being and that of not-being. The "I am" is unable to endure this dual perspective: that in which "I am" is subject to change, and since being and the intellectual movement ("in which" I am) are not separated, this being is likewise subject to change. The "former" state of being is past and has given way to the present state of being. This means that the being of which I am conscious as mine is inseparable from temporality. As actual being . . . [i]t is a "now" in between a "no longer" and a "not yet." (FEB 37)

If there is a movement or change from being to nonbeing, for Stein, following Aristotle and Thomas Aquinas, we must also posit both possible being and actual being, potency and act, *dynamis* and *energeia*. Being itself and its changes and movements enclose within themselves a potential to be that can actualize itself; this actualization passes into nonbeing, which signifies the completion or finite end of an act of being as it moves into nonbeing (FEB 1–2, 31–34).

Both Perone and Stein recognize the potential in being and both understand the position of the lived past in relation to the past and the future, but it is the experience of the present that is somewhat different in the two philosophers, especially as they both are responding to what they see as Heidegger's privileging of the future and his critique of traditional philosophy's emphasis on full presencing of the present. For Stein, the present is not a threshold experience marked by both dilation and rupture; rather, she wishes to argue that the present is an experience of unification and radical alterity. The present is phenomenologically described as manifesting three unique aspects: becoming, the being of pure I or ego-subject, and a radical Other, whom Stein calls God.

How does Stein account for becoming? What is it? While it is true that we experience ourselves as both being and not-being, we also experience ourselves as perduring or persisting through time: time moves relative to our own being. Citing her fellow phenomenologist Hedwig Conrad-Martius's work on time, *Die Zeit*,[9] Stein writes about the ontic birth of time, a birth that happens in the present. It is true that time conditions being, especially as we exist in time, but time too is also transformed as it comes into contact with being. Stein powerfully observes, "The peculiar nature of enduring being cannot be understood from the point of view of time, but rather, conversely, time must be understood from the point of view of non-dimensional actuality. The 'ontic birth of time' takes place 'in the fully actualized present,' in that actual existence . . . which establishes a contact with being . . . at only one point," as something that is given and that in its "givenness is simultaneously something privative": a "being suspended between not-being and being" (*FEB* 40).

Though one is in between being and not-being, which is like Perone's threshold, Stein posits an enduring or becoming that is an "actual existence"; that is, one lives an enduring point that actually exists. Perone emphasizes a real fleetingness of being, whereas Stein sees becoming as an actual state that is marked by a kind of enduring being. But here we meet with a great difficulty: If temporal being always immediately passes over into nonbeing, and if thus nothing that is past can "stand firm and remain," is it then not meaningless to speak of enduring units? How can we arrive at a unit that extends beyond the fleeting moment? The life of the ego thus appears to be nothing but a continuous living-from-the-past-into-the-future whereby the potential is constantly actualized and the actual constantly sinks back into potentiality. Or, to express it differently: that which is not fully alive reaches the height of its vitality, and that which is now fully alive becomes, a moment later, "life that has been lived" (*FEB* 44). If time is a flow, it admits becoming. To view time as constituted by three moments, or ecstases, to borrow Heidegger's terminology, is to misunderstand the unfolding of time. Stein maintains that instants of time such as "now," "past," and "future" are experienced only from the perspective of the completion of time accomplished as opposed to time unfolding. Stein ascribes to each of the modes of time a durational quality: the past has duration, as do the present and the future. Stein writes,

> To be sure, we constantly take it for granted that there are such enduring units. And, moreover, by "present" we mean not only the fulfilment of the present moment, nor do we mean by "past" and "future" only what precedes and follows this moment within the circumference of an enduring experiential unit, but we must also call present, past, and future such individual enduring units as are experienced in acts of deliberation, of fear, or of joy. We

then designate as past an experiential unit which in its entirety has "moved into the past" and thus is no longer organically and structurally active; we designate as future an experiential unit which has not yet reached the height of the present [*Gegenwartshöhe*]; and we call present an experiential unit which, though not fully alive in its entire extension, is engaged in a vital process of becoming and is at every moment in vital contact with the fullness of life. (FEB 44)

Stein here introduces a Bergsonian perspective on the psychological experience of becoming as a kind of duration whose constitutive moments or aspects are not necessarily distinct, even though one experiences the flow of becoming. Perone's threshold bifurcates being and not-being and situates becoming within them. Stein sees becoming happening within the past, present, and future, which ultimately means that possibility, being, and nothing also become and admit duration. Stein gives the example of joy. The lived and actual experience of joy moves, and as it moves it becomes past, then present, and can even anticipate future moments of joy (FEB 45, 47). Whereas Perone's threshold divides, Stein's present is one of becoming: it is marked by the unity and connectedness of the flows of content or experience as they alter in time.

Though lived experience and being admit durational becoming, they still require being for them to manifest as the distinct and clear experiences of being truly or really present, past or future. Some parts of the whole of a becoming must attain fullness of being in order for the experience of being to keep moving into nonbeing and to keep moving *tout court*, otherwise we would lapse into an eternal present devoid of the flow of time. "Owing to the fact that one or another part of such a unit steadily—though only for a brief moment—reaches the height of being, the whole unit receives a share in being and reveals itself as actually present, i.e., as something actual" (FEB 46). In short, human beings experience being, and their being in particular, as a whole becoming, whose constituent parts are moving in units of greater or lesser intensity as they become more distinct from one another. As it moves through time, being admits duration. Duration means that parts of being are becoming past, present, and future while other parts are fully or actually past, present, or future. Stein has introduced a unifying durational becoming into the classical concept of constituent instants of time.

We come now to the second aspect of Stein's understanding of the present. Perone argues that the threshold demands a subject. For Stein, the subject, understood in Husserl's sense as the pure ego, is given: it accompanies all experience of being and has a unique being that is its own; it has a life. "This ego is alive, and its life is its *being*. It lives perhaps right now in the experience of joy, a little while later in longing, and again a little later in thoughtful reflection, but most of the time in several such experiential units simultaneously. But while joy fades away, longing dies, and reflection ceases, the ego does not fade or pass away: It is alive in every now. This does not mean, however, that it possesses eternal life" (FEB 48). For Perone, the subject has the potential and the initiative to dilate the present, whereas for Stein, the durational present requires the life of the ego in order for it to have being. The ego stands in a relation to its own being and the being that it experiences:

> The fact that the experiential contents attain to real being, although they touch it only punctually [*punktuell*] at any given moment, may now appear a little less enigmatic. The real being they touch is in fact not *their* being, since in and of themselves they are incapable of real being. The experiential contents receive a share in respect to what owes its being to the ego and rises to the level of being by virtue of and within the ego, the latter thus exists in a preeminent sense. The ego is not, to be sure, *existentially superior* in the sense that it could be said to embody the *height of being* (as compared with *rudimentary degrees of being*) but rather in a sense that indicates a relationship existing between a *carrier* and the *thing carried*. (FEB 49)

The ego-subject, for Stein, allows the experience of being to persist in consciousness, but the very being of the ego itself, as it lives, is an actual being.

For Stein, it is the being of the ego that introduces a limit, which brings us to the third aspect of the present. Whereas Perone's present is marked by the limits of finitude, Stein's view of the present made while living in an ego admits a finitude that requires it to be constantly held in being: being needs to be given to the finite ego in order for it to live, especially as the ego's life is subject to passing and, therefore, nonbeing. The actual living of the ego from moment to moment in the actuality of the lived experience is only temporary and, therefore, fleeting. The ego can never stop the flow of lived experiences, and as such is never in control of its own being. The pure ego receives experiences and, therefore, experiences itself as received in experience. The being of the ego is experienced as an *empfangenes Sein*, a received being.[10] The ego does not call itself into being; rather, it finds itself already "thrown into being" (FEB 54). What started off in a very Husserlian fashion with a meditation on the nature of lived experience and what lies behind experience, namely, the pure I, is now elaborated. Stein goes on to analyze the very being of that I through the Heideggerian inspired notions of time and being. Temporality reveals both that our being is fleeting and also that we are not in full possession of our being.

What, then, is the nature of this received being? Stein begins to speak of this received being as a nihilating being (*nichtiges Sein*) because this being is fleeting. Moment to moment this being that I find myself immersed in disappears (FEB 53). Yet despite this nonbeing, I continue to exist. One finds oneself continuing to be as well as experiencing a fleetingness of being. For Stein, however, this being of the *nichtiges Sein* points to a fullness (FEB 53). The fact that being possesses the doubleness of not-being and being concomitant with the fact that there is a continuous flow of this experience of being suggests that being is also a becoming. As one moment disappears, another moment is given. The I is that concrete unity that makes the experience of the moments of being livable, not as mere unconnected moments, but as a whole-life unified within the dynamic of the I.

Having accepted Husserl's understanding of the pure I as unifier of experience and Heidegger's insight into the fleeting nature of being as a *nichtiges Sein*, Stein goes on to give her own phenomenological description of the being of the I, namely: the I as being-held-in-being (*im Sein erhalten*). Stein experiences the being of the I not only as fleeting but also as constantly reaffirmed because one is held-in-being. This being-held-in-being is experienced as peace and security, the sweet and content security of a child. Being is constantly being given to the I. Stein says that Heidegger's notion of *Angst* as a fundamental *Lebensgefühl* (sense, feeling of life) is given far too much emphasis (FEB 56). Rather, *Angst* is a legitimate feeling when one thinks of the imminent death that plagues us all; however, it is not the only experience.[11] The experience of our beings constantly being held-in-being and the security that our beings will be definitely held-in-being signify a comfort or security in our being: a *Seinssicherheit* (FEB 58).

The experience of being-held-in our being and the sweet security that accompanies such an experience of the being of the I causes Stein to question her experience more fully, thereby opening up further the field of experience. From whence does my being receive its being? In other words, what or who keeps my being continually becoming until my death, especially given that I experience myself as not being capable of giving myself being? Stein affirms that there is an other who preserves my being (FEB 57–58). The being of the I is experienced as "stopping in" and grounded in a being who is groundless and "stopless": an eternal being. Stein's phenomenology of the I opens up the field of experience to reveal that our beings are preserved in a being that is experienced as endless and groundless. Philosophy and phenomenology stop here, for Stein. They can go no further in naming this experience of being-preserved-in-being by an eternal Being who continually gives our being to us despite the very fleetingness of being. This existing despite the fleeting moments of being into nothingness is confirmed in the very experience of the ego to identify itself as "I am" despite the fleetingness of my being.

When philosophy and phenomenology reach their human limit, Stein appeals to the knowledge of faith. Faith is not to be conceived as blind consent, for that would result in a fideism of the worst sort. Rather, faith is to be conceived as a kind of knowing, which is based on spiritual sensibilities.[12] It is not like rational or intellectual knowing although it draws on these human faculties. Faith is to be understood in the English sense of "belief" wherein one need not have confirmation of every fact in order to make a more or less true claim about reality. Someone may ask me, "Where is John?" I respond, "I believe that Johnny is out playing in the yard." I make such a statement not as an absolutely verifiable empirical fact. I take certain evidence, like Johnny's having exited the back door with his croquet balls and mallet, along with the knowledge that Johnny likes spending his summer afternoons playing croquet in the yard, and I make a reasonably intelligent conclusion. It is a conclusion that is most likely true even though I have not gone out to confirm that John is indeed playing croquet in the yard. Perceptual faith is similar. I know that something is such and such a color without having to confirm it each and every time. Stein's notion of faith follows very much the Thomistic and Scholastic line of thought wherein faith works within the dynamic of human reason and will; that is, *fides quaerens intellectum* (faith seeking understanding). Faith, then, is not to be conceived as opposed to rationality. Rather, it is another way of knowing.

Stein claims that there are two ways in which one can describe the experience of the other that holds our beings in being. First, one can turn to Revelation given in Faith. This other, then, becomes identified as the personal God of Scripture and Tradition (*FEB* 58). The second way in which one can identify the Eternal Being who preserves us in our being is by appealing to thought illumined by faith, which is a more philosophical approach. One can, like Thomas, try to give proofs for the existence of the Eternal Being. This Eternal Being is described as First Cause, Pure Being, First Mover, Ultimate Telos, and so on. Through thinking about proofs for the existence of God, one comes to a deeper understanding of the nature of the Being who preserves our being as an "I am" despite the fleeting of our being into moments of nonbeing or nothingness (*FEB* 58).

Lingering and Security in Being: A Dialectical Relationship?

Perone and Stein's analyses give us a present in which we can linger, in which we can feel ourselves being given more being. I see these two ways of being as interrelated in that lingering is made possible by a feeling of ease, comfort, and security: we can linger a while, we can think for a while, when we know that there is no future task that requires attention or when there is a lack of Heideggerian anxiety over the radical finitude (death) of time, as both Perone and Stein, *contra* Heidegger, point out. Lingering and the safe expectation that being will be given imply an opening of a time-space in which one can be in a moment, a moment that can be experienced in a durational sense. This time-space has to be open; that is, it has to be experienced with both beginning and end receding into a background in order for one to live fully in that present moment. In addition to the aforementioned two aspects of the present that Stein and Perone uncover, it must be noted that both lingering and security stand in an important relation to one another. The security in being permits a lingering, but the lingering also reinforces the awareness that being is constantly being given to us in that very lived experience of the present. The lingering as the threshold of the present can be rendered more intense with the knowledge and/or feeling that this threshold of possibility can persist. The certainty that comes from a security in being can, in turn, make more possible the initiative of being a subject and of dilating the present.

Possibility and impossibility are subject to time. Possibility and impossibility are experienced and lived not only quantitatively, that is, in a measurable time of instants, but in the qualitative sense of a Steinian durational content of becoming, as a lived experience. For example, in a threshold experience, the subject can choose to dilate the present by making present a possibility for its being; but if that possibility of being is simply fleeting or if it really moves and grasps the subject, this experience reveals a certain intensity to a possibility, an intensity of personal being, which Stein has called "depth."[13] The experience of a qualitative experience of possibility can be more or less possible, realizable, or achievable. The possibility can also resonate with one aspect of the subject's being or even with the whole or with no part of the subject's being at all. For example, in a threshold experience, a possibility emerges: the wish to be a writer or poet. This desire can move my entire being: it can be seen as a vocation, understood in the traditional sense as a way of being or even a personal identity. In the same threshold experience, the possibility of writing may emerge in a less intense way, perhaps as a fleeting desire: it would be nice to be a writer, but I know that I do not possess the talents. I consider simply for a brief time, in the present, this possibility, which I then dismiss. My dismissal results in a closure of a possibility for the subject arrived at in the threshold experience.

What contributes and helps to intensify possibility, what helps possibility seem more achievable, which ultimately will cause the maximal dilation of the possible present? Stein is right to affirm that the degree of depth of the experience of possibility helps make it seem more real or possible, but I also think that her discussion of security in being and the transcendence it announces can make the experience of possibility more realizable, more possible. The security that derives from the awareness that being is given and will be given from moment to moment can give to the very experience of possibility in the threshold or in lived experience of the duration a strong foundation in being that renders the very experience of possibility more solid, more achievable, closer to our being, and more meaningful. The more a possibility is held secure in being, the more it seems realizable, the more it seems real, and the less it appears as impossible. When possibility emerges within a Heideggerian framework of being-toward-death and anxiety, then possibility will more easily, and perhaps even more intensely, turn to impossibility. What allows possibility to linger, what allows it to flood the depths of our being, thereby making it more possible, is the fact that it is not erased by anxiety or by the closure of the present moving into a having been of the past. The feeling and knowledge that the possibility can endure in the present gives us hope and confidence that it can be achieved, that it is not impossible. Stein gives to Perone's possibility of dilation the experience of security in being, which can ultimately color the way the dilation happens, with more or less depth, with more or less intensity, and therefore with greater or lesser possibility. The depth and the intensity of the lived experience of possibility is directly affected by the way it is lived psychically and existentially. The comfort and ease that comes with a Steinian security in being conditions the very quality of the possibility announced by Perone's threshold experience.

Furthermore, Stein's argument that a security in being points to another kind of being that gives being to us and holds us in it, namely, God, creates in us a knowledge of our own finite limits, which are being held in being by an eternal, infinite being. Stein admits that in the experience of our very being, we expect and indeed hope that our being will persist, that more being will come. We trust that it will; there is hope and confidence that our being will continue. Hope and expectation are built into the very structure of our being, according to Stein, as we anticipate that God will not only hold us in being but also preserve us in being. Our finitude, in a deep sense, is constantly being given the potential to be and live; in every moment that being is being given, that we are being held in being, we transcend our own finitude. This experience of the transcendence of our very finitude can bend back to color our own experience of possibility.

Here, we uncover the deep structure of ultimate hope, a hope that things may be possible even though we have come to a limit, the limit of our very own finitude. The radical transcendence announced by Stein in her analysis of the living present gives to the experience of possibility an ultimate possibility, namely, that impossibility may be transcended, may be overcome through God's giving another possibility to us in the very form of the givenness of being, a being that we anticipate moment to moment as we rest secure in our being. Possibility, then, need not simply be framed within the extension of our own finite limits, but also can be altered radically by God's making possible that which is impossible for us. Hope, ultimate hope, cannot simply be understood as a possibility within the realms of all possible finite possibilities. Ultimate hope requires a radical break with all that is possible in a given realm. For Stein, our finitude, the very structure of who and what we are as beings, is constantly being given being that finite beings cannot give themselves, namely, life. With every new moment of life comes the possibility of God's giving more possibility to a finite being, possibilities that may transcend the limits of our possibility. Stein's analysis of the security in being and the givenness of being by God adds to the threshold experience of the subjective dilation of possibility a maximum possibility, namely, the possibility of overcoming that which may appear impossible, which is the true sense of hope. Hope is the ultimate and maximal form of possibility that, Stein believes, lies within the very experience of durational present. This radical hope of possibility that can transcend the impossible can condition the very possibility announced in Perone's threshold experience of the subject's dilational present, ultimately giving to the subject the possibility of radical transcendence.

Notes

1. Ugo Perone, *The Possible Present*, trans. Silvia Benso with Brian Schroeder (Albany, NY: State University of New York Press, 2012); hereafter referred to as *PP*.

2. Edith Stein, *Finite and Eternal Being*, trans. K. Reinhardt (Washington, DC: ICS Publications, 2002); hereafter referred to as *FEB*.

3. Perone remarks, "[The present] cannot be a simple limit, that is, [it cannot be] the extreme line either of a contact defining itself through separation or of a being whose consistency is given through exclusion or of an encounter stiffening differences. Nor is it properly a barrier, because the barrier is simultaneously

insurmountable and independent from me. The divide is instead mobile, and a constructive trait of the deciding subject. Nor is [the divide] of the absolute that tangentially encounters the infinite, the *eschaton* that becomes time, because the divide does not discriminate absolutely but rather chooses on the basis of finitude, reorients finitude, and arranges it within the order of time" (PP 16).

4. Luigi Pareyson, *Esistenza e persona* (Genoa: Il Melangolo, 2002), 168.

5. See Enrico Guglielminetti, *Interruzioni, Note sulla filosofia di Ugo Perone* (Genoa: Il Nuovo Melangolo, 2006), 18.

6. Ugo Perone, *Nonostante il soggetto* (Turin: Rosenberg and Sellier, 1995). See also Ugo Perone, *La verità del sentimento* (Naples: Guida, 2008); and Ugo Perone, *Ripensare il sentimento. Elementi per una teoria* (Assisi: Cittadella Editrice, 2014).

7. Perone observes, "The present, however, cannot be deferred, that is put off to a new role. Perhaps it can be prolonged through lingering, which expands [it] and gains new time. Lingering remains within the present and prolongs it. Conversely, deferrals feed on indifference. Because all things are the same, times too are the same, and everything slides away and is deferred. The present is instead here, it impends, and it demands a subject that handles it. The time centred on the present is not cosmological but rather human time, which presupposes a subject (not a master) of time. This subject that ventures through time is no longer the solipsistic subject. Having risked itself in existence, having trusted itself to temporality, the subject has encountered the extension of the self. Yet this extension that, as the figure of the threshold has shown to us, always occurs within an alternative between oppositions (outside/inside, past/future) unfolds but not like an inertial expansion. It knows oppositions, fatigue, and rough rubbing. In principle (without wishing to account properly for this here), the subject from now on inevitably finds itself confronted with its own and the other's alterity; thus it is open to a possible intersubjectivity first of all because it is indeed implicated in a tangle of intersubjectivity" (PP 27).

8. Ugo Perone, "The Risks of the Present: Benjamin, Bonhoeffer, Celan," *Symposium: Canadian Review of Continental Philosophy* 14, 2 (2010), 19–34, 33.

9. Hedwig Conrad Martius, "Die Zeit," *Philosophischer Anzeiger* 2 and 4 (1927–28): 143–182, 345–390.

10. Received being stands in opposition to Heidegger's *Geworfenessein*.

11. See Sarah Borden Sharkey, *Thine Ownself: Individuality in Edith Stein's Later Writings* (Washington, DC: ICS Publications, 2009); Ken Casey, "Do We Die Alone? Edith Stein's Critique of Heidegger," in *Intersubjectivity, Humanity, Being: Edith Stein's Phenomenology and Christian Philosophy*, ed. Mette Lebech and John Haydn Gurmin (New York: Peter Lang, 2015), 334–338; and Vincent Wargo, "Reading against the Grain: Edith Stein's Confrontation with Heidegger as an Encounter with Hermeneutical Ontology," *Journal of the British Society for Phenomenology* 42, 2 (2011): 125–138.

12. See Edith Stein, *Ways to Know God*, trans. R. Allers (New York: Edith Stein Guild, 1981), 37–51.

13. Edith Stein, "Der Aufbau der menschlichen Person," in *Edith Steins Werke*, ed. Lucy Gelber and Michael Linssen (Freiburg: Herder, 1994), 16:114.

5

Failing to Imagine the Lives of Others
Remo Bodei and Jean-Luc Nancy on
Citizenship and Sancho Panza

Alexander U. Bertland

In *Living Thought: The Origins and Actuality of Italian Philosophy*, Roberto Esposito describes the tradition of modern and contemporary philosophy that has developed in Italy. He emphasizes that this tradition does not exist as a community isolated within its borders. Instead, these Italian philosophers step outside political boundaries and intellectual disciplines to enrich their thought. This "opting for engagement with the outside world" can be traced back to Niccolò Machiavelli and Giambattista Vico.[1] Because these philosophers always consider their work in the context of a larger political environment, they carry with them a sense of practical urgency.[2] Esposito writes, "But what characterizes both modern and contemporary Italian philosophy is the awareness that the ontology of actuality is furrowed by alternatives that cannot be mediated and that demand a decision."[3] This sense of urgency can be found in the writings of Remo Bodei. He crosses boundaries between psychology, literature, history, philosophical issues of personal identity, and the postmodern discussion of the subject as a singular.[4] This drives Bodei to argue that discussions of identity ought to be directed toward attainable political activity.

In *Immaginare altre vite. Realtà, progetti, desideri* (*Imagining Other Lives: Realities, Projects, Desires*), Bodei explores a curious topic in order to expand the political discussion of the singular.[5] Imagining how others live seems like an ordinary and innocent activity. Nevertheless, there are at least two important reasons to look deeper. First, these acts of fantasy may have negative political consequences. The destructive collective movements of the twentieth century often relied on the use of leaders as role models. These abuses need to be studied and avoided. More positively, however, imagining the lives of others sits at an important intersection between one's own identity (*l'identità propria*) and being-with-others. The constant presence of others encourages the investigation of new paths, experimentation with alternative solutions, and reshaping ourselves. Those we live with and those we watch on the media shape and become part of the horizon of our life world. Our existence as interconnected singulars makes imitating the lives of others essential for considering what our identity can be.

In *Immaginare altre vite*, Bodei argues that it is politically vital to imagine the lives of others in an effective way. These imaginative acts teach how to be a citizen with political responsibilities. Failure to fantasize properly about other lives could have grave consequences. If singulars do not dare, with enough boldness, to visualize other ways of being, society could fall into complacency. Alternatively, if their daydreams are too wild and extreme, they could focus on unrealistic and unrealizable goals for social change. Bodei holds that our imaginations must be used to help open ourselves to new perspectives and possibilities that can be experienced only through encountering others. We must do so, however, in a practical way that acknowledges the way in which we are situated in the world.

This chapter will explore Bodei's argument by contrasting his account with that of Jean-Luc Nancy. In *Immaginare altre vite*, Bodei reveals a deep concern about poststructuralism. He worries that a range of authors, from Gadamer to Derrida, have devalued facts and convinced people that history is malleable (*IAV* 176). This, Bodei contends, has contributed to the current cultural trend that has driven the imagination further away from its practical function. Bodei does not include Nancy in this group. Instead, he shares Nancy's ontological account of the singular and, in the very few places where Bodei mentions Nancy in this particular text, he praises him for connecting the question of the singular to identity (*IAV* 196). Nevertheless, there is a divide that separates these two authors, and it will be profitable to trace the points of division. Since the two authors use a similar ontology, it will be helpful to see where Bodei's more practical orientation informs Nancy's project.

This chapter will examine how Bodei gives Nancy's ontology a sense of practical urgency. Nancy certainly does not ignore the practical or the political. Nevertheless, his commitment to an ontology that prioritizes the openness of the singular makes it challenging for him to present a positive account of political action.[6] It is unclear how Nancy calls us to orient our lives, given the ontology he has unveiled. There will not be space here to analyze fully Nancy's writings on this subject. Instead, I will explore the ontology of openness of the singular plural in order to show how Bodei develops its practical implications for political engagement in regard to imagining the lives of others.

One of the most important aspects of Nancy's ontology is that it forces us to recognize the value of the unique singular and the value of finite thinking. Nancy encourages us to embrace the openness that lies before the singular and not to let ourselves be restricted by the past. Bodei embraces this presentation of the singular as existing as exposed to others. While he does not fully use Nancy's terminology, he always stays far away from any depiction of the singular as having an essence that it must authentically present. He agrees that people should not be restricted by political traditions. Nevertheless, he wants to place the openness of the singular in the context of a psychological and political situation that allows for responsible action. Bodei's concern is that too much emphasis on the openness of the singular without the acknowledgment of practical and psychological concerns that shape a context will lead to debilitating insecurity and idle fantasizing. Rather than rejecting the past entirely, Bodei holds that the singular should mediate both the past and the future. In this way, one can be open to the future and have the possibility of radically reinventing the self or culture while not entirely fragmenting the self. This, according to Bodei, allows one to fulfill moral obligations.

Ontology of the Singular

To construct the conversation between the authors, it is helpful to start from their common ground. Both use the notion of the singular to combat any attempt to justify political collectivism. In *The Inoperative Community*, Jean-Luc Nancy presents his critique of communism, arguing that shared experiences of work cannot artificially construct a collective that merges fundamentally unique singulars.[7] In *Destini personali* (*Personal Destinies*), Bodei calls for philosophy to reinforce the uniqueness of the subject in order to prevent a reoccurrence of the twentieth-century attempts at political collectivization.[8]

Ontologically, however, neither author returns to a modern sense of the individual as isolated from a community. Nancy claims that there is no separation between the singular's being and the singular's being-with others. The existence of others is not given in addition to the being of the singular but is already contained within the being of the singular. For Nancy, to understand this requires a rethinking of how singulars interact.

Traditionally, community is thought of as a network of relations that connect separate individuals. Nancy rejects the possibility of community in this sense. While singulars can never be reduced to one another, he denies the existence of an initial void that separates them. Singulars already reside in a space together. This common space is the being-with of the singular.[9] Nancy writes, "Not only must being-with-one-another not be understood starting from the presupposition of being-one, but on the contrary, being-one (Being as such, complete Being or *ens realissimum*) can only be understood by starting from being-with-one-another."[10] The ontological being-with of the singular precludes any possibility of imposing a community onto it. As Greg Bird explains, there is no way for a singular to become alienated from the being-with-one-another and so there is no way for a community to appropriate the singular.[11] So, there is no way of thinking ontologically about community as bringing people together to form a collective since singulars are inherently being-with.

Nancy emphasizes that relationships among singulars must be understood as part of each singular and yet as never reducing the singulars to one another. At times, Nancy refers to this as "compearance." Singulars, as part of their being, always share their appearances with each other, but they can never appropriate another.[12] In his later works, Nancy refers to the relationship among singulars as "touching" in order to represent the sharing between irreducible singulars. Bird writes, "It is the sharing/division of bodies exposed to each other as simultaneously singular and plural. The 'with' is nothing but shared/divided incorporeality; the modality of the 'with' is nothing other than touching (neither taking-giving, nor holding-letting go), just touching."[13] Nancy is primarily interested not in the way in which separate individuals communicate by sending messages, but rather in how singulars already exist in relation to one another.

It is a popular idea that a community requires a *sensus communis*, that is, a shared tradition that allows its members to communicate and work together. The challenging idea within Nancy's ontology is that the being-with-one-another of the singular does not produce a collective of singulars but instead demonstrates the impossibility of such a collective. The identities of singulars could only actually merge if the traditional *sensus communis* were to become so powerful that it could somehow replace the intertwining of the being-with. Since communication depends on the being-with-one-another but cannot appropriate it, there exist borders that prevent singulars from communicating transparently. The borders among the singulars are shared but impassible boundaries that are frustrating and serve to protect each singular's uniqueness. Consequently, Nancy rejects the idea that groups should reinforce or impose traditional tales or rituals on one another in order to create a collective community.

Nancy develops this point further. He describes the singular as a happening at a particular temporal point rather than as a being with an essence that unfolds over time. Each manifestation of a singular or happening is a point that is connected to the course of time and so, in a sense, is inseparable from it. Nevertheless, each moment has its own unique existence, which is separate from the underlying flow. Nancy writes, "The singular is a plural. It also undoubtedly offers the property of indivisibility, but it is not indivisible the way each substance is indivisible. It is, instead, indivisible in each instant, within the event of its singularization."[14] Therefore, the singular is unique but contains the borders that establish its uniqueness within its being. Nancy writes, "A singularity does not stand out against the background of Being; it is, when it is, Being itself or its origin."[15] In this sense, the singular is integrated into the flow of Being, but it manifests itself at particular instants as a unique entity.

Nancy defends his characterization of the singular in the following manner. He argues that nothing would have meaning if it were not held in contrast with something else. Every object, plant, and animal can only be understood if it is put into a comparison with something else. In this way, the context of the singular becomes part of the singular.[16] A truly distinct being has never existed as a separate entity apart from the plurality. It has always been a being in a particular position and, as such, needs that position to express what it is. Nancy proclaims, "*The plurality of beings is at the foundation of Being.*"[17] To ask what gives a person an identity separate from a particular context and situation does not make any sense, for Nancy, because nothing can be understood outside a context. Yet this does not deny the fact that borders exist between singulars that prevent transparent communication or appropriation.

Bodei does not enter fully into Nancy's ontological discussion and instead engages in wide-ranging sociological, literary, and historical analyses. Nevertheless, he accepts major aspects of Nancy's ontology. Specifically, Bodei wants to integrate the notion of being-with into a discussion of identity. He briefly traces the history of the term "identity" back to the origin of the idea of personal identity in John Locke. He makes clear nonetheless that his goal is to understand identity in the context of an ontology of the singular. He writes, "The examination of what we become reveals our plural nature and permits us to recognize the fact that our life is essentially integrated with those of others, it gives and receives meaning reactively from their needs, hopes, fears, inadequacies, and cruelties" (*IAV* 27). Bodei holds that it is necessary to think about the identity of the singular as it resides in the interconnections with the plural. He examines neither communication between individuals nor the way in which an individual might appropriate the essential identity of another. Instead, he wants to explore identity in the context of "compearing" singulars, to use Nancy's expression. Bodei emphasizes this point when he explains why he does not develop a semiotics. He distinguishes himself from Umberto Eco, "who sees the novel as a 'lazy machine' that needs interpretive cooperation on the part of the reader" (*IAV* 69). Instead of explaining how such a machine works, Bodei describes how the life of a reader changes when a text is introduced to it (*IAV* 69). The crucial point is not how meanings are communicated but how texts become absorbed into the being-with.

When Bodei discusses imagining the lives of others, he does so to explore the activity as part of being-with-one-another. He certainly does not think that this act of imagination can reveal the essence of another. He is also not focused on fully self-aware attempts to study the way another acts in the world. Obviously, there are times when one consciously decides to imagine how another experiences the world. These reflective choices, however, are not Bodei's primary concern. Instead, Bodei makes clear at the beginning of his text that he is interested in the way our everyday observations lead us to imagine sympathetically what others experience. We continually integrate these observations into our personality, often with little critical reflection. Our imaginations are continually watching and remembering the actions of others so that when we find ourselves in similar situations, we draw on this bank of the experiences of others. Those with more active imaginations, therefore, inhabit a richer world.

Bodei uses a musical metaphor to describe this conception of imagining the lives of others: "In the best cases, with respect to a life effectively lived, imagined lives resonate as the natural harmonics in music, as vibrations that accompany the fundamental note, enriching the timber" (*IAV* 16). For example, when someone who has not developed an imaginative ability walks down the street or searches the Internet, that person will see simply what is there. As one develops one's imagination, these places become richer because the imagination will connect physical images to opportunities and risks. Thus, imagining other lives enters into the horizon from which one sees the world.

In *The Inoperative Community*, Nancy also uses a musical analogy to describe the way in which myths continue to exist in our culture. Myths cannot be reused or reinvented to create a community because no new myth can replace the original myths that lie at the center of culture. Myths also cannot be fully extinguished from culture since they have an existence within the coappearance that exists as part of the being-with. The echo of myths continues to reverberate down through the ages in poetry and literature. Nancy writes, "The mythological presentation is ended, it no longer holds good and no longer works (if it ever worked in the way we thought it was supposed to work, in our functional, structural and communal mythology). But in some way the interrupted voice or music imprints the schema of its retreat in the murmur or the rustling to which the interruption gives rise."[18] The tones that myths leave behind continue to provide ground for sharing among singulars even though the myths are interrupted and thus unworkable.

Nancy and Bodei are both ontologically committed to understanding the singular as residing within the plural. They are not interested in how singulars communicate as much as in how they continually experience the plural. Bodei pushes Nancy's position by incorporating the activity of imagining the lives of others into that experience. The divide between these authors opens, however, as they describe the singular as unique. Specifically, they disagree on the extent to which one can know the uniqueness of a singular.

Nancy on History and Being-With

Once one accepts the idea of the being of the singular as a being-with, one encounters a major problem in understanding identity. The plural cannot be fully known or understood. As far as it constitutes the being-with of the singular, it curtails the possibility of full self-knowledge. Since social influences cannot be fully grasped and those instances are part of the being-with of the singular, the singular also can never be transparently known. The question becomes: what does one strive to know given our inability to grasp self-knowledge?

Nancy is content to steer the singular away from the traditional question of self-knowledge, and he does not appear worried about the anxiety this may instill. Instead of trying to grasp the being of others to understand the self, Nancy thinks our task is knowing the "with" of being-with. This is the boundary that singulars share with one another. Nancy writes, "Only the limit is common, and the limit is not a place, but the sharing of places, their spacing."[19] Since we cannot share with others across limits, our awareness of the being-with comes precisely from the shared limits themselves. Nancy writes, "To reach the origin is not to miss it; it is to be properly exposed to it. . . . We reach it to the extent that we are in touch with *ourselves* and in touch with the rest of beings. We are in touch with ourselves insofar as we exist. Being in touch with ourselves is what makes us 'us,' and there is no other secret to discover buried behind this very touching, behind the 'with' of coexistence."[20] For Nancy, there is no deeper significance behind the being-with. One does not approach the border to see what is behind it. All there is to experience is the border itself.

In exchange for this loss of identity, Nancy holds that we receive an openness to ourselves and the world. When one considers the "with" without going beyond it, one sees that the borders of the singular change and grow continually. Rather than having a base personality that one is tied to, each singular actually creates itself anew at every moment. As Marie-Eve Morin writes, "For Nancy . . . to be free is not to be absolutely self-determined but to be absolutely without 'why.' . . . Freedom is the unfounded (*défondée*) factuality of an existence that surprises itself in existing."[21] Because the singular is not tied to any essential identity, it is free to reshape its personality in ways that will allow it to have radically new experiences.

Nancy pushes this point farther by disconnecting the singular from any anchoring notion of origin; and since the singular is not tied to an essential notion of origin, it can reshape its own origin at any time. Nancy writes, "At this exact point, then, one becomes most aware of the essence of singularity: it is not individuality; it is, each time, the punctuality of a 'with' that establishes a certain origin of meaning and connects it to an infinity of other possible origins. Therefore, it is, at one and the same time, infra-/intraindividual and transindividual, and always the two together."[22] At every moment, one establishes a new origin for oneself based around the borders that appear at that moment. That origin is one out of many that could be selected. At the next moment, a new origin arrives. This gives singulars a radical freedom in the sense that they should not allow artifacts of the past to constrain them.

Nancy draws out implications of this for history and politics. Nancy admits that the practical work of historians and scholars has an intrinsic value.[23] Nevertheless, he also claims that history is not something that can be fully known or that can define us. He writes, "Memory is the (re)presentation of the past. It is the *living* past. History begins where memory ends. It begins where *representation* ends. The historian's work—which is never a work of memory—is a work of representation in many senses, but it is representation with respect to something that is not representable, and that is history itself."[24] The historian cannot know the past and instead always creates new representations of the past. Because these representations always happen in the present now, they themselves are not in a flow of history but instead each fills the present now. Nancy writes, "A time full of 'now' is a time full of openness and heterogeneity. 'Now' says 'our time'; and 'our time' says 'We, filling the space of time with existence.' This is not an accomplishment; this is a happening. Happening accomplishes—happening. History accomplishes—history."[25] Hence, one should not search history for meaning but should use the activity of doing history to create meaning.

Nancy's account of history shows how he connects finitude to openness. If one could understand from an infinite perspective what the events of history were, then there would be knowable essences. Because singulars are finite, they cannot know history from this perspective. This is not cause for anxiety but instead opens up a life in which a range of possibilities can be encountered. As Morin writes, "To think history is to think finite and discontinuous happening, the opening of a space of time where we happen, we come to be. The space of time where 'we' happen is without origin or end."[26] This embracing of finitude allows for the possibility of constant renewal and encounters with the new.

Politically, this implies that singulars exist apart from their history and so are not tied to a tradition. H. B. Hutchens describes how Nancy's ethics is constituted by an archi-ethics that is based on a narrative form that always asserts the singular within a community in which individuals are not bound by a communal essence but have, instead, a common area within which to assert their individual freedoms. This form of narrative implies a resistance to the reabsorption of history that would prevent one from understanding one's current self through the past.[27]

Bodei and the Need for Role Models for Navigating Life

Bodei agrees with Nancy's fundamental point that identity must be thought of as open-ended. Singulars do not have definite essences buried within them that are naturally opened up through a process of maturation. Instead, identity is "an open work in progress (*cantiere aperto*)" (IAV 49). Nevertheless, Bodei makes a subtle shift in his account of the singular that drives his ontology in a direction different from Nancy's. For Bodei, the singular is open but, at the same time, must be thought of as having a direction or at least a practical orientation. This is the moment when Bodei brings the Italian sense of practical urgency to Nancy's ontology. For Bodei, singulars are thrown into a world where they have to adapt, develop outlooks on that world, and make decisions that have real consequences.

Bodei uses the image of the *navigatio vitae* (the voyage of life) to describe the singular's placement in the world. The singular is always on a course that is constantly battered by a variety of unexpected and potentially dangerous forces. He writes, "Between the departure and arrival of the voyage of life, there arrive, symbolically, tempests, rocks, shallows, periods where the ship is becalmed, stormy capes to cross, and possible shipwrecks" (*IAV* 22). Despite advances in science and technology, not all dangers can be accurately foreseen. Fortunately, there exist many institutions that create opportunities to imagine the lives of others to help predict crises and respond to them. Schools, churches, and television are some of these institutions (*IAV* 23). Yet given the uncertainty of the future, there always exists a need for the singular to orient itself in a particular direction. This sense of practical urgency drives Bodei to consider imagining the lives of others in a way Nancy does not.

While Nancy certainly does not ignore the stress that his ontological account could create, he sees the constant re-creation of the singular's origin and the associated openness to the world as a generally positive thing. Bodei, on the other hand, is deeply concerned about the insecurity created by the singular's lack of origin and identity. If the singular is too fragmented, the ensuing anxiety will impede its freedom. The contemporary world, through globalization and the growth of diverse forms of media, has greatly expanded the number of possible lives that can be imagined. Bodei writes that "identity is always intrinsically in conflict" as many different forces pull and adapt it in diverse ways (*IAV* 50). In the past, this was limited by the lesser diversity of religions and cultures to which one was exposed. But as access to the lives of others has grown across continents and institutions, the amount of content has also expanded. Not only do people have access to lives in a greater number of cultures, but the availability of historical evidence makes it easier to imagine lives in other epochs (*IAV* 145–146). These influences increase the conflict and instability within the self as well as a growing concern about which of the many options one should assume as one moves toward the future. For Bodei, this openness needs to be grounded.

In accord with Nancy, Bodei does not hold that this ground could be found in history or a notion of essence. Nevertheless, he thinks that singulars have a psychological context that cannot be ignored. He concludes that singulars must imagine the lives of others, but they must do so in a way that acknowledges the presence of current psychological concerns in both the one doing the imagining and the life being imagined. Obviously, it is impossible to imagine fully the way any other person lives, and that should not be the objective. Yet this should not be taken as a license to imagine another's life in any way possible. Instead, a practical sense of context and limitation must guide the singular's orientation. This may seem like an obvious point, but it is one that runs counter to Nancy's view of politics and history.

Bodei has many arguments to defend his position, and two key arguments seem to respond most directly to Nancy. These arguments are a call both to examine the dangers lurking in contemporary social institutions and to avoid the arbitrariness with which poststructuralism seems to use history. Bodei's first argument is more theoretical and refers to the need for mediation in developing a sense of identity. His second argument is practical and depends on a critique of contemporary culture. This argument contains valuable insights into the way role models are currently deployed.

The theoretical argument that Bodei advances undercuts Nancy's idea that the I can continually reinvent its origin. Instead, it works from a traditional problem found in the search for identity. When one reflects on oneself, one creates a divide in the self. There is part of the I that treats itself as an object of reflection. This I becomes separate from the prereflective I, the *tactus intimus* (inner sense or feeling or, literally, touch) that exists underneath the act of reflection, outside the realm of sensation (*IAV* 76–77). It is unclear how the reflective I can come to know or even connect to the *tactus intimus*. Fichte tried to do this but ended up with a bad infinity as a continual string of self-reflecting identities continued to expand (*IAV* 53–54, 73). Bodei is unsatisfied with this solution.

Instead, Bodei contends that the reflective level and the prereflective level must be mediated. It is not as if the prereflective level is an essence that must somehow be discovered. This is because the *tactus intimus* is malleable. Nevertheless, if these two aspects of the self are disconnected, this will impede the singular's freedom to be open to the world. The disconnect between what the singular thinks and does can be so great that the singular may crumble such that what it chooses to do and what it actually does are separate. This blocks the singular's capacity to expand in positive directions.

The *tactus intimus* may not be known directly. Nevertheless, by looking at the history of the self and its actions one can develop a sense of its stable content. Bodei writes, "It happens as when a pianist, after long and tiring exercises, learns to play a difficult piece without even looking at the score" (*IAV* 78). In this way, the two levels of the self can come into contact and, while inevitably in conflict, work together. Without this connection, the reflective I will float off like an astronaut who suddenly realizes the importance of gravity (*IAV* 77). This knowledge will never be so perfect that one knows perfectly one's essence and so becomes trapped in a defined personality, yet it does allow parts of the self to work in a harmony that is practically effective.

As a response to Nancy, Bodei suggests that focusing simply on the "with" of being-with misses the value of this mediation. It ignores the existence of the *tactus intimus* as an anchor from which a singular can work and tries to replace it with the borders that exist between singulars as what provides stability. Yet these borders are themselves in such transition that they cannot provide stability. The singular, as Nancy portrays it, is the astronaut in need of gravity. As another example, Bodei presents the schizophrenic who is aware of psychic contents and the facts of the world but cannot refer them back to a subject and as a result cannot function (*IAV* 77).

To prove his point, Bodei works through a series of models that describe the experiences of psychological growth and development. Bodei suggests that these models combine to give a depiction of psychological growth that helps to develop the practical dimension of Nancy's ontology of the singular, appealing both to psychological evidence and to our own experiences to develop his account. This has a ring of circularity to it since Bodei uses an appeal to experience in order to justify his position that we should ground our imagination in actual psychological experience. Nevertheless, the models he presents speak to events that appear to be common in human life, and therefore it seems that they should have philosophical value in an argument.

Each model reveals the importance of mediation between the reflective self and the *tactus intimus*. There is always conflict between the two levels since the *tactus intimus*, as the underlying substratum of the psyche, wants to maintain stability while the reflective self wants change. All the models show the desire to maintain this conflict since that is necessary to continue growth. Yet these models also suggest a need for a certain amount of cohesion since too much conflict creates different types of paralysis or, at least, impediments to productive behavior. Bodei goes into the models in some detail, but here it will be helpful simply to review them briefly to see how they function in his argument.

The first model is the Freudian model of the development of the psyche as a sort of condensation (*IAV* 78–79). As different versions of the I develop, the older versions are condensed and subsumed into the new version. The past is thus conserved in the I while, at the same time, the way is made ready for an even newer version of the I to develop with the current model condensed into the new one.

The second model describes two psychic realms that are at odds with each other. One realm is committed to maintaining a consistent substrate in changing environments, and the other is the alert consciousness that tries new experiences. These two realms simultaneously conflict and cooperate.

Anyone who has made a decision radically to change the direction of his or her life understands this feeling. There is a push to change oneself to match the new environment but also a simultaneous longing to hold onto elements of the past by incorporating them into the new (*IAV* 79–81).

The third model is based on Foucault's account of the development in the psyche through the metaphor of looking at a mirror. The mirror image is the ideal image of the self, and it is necessary that one first create this ideal image before being able to manipulate the bodily self. Yet this ideal image can only have meaning if it originates in the actual bodily self. So, again, both levels are necessary (*IAV* 81–84).

The fourth model draws on Proust's account of involuntary memory. The reflective mind can choose to remember or also to forget events. There are times, however, when a sensual trigger causes the prereflective mind to present a memory that had fallen into forgetfulness. This makes the subject aware of the gap between the choices of the reflective self and the underlying reality of the *tactus intimus* (*IAV* 84–86).

The fifth and final model comes from Plato's *Gorgias*, where he describes desire as the attempt to fill vases that have holes in them. Callicles argues convincingly that the only life worth living involves filling our most strenuous desires, even if the pleasure is only temporary. Yet, Callicles's view is decadent if it is not understood alongside Socrates's claim that there is a necessity of the soul that must be recognized (*IAV* 86–88).

This summary of the five models suggests experiences in psychic life that Nancy seems to overlook. Nancy's account illustrates how singulars must be open to the world, and these models also describe this aspect of openness. Bodei draws our attention to the fact that this openness must occur within a psychological context that we cannot experience directly, and yet we still feel its effects. We can radically change our lives, but we cannot do it without a sense of loss and without feeling the need to incorporate the past into our new selves. We can move on from past events and forget they happened, and yet triggers occur that bring repressed memories back. This need for mediation between the reflective and prereflective self exists. This implies, therefore, that when one imagines the lives of others, one must take into account both the mediated aspects. There is a reality to the *tactus intimus* that governs, to an extent, what choices are possible. When we imagine how others live, we must be realistic about the choices the other makes and what choices we can make given our psychic reality.

Bodei refers to Hannah Arendt, who describes judgment as that which allows the mind to connect the general to the particular. Without this, the mediation would remain completely in the abstract. Bodei writes, "Differently than the 'hermeneutic circle,' this form of judgment does not subtract from the responsibility of actively taking a position. The formulation of judgments then needs the imagination both for interpreting and rectifying sense data and thought and also for fulfilling moral responsibilities" (*IAV* 89). If these moral responsibilities are going to be fulfilled, the imagination must operate with a ground in actual psychic experience. This leads to Bodei's second argument, in which he outlines the practical benefits of imagining the lives of others and discusses particular dangers our society faces when this is not done in a way that is grounded in practical reality.

Bodei gives an extended account of the benefits of imagining the lives of others, which is necessary given the accompanying fear of collectivization (*IAV* 60). His account of Don Quixote encapsulates this account in a way that emphasizes the mediation of the prereflective and reflective self. People fault Don Quixote for allowing his imagination to get the better of him, but Bodei suggests that this assessment misses the point. On his deathbed, Don Quixote has a conversion to Christianity. He does not regret the fact that he spent his life fantasizing. Instead, he laments that he fantasized about imaginary knights rather than God and his own eternal soul. The point is not that imagining the lives of others is in itself bad but rather that this activity needs to be grounded in actual psychic experience. Sancho Panza suffers because he lacks imagination. He cannot use his imagination to envision another life and so is trapped in the routine of ordinary life. Don Quixote was right to imagine the lives of others, but he should have done so in a more effective way (*IAV* 34).

According to Bodei, great literature allows the imagination to melt the texture of the real so that it produces images that devalue our ordinary existence. In this way, the imagination can inspire people to go beyond their given situation (*IAV* 70). This act of imagination can only be practically effective, however, if there is a common ground between the reader and the author. As established in the earlier discussion of the relation of the singular to the plural, this common ground does not come about through intentional communication or appropriation but rather through spontaneous similarities that people automatically recognize. Bodei writes, "In common places, great literature succeeds in giving clear form and an abundance of meaning; above all, it is capable of expressing it in an articulate and intimately cohesive way. It constitutes the point of equilibrium between that which the author says and that which the reader can comprehend almost instinctively if the reader has had analogous experiences and is therefore capable of connecting the other's words with the reader's own experiences" (*IAV* 65). Great literature can express this common ground in a way that links to the *tactus intimus* of the reader. This is not to deny Nancy's point that literature must share borders and cannot produce a complete transfer of meaning. It does suggest, however, that there is something that can be shared beyond simply the border that separates the authors: there must be a connection of psychic contents.

Bodei fears that contemporary society does not provide the means through which these psychic contents can be shared such that they allow people to effectively imitate the lives of others. The proliferation of ways of gaining access to the lives of others and the associated weakening of traditional institutions have increased internal conflict in the psyche (*IAV* 48). As people lose touch with the *tactus intimus*, they become insecure and the wide range of options before them becomes debilitating rather than uplifting.

The insecurity of the contemporary world drives people to fantasize in ways that point in the direction of either Don Quixote or Sancho Panza. To distinguish Bodei's position further from that of Nancy, it will be helpful to dwell on a couple of the ways in which Bodei traces the negative consequences of this. Those leaning toward Sancho Panza find the quantity of possibilities so overwhelming that they abandon fantasizing in ways that could effectively change their existence. Instead, they fantasize about trivial ways in which daily life can be enhanced (*IAV* 143). They focus on establishing work routines, controlling their diet, and organizing their houses. They fantasize about people on television who have perfectly organized lives and not about people who fulfill, in a productive way, their moral obligations to others.

Those leaning toward Don Quixote engage in escapist fantasy and come to desire instant celebrity through institutions such as sports or the Internet. Bodei discusses at length how this desire stems from an inherent desire for recognition (*IAV* 149–154). The immediate problem, however, is that popular celebrities often lack social value (*IAV* 141). It is not so much that athletes and actors are bad people but rather that these figures do not appear to engage in productive citizenship. Hence, people who imagine these lives do not learn how to work for real social change.

A key symptom of this is the development of what Bodei calls the "impotent phenomenon of volunteerism" (*IAV* 163). This movement shows the apathy and cynicism of the younger generation, which contributes to the community because of a sense of self-important generosity rather than civic duty. Because it lacks models to imitate, this generation has not learned to act out of a sense of obligation to democracy and instead remains distant and unengaged. Bodei ties this to contemporary heroes, such as superheroes, who are often praised for doing what is good not because they have any actual commitments to a community, but rather because they choose to be generous (AIV 126). He writes, "The apathy, the infantilization of the public, the protests without purpose exist today in a worrying amount and they constitute the principle pathology of democratic citizenship" (AIV 163). To remedy this, at least in part, it is necessary to promote model lives that can suggest real social change.

In response to Nancy, then, Bodei holds that it is not enough to be open to the world and to contemplate the borders that we share. We must also (but not only) try to ground our imagination in our experience of the world. We must acknowledge the need for mediation between the reflective self and the prereflective self in a way that gives us the security to fulfill moral obligations to the world. The conversation between these two authors, obviously, does not end here. Nancy has a good deal more to say about what it means to share the "with" of being-with that might be able to serve as the ground that Bodei desires. Further, it is always possible to reopen the hermeneutic question and challenge Bodei about our ability to know our own psychological reality. Nevertheless, it will be poignant to end this chapter by comparing the two authors' interpretation of Nietzsche.

Both authors present a subtle view of Nietzsche that does not accept him as merely a relativist who entirely dismisses the possibility of history. For Nancy, Nietzsche recognized that history's emphasis on knowledge outside itself does not allow it radically to question its own activity or the full extent of its political influence. Nancy writes, "But, as Nietzsche already knew, the more history becomes a broad and rich knowledge, the less we know what 'history' means, even if historical knowledge is also an excellent critical and political tool in the fight against ideological representation and their power."[28] Hence, for Nancy, it becomes necessary to step outside history and critically analyze its political meaning.

Bodei, in a way that reflects the practical urgency that Esposito finds in Italian political philosophy, reads Nietzsche differently. Nietzsche famously claimed that there are no facts but only interpretations. Bodei does not think this represents the abandonment of facts. He writes, "As an 'old philologian' that believed in facts, Nietzsche repeated many times, especially in the last years of his life, that whenever laying claim to the honesty and courage of one who searches for truth and declaring error to be an expression of cowardice, one so maintains the tension between truth and suspicion" (IAV 176). Bodei's point is that one needs to continue to search for facts and for a ground in history, otherwise one will not grasp the accompanying suspicion that goes with that search. A truth must be searched for in history and in the self, not so much to find it, but rather to understand what its openness means. This way leads to finding possible political change.

Notes

1. Roberto Esposito, *Living Thought: The Origins and Actuality of Italian Philosophy*, trans. Zakiya Hanafi (Stanford, CA: Stanford University Press, 2012), 10–11, 18–19, 25.
2. Esposito, 11.
3. Esposito, 25.
4. Esposito briefly characterizes Bodei's interest in this. See Esposito, 277.
5. Remo Bodei, *Immaginare altre vite. Realtà, progetti, desideri* (Milan: Feltrinelli, 2013); hereafter referred to as *IAV*. The translations are my own.
6. Greg Bird analyzes Nancy's politics on the way to a discussion of how Agamben and Esposito build on it. He concludes that the politics is weak because it is "tasked with holding open the space that is necessary to exist in-common"; see Greg Bird, *Containing Community: From Political Economy to Ontology in Agamben, Esposito and Nancy* (Albany: State University of New York Press, 2016), 101.
7. Jean-Luc Nancy, *The Inoperative Community*, trans. Peter Connor, Lisa Garbus, Michael Holland, and Simona Sawhney (Minneapolis: University of Minnesota Press, 1991).
8. Remo Bodei, *Destini personali. L'età delle colonizzazione delle coscienze* (Milan: Feltrinelli, 2009).
9. Ian James makes a helpful distinction between Nancy's view of space and Heidegger's view that helps to show how he conceives the relation among singulars as an opening. He writes, "Against the thinking of being as gathering, sheltering, or oneness [as in Heidegger], Nancy seeks to maintain, and to hold open, a movement of opening, in which the event of being as *sense* is always a movement to, onto, or a passage and spacing of sense, which is irrecoverable and ungraspable, but which nevertheless *is* the space of the world as meaningful, intelligible, and experiencible as such"; see Ian James, *The Fragmentary Demand: An Introduction to the Philosophy of Jean-Luc Nancy* (Stanford, CA: Stanford University Press, 2006), 102.
10. Jean-Luc Nancy, *Being Singular Plural*, trans. Robert D. Richardson and Anne E. O'Byrne (Stanford, CA: Stanford University Press, 2000), 56.
11. Bird, 91–92. See also his discussion of Nancy's critique of the traditional sociological idea of community, 87–90.
12. Bird, 72.
13. Bird, 92.
14. Nancy, *Being Singular Plural*, 32.
15. Nancy, *Being Singular Plural*, 32.
16. For a discussion of this argument, see Marie-Eve Morin, *Jean-Luc Nancy* (Cambridge: Polity Press, 2012), 36–37.
17. Nancy, *Being Singular Plural*, 12.
18. Nancy, *The Inoperative Community*, 62.
19. Nancy, *The Inoperative Community*, 73.
20. Nancy, *Being Singular Plural*, 13.

21. Morin, 35.
22. Nancy, *Being Singular Plural*, 85.
23. Jean-Luc Nancy, *The Birth to Presence*, trans. Brian Holmes et al. (Stanford, CA: Stanford University Press, 1994), 146.
24. Nancy, *The Birth to Presence*, 161.
25. Nancy, *The Birth to Presence*, 165.
26. Morin, 32–33.
27. B. C. Hutchens, "Archi-Ethics, Justice, and the Suspension of History in the Writing of Jean-Luc Nancy," in *Jean-Luc Nancy and Plural Thinking: Expositions of World, Ontology, Politics, and Sense*, ed. Peter Gratton and Marie-Eve Morin (Albany: State University of New York Press, 2012), 129–141.
28. Nancy, *The Birth to Presence*, 147.

6

A Political Gesture

The Performance of Carlo Sini and Michel Foucault

Enrico Redaelli

> The abolition of the sign dazzlement depends solely on us.
> —Carlo Sini, *Figure dell'enciclopedia filosofica.*
> *L'origine del significato*

Philosophy as Performance

In this chapter, I show how the thought of Carlo Sini is to be understood as a *political gesture*. Such a gesture is analogous to, but also, in certain respects, more radical than the gesture that concretizes Michel Foucault's philosophical practice.

Like French poststructuralists such as Derrida, Foucault, Deleuze, and Lacan, Sini considers the subject to be an outcome. As subjects, we are instituted and dazzled by historically determined practices, which Foucault calls *"dispositifs"* (apparatuses) and Deleuze terms "machines." These practices have shaped and transformed us, orienting our ways of living, thinking, and acting. The intertwining of practices, with its inherent or constitutive dazzlement (*abbaglio*), is constantly at play, ultimately originating specific, yet always contingent, relations of force. Sini's philosophy can be viewed as a political gesture that abolishes the aforementioned "sign dazzlement (*l'abbaglio del segno*),"[1] to borrow the expression used by Sini himself.

Before proceeding to a discussion of the sign dazzlement, we must clarify what we mean by the term *political gesture*. As for Foucault, for

Sini too, philosophy is a concrete exercise of self-emancipation, that is, of self-deconstruction and reacquisition. The "abolition of the sign dazzlement" is, hence, not a project. It is not a theoretical proposition, a manifesto of intents to be eventually translated into a practice. It is not a matter of voicing or promoting, on an intellectual level, an idea (such as "Let us abolish the sign dazzlement!") that some others should then pursue and concretize in their own habitual acts or daily "undertakings (*fare*)."

Traditionally, the philosopher, who is a person of theories, elaborates certain reflections that form a "political project" that someone else (for example, the politician) then concretely applies to the world. Therefore, when one hears the word *project*, one also hears the implicit distinction between theory and practice, reflection and action, word and reality.

Projects find their ultimate meaning elsewhere, outside themselves, namely, in the actions that concretize them and bring them into being. Projects still imply the abstract and universal gaze of the *theorein* (theorizing or speculating) and dwell in the fissure, which is typically metaphysical in nature, between the theoretical-discursive sphere and the practical-applied sphere.

In this traditional way of understanding the relation between philosophy and politics, one finds the figure of the philosopher understood as the "enlightened guide," that is, as the wise counselor of princes in modernity and the engaged intellectual in our contemporary age. This image of the enlightened guide has its origins in Plato and his visit to Syracuse. The failure of the Platonic project, though—that is, influencing the politics of the tyrant Dionysius in order to actualize the ideal city—already contains within itself the failure that is common to all projects: the failure that is inscribed in the fatal breach between political theory and factual actions. In Sini's philosophy, there is no "political project" in this sense; rather, one could say that in his thought, one finds a political *gesture*.

To speak of gesture means to move beyond the traditional distinction between theory and practice, word and reality, speaking and doing. Gestures are already, in themselves, actions and need no further "addition" or practical application. This does not mean that one cannot take hold of a gesture and repeat it in other contexts. Yet gestures do not find their sense elsewhere, in other contexts. The sense of a gesture is achieved there where it *finds* itself, in its *performance*.

If, as Roberto Esposito writes, "Italian thought seeks to achieve an immediate relation with that which it affirms,"[2] this is all the more true for Sini's work, for Sini's thought is to be considered as action *in act*. The abolition of the sign dazzlement, understood as the core of Sini's philosophy, must be considered as a *performative gesture*. In order to understand this gesture, we must examine the very problem of sign dazzlement.

Sign Dazzlement

Like Foucault,[3] Sini makes reference to practice (both philosophers are drawing from Husserl's *Crisis of the European Sciences*) in order to indicate a determined, pragmatic horizon that is historically situated and in which a specific object and correlative subject are inserted.[4] The subject is a "role" that every practice institutes in a specific and always determined form.[5]

Together, both philosophers raise the problem of subjectivation: we become subjects within practices that produce, time after time, peculiar effects of truth and corresponding forms of life. We are, therefore, subjected to an "invisible power."[6] Practices are like self-moving "machines"[7] that give rise to, and govern, the actions of the living body.

For Sini as well as for Foucault, the work of the philosopher is genealogical. It is a matter of untangling the concatenations of practices, intertwined in the interconnections of knowledge and power, that have come about through historical stratifications and of disclosing the invisible dynamics to which we have been subjected. The goal of the philosopher's work is to bring about an "ethical transformation" in the reader,[8] which Foucault would call a "*déprise* (detachment),"[9] and that problematizes all that appears to be true, obvious or natural, or institutionally accepted and guaranteed.

Drawing on his studies of American pragmatism,[10] Sini interprets the Husserlian-Foucaultian concept of practices in terms of Peirce's semiotics.[11] Each practice can be understood as a specific "sign relation." In signaling or giving a sign (*facendo segno*), each practice directs the subject toward the object, which the practice itself posits. This is where the sign dazzlement occurs. Practices refer to the object and deflect away from themselves, hiding themselves from our attention (that is, they divert from their own happening and from the interconnections of practices that support them). Insofar as we are subject *to* practices (to their goals and to the objects manifested within them), we do not pay attention to the practices' own implementation, that is, to the interweaving of operations that at every moment directs and orients us within the very doing we are performing. The "invisible power" of practices and their constitutive dazzlement, therefore, have a nature that can be defined as a "*sign reference* (*rinvio segnico*)."

There is one particular type of dazzlement that Sini's thought wishes to abolish, namely, "superstition," which consists in abstracting the object from the practice that placed it into being.[12] This specific type of dazzlement is found only in some specific practices, namely, the practices of knowing in connection to words: *knowing-how-to-say-or-speak* and *knowing-how-to-write*. Prior to these two levels of experience, however, there is a silent *knowing-how-to-do* (*saper fare*), which, within its own sign references and pragmatic horizons, does what it does, forming compliant subjects without any superstition.

Let us take as an example the practice of touching. This practice too *gives a sign* of its proper object and configures a related subject. In touching, the subject experiences the world and thereby fundamentally modifies itself through its encounters with the "touched" world. Yet there is no superstition here. The practice of touching is, following Foucault, a "*dispositif* of subjectivation." The problem does not lie in this, however. The subject is a result of experience. Without experience, there would be no "free, emancipated" subject, that is, a subject that is no longer subjected to powers that be; without experience, there would be no subject at all.

Furthermore, the practice of touching hides itself, allowing the object to emerge (as the "touched" world). Again, though, in this case there is no problem. The revelation of a world, which (speaking with Heidegger) *unveils* the object and *veils* the conditions of the object's appearing (a revelation that *refers* but also *defers*), consumes itself in the concrete circumstances of its happening. The object of touch, for example, the touched table, is not assumed outside the practice of touching that reveals it. On the contrary, the object of touch disappears as soon as I remove my hand from the table.

If subjectivation occurs, therefore, at "every instant," as Foucault writes,[13] nevertheless it does not call for a critical instance of liberation at all times.[14] In contrast to the French philosopher, Sini indicates the precise point at which the power of practices of subjectivation becomes a problem that needs to be overcome. Such a point arises when practices generate "superstition" (that is, an abstraction of the object from the practice.)

The problem emerges when experience is translated into a linguistic practice; that is, the problem arises in the passage from knowing-how-to-do to knowing-how-to-speak. The practice of words takes on the objects of other practices and converts them into "meanings" that endure outside the concrete operations that placed them into existence (and they endure insofar as they can repeatedly be reinvoked by the voice; for example, "Here is the table"). Superstition begins with language.[15]

In the passage from *knowing-how-to-speak* to *knowing how-to-write*, one adds the superstition of writing, which produces a particular sign dazzlement, to the superstition of oral language. Insofar as the written sign is objectivized and fixed onto a material support, it is the *analogon* of a crystallized meaning that is posited as a reality in itself and that is valid for all past, present, and future humanity. The practice of writing refers the subject to significations that are allegedly permanent and exist objectively and universally as such (the "universals" that Foucault distrusts). This creates the illusion that their meaning has always existed as it has been determined and that it exists apart from all circumstances and concrete practices that are at the origin of such meaning.[16]

The superstition generated by the written sign affects the subject who writes and reads far beyond the actual and limited circumstances within which such practices of writing and reading take place. Because practices create chains, writing retroactively acts on speech practices and transfers writing's own superstitions into such oral practices. For example, philosophers, scientists, intellectuals, politicians, and so on all speak and deploy forms of speech that are based on a culture of writing. Even when scientists or metaphysicians deploy the practice of oral discourse, they are able to speak of "reality in itself," of the "past in itself," of "atoms themselves," and so forth, thus referring to supposedly absolute objects; that is, to "free, independent" objects that are freed from the chains of their contexts of operation. Hence, our mode of thinking and, consequently, of acting are often enslaved to the dazzlement of the written sign, even when we are not writing.

Political Implications

The problem with the sign dazzlement that is at work in writing and speech, which Sini defines as "superstition," must not simply be understood within the framework of intellectual honesty. Ever since the publication of the six volumes of *Figure dell'enciclopedia filosofica, 2004–2005* (*Figures of the Philosophical Encyclopedia, 2004–2005*), Sini's work has sought to explain the wide range of consequences that ensue from an uncritical and superstitious engagement with different forms of knowledge and their entwinement with scientific, engineering, technological, and economic practices. The sign dazzlement is, in this sense, a political question.

A clear example of this claim can be seen in Sini's book, *La materia delle cose. Filosofia e scienza dei materiali* (*The Matter of Things: Philosophy and the Science of Materials*).[17] The volume begins with a critical analysis of the scientific and professional formation of engineers. Under investigation is the specific discipline of the science of materials. Sini carries out a genealogical examination of this branch of knowledge by investigating the academic textbooks that are in use in various polytechnic institutes. Here, one finds a conglomeration of ideologies and dogmatic presuppositions that have (very concrete) effects on social and political domains. In fact, it is on the basis of such ideological presuppositions, given as obvious and never challenged, that engineers institutionalize their practices, which have become increasingly technological and crucial for the future of the planet.

One may consider, for example, the so-called materials and resources cycle described in textbooks on materials sciences. There, one finds a representation of reality that is based on typical dogmas of "naturalism" and "objectivism." Yet this representation is offered to future engineers as a description of the world "in itself" or as it is "in nature." Sini's reading of such a representation aims to show how, in this configuration of the world, the relation between theory and practice is surreptitiously reversed. The thing in this cycle that is offered as "the world" (with its resources, materials, and their properties) is far from being a "necessary truth" that the scientific gaze simply observes and records; rather, the very configuration of the world depends on human practices. The "theory" offered by the textbooks is the result of concrete scientific-technological practices that are carried out on the grounds of entirely arbitrary economic and financial interests. After presenting his genealogical reconstruction of the foregoing representation of reality, Sini concludes as follows:

> It is nation states, international cartels of producers and distributors, the interests of financial capital, the markets, and the global stock markets that decide what constitutes "materials," their "reserves," their preferable "sources," their technologically advantageous transformations, the methods, timelines, and, above all, the places of their toxic smelting. Hence, the real lifecycle of materials is not at all exhausted by the processes we can see: this is a typical fiction of "objectivistic" naturalism and is a lie that covers over a much more complicated reality, a "political" reality that contains explosively conflicting elements; such elements are largely "subjective" (and not necessary and unmodifiable ones) as well as historically contingent. . . . This is how the correct and shared preoccupation with imparting a scientific culture to young people (and not only them) turns into a cultural monstrosity and into an involuntary transmission of a dogmatic and acritical spirit.[18]

We see here the political consequences of the sign dazzlement. Material sciences aimed at forming future engineers assume, within their operations, a series of objects such as "materials," with their "properties" and their "sources" or "reserves," without making explicit the concrete practices that constitute these objects in the first place. The sign dazzlement, which directs our attention to meanings, erases the context of origin and the practices that generate such meanings. This erasure is, in fact, a political masking. The objects of the aforementioned science, which are presented as natural givens and factual necessities, are, in truth, the fruit of decisions and interests that are contingent, and in no way "objective" or "neutral." What is cancelled out is the political nature of the objects, a nature that is instead marketed as a reality "in itself." As is the case with Foucault's genealogy, the problem before us is both epistemological and political. What is at stake is how the world is concretely redesigned and transformed by engineers' practices, with an ever-growing impact on the environment, society, and the world population, on the basis of an ideological representation of reality grounded on "partisan" economic interests.

The sign dazzlement transforms games that are arbitrary, "separate, and partisan" into seemingly irrevocable "facts" (that is, as Foucault says, "the arbitrary under the guise of knowledge" is "violence, understood in terms of power").[19] To abolish the sign dazzlement is not, therefore, a matter of intellectual honesty; rather, it is more a matter of honesty *tout court*. The search for truth is the search for the common good. The struggle against opinion and false beliefs and the struggle against injustice are one and the same.[20] The gesture that abolishes the sign dazzlement, then, is both and simultaneously theoretical and ethicopolitical.

The Turning Point

If superstition is a political problem, and not only a theoretical issue, what are we to do? What does it mean to abolish the sign dazzlement? Who will do this, and how? Before we can even think about the aforementioned engineering practice—its dogmas and "public" consequences—we must note that the philosophical discourse that seeks to abolish the sign dazzlement is itself constituted of signs that have their own references and dazzlements.

Sini always underscores that his own philosophical practice, which concretizes itself in his own texts and speeches, is a network of signs that refers back to specific meanings and orients subjects toward the very objects that the practice itself posits. Sini's philosophical practice is a "dispositive of subjectivation" and, in this sense, it is no different than any other practice. In it, too, we find at work a sign dazzlement that makes subjects—that is, its readers—conform to itself; it makes readers subject *to* the genealogical practice and *to* that which is revealed in it.

A clear point of deviation of Sini from Foucault, however, must be noted here. After the publication of *The Archaeology of Knowledge* (1969), Foucault raises the same question as Sini does, namely: What is the status of the objects of the archaeological practice ("enunciation," "discursive formations," "rules," "epistemes," "archives")? In the 1970s, Foucault is aware that the objects of his own philosophical discourse are dazzlements ("fictions" as he often claims) posited by his own very practice.[21] Whereas these fictions are not problematic for Foucault, for Sini this becomes a decisive turning point (the point at which the negative is transformed into a positive action).

Let us first examine the negative side. The very philosophy that diagnoses the disease of superstition and tracks it down to something other than philosophy (for example, to the work of the scientist or the engineer) ends up finding that very same disease at the core of the philosophical practice itself. Even worse, in the attempt to diagnose and denounce it, such a philosophical practice does nothing but spread the disease, fueling the contagion. Rather than bringing us closer to a solution, philosophy, here, seems to distance us from the possibility of finding such a way out: to one problem (namely, the epidemics of superstitions that spread from one practice to another), another is added (that is: all attempts at a cure are in themselves potential incubators of the epidemic).

Here we reach a crucial turning point, however. It becomes clear that we can no longer limit ourselves to denouncing superstition. It is a question of coherence as well as of effectiveness. First, there is the problem of coherence: we cannot denounce the sign dazzlement within this or that specific practice (whether it be the discourse of the scientist, the engineer, or the metaphysician) while continuing at the same time to attend (and be subject) without impunity to the sign dazzlement.

Second, there is the problem of effectiveness: if we limit ourselves to denouncing the sign dazzlement of this or that specific discipline (for example, the materials sciences or engineering), we not only remain on the plane of saying (*dire*), which means that nothing *happens*, but also the dazzlement will reestablish itself at the very moment when we seek to destroy it. It will do so through the very same gesture through which we say we are eliminating it, ultimately giving rise to a performative contradiction that is simultaneously a coercion to repetition. As Tolstoy remarks, "One cannot extinguish fire with fire, dry up water with water, combat evil with evil."

Only when one is radically consistent can one be effective, and vice versa. This statement means that the abolition of the sign dazzlement must first happen *here*, that is, within the practice that one executes in the first person, within the *dispositifs* that one uses and that orient the philosopher at the very moment of beginning to speak. The abolition of the sign dazzlement must either be put into practice, that is, it must be enacted or, if it is only denounced, enunciated, or proclaimed, it will have neither validity nor efficacy.

What constitutes, then, Sini's sharp deviation from Foucault? For Foucault, the exercise of philosophy finds its ultimate meaning in the production of an experience, a certain effect on the reader.[22] In this experience, we undergo a decentering and estrangement from certain ideas and notions, from objects within practices, that were acritically assumed to be obvious and were taken for granted (for example, a certain idea of madness that may be operative in the practice of psychiatry or a certain idea of the human that is at work within the human sciences, and so on).[23] In this respect, Foucault's genealogical practice is certainly a political gesture.[24] Foucaultian practice aims to deactivate the foregoing *dispositifs*, abolishing their dazzlement and the related effects of subjectivation. This was precisely the effect, for example, of *Madness and Civilization*: the genealogical deconstruction of the object "madness" (as acritically understood by the psychiatric practice of the 1950s) produced a transformation in its readers, decentering and disenchanting them from their superstition and ultimately contributing to the battles of the antipsychiatry movement.[25] Yet Foucault's genealogical practice does not put itself into question (as a discursive practice with its own particular objects of knowing).[26] It does not manage to show itself as a *dispositif* with its own particular dazzlement.[27]

Sini's genealogical practice, on the contrary, offers itself as an exercise of self-decentering focused not only on deactivating other *dispositifs* (such as the practices of scientific and technological knowledge with their subjectivating effects as they become the target of Sini's genealogical practices), but also on deactivating Sini's own practice (namely, his very own genealogical discourse at the precise moment when it is *acting*). Sini's genealogical practice seeks to produce a double effect on the readers, forcing them to undertake a vertical, acrobatic exercise consisting in disenchanting themselves from the objects of the practices that are being examined by the genealogical investigation and also from the very objects that the genealogical practice itself ultimately delineates within its own discourse.

How is such an exercise concretely carried out? And what is its political significance? We can understand it if we first keep in mind that the abolition of the sign dazzlement can only start at this point, *here*. But what does "here" mean?

Shifters

Let us briefly examine the word *here*. Modern linguistics situates this adverb in a class of particular signs, namely, in what Benveniste terms the *indicators of an enunciation* or, in Jakobson's terms, *shifters*. We are dealing here with particular linguistic signs whose meaning can be determined only with reference to the context of the discourse that contains them and renders them effective. Taken by themselves, such signs are "empty." They become "full" only in the actual act of speaking. One easily understands the particularity of shifters if one compares substantives such as *Paris*, *tree*, and *friendship* with pronouns such as *I* and *you*. The referent of the linguistic signs *I* and *you* is "filled" (and their signifying reference becomes actualized) only in reference to a concrete discursive context (in reference to a concrete *instance of discourse*, Benveniste would say). To this class of terms belongs, in addition to personal pronouns, the demonstratives (*this* or *that*, and so on), adverbs such as *here* and *now*, and a great number of simple or complex terms such as *today*, *yesterday*, *tomorrow*, and *in three days*. These are all incomprehensible if they are removed from the enunciative contexts within which they are inserted.

Jakobson traces such linguistic elements back to the Peircean category of symbols insofar as these elements belong to a conventional code for communication ("I" can also be said as "*Ich*," "*je*," or "*io*," according to different linguistic codes). At the same time, though, Jakobson notes that these elements cross over the code as the code is insufficient to define them. And they overstep it precisely when the elements deictically refer to the discursive context in which they are expressed. It is this deictic reference that renders these elements indices in the Peircean sense.

Between symbols and indices, shifters bridge *la langue* (the language code) and *la parole* (the act of speaking). As Agamben remarks, shifters make the passage from signification (the *propria* of symbols) to the deixes (the *propria* of indices).[28] In Heideggerian terms, we move from saying (*Sagen*) to showing (*Zeigen*). When I say "here," it is as if I were pointing my finger to the floor. I am not *saying*; I am *showing*. Better still, the "here" is a *symbol* that, while referring (so that it can be understood) to the proper discursive context (or *instance of expression*), transforms itself into an *index*, thereby making the passage from saying to showing. In this sense, shifters appeal to the *event* of the concrete linguistic practice, which contains and supports them; that is, the very linguistic practice that is in *act* at the very same time that they are expressed.

The Abolition of Dazzlement in Act

When we say that the abolition of the sign dazzlement must happen *here*, we mean that it must act on the practice that is currently *in act*. If we refer this to Sini's own philosophical practice, it has to operate on the very same sign reference that Sini's discourse effects on its subjects (that is, on its readers).

In Sini's books, this "abolition" begins concretely through a series of referrals that function like shifters. This occurs in passages—appearing very frequently in Sini's works—in which the discourse, folding on itself, refers the reader to the instance of expression that is operative at that very moment (in Sini's terms, it refers to the event of the practice in act). What happens on the plane of signification with this type of reference?

Let us explore some examples. In *L'origine del significato* (*The Origin of the Signified*), after introducing his own theory of practices (through the notions of *event*, *threshold*, and *detachment*), Sini makes a remark that produces the complex effect of a shifter:

> Now let us look at *this* description that we have just given and that makes its own implicit claim of showing us how we live, how we practice, and how we remember, and of establishing the meaning of these actions. This description is obviously an *interval*, the event of sense of a threshold. It too practices a particular practice, which derives from present and past weavings and from the synergy of innumerable thresholds that have been continually crossed and differentiated. It is this "happening" that allows us to practice the practice that we are here practicing, in all of its senses and modes. Obviously, we are dealing here with a practice of philosophical writing, and we have to see exemplified in it, applied to it, the very double experience of truth of which we spoke: we certainly cannot exempt it from this "labour."[29]

A second example is in the volume *Gli abiti, le pratiche, i saperi* (*Habits, Practices, and Forms of Knowing*). The first part of this work presents a genealogy of self-consciousness and the second part is devoted to a theory of practices that ultimately leads to the peculiar practice of philosophical knowing. Here, we find the shifter at work: it refers back to the whole discourse undertaken from the very beginning of the book. Sini observes, "What is this knowing? Let us think, for example, of the first part of this book, in which we traced the genealogy of self-consciousness from the gesture of the voice and the habits that follow from it. After we have tackled the question of practices, what do we make of all that we have put forward?"[30]

Through these shifters,[31] which imply a deictic referral to the instance of expression, Sini's texts call for the application of the discourse of practices (by which "every practice posits its own objects, which do not exist outside the practice itself") to *this* specific practice in act (practice that is qualified, each time, as "this" on the grounds of the context and concrete circumstances of its use).

This is the self-reflexive gesture that Foucault never recognized as a possible exercise, but which Sini considers as the true and proper political-pedagogical exercise. The reader is forced into a "second reading." Sini's *shifters* invite the reader to carry out a concrete exercise on that which has been said up until that point and on that which will be said in the rest of the text. It is a "second" operation in addition to the genealogical work carried out by Sini himself and followed up to the specific point. This "second reading" consists in rereading the text from the beginning and in leading all the text's meanings back to the event of the practice that has placed such meanings into being.[32] This implies deactivating the words in their signifying function: we have to suspend all the theories, all the genealogical explanations, all the interpretations contained in Sini's text; we have to subject them to an *epoché*. A reader who does not carry out this act will be lost; having not understood anything of Sini's works, ultimately he or she will remain infected by the disease of superstition. If the reader carries out what Sini proposes, though, what will happen?

What will happen is that all the significances of the text, insofar as such significances are led back to the instance of their expression, will *change their signs*. The exercise that is carried out in the "second reading" (and that the text itself invites the reader to carry out) is the proper operation of *shifting*, which, in referring the reader back to the discursive context (or the *instance of expression*), actualizes the passage from signification to deixis. Through such an exercise, all the significances that are present in Sini's text become, once they are "anchored" to the event of the practice in act, automatically converted into *indices*.

Let us consider the expression, "Look here." I must first understand the word "here" on the plane of *signification* (that is, I must grasp "here" within the significance that is lodged within the code of the English language) in order to understand the word correctly as an indication (that is, in order to be able to turn the gaze to the place where the word points). The moment I have understood their signification, the *significance* of the words "look here" drops its *significance* and takes on the role of a simple *index*.

In the same way, the significances working in Sini's text (the objects of his practice) disappear once they are reread in the deictic sense. He writes, "That which is said here is nothing insofar as it is said. . . . That which is said here is something only insofar as it is 'put into action,' or made to fall and left to fall out, which is proper to all ascetic exercises and to all ways of beginning that are radically autonomous and carried out for themselves."[33]

The "second reading" is complete when all the words of the text have been converted from *symbols* to *indices* or when the signifying function of the whole text has been deactivated and reincluded at the level of deixes (that is, of indicating/showing). At this point, the sign dazzlement in act (the sign dazzlement that Sini's practice of words produces) is abolished. Superstition consists in attending to the words while abstracting significations from the practices that lie at their origin. Moreover, the particularity of the shifters lies in their ability to transform the signifying value into an index so that their significance remains "anchored" to the instance of expression. It is this "anchoring" that abolishes the sign dazzlement and deactivates superstition.

Shifting, which carries out the passage from signification to deixis, enables language to "regress" from *knowing-how-to-say* to *knowing-how-to-do*. In mere *knowing-how-to-do*, there is no superstition because its "objects" are not separate from the concrete circumstances that place them into being (the "touched" table cannot be assumed to lie outside the practice of touch that reveals it). In the same way, the objects that emerge within Sini's practice of speech, once they are converted into an index, remain "anchored" in the *instance of discourse* (in the event of the practice) that produced them and cannot be (or be comprehended) outside such an instance (just as it is impossible to comprehend the significance of the word "here" outside of the act of speaking that expresses it). Superstition is abolished, therefore, *only if* the "second reading" (to which the "Sinian *shifters*" refer) is effectively achieved and the exercise (which the text itself invokes) is concretely actualized.

If this abolishment comes about, nothing will remain of Sini's "theories." More precisely, nothing will remain on the *plane of signification*. If correctly understood (that is, if transformed into a deictic sense), Sini's apparent "theories" (for example, the theory he develops in *The Ethics of Writing*, which is focused on the origin of *logos* from the practice of alphabetic writing,[34] or the theory on the origin of self-consciousness, which stems from embodied graphemes,[35] and so on) cease to *signify* that which they *signify* (for example, that there is a historical development in which the events described by theory are produced or that there is an interweaving of practices that has occurred according to the modes illustrated by theory). The ceasing of signification may pose problems for the historian of philosophy who wishes to reconstruct the objects of Sini's "theorizing" and relay what Sini has said. Nothing, in fact, remains of "the said" once the operation of conversion required by Sini's own texts is over (and this is what Foucault had hoped for his own books: "I would like my books to become a sort of scalpel, a Molotov cocktail or a series mines, which, when used, destroy themselves, just as fireworks do").[36]

What remains, though, is a series of *indices* (or "indicators of direction"). Like all *indices*, the remaining indices refer back to practices (if I point my index finger to behind your shoulders, this indicates that I wish you *to do* something, that is, that you turn in the direction that I indicate; there is nothing to "know" about my finger itself). And the practice to which indices refer is precisely the placing into work, always again, of that operation of shifting that at every instance abolishes the sign dazzlement that is currently in act.

For example, let us look again at the theory of practices. Ultimately, it must be understood solely as an *index* or, as Sini notes, as a "practical expedient."

> I say: Look at your very doing, at your very practice. You reply: You are not going to impose on me the question of practices. No, there is no imposition. It is as if I were to give you a mirror with the invitation to look at yourself and you were to object: The image I see before me is not the real one. Certainly, it is not the real image, nor do I wish to claim that it is. But there is nothing like a "real image." Every image, mirror included, is a trick. My discussion of practices is also a trick. But just as the mirror is a practical expedient of control (it is a way to look at myself from the outside so that I may see myself as others would or could presumably see me, even though it is I that look and look at myself, pretending to grasp the gaze of the other), so too is the practice of which I speak: it is an occasion, a circumstance, and a provocation of ethics.[37]

Political Consequences

If the abolition of the sign dazzlement is a *gesture*, that is, a practice that Sini's texts concretely execute, it remains to be understood in what sense this gesture may be read as *political*. We may ask: What happened to the engineer? The gesture that abolishes the sign dazzlement may be carried out by philosophers on their own practices; what about other practices though, especially those that greatly affect the world and, through ideological procedures, transform it right under our eyes? Does the political instance not end up losing itself in self-reference, in the refolding of the philosopher, that is, Sini, onto himself?

The gesture is political because it leaves a *trace* of itself. It does not vanish with its performance (the performance, for example, that Sini enacts in his own philosophical practice and that the reader of Sini's texts is forced to perform on Sini's very practice of reading). But where does the gesture leave its trace? It leaves it neither in written signs nor in books (there, what remains, if anything, is the significances, which, when they are not converted into a deictic sense, persist as *caput mortuum* [worthless remains]);[38] rather, the gesture leaves its trace in the subject.

For Foucault too, the philosophical word finds its meaning only in the effects that it produces. Whereas Foucault considers his works as an experience that aims to produce a desubjectivation (*déprise*) in the reader, for Sini (who understands his own books as a fitness gym),[39] the issue is instead that of producing a desubjectivation "*squared*": it is a gymnastics that: (1) readers perform in the first person and on their very own practice of reading *in act* so that (2) eventually readers become capable of replicating this exercise autonomously.

The gesture leaves a trace in the subject, for every practice produces a compliant subject. Every practice *refers* the subject, who constitutes him- or herself in a determined way (as a specific subject) on the basis of a sign reference that is operative in the practice itself. The sign reference at work in Sini's practice is precisely the kind of reference belonging to the shifters, which converts the signified into an ostension.

What happens when, turning to my interlocutor, I point my finger behind his or her shoulders? He or she turns around and looks. Deixis produces an immediate effect on the subject, forcing him or her to turn his or her gaze, to change his or her stance (the subject must turn the neck or torso to look behind).

The "deictic" effect of the *shifters* that we find at work in Sini's texts produces an analogous shift of one's stance. By operating as symbol-indices (making the passage from signification to ostension), the shifters continually refer the subject to the instance of their expression (to the event of the practice), ultimately habituating the subject to that turning back that time after time anchors the significances to their happenings in act.

The political consequence of this practice consists, therefore, in the production of subjects that *conform to this practice*;[40] that is, subjects that are habituated to a different stance and that repeat the gesture of such a stance. This "habit," if constantly performed, moves beyond the book and the philosophical practice.[41] The gesture can be repeated in other contexts and circumstances, changing profoundly the sense of the practices to which it is applied. Since practices form a chain, they open the performers to unknown interweavings of meanings and unforeseeable transformations.

Is the practice of engineers also affected by this insight? We are unable to say, because engineers will do what they will happen to do and not what the practice of words abstractly theorizes. But that which "they will happen to do" depends greatly on the interweaving of practices that they find on their paths of life and on the transformations that such practices will have undergone.

Once we have worked through Sini's works, there is nothing "to know" and there is not much "to say." But, certainly, there is much to do.

Translated by Antonio Calcagno

Notes

1. "Sign dazzlement" translates the Italian expressions "abbaglio del segno" and "abbaglio segnico"; albeit unusual, the form "sign dazzlement" seems preferable to "dazzlement by the sign" or "dazzlement of the sign" because although the dazzlement has to do with the sign, it is not ultimately clear, in Italian, that the sign plays an active function in causing such dazzlement.

2. Roberto Esposito, *Da fuori. Una filosofia per l'Europa* (Turin: Einaudi, 2016), 14.

3. See Michel Foucault, *L'archéologie du savoir* (Paris: Gallimard, 1969).

4. On the constitution of the subject in relation to the object, in addition to Foucault's *L'archéologie du savoir*, also see Michel Foucault and D. Trombadori, *Colloqui con Foucault. Pensieri, opere, omissioni dell'ultimo maître-à-penser* (Rome: Castelvecchi, 2005), 50–51. Foucault speaks of a "correlative constitution" in Michel Foucault, "Foucault," in *Dictionnaire des philosophes*, ed. D. Huisman (Paris: PUF, Paris 1984); and in Michel Foucault, *Discourse and Truth: The Problematization of Parrhesia* (Evanston, IL: Northwestern University Press, 1985).

5. For more on the subject as "role," see Carlo Sini, *Transito Verità. Figure dell'enciclopedia filosofica* (Milan: Jaca Book, 2012). On the subject as "form," see Michel Foucault, "L'éthique du souci de soi comme pratique de la liberté," *Concordia. Revista internacional de filosofia* 6 (1984): 99–116.

6. On the notion of an "invisible power," see Carlo Sini, *Inizio* (Milan: Jaca Book, 2016), 21ff.

7. A term used by Sini; see *Inizio*. Deleuze and Guattari also speak of machines in various works; see Gilles Deleuze, *Logique du sens* (Paris: Éditions de Minuit, 1969); and also Gilles Deleuze and Félix Guattari, *L'anti-Œdipe: Capitalisme et schizophrénie* (Paris: Éditions de Minuit, 1972); *Kafka. Pour une littérature mineure* (Paris: Éditions de Minuit, 1975); and *Mille plateaux. Capitalisme et schizophrénie 2* (Paris: Éditions de Minuit, 1980) to indicate that which produces the subjectivation of the living body. The machine in Deleuze and Guattari is similar to Foucault's concept of the dispositive or apparatus. For Sini, Deleuze, and Guattari, machines arise from the concatenation and intertwining of other machines.

8. Sini, *Transito Verità*.

9. Michel Foucault, *L'usage des plaisirs* (Paris: Gallimard, 1984), and "Le souci de la vérité," *Magazine littéraire* 207 (1984).

10. Sini, *Il pragmatismo americano* (Rome-Bari: Laterza, 1972).

11. Sini, *Transito Verità*.

12. Carlo Sini, *Gli abiti, le pratiche, i saperi* (Milan: Jaca Book, 1996), 83–84.

13. Michel Foucault, *A verdade e as formas jurídicas* (Rio de Janeiro: Editora Nau, 1973), 10.

14. For an analysis of the omnipresence of power in Foucault, see Deleuze, "Désir et plaisir."

15. Carlo Sini, *Figure dell'enciclopedia filosofica. L'origine del significato: Filosofia ed etologia* (Milan: Jaca Book, 2004), 3:38.

16. Here, we can refer to the Derridean critique of logocentrism, but the notion of the origin discussed earlier is different than the genealogical account (which is absent in Derrida) of concrete practices in which language and writing concretely incarnate themselves (as discussed by the studies of E. A. Havelock and W. J. Ong). The critique of Derrida is taken up by Sini in *Ethics of Writing*, trans. S. Benso and B. Schroeder (Albany: State University of New York Press, 2009).

17. Carlo Sini, *La materia delle cose. Filosofia e scienza dei materiali* (Milan: Cuem, 2004).

18. Sini, *La materia delle cose*, 43–45.

19. Michel Foucault, "Qu'est-ce que la critique? (Critique et Aufklärung)," *Bulletin de la Société Française de Philosophie* 2 (1990).

20. Enzo Paci, one of Sini's teachers, read Marx and Husserl as saying the same thing, ultimately making way for a fertile encounter between Marxism and phenomenology.

21. "I fabricate, as I can the instruments that are destined to make appear the objects. The objects, however, are in part determined by the instruments, good or bad, fabricated by me. And these objects are obviously false, if my instruments are false"; Michel Foucault, "Kenryoku to chi" (interview with S. Hasumi), *Umi*, December 1977: 240–256. Foucault speaks of "fictions" in Foucault and Trombadori, *Colloqui con Foucault. Pensieri, opere, omissioni dell'ultimo maître-à-penser* (Rome: Castelvecchi, 2005); Foucault, "Foucault Examines Reason in Service of State Power," *Campus Report* 12 (Oct. 24, 1979): 5–6; and Foucault, "Les rapports de pouvoir passent à l'intérieur des corps," in *Dits et Écrits, 1954–1988* (Paris: Gallimard, 1994).

22. Foucault makes this point numerous times. In an interview, he speaks of his own books as an experience from which "one can come out transformed"; see Foucault and Trombadori, *Colloqui con Foucault*, 22. He remarks, "An experience that permits a change, a transformation of the relation we have with ourselves and our cultural universe" (35).

23. Foucault, "Qu'est-ce que la critique?"

24. "My books," says Foucault, "function as invitations, as gestures, both made in public"; Foucault and Trombadori, *Colloqui con Foucault*, 37.

25. Foucault speaks of his work *Madness and Civilization* in this way. See Foucault and Trombadori, *Colloqui con Foucault*; Foucault, "Kenryoku to Chi"; and Foucault, "Foucault Examines Reason in Service of State Power."

26. H. Rabinow and P. Dreyfus, *Michel Foucault: Beyond Structuralism and Hermeneutics* (Chicago: Chicago University Press, 1983).

27. See my analysis in Enrico Redaelli, *L'incanto del dispositivo. Foucault dalla microfisica alla semiotica del potere* (Pisa: ETS, 2011).

28. See Giorgio Agamben, *Il linguaggio e la morte* (Turin: Einaudi, 1982), 36.

29. Carlo Sini, *Figure dell'enciclopedia filosofica: L'origine del significato. Filosofia ed etologia* (Milan: Jaca Book, 2004), 3:66. Emphasis mine.

30. Sini, *Gli abiti, le pratiche, i saperi*, 90.

31. The term *shifter* (as we call it here) is often used by Sini in his works starting in the 1990s.

32. "I realise that I am asking you to carry out an impossible exercise. On the one hand, I am asking you to faithfully listen to that which I am saying. On the other hand, I am asking you not to trust wholly in what is being said, because ironically this is what is being said: we need to follow the unfolding logic of the significances and, through them, observe the drama of the practice of writing that governs and grounds the significances themselves" (Carlo Sini, *Teoria e pratica del foglio-mondo* [Rome-Bari: Laterza, 1997], 173).

33. Carlo Sini, "Filosofia teoretica," in *Filosofia (Prolusioni di Karl Otto Apel, Giulio Giorello, Carlo Sini, Vincenzo Vitiello)*, ed. Carlo Sini (Milan: Jaca Book, 1992), 31.

34. Sini, *Ethics of Writing*.

35. Sini, *Gli abiti, le pratiche, i saperi*.

36. Michel Foucault, *Dalle torture alle celle* (Cosenza: Ed. Lerici, 1979), 21–22.

37. Carlo Sini, *Filosofia e scrittura* (Rome-Bari: Laterza,1994), 148.

38. Sini, *Transito Verità*, 27.

39. Sini, *Transito Verità*.

40. See Carlo Sini, *Figure dell'enciclopedia filosofica: "Le arti dinamiche"* (Milano: Jaca Book, 2005), 6:215.

41. In *Inizio*, "habit" is defined as an accompaniment that "fatally ends up modifying the meaning and way of my everyday acting"; see Sini, *Inizio*, 47.

Part Three

Thinking, Estrangement, Ideologies

7

What Does It Mean to Think?

Antonio Gramsci and Gilles Deleuze

Richard A. Lee Jr.

Introduction

From a certain perspective, which is decidedly modern, Aristotle's *De Anima* proceeds with some naïveté. He assumes, already from the beginning, that any soul is a way of encountering, engaging, and, quite literally, incorporating the world in which it finds itself. It is not frequently noted that Aristotle's account of the soul presents but one general structure. Since the soul is the principle by which living things are living, every soul must engage in the "business" of living. What separates the living from the nonliving? A rock, for example, cannot sustain itself by reaching out to the world and bringing back to itself the resources that might support its continued existence. Plant souls, animal souls, and intellective souls are all "souls" precisely because they can go out into the world and bring back what is found there in order to sustain the existence of that on account of which they are living. Perhaps because the insight seems so obvious, it often goes unnoticed: living things live by "incorporating" the world, that is, by somehow bringing what is outside into the inside and making it the living thing's own. What constitutes life, therefore, is the ability of a thing to make the world in which it finds itself its own body.

The division of different souls, consequently, is a division according to different ways in which the soul goes out to the world, encounters "something," and brings it back to make it the soul's own. This general description of soul, whether plant, animal, or intellectual, means that, for Aristotle, the soul is always in the world, engaging the world, and appropriating the world. One would never ask whether, when a plant absorbs nitrogen from the air, it is appropriating "real" nitrogen. The relation between a plant and the world does not seem to allow for questioning whether the plant "gets it right." Yet the general description of soul means that we cannot, for Aristotle, equally question whether the intellective soul "gets it right" when it reaches out to the world and grasps the "what-it-was-being," the essence, of the thing. *Nous*—the mind, thought, or intellect—cannot err. It either grasps the essence of what is or it does not. In this case, for Aristotle, there is never really a question of whether or how "thought" grasps the real.[1]

If, beginning with Aristotle, thought, at least in the form of *nous*, grasps what is as a lion grasps a gazelle, then how could the question, "How can thought grasp/think the real" ever arise? There is almost a ready-made story: Descartes separated the thinking thing, the *cogito*, from the world, invented dualism, and bequeathed to us the problem of whether we can ever be assured that what happens in thought is related to what is "outside" thinking. The difficulty of this story is twofold. First, it starts with a received story about Descartes that does not match the complexity of his texts. Second, and perhaps more important, Descartes's method uncovers a crucial question: What if everything that is real does not "exist" in the normal sense in which we take that word? What if, for example, class does not exist, in the sense that it cannot be "on the mat"? And, for all its nonexistence, what if class still has effects in the world? Does the fact that class might have effects not force us to count it as real?[2]

An Explanatory Apology

Gramsci is not an author to whom Deleuze refers frequently, if at all. Although Marx plays a pivotal role in Deleuze's philosophy,[3] there really is no evidence that Gramsci's reading of Marx was particularly influential for Deleuze. My goal here is to show neither the relation between Deleuze and Gramsci nor the influence of the latter on the former. Rather, my concern is with how they both struggle with the general problem of how to think the real. There are multiple places at which Gramsci and Deleuze circle around similar points, insights, and even terms. Therefore, my goal here is to show how productive a conversation between Gramsci and Deleuze on this difficult topic might be.

What makes the question particularly difficult is that it plays on a metaphysical or ontological field that is not so easily delineated. Although Deleuze is not a Cartesian,[4] there is a single author from which they both emerge: Duns Scotus. While Scotus is, perhaps, best known for his argument that being is predicated univocally of everything that is (including God) and for his concept of irreducible singularity or *haecceitas*, both these notions turn on a more fundamental insight in his philosophy. The notion of "thisness," of *haecceitas*, is his conclusion that what makes individual things individual must be some element—Scotus calls it "beingness," *entitas*—that is neither further reducible to, nor, therefore, understandable in terms of something other than, itself. While all stones are really stones, this stone is just this one because of, well, "thisness." This is a remarkable position. However, Scotus comes to it because he had already argued that something like an essence or quiddity is *real*. This stone really is a stone, and stone is what it is for it to be. However, Scotus insists that the reality of a quiddity is not identical to its actual existence; that is, while essences (Scotus calls them "common natures") are real, they do not "exist": they do not have what he calls *esse existentiae*, or the being of existence.

The notion that there can be something that is real but that is not also existing is not so easy to grasp nor to put into further words. Descartes, for his part, is forced to speak in indirection: even if such "things" do not exist, they are not, nevertheless, nothing. Descartes recognizes that between existence and nothing there is some space that what is real might still occupy. For Descartes, this space of the real opens the moment at which we are forced to acknowledge that what we think "is not, nevertheless, nothing," even if it does not exist.

Illustrations

Medieval Perspectivism

We can take three experiences: (1) a straight stick submerged partially in water appears bent; (2) a stick that has been lighted on fire, when swung rapidly in a circle, appears to draw a "circle of fire"; and (3) when I look at myself in a mirror, I appear to be "in" the mirror. These three experiences, and even more, were known to the medieval tradition of "perspectivism" to present ontological difficulties. The bent stick, the circle of fire, and myself in the mirror do not "exist." However, each of them is not nothing. We can also note that, while we can describe or analyze all of them by means of physics or even neuroscience, that analysis must always set out from, and, perhaps, conclude, that the reality of what appears is "not, nevertheless, nothing." We are forced, in these cases, to acknowledge that there is something real (e.g., the stick "really" does appear bent) that does not exist (i.e., there is no existing bent stick). In this case, effecting turns out to have something to do with reality, even if what is effected does not exist.

Structural Causation

Social classes are not actually existing things. Nor, for that matter, are races or genders. There "is" no "proletariat," no "white race," no "male." However, as much as all these "things" lack existence, they seem not to lack effective power. As I put the final touches on this chapter, several more black men have been murdered by the police in the United States. Blackness does not exist, but it is clearly not, nevertheless, nothing. The chief executive officer and majority shareholder of a major U.S. corporation can declare bankruptcy as a "smart business strategy," meaning that most of the company's creditors do not get paid, or at least not in full. At the same time, middle- and working-class homeowners who cannot pay their mortgage are turned out of their houses. Class does not exist, but it is not, nevertheless, nothing. The list can go on, but every item points in the same direction: existence is insufficient to account for reality.

Marx's Ghosts

In *Specters of Marx*, Derrida argues that Marx's corpus is haunted by ghosts. Besides the famous opening of *The Communist Manifesto*—"A specter is haunting Europe"—Derrida also points to Marx's *The German Ideology*. In that text, Marx is struggling with a nagging problem raised by the Idealist neo-Hegelians. As Marx points out, the problem such Idealists present is that ideas have escaped their heads and are parading around in the world as if they were things. How better to describe this situation than to talk of the haunting of ghosts? Marx's argument is that ideas are not bodily things and therefore cannot, it seems, interact with our world. However, when ideas "slip out of our heads," they enter into our world and have an effect on things that they otherwise should not be causally related to. A ghost is that which only ever just appears. It is the "mere appearance," the *Erscheinungsform* of something that is, considered in itself, not present. The spectral, as Derrida argues, is a kind of virtuality itself in that the ghost, the shadow, the specter, is an appearance of an appearance and, therefore, always puts off the question of the "reality" of what appears. A ghost, therefore, must always appear as other than itself, that is, it must take on a "form of appearance" that is other than what it is. As Derrida shows, masks, visors, costumes are required in order for the ghost to do its haunting work.

What is frustrating, however, in Derrida's account, is that he locates the ghostly and the spectral only in the one line from the *Manifesto* and from his reading of the *German Ideology*. Marx, for his part, is as worried about the ghost produced by philosophers as he is by the ghosts that are produced by our society, which is constituted around a peculiar and specific form of production. As Marx argues at the beginning of *Capital*, commodities take on a value in being exchanged—a value that is not only other than the value attached to their usefulness but, in fact, in contradiction to that value—that is unattached to any material, physical, sensuous characteristics of the object whose value it is. As immaterial, this value is already something like a spirit. However, its lack of materiality does not prevent it from functioning in the material world. It must do so by becoming an apparition, by taking on a form of appearance. Ontologically, ghosts are, according to Marx, a *gespenstige Gegenständlichkeit*—a ghost-like objectivity. The objectivity arises from what we might call the haunting of the ghost of exchange value: it has real effects in the real world. It is, however, ghost-like because, although it appears as a thing, as an object, it is, in fact, nothing of the sort.

We should, however, be a bit more patient in order to see that this ontological region is not unique to the critique of capitalism. A commodity is defined as "an external object, a thing which through its qualities satisfies human needs of whatever kind."[5] It is the satisfaction of needs that requires of the commodity that it be an external thing that is material and has sensuous qualities that are appropriate to fulfilling certain needs. Because things satisfy needs, they have a use-value that is realized only when the thing is consumed. When two material things, two commodities are exchanged, they are exchanged on the basis, at first, of their use-value. We only exchange one thing for another for which we have a need. However, it is precisely the use-value that makes exchange difficult, almost impossible. If we keep in mind that what makes any given thing useful arises from the unique and specific sensuous and material qualities that belong to it, then exchange would be the exchange of two entirely singular and unique things. On what basis, therefore, is the exchange possible? How do I determine that one yard of linen equals one quarter bushel of corn? The equation itself, which is required for exchange, contradicts the use-value of each thing. Their use-value says linen does not equal corn. Yet the act of exchange is only possible when one yard of linen *is* one quarter bushel of corn. Formally, we have here a contradiction: A *is* not A at the same time in the same way. The difficulty with this situation is that we have been taught, since Aristotle, that the principle of noncontradiction is ontologically binding:

nothing that *is* can be a contradiction. However, in this situation of the relation of exchange, Marx has shown that the principle of noncontradiction is not, at least always, binding.

It is for this reason that Marx's insight is not limited to the economic situation with which it begins. Rather, if it turns out that the principle of noncontradiction is not binding ontologically, then it turns out that it is a merely logical principle. Yet this leads to a further conclusion: logic is unmoored from what is. That is, the principle of noncontradiction is binding in terms of what is thinkable but not in terms of what is actual. Even though the commodity was the origin of Marx's insight, the conclusion he reaches goes to a more fundamental problem: the processes, determinations, and principles of thinking are not identical to those of what is. In this way, Marx uncovers an expansive philosophical problem, namely, that if thought operates in a way that is not identical to the way things that are operate, it might turn out that we are unable to think what is.

The problem only gets worse. As Marx continues his analysis of the commodity, the issue of this identity-within-contradiction comes to the fore. One yard of linen is one quarter bushel of corn only if we do not consider all those things that make linen and corn the very things they are. If the linen and the corn are identical—which is required at the moment they are exchanged—then some abstraction must be made away from those sensuous, material qualities that make them singular things. Yet notice that the abstraction does not occur in thought: it is not a philosophical gesture. Rather, the abstraction occurs as a prior condition for the exchange that actually takes place. But if there is abstraction, then we must ask two questions: from what and, *more important*, to what or where? We have already seen the "from." We abstract from whatever makes a thing the very thing it is. But where do we drag or draw the thing? Marx's answer is that underlying the act of exchange is a third that is not immediately obvious in the act of exchanging. That is, if one yard of linen is one quarter bushel of corn, then this equivalence, indeed, identity, is based on some other, outside the two, to which each is equal and identical. In other words, the condition for the possibility of exchange is not borne by either of the things being exchanged. "Both are therefore equal to a third thing, which in itself is neither the one nor the other. Each of them, so far as it is exchange-value, must therefore be reducible to this third thing."[6]

The third, however, is precisely that which exacerbates our earlier problem. Exchange was made possible on the basis of the identity of two things that, necessarily and by definition, are not identical. What is this third in relation to which two things can be identical? When the context is the exchange of commodities, the third cannot be anything that would make of each a use-value. Therefore, "if we disregard the use-value of commodities, only one property remains, that of being products of labor."[7] The value, therefore, that emerges in exchange depends on labor; it is the crystallization of labor and, therefore, this value is social. It is social because in order for exchange to be possible, individuals need to produce things that they themselves do not need and, therefore, have no use-value to the people producing them. But the possibility of producing things that are not useful to the one producing them emerges only if labor has been divided, that is, if, as a society, we can arrange for the production of all useful things across the individuals in that society. In this way, exchange value—which is just value in any society that produces commodities for the purpose of exchange—is a social value that is measured by the "amount of labor time socially necessary, or the labor-time socially necessary for its production."[8] It is here that the ontological problem comes to the fore. The fact that the principle of noncontradiction is not ontologically binding is the very origin of the haunting of ghosts. A commodity can only be exchanged because, for someone other than the producer, it is useful. For the producer, however, it is not useful. This condition is doubled because one commodity is being exchanged for another. Thus the exchange depends on the usefulness of the thing and, at the same time, its nonusefulness. Use, as we have seen, is what belongs to the thing in its material, sensuous existence. It is this, however, that prevents the identity that exchange requires. Thus, outside of the material, sensuous existence of each commodity is a third that is the basis of the exchange. That third cannot be sensuous and material—yet it must be real because the things are really exchanged. It is, therefore, a ghost.

The commodity is not a ghost but is, rather, the means of the apparition of that which cannot otherwise appear. The commodity is, at the same time, congealed labor-time and the form of appearance of exchange value. Neither of these can appear, as they are not material, sensuous things. They haunt our world by appearing in things, in commodities. Yet as apparitions within commodities, such immaterial, nonsensuous things are effective and, therefore, *real*.

These illustrations show that "thinking the real" is not as simple as it seems. It requires, it seems, attentiveness to at least three themes: (1) the real is constituted by effectivity, and therefore is not exhausted by what exists; (2) structures are, consequently, real and their effectivity must be grasped if we are to think the real; (3) identity, what makes something what it is, does not come before—temporally, logically, or ontologically—effectivity.

It is in relation to these three themes that I think the conversation between Deleuze and Gramsci can be most productive. These themes, however, can be recast around terms or concepts that are shared by both philosophers, namely, creativity, assembly, and reality.

Creativity

Deleuze defines philosophy, if definition is something that is significant in Deleuze's philosophy, as "the art of forming, inventing, and fabricating concepts."[9] As such, philosophy is constructive, creative, and not receptive or passive. The characterization of philosophy as creative or constructive distinguishes it from science (and, perhaps, also journalism), whose task is to record "facts." If, however, a fact is "what has been done,"[10] then science stands outside bringing about the creativity of that which it records. We might paraphrase Deleuze in this way: "it is effectivity all the way up and down; philosophy, therefore, is no less productive than anything else."

The constructivism or creativity of philosophy can be approached from a different direction. If it is the case that thinking belongs to what it is to be human, then we can ask:

> Is it preferable "to think" without having a critical consciousness [*consapevolezza*], in an occasional and segmented [*disgregato*] way, that is, "to participate" in a conception of the world "imposed" mechanistically by the external environment [*ambiente*], and that is by one of the many social groups in which everyone is automatically involved all the way from their entry into the conscious world . . . or is it preferable to elaborate one's own conception of the world consciously [*consapevolezza*] and critically and, thus, in connection with such labors of one's own brain, to choose one's own sphere of activity, to participate actively in the production of the history of the world, to be the guide of oneself and not already passively and supinely accepting from the outside the imprint on one's own personality.[11]

Here, Gramsci moves on the same terrain as Deleuze. For Gramsci, philosophy, which belongs to everyone, is a "determinate conception of the world."[12] The fundamental question, for Gramsci, is whether that conception will itself be an effect, a mechanistic result, or productive of the history of the world.

There is a simple, but not, for that reason, easy insight that stands at the beginning of this Gramscian-Deleuzean path. Philosophy should not concern itself with what is. We might say that what is "takes care of itself" or is not in need of analysis, let alone justification. As Gramsci points out here, the mechanistic "imposition" of a conception of what is prevents the construction of one's own sphere of activity: "what is" impedes activity, creativity, the production of the "history of the world." While "understanding" might be a task that philosophy sets for itself, living, going on, indeed constructively engaging the world, is a task presented to living things. This task requires activity and activity requires concepts that are not received but rather are created.

The creation of concepts is never "from nothing."[13] For both Deleuze and Gramsci, the creativity, the productivity that characterizes philosophy—the construction of concepts—is always in relation to a *problem*. Therefore, a problem is what calls for, and perhaps even calls forth, new concepts. "One's own conception of the world responds to determinate problems posed by reality that are determined and 'original' to their actuality."[14] The critique that philosophy favors presence and, therefore, eternity is right in its conclusion, if not always in its presuppositions.[15] It could, perhaps, be the case that if nothing ever happened, that is, if there were no effectivity—if there were no change and being affected, if there were no labor—then the task of philosophy could be simply to record, even in the form of representing, what is.[16]

The creativity/constructivity of philosophy, therefore, has to do with effectivity: labor and activity.[17] Gramsci and Deleuze each show that the task of philosophy must be adequate to the reality of what is. That adequacy, however, is not to those traditional metaphysical posits—substance, essence, presence, eternity—but to a world in which, to sum up the basic Deleuzean insight, force is what it is to be and force just is what it does.[18] The "other world," the world of enduring, the eternal, the leisurely, is the world that uses these concepts normatively (and therefore statically and representationally); that is, from the perspective from which labor, effectivity, and force are all expressed by means of their denial. In Gramsci's terms, the question is one of hegemony. As long as labor is subaltern, it is "deprived of all historical initiative."[19] Therefore, the creativity of philosophy must be its defining feature:

> Might it not be said in a sense and up to a certain point that what nature provides the opportunity for are not discoveries and inventions of pre-existing forces—of pre-existing qualities of matter—but "creations," which are closely linked to the interests of society and to the development and further necessities of development of the forces of production? . . . In reality, the philosophy of praxis does not study a machine in order to know

about and to establish the atomic structure of its materials or the physical, chemical, and mechanical properties of its natural component (which is the business of the exact sciences and of technology) but only insofar as it is a moment of the material forces of production, is an object of property of particular social forces, and expresses a social relation that, in turn, corresponds to a particular historical period.[20]

From Creativity to Assemblage/Ensemble

The passage that was just cited goes on to say, "The ensemble [*l'insieme*] of the material forces of production is the least variable element in historical development."[21] Deleuze expresses a similar connection between concepts, which, for him, are always created/constructed, and an ensemble/assemblage: "Concepts are concrete assemblages, like the configurations of a machine."[22] That concepts are creative is, therefore, related to their also being an "assemblage," an "ensemble." In an interview, Deleuze insists that the notion of assemblage is, perhaps, the most important concept in *A Thousand Plateaus*.[23] For him, "assemblage" provides a more fruitful manner to understand the ways in which effects are produced by forces, regardless of the question of "what" that agent is, that is, apart from the metaphysical question of identity or essence. The insight here is that "agent" can only be identified retrospectively on the basis of what it does, not what it "is"—let alone "what-it-was-being." The move from effect back to cause, Deleuze and Guattari show, does not require, at the same time, that the cause be "something" in the sense that is has a form or essence on the basis of which its actions are determined.

It is this move, that is, from effectivity back to essential/substantial identity, to a "what-it-is," that Gramsci and Deleuze challenge. For example, a body is, according to Deleuze, "not defined by the form that determines it nor as a determinate substance or subject nor by the organs it possesses or the function it fulfills."[24] In this way, a body is not a "what," nor is it teleologically identified. Rather, it is "nothing but affects and local movements, differential speeds."[25] Deleuze gives the Scotistic name "haecceity" to that which is what it is because of its effectivity. It is a "this" but not a "what." Scotus invents the term *haecceitas* to show that whatever is an individual is such independently of its essence: individuality, singularity, must necessarily be independent of form or essence. If essence, "what-it-was-being," is Aristotle's answer to the question "What is it?," haecceity answers that question with the indexical "this." Yet that individual is not—either for Scotus or for Deleuze or for Gramsci—simple, uncomposed. That something—a body, for example—can be, at the same time, a coming-together of many "things" that are also just "this" is what leads Deleuze to the concept of assemblage and Gramsci to the "ensemble," *l'insieme*.

As Gramsci argues:

> One could say that each one of us changes themselves, modifies themselves insofar as they change and modify the whole complex of relations of which they are the center of the nexus [*annodamento*]. In this sense, the real philosopher is and cannot be other than the politician, that is, the active person [*l'uomo attivo*] who modifies the environment, meaning by environment the *ensemble* [*l'insieme*] of connections of which every individual enters to take part. If one's own individuality is the ensemble of these relations, to make a personality means to acquire consciousness [*coscienza*] of these relations, to modify one's own personality means to modify the ensemble of these relations.[26]

As with Deleuze, Gramsci sees that an individual is not simple but rather complex, the coming-together of a multiplicity. This multiplicity is designated here as an *ensemble* of relations. Gramsci's analysis begins, as does Deleuze's, with the question of effectivity: how can a thing change or modify itself? The difficulty is that the individual is what it is because it brings together—or, perhaps, just is—a "complex of relations." While Gramsci here is referring to a person and the social relations in which it is knotted (another meaning of *annodamento*), his point is expanded by Deleuze to a larger metaphysical horizon. As Deleuze points out, a human body is, itself, an assemblage in the sense that a liver, for example, is not for the sake of the body as a whole nor, conversely, does its function and "purpose" in relation to the whole define what a liver is. Yet the body is an arrangement of a multiplicity that is effective in some ways such that its effectivity makes it "this."

Yet Gramsci points out the specifically social dimension of the ontological position.[27] Even if an individual is a body that is, as such, simply a nexus of the relations of the elements, it is also within a nexus of effectivities, of effective elements that may not be, or may not be exhausted by, their material constitution. Marx's analysis of exchange value exposes just this ontological problem. Gramsci's concept of ensemble (*l'insieme*) operates within this ontology. If relations (or, to put this in Deleuzian-Guattarian language, lines of flight, affectivities, smoothing of striated space, and so on) can produce without themselves being "something," then the task of human activity, the sphere of the activity of a person, is one that must be able to operate outside substance or subject. In fact, both Gramsci and Deleuze show that the essential, substantial, identity of things is irrelevant at best. At worst, essence and substance as concepts are effective in their own right, demanding of the "person of action" (*l'uomo attivo*) that they demonstrate the ground, that is, the "what" that grounds his or her action. The thriving of an individual, however, is never dependent on such a ground.

Gramsci's conclusion circles back to the role of concepts, the role of thinking, in this web of effectivity. In this way, he prepares the way for Deleuze's Spinozism.[28] As Gramsci notes, this nexus of effectivity requires thought or, in his term, consciousness. That is, the creativity of philosophy in relation to the effectivity of what is forces us to recognize that what is real is not entirely exhausted by what actually exists.

The Real and Thought

As I showed in the section on Marx's ghosts, the challenge that exchange value poses to most customary ontologies is that it forces an expansion of ontological categories. This expansion, however, is not peaceful in the sense that once we are forced out of the customary ontological categories, which are almost always presented as dichotomies (being/nonbeing, substance/accident, actual/potential, necessary/contingent, existing/nonexisting), we come to see the limitations, if not outright failure, of customary ontology to account for all that is effective and that, since effective, must be counted as real. The opening sections of *Capital* appear, in many ways, as a traditional—sometimes even scholastic—discussion of ontology. Setting out from the concept of substance, it begins by assuming that the "what" of commodities must belong to their substantiality. However, Marx goes on to show that what makes a commodity what it is turns out to be its exchange value, which is, in turn, a strange kind of reality: a "ghost-like objectivity." The substantiality of the commodity is insubstantial and yet, contrary to traditional ontology, both effective and essential to what it is.

Marx's analysis, therefore, shows that the most substantial element of substance might be insubstantial, that that insubstantiality of substance means that the identity of something—its essence—is entirely inessential in analyzing what it does, and finally, that things that do not exist might nevertheless be real. How are we to think what is real if, in Deleuze's language, the usual "images of thought" are shown to be, at best, impotent?[29]

In this sense, conceptual philosophical thought has as its implicit presupposition a pre-philosophical and natural Image of thought, borrowed from the pure element of common sense. According to this image, thought has an affinity with the true; it formally possesses the true and materially wants the true. It is *in terms of* this image that everybody knows and is presumed to know what it means to think. Thereafter it matters little whether philosophy begins with the object or the subject, with Being or with beings, as long as thought remains subject to this Image which already prejudges everything: the distribution of the object and the subject as well as that of Being and beings.[30]

Here, Deleuze aims his hammer at any philosophy of representation, that is, at any philosophy that assumes that the problem *for* philosophy is how to present again (re-present) something that is given from "outside," something that would, therefore, be prephilosophical. This is, by no means, a simple trajectory to follow, for Deleuze is insisting that any "image of thought" that works on the model of representation is already, to borrow a term from Scotus, "indifferent" to those distinctions that have seemed most important to philosophy: set off *either* from the subject *or* from the object; beginning with *either* beings *or* Being. Deleuze's argument is that these decisions, which seem so important from a certain philosophical perspective, are actually indifferent in that they all repeat the same image: how can thought best present again the very thing it thinks?

The dead end into which thought imagined or imaged as representation drives is that it will always, necessarily, assume something outside of and other than itself: the "rightness" of thinking (a moral presupposition) and/or the belonging-together, if not identity, of thought and what it thinks (perhaps a political presupposition masquerading as an ontological principle). Whether in the form of an "ontological difference" between beings and Being or in the form of the contestation between objective and subjective Idealists, Deleuze argues that the same assumption is operative: how to "get" what is outside or other than thought into thought.

Against this image of thought, Deleuze insists that thought is already different and, therefore, is already operating with a difference that is not repetition. It is difference because it "is trespass and violence, the enemy, and nothing presupposes philosophy: everything begins with misophy."[31] That thought emerges at all indicates that "something in the world forces us to think." Thought is, therefore, this difference between that which forces thinking and the thought that emerges. Thought is, to use a phrase

I think Deleuze would find problematic, originary difference. That there is thought already shows that there is an other to thought.[32] In a move not unlike that which Adorno makes in *Negative Dialectics*, Deleuze recognizes that thought runs up against that which is fundamentally different from it, "the absolute contingency of an encounter with that which forces thought to raise up and educate the absolute necessity of an act of thought or a passion to think."[33] This "encounter," Deleuze argues, is with that which can only be sensed; that is, it is not originally a "thought-thing" and, as such, it gives rise to sensibility rather than the reverse.

As Deleuze insists, this encounter with this "other" is violent from the perspective of sensibility and, perhaps even more so, of thought. A "faculty" is brought to its limit by this encounter because the other that is encountered is encountered as *intensity*, which marks an originary difference. The notion of intensity emerges in Deleuze's thought through his encounters with both Duns Scotus and Spinoza. For Scotus, the notion of intensity belongs to what he calls "modes" and, most important, to "modes of being" (*modus essendi*). What characterizes God, for example, is that God's being (*esse*) is infinite. Here, "infinite" characterizes the way in which God is in distinction to the way in which, for example, I am (that is, finite). Infinite, therefore, names a sort of measure of that mode, that is, an intensity of it. Scotus frequently uses the example of color to illustrate this. Two things might both be white and "what" that whiteness is will be identical for each. However, one may be more intensely white than the other. In this way, intensity is nothing other than a marker of difference: but not, however, of *essential* difference. Intensity emerges precisely among those things that are essentially identical, and it marks a difference that is not reducible to the "what" of the things that are involved. It must, therefore, be a mark of difference of power or force. Intensity of force, violent encounter, all of this points back to the original difference between thought and what it thinks.

Intensity, therefore, marks a difference that is not a negation. The difference between two intensities is not that of A and ~A but rather, as Deleuze insists, dx, that is, a differential. Thinking the real, thinking this encounter of violence, therefore, requires a thinking of the differential. Deleuze develops a notion of Idea as the thinking that is operative within this differential origin of thought in relation to its encounter. Ideas are, for him, not the grasp of an identity—substantial, essential, or even numerical—but rather "multiplicities." A multiplicity is, for Deleuze, not a relation of many such that they constitute one thing. The multiplicity is in no need of unity in order to operate.[34] As Deleuze argues, multiplicity is just variety; "in other words, difference."[35] Ideas, therefore, as differentials are a way to think the real that is encountered in this originary forceful encounter that thought has with the real.

On the one hand, the representational image of thought—indeed, of all images of thought that insist that thought has its origin in itself—leads to the inevitable problem that thought cannot get at anything other than itself. No wonder subjective idealism has such an affective draw! Such images of thought take the original difference, and therefore violence, in the encounter of thought with the real as an embarrassment, one that is ultimately overcome in the insistence, in the need, for thought to be in full possession not only of itself, but also of the real. On the other hand, any image of thought that plays on the field of subjective idealism also has a draw, a pull, that cannot be denied.

Gramsci identifies the pull of subjectivism directly in relation to what Deleuze identifies as the power of Ideas: it is only through subjectivism that the causality of structure can come to the fore. In this way, Gramsci allows us to see why Deleuze turns to the Idea despite its role in Plato, Kant, and even Hegel. What Deleuze shows is that thought is an effect of a violent encounter with what can only be a multiplicity. Yet "multiplicity" is not just one damned thing after another; it is not a heap. Its effectivity emerges through its structure. This entails that the effectivity of the multiplicity is not reducible—metaphysically or analytically—to the effectivity of each of its elements. However, its effectivity is not reducible—metaphysically or analytically—to a unity or identity. Therefore, the effectivity of a multiplicity is a result of the relation of the elements and that relation is, as Deleuze points out, a structure. It is for this reason that Deleuze remobilizes Idea with a difference. Idea is the traditional and effective way of thinking the operation of a multiplicity, that is, the effectivity of structure. Deleuze's remobilization, however, turns the Idea toward the system or the structure that is itself a multiplicity. In this way, Deleuze's Idea, much like the notion of "concept" in *What Is Philosophy?*, opens up something like structural causation, that is, that kind of effectivity that emerges from a structured multiplicity that is not reducible to any of the elements and does not characterize a "what"; in other words, an identity.

Gramsci, however, points out that it is the image of representation and its related notion of recognition—that is, the "subjectivist" philosophy of Hegel—that first brought this critical function of thought to the fore. "It must be demonstrated that while the 'subjectivist' conception has had its usefulness as a criticism of the philosophy of transcendence on the one hand and the naïve metaphysics of common sense and of philosophical materialism on the other, it can find its truth and its historicist interpretation only in the concept of superstructures. As for its speculative form, it is no more than a mere philosophical novel (*un mero romanzo filosofico*)."[36] Two things should be noted here. First, Gramsci sees in Kant and, perhaps even more so in Hegel, a genuine contribution to a critique or a critical philosophy—Gramsci frequently uses the phrase "philosophy of praxis (*filosofia della praxis*)." That critical aspect moves in two directions. On the one hand, it provides a critique of transcendence, that is, a critique of the notion that the correct philosophical account of the world needs to point outside that world (either to God or to a realm of Ideas). On the other hand, it also provides a critique of what Gramsci here calls "philosophical materialism." This leads to the second point. Gramsci, much like Althusser later, is, as we have seen, intensely critical of the kind of materialism frequently associated with Engels, a blunt and even naïve materialism that insists that only that is real that is a material thing. For Gramsci, as for Althusser, this blunt materialism is not unrelated to "economism," that is, to the claim that there is a strict *and uni-directional* causality from the economic base to the cultural superstructure.[37] What Gramsci sees in this image of thought is the analysis of structure as crucial to philosophy. It is this analysis that both the philosophy of transcendence and blunt materialism fail to see.

For Gramsci the real is always an ensemble and, as such, is never simple and never blunt. As an ensemble, the real requires a thinking that recognizes the effectivity of structures, even if such structures do not "exist" in the usual sense. He deploys a telling example:

> To understand exactly what might be meant by the problem of the reality of the eternal world, it might be worth taking up the example of the notions of "East" and "West," which do not cease to be "objectively real" even though analysis shows them to be no more than a conventional, that is "historico-cultural" construction (the terms "artificial" and "conventional" often indicate "historical" facts that are products of the development of civilization and not just rationalistically arbitrary or individually contrived constructions). . . . It could be objected that without thinking the existence of the human one cannot think of "thinking," one cannot think at all of any fact or relationship that exists only insofar as the human exists. What would North-South or East-West mean without the human? They are real relationships and yet they would not exist without the human and without the development of civilization.[38]

Here, Gramsci shows that the question of the "real" is certainly never determined completely by the question of what exists. A native of Shanghai is certainly not a native of the "East." In this sense, the concept, the category "East" does not exist. And yet, Gramsci is pointing out that the "East" is most certainly real as it has effects in the world that matter and must, therefore, be real. To say that the Idea, concept, structure, is arbitrary or a mere phenomenon of a certain cultural perspective—Europe—leaves us impotent in analyzing its productive capacity. If this cultural, historical categorization is found, metaphysically, not to exist, this must not be the end of the analysis—it is not, nevertheless, nothing. It is not just that "East" and "West" are ways of theorizing or conceptualizing the world. It is that such structures matter in the movement of peoples, the allocation of resources, and the ability of individuals to make their way in the world. In a way that speaks to our *today*, Gramsci continues, "Thus Italians often, when speaking of Morocco, call it an 'Eastern' country, to refer to its Muslim and Arab civilization."[39] There is probably today, as there was when Gramsci wrote this, no "Arab." And yet, the structure of "the Arab" is operative and, as Gramsci indicates, "the references are real; they correspond to real facts, they allow one to travel by land and by sea."[40]

For Gramsci, as for Deleuze, the crucial philosophical question is how to engage in thinking the effectivity of structures and systems that may, in fact, be more effective the less actual—the less "existing"—they are. In short, Gramsci and Deleuze are recognizing that the real is haunted. They variously deploy the notions of assemblage, ensemble, multiplicity, structure, and system to insist that thought cannot merely re-present—that is, present again—if that means a mechanical "registration" or representation of what is, because what is, in its reality, is not merely what is given to thought in the way that its being thought is unproblematic. Gramsci's example of the "East" and the "Arab" show the stakes of this "merely" philosophical debate. What is needed, according to Gramsci, is the historicization of philosophy. This does not mean that, on his account, philosophy refuses the notion of "Idea" and the structure it brings to thought. Rather, the issue is to historicize the Idea and, thereby, to bring forth "a new way of philosophizing that is more concrete and historical than what went before it has begun to come into existence."[41]

The question of thinking the real emerges, therefore, precisely when we recognize that the real operates as a multiplicity that is not reducible to identity or unity. From Plato and Aristotle through Descartes, Kant, and Hegel, philosophy has operated with an image of thought in which thought is *causa sui*, its own cause and, as in possession of itself, is the determining condition of what is. For Gramsci and Deleuze, this image of thought will never get at the real. Thought, on this model, misses the original difference between itself and what calls it forth (and for Deleuze, does so violently). The encounter with something other calls for thinking, and that thinking must operate *on the basis of*, rather than against, that encounter.

The Social Difference

I have tried to show the ways in which Gramsci and Deleuze are both attempting to reorient philosophy in the direction of a creativity that strives to regard the encounter with a multiplicity, ensemble, or assemblage that gives rise to philosophy. To this end, I have endeavored to steer clear of a "comparison and contrast" of their philosophies. It seems clear that Gramsci and Deleuze are both intervening in philosophical discourse at its most crucial moment—asking how can thought think something other than itself?—and it is even clearer to me that these issues are quite fundamental and profound. Their philosophies strive to show that something like "method" is not divorced from ontological, epistemological, and critical issues. For this reason, presenting their common field, their common problematic, proves fruitful. There is, however, a striking difference between the two, which is not without its own importance.

Indeed, the difference between the two philosophers plays out in all three of the domains I investigated earlier: creativity, assemblage/ensemble, and thinking the real. The difference, in short, is society. The concept of society and social theory in general is almost entirely absent from Deleuze's thought.[42] For Gramsci, however, the "philosophy of *praxis*" is constituted precisely by its recognition of the causal power of society on all aspects of life. The creativity of philosophy, the concept of ensemble, and the problem of thinking the real are all thought by Gramsci in terms of society and its concrete historical development. In short, I have made Gramsci play Deleuze's game.

The difficulty, however, is that it is almost impossible to make Deleuze play Gramsci's game. It is, perhaps, one of the great achievements of Deleuze's thought that he deploys seemingly normative concepts completely free of any normative operation. In this sense, Deleuze is thoroughly Nietzschean. However, putting Deleuze in conversation with Gramsci might bring us to reinsert society into Deleuze's thought. What if society operates in the same way as the real? What if society is nothing and, yet, nonetheless effective—that is, real? What is a social structure capable of producing? How does its effectivity operate?

It could be argued that the fundamental insight of Gramsci's social thought is the relation between the hegemonic and the subaltern. For Gramsci, the social ensemble is, to borrow a phrase from Deleuze, striated. There are institutions through which lives are affected, force operates, and the determination of what counts as "force" and what counts as "just the way it is" emerge.[43] For Gramsci, these institutions are something like machines through which force operates and life is organized. As such, the question of their deployment is crucial. Gramsci uses the term *hegemony* to refer to the ability to deploy institutions and, through that deployment, determine a society. Hegemony, however, entails that there are others who are dispossessed from the power to determine: the subaltern. The main issue to which Gramsci returns over and over again is how the subaltern can seize hegemony. That is, he is interested in how the subaltern, dispossessed as they are, can come into full possession of the institutions that determine society.

The question of the social analysis of force in the form of institutions and social determinations might be possible in a Deleuzean register.[44] Yet one must wonder what effect this might have on Deleuze's thought. Is it not possible that, once society is brought into Deleuze's thought, it might not have an autoimmune response? What if labor was not just a form of effectivity but rather a class? Can Deleuze think class? In all of his tarrying with Marx throughout his corpus, the issue of class almost never appears. What effectivity has brought this strange situation about? Perhaps Gramsci can outplay Deleuze, here, in his own game.

Notes

1. There is another, and perhaps more important, reason why *nous* cannot go wrong. Since *nous* grasps the what-it-was-being and since the essence is not "put together," it cannot err. Error arises only in those contexts in which something is said of something else. The cases of "putting together" are those in which an accident is said of a subject, including a relation, as, for example, the much used "The cat is on the mat." In the case of understanding, there is no case of "X is Y." Understanding "human" is not the same as knowing that a log is white.

2. While it would take me too far afield to pursue it here, I would argue that Descartes's fundamental insight has to do with distinguishing what is real from what actually exists. Descartes frequently insists that even if something does not exist, "it is not, nevertheless, nothing." He uses this phrasing frequently in relation to "objective reality," that is, the reality that must be acknowledged as belonging to anything that can be "thought," that is, imagined, willed, willed that not, and so on. If I perceive something and, on some extraneous measure, that turns out not to be,

that fact that that something "is" in my perception is "not, nevertheless, nothing." Spinoza will come to see that this reality is worthy of analyzing in more detail.

3. One need only point to Gilles Deleuze, *Difference and Repetition*, trans. Paul Patton (New York: Columbia University Press, 1995), where Marx's *Contributions to the Critique of Political Economy* plays a decisive role, as well as to *Anti-Oedipus* and *A Thousand Plateaus*, both of which can be read as Marxist interventions. See Gilles Deleuze and Félix Guattari, *Anti-Oedipus: Capitalism and Schizophrenia*, trans. Robert Hurley, Mark Seem, and Helen R. Lane (Minneapolis: University of Minnesota Press, 1983), and *A Thousand Plateaus: Capitalism and Schizophrenia*, trans. Brian Massumi (Minneapolis: University of Minnesota Press, 1987).

4. Deleuze argues, in *What Is Philosophy?*, that philosophy is the creation of concepts that do not "fit together" like puzzle pieces. One way he illustrates this is by means of the Cartesian *cogito*. In that presentation, Deleuze shows why he (or anyone else today, for that matter) cannot be a Cartesian. We think on a different plane. See Gilles Deleuze and Félix Guattari, *What Is Philosophy?*, trans. Hugh Tomlinson and Graham Burchell (New York: Columbia University Press, 1996).

5. Karl Marx, *Capital*, trans. Ben Fowkes (London: Penguin Books, 1976), 125.

6. Marx, 127.

7. Marx, 128.

8. Marx, 129.

9. Deleuze and Guattari, *What Is Philosophy?*, 2.

10. This is not only an etymological point. It is the case that the Latin origin of the word "fact," *factum*, is the perfect passive participle of *facere*, that is, "to do" or "to make." Vico is, perhaps, the first to point out that if what is has been brought about, then we must insist that *verum est factum*, that is, the truth is what has been done or made. To that extent, any theory of truth that does not acknowledge that what is has been made, been brought about, will never capture what is. Since what is has been brought about, a theory of knowledge must also be constructive/creative.

11. Antonio Gramsci, *Quaderni del carcere* (Turin: Einaudi, 1975), 1375–1376; Antonio Gramsci, *Selections from the Prison Notebooks*, trans. Quentin Hoare and Geoffrey Nowell Smith (London: ElecBook, 1999), 626–627.

12. Gramsci, *Selections from the Prison Notebooks*, 626.

13. Deleuze and Guattari, *What Is Philosophy?*, 19.

14. Gramsci, *Selections from the Prison Notebooks*, 628.

15. I have in mind two main critiques of presence and the "atemporality" that attends it: Adorno's and Heidegger's. For Heidegger, the critique of presence sets out from the recognition that any form or mode by which something comes to be present requires, as almost a condition, some form or mode of coming to be absent. For Adorno, the critique is more immediately temporal and, as a result, related to the philosophical preference for leisure over labor. While the argument is obviously more complex, the main steps involve the unmoved mover. Since the unmoved mover is actuality as such or, at least, "most actual," or pure actuality, and since the unmoved mover is also defined primarily by lack of labor, actuality

turns out to be fundamentally connected to leisure. If what is turns out to relate to actuality (or even be defined by actuality), and if actuality is exemplified most of all by leisure, and if that leisure is what leads to the conclusion that actuality is measured in proportion to eternity, then labor, or activity, is a mark of falling away from actuality: labor is a way of nonbeing. I will return to the question of labor later in this chapter. For now, it is sufficient to note the connection between effectivity and reality that stands at the center of both Gramsci's and Deleuze's arguments. This is in marked contrast to the Heideggerian argument.

16. For this reason, one can see why Deleuze, in *Difference and Repetition*, is critical of thought as representation.

17. While in *The Human Condition* Arendt distinguishes between labor and activity, I bring the two together at this point. It would take me too far afield to properly address this issue here. I would, however, argue that Arendt's concept of labor is based either on a metaphysical assumption that is not stated or a social assumption that, I believe, permeates her work. If the Spinozian insight that "everything strives to maintain its existence" is correct, then labor belongs to all things that are. Labor might be nothing more nor less than the way in which existing things are effective and, therefore, real. See Hannah Arendt, *The Human Condition* (Chicago: University of Chicago Press, 1998).

18. For this last insight, I am indebted to Jeffrey Nealon, who drove this point home over and over again before I ever realized its fundamental importance.

19. Gramsci, *Selections from the Prison Notebooks*, 734.

20. Gramsci, *Selections from the Prison Notebooks*, 837.

21. Gramsci, *Selections from the Prison Notebooks*, 837–838.

22. Deleuze and Guattari, *Qu'est-ce Que La Philosophie?*, 39; Gilles Deleuze and Félix Guattari, *What Is Philosophy?*, 36. I will not take issue with the translation of "*agencement*" as "assemblage." Beyond the choice of translation, what is clear is that an assemblage is a relation of elements that are, considered in themselves, a multiplicity. The only "identity" that an assemblage gives to its components emerges in the production of effects that no single element produces by itself. Much the same is true of Gramsci's notion of "*l'insieme*": the "together" or "ensemble."

23. Gilles Deleuze, *Two Regimes of Madness: Texts and Interviews 1975–1995*, ed. David Lapoujade, trans. Ames Hodges and Michael Taormina (New York: Semiotext(e), 2006), 176–177.

24. Gilles Deleuze and Félix Guattari, *A Thousand Plateaus*, 260.

25. Deleuze and Guattari, *A Thousand Plateaus*, 260.

26. Gramsci, *Selections from the Prison Notebooks*, 670.

27. In the conclusion, I will argue that Deleuze seems not to think the effectivity of a given society, that is, he never analyzes society as a "machinic assemblage."

28. The two texts Deleuze wrote on Spinoza do not exhaust his basic and pervasive commitment to Spinoza's thinking. *Difference and Repetition*, *A Thousand Plateaus*, and even *What Is Philosophy?* are replete with affirmations of Spinoza. To my mind, Deleuze's commitment to Spinoza frequently circles around three insights he finds in Spinoza's thought: a thing is what it can do (*conatus*); thought

is parallel to, and therefore not reflective of, matter; and, as a result, thought is as effective/productive as material things. Related to these are other crucial insights of Spinoza's thought: the ubiquity of infinity, the centrality of intensity, and the denial of a distinction between force and being. These latter are shared between Spinoza and Duns Scotus.

29. I cannot pursue here the seemingly "negative" connotation of "concept" with which Deleuze operates here in contrast to the more "positive" valence operative in *What Is Philosophy?* Dan Smith once suggested to me that "concept" in *What Is Philosophy?* might be a mode of operation of what Deleuze, in *Difference and Repetition*, calls an "idea."

30. Deleuze, 131.

31. Deleuze, 139.

32. This is an insight that Adorno expresses in *Negative Dialectics*. It might be that Adorno forms the passage between Gramsci and Deleuze on this issue.

33. Deleuze, 139.

34. In this way, the very notion of multiplicity relates back to the notion that what is just is what is effective. Multiplicity is a way of thinking effectivity without unity or identity.

35. Deleuze, 182.

36. Gramsci, *Quaderni del carcere*, 1415.

37. The critique of this materialism and economism is most trenchant in Louis Althusser, "Contradiction and Overdetermination," in *For Marx* (New York: Verso, 1996), 87–128. For a discussion of the relation between this critical and structural causation, see Vittorio Morfino, "The Concept of Structural Causality in Althusser," *Crisis and Critique* 2, 2 (2005): 87–107. On precisely this issue, Althusser refers to Gramsci.

38. Gramsci, *Selections from the Prison Notebooks*, 809ff.

39. Gramsci, *Selections from the Prison Notebooks*, 810.

40. Gramsci, *Selections from the Prison Notebooks*, 810.

41. Gramsci, *Selections from the Prison Notebooks*, 811.

42. This is not to say that Deleuze is not interested in, for example, the difference between society and kinds of society. He is, for example, aware that nomadic societies can provide philosophy with certain crucial tools for thinking the real. Rather, what I will argue is that society does not come under analysis and, therefore, one does not see Deleuze consider the role that it plays, for example, in the representational image of thought. Philosophers frequently appear in Deleuze's texts as sui generis. What is more, his attempt to think about a *socius* otherwise than as a prestate structure seems to fall short of the attempt to analyze society in the way its forces currently operate. This seems to be a precondition for thinking an "otherwise."

43. If it seems that the notion of "institution" is not really at home in Deleuze, we can simply note that an institution is itself an assemblage, a multiplicity that is effective as a structure.

44. In fact, many social theorists have taken the notion of assemblage in this direction.

8

Herbert Marcuse in Italy

Michael E. Gardiner

Introduction

In his 1963 lecture "The Obsolescence of the Freudian Concept of Man," Herbert Marcuse states that many "basic assumptions" of Freudian theory are now antiquated because, in the contemporary social world, the human psyche no longer conforms to the classical "psychoanalytic object."[1] Rather than analyze systemic social contradictions, Freudianism treats them as individual problems to be "managed" by therapeutic means, thereby bolstering the status quo. It is not our intention to suggest that Marcuse's critical theory has become similarly "obsolete" in the context of the twenty-first century. But we might want to consider the possibility that major changes in the mode of production over the last forty-odd years have problematized Marcuse's account of "contemporary industrial civilization" and that, much as he counseled a radical rethinking of Freud, a reconsideration of key Marcusean themes and ideas might be similarly countenanced.

This chapter proposes to initiate such a dialogue by reading certain features of Marcuse's thought through the lens of "Autonomist" Marxism. Autonomism (and its offshoots) is a variegated intellectual movement that developed originally as a strategic response to the specificities of the Italian postwar political and socioeconomic situation.[2] Since the 1970s, however, and especially after the start of the world financial crisis in 2008,[3] Autonomism has inspired more general analyses of global capitalism, as well as theorized potential modes of resistance to it. Accordingly, the key thinkers of this tradition—most famously Antonio Negri (often in collaboration with Michael Hardt), but also Maurizio Lazzarato, Christian Marazzi, and Paolo

Virno—have begun to exercise a powerful attraction for a new generation of politically engaged writers, artists, and activists. Here, we will focus on one Autonomist theorist in particular, Franco "Bifo" Berardi (hereafter "Bifo"). The reason for this is straightforward: Bifo articulates a challenging and, at times, counterintuitive critique of Marcuse, especially his reliance on the paired concepts of "repression" and "alienation." To Bifo's way of thinking, these concepts have become largely redundant in a world now dominated by what he calls "semiocapitalism," a socioeconomic system that relies not on the containment or distortion of human desires and libidinal energies, but rather on their unending and virtually limitless hyperstimulation and co-optation by a technologized, networked capitalism. As such, the nature of work, production, and leisure have been transformed dramatically since Marcuse's death in 1979, especially in the most advanced sectors of the global North.

Bifo develops a number of strong arguments and insights but, at the same time, there are certain weaknesses in his account of Marcuse, particularly in two main areas. First, Bifo downplays the concept of "repressive desublimation" as articulated in Marcuse's *One-Dimensional Man*, which is arguably a more nuanced position on repression than found in such earlier works as *Eros and Civilization*. And second, Bifo overlooks completely Marcuse's fairly extensive treatment of Marx's *Grundrisse*, which is ironic because this is a canonical text for virtually all Autonomist thinkers, and also insofar as Marcuse anticipates many of the same technosocial and political tendencies that Bifo identifies as intrinsic to semiocapitalism. What emerges from this discussion of certain blind spots in regard to Bifo's interpretation of Marcuse is the possibility of a closer theoretical alignment between them than might otherwise have been anticipated. In what follows, we will begin by summarizing Marcuse's position on labor, repression, and alienation; move to an assessment of Bifo's rejection of central Marcusean ideas together with a consideration of the limitations and omissions already mentioned; and conclude by reflecting on the ways in which Marcuse's critical theory dovetails with both the style and substance of Bifo's thought.

The Alienation/Repression Problematic

In his 1955 text *Eros and Civilization*, Marcuse accepts much of Freud's philosophical anthropology, especially the image of the human organism as a dynamic entity animated by vital (if often contradictory) impulses and instincts.[4] As is well known, one of the main drives is the "pleasure principle," which for Marcuse ideally takes the form of a playful, uninhibited deployment of the human senses and imagination. For Freud, an unrestricted adherence to the pleasure principle threatens to undermine the very civilizational fabric itself, therefore requiring complex and far-reaching modes of repression and sublimation to either contain or redirect such energies into more "constructive" pursuits. If successful—and oftentimes it is not—such a process results in the tentative reconciliation of humankind with an overarching "reality principle," one that, however much unhappiness on an individual basis it might cause, is necessary for the survival of the species. Marcuse's counterargument is that the development of the productive forces, specifically the high levels of automation and technical efficiency necessary for competitive manufacture in advanced capitalist societies, has rendered virtually all this repression unnecessary and, thus, ultimately eradicable.[5] Humanity has, over the course of centuries of capitalist accumulation, created inadvertently the material conditions for our universal liberation from the burdensome work imposed by capitalism. Inasmuch as the mechanism of repression is a historically specific phenomenon, its supersession would entail the cultivation of authentic or "true" needs through spontaneously inner-directed and creative forms of nonrepressive labor, undertaken in a peaceful and consensually organized fashion. The problem, of course, is that the maintenance of vested class interests demands the ongoing disinvestment of libidinous energies with respect to the pleasure principle and their redirection toward alienated work and avaricious consumption for its own sake. Therefore—and on this point Marcuse is in full agreement with Freud—the continual expansion of capitalist production, and the attendant concentration and centralization of wealth, power, and resources, requires the intensification of repression itself, turning on the "introjection" of dominant values into the very subjectivity of the individual. Yet, however much we drift toward the consolidation of a "totally administered society," one marked by increasing regimentation, routinization, and social-bureaucratic control, Marcuse always subscribed to the notion that the contradictions manifested by such an apparatus remained volatile and at least latently transformative. Countervailing tendencies of negation and revolt do exist, registered in myriad resistances that were particularly evident by the late 1960s, which explains his qualified support for the New Left, feminist, and anti-colonialist movements. As Anthony Elliott characterizes it, we witness a shift over time in Marcuse from a focus on "repressive sublimation" to that of "libidinal rationality." The latter holds the promise of reconciling such apparent antimonies as self and society, humanity and nature, and the reality and pleasure principles, although of course its full actualization would only become completely apparent in a postcapitalist era.[6]

 At the same time, encoded in this narrative are a number of assumptions that many in the Autonomist tradition, including Bifo, would treat with skepticism. Marcuse, as we know, came to intellectual maturity at a time when modern industrial capitalism was in the throes of its classical "Fordist" phase. Under this regime of accumulation, things like profits, salaries, and prices were subject to considerable oversight and regulation, especially as pertains to the relation between socially necessary labor time and value. Production at this stage is governed by the principle of measurable and homogenous linear time, wherein human subjectivity and action are orientated toward the instrumental organization of physical matter, tasks, and outputs, necessitating the disciplinary surveillance and control of the laboring body and ultimately conforming to what Marcuse called the "performance principle." Marcuse's favored metaphor to describe this form of bureaucratically organized capitalism is that of the "apparatus" or "machine." As he writes in the opening pages of *One-Dimensional Man*, "The machine [is] the most effective political instrument in any society whose basic organization is that of the machine process."[7]

Arguably, however, we have left this "machine paradigm" behind. A central Autonomist proposal is that, at the tail end of the Fordist era, around the mid-1970s the burgeoning power and growing militancy of workers threw capitalism into a profound state of crisis. Capital responded by implementing technologically driven changes to the production process, thereby dramatically reducing the need for physical labor. This, combined with an economic downturn and the mass layoffs that followed, made the industrial working class increasingly redundant vis-à-vis the process of production itself, and the locus of struggle shifted outside the factory walls. The replacement of "living labor" by increasingly sophisticated computer-controlled systems radically transforms the very conditions of production and places the process of value-creation on an entirely new footing. One consequence is that labor and its products become ever more "immaterial,"[8] inasmuch as the physical side of production is taken over by automated techniques, and all aspects of the collective worker's affective, desiring, and cognitive capabilities, as these are located in the "social factory,"[9] are now brought to bear on production itself. Although such changes are riddled with paradox and countervailing tendencies, any clear connection between necessary labor time and measurable values or outputs has now been cast into doubt. This is a dual consequence of the explosive growth of immaterial labor in the post-Fordist era, wherein "mind, language and creativity [are] primary tools for the production of value,"[10] but also because the circulation of digital and symbolic goods has become the norm, which effectively problematizes capitalistic notions of proprietary control and ownership.[11]

As a result of these and related factors, capitalism is plunged into ever deeper crises of overproduction, indebtedness, financial instability, and resource depletion,[12] which would seem to cast doubt on some of Marcuse's predictions that such contradictions have become more or less successfully managed by contemporary industrial society. But more germane to our central focus, how do these socioeconomic transformations bear on Bifo's critique of the dual problematic of alienation/repression? For Bifo, the latest modes of capitalist valorization create a new kind of neoliberal subject, which in turn fundamentally reshapes the mass formation of affective and psychic life. The new "fixed capital" is not so much tools, machines, or factories, but quite literally the brain of the worker or, to be more precise, the "general intellect" of cognitive workers, which is combined with living labor to make productive activity possible.[13] The shared intellectuality of the workforce is the central resource of post-Fordist enterprises, but such capitalist organizations require the means to identify and capture this factor and make it a tangible asset. In Autonomist parlance, this marks the transition from "formal" to "real" subsumption: essentially, a shift from the politico-juridical subjugation of laborers in the physical workplace to the confinement of workers' entire lives by the flows of capital accumulation through techno-economic means. Activity in the sphere of work increasingly requires not a slavish devotion to inflexible rules in hierarchical bureaucratic settings, but rather interpretive and communicative skills that shape flows of knowledge about consumer tastes and preferences, foster problem-solving abilities, promote individual and group initiative, and facilitate endless adaptability to changing market and productive conditions. For Bifo, this means that what he calls semiocapitalism, wherein "informational technologies make possible a full integration of linguistic labor with capital valorization,"[14] moves away from the overt disciplining of the body toward something closer to an architectonics of the "soul."

According to Bifo, there are clear reasons why semiocapitalism has so effectively captured the affective, desiring, and cognitive qualities of immaterial labor. In the Fordist era, factory work generally does not engage the intellect; its tasks are routinized and can be performed by virtually anyone, and hence work here is seen as malign and dehumanizing. Post-Fordism represents a very different scenario: cognitive workers, especially the high-tech vanguard, now typically see their labor as an "enterprise"—the free and creative disposition of their imagination and energies—even if they are ultimately wage-earning employees of a firm. The so-called "enterprise culture" has become a ubiquitous principle and the primary site of the investment of desire. And, although all the available empirical evidence shows that time spent laboring, both inside and outside the workplace, has increased dramatically over the last thirty years, there has been little in the way of generalized social opposition to this trend. As Bifo usefully summarizes it, while industrial workers "invested mechanical energies in their wage earning services according to a depersonalized model of repetition, *high tech* workers invest [fully] their creative, innovative, and communicative energies in the labor process."¹⁵

The relevance of Bifo's analysis for Marcuse's central thesis in *Eros and Civilization* should be obvious enough. Marcuse argued that "surplus" repression was integral to the tightly regulated system of industrial production and exchange and that the liberation of such instincts and drives in polymorphously sensuous and imaginative forms threatened the viability of capitalism itself. Bifo's position, by contrast, is that the very success of this new phase of semiocapitalism lies in its ability to effectively capture precisely those libidinal and creative energies in the service of capital accumulation. Work under the aegis of semiocapitalism *is* a libidinal rationality, at least in some respects. Lest there be any potential misunderstanding here, Bifo is acutely aware that all manner of invidious distinctions and inequities are involved in the deployment of cognitive labor. Much of it, such as data entry, is rote and mechanical in nature, which is why we have to distinguish between "brain workers" and "chain workers."¹⁶ Furthermore, it does not mean that degrading forms of manual labor have simply disappeared, although they tend to shift to economically less-developed regions, or that the "immateriality" of cognitive work does not concern bodies at all. Bifo does not believe that semiocapitalism is a more just or humane socioeconomic system than its Fordist predecessor. On the contrary, Bifo argues that unlike liberal democratic societies that allow for at least the limited individual pursuit of relative happiness, post-Fordist capitalism is a "totalitarian" social order. This is so not only in its all-encompassing reach—which is both extensive, or global, and intensive, saturating all of everyday life—but also inasmuch as it harkens back to the Stalinist or fascistic expectation that all citizens *must* participate enthusiastically in what our society defines as the only possible avenue to happiness.¹⁷

The key to this "new totalitarianism" is that virtually all work is now contained within a network of digital infrastructures. Exploitation is no longer exercised exclusively in hierarchical, bureaucratically organized systems found in a specific time-space, such as the factory during working hours, but has a "transversal, deterritorialized function, permeating every fragment of labor time."¹⁸ Work might be vaunted today as self-directed activity of intrinsic value, but although formal hierarchies and clear-cut directives have waned considerably, what takes its place is more insidious and all-encompassing, conforming to a "chain of automatisms" embedded in a network. These digital networks coordinate each subjective aspect of the worker, every deployment of desire and attention, suturing them into a totalizing but fluid and endlessly manipulable process. Hence, what is important for theorists like Bifo is not the automation of production per se, which has been happening for a long time, but rather its *computerization*. Digital technologies are capable of modeling every event or process in infinitely replicable ways, thereby creating virtualities that effectively reduce the productive process to bits and bytes of information. For Bifo, this means the emergence of something resembling a new form of "bio-info-production."[19] Fordist techniques had "autonomic" subsystems and cybernetic modes of information monitoring and retrieval, but such individual subunits were not linked via a quasi-biological info-sphere, akin to the neurons connecting the brain into an organic whole. In semiocapitalism, the feedback loops of systems theory mesh with biogenetics to create a new posthuman landscape, as the digital nervous system progressively insinuates itself into its organic counterpart, recodifying the latter to suit its own needs. As a result, human rationality and agency have now been effectively abandoned to a series of internalized technosocial automatisms, wherein human beings "are tending to become the ruthless executors of decisions taken inattentively."[20]

If the crux of semiocapitalism is the subsumption of human desires, imaginative capabilities, and affects in ways that directly augment modes of capitalist valorization, for Bifo it means that the Freudian-Marxist concept of "alienation"—positing the repression of "authentically" human essences leading to neurotic symptoms, and which only need to be released or "liberated" by dialectical fiat to bring about universal happiness and fulfillment—must now be abandoned. The mass psychopathologies that afflict us now, especially anxiety, panic, and depression, are not neuroses that stem from the curtailment of libidinal energies, but the reverse: they are symptoms of the sort of hyper-enervation and semiotic overload demanded by the constant ratcheting up of our psychic and bodily investment in ever-accelerating modalities of work and consumption. Hence, they are best understood as "schizo-pathologies" and cannot be challenged effectively by the unleashing of desire or its social investment elsewhere, much less a frontal assault on the power structure, but rather through a process of libidinal *disinvestment* that Bifo labels, provocatively, a "poetics of exhaustion." Such a position also underscores Bifo's reservations as to the long shadow cast by Hegel's thought over humanistic Marxism. For Bifo, the main problem with the Hegelian legacy in Marxism is that it sees the working class as the living embodiment of the principle of communism and, hence, as a transcendental figure, an eschaton or "radical beyond representing the truth to be realized outside the contradictions of the existing [world],"[21] a perspective that is insufficiently attentive to the "social and technical history of the conflict between workers and capital."[22]

Autonomists, by contrast, prefer the Spinozian-derived concept of *immanence* to that of Hegelian *transcendence* and insist that workers are an active force that strive against the imperatives of capital, thereby forcing the latter to constantly adapt to innovative forms of resistance on the part of laborers. This helps to explain why Bifo prefers the term *estrangement* to that of *alienation*. Although this might seem an overly nuanced distinction since the two are often used interchangeably, estrangement for Bifo implies an active confrontation of the object of domination in determinate sociohistorical conditions, whereas alienation is understood as an externally induced, abstract, and essentially passive phenomenon. In this reading, estrangement is not the loss of some putatively authentic and universal human essence, the negation of an original "wholeness" that must be rendered complete again, via dialectical synthesis, at some abstract future time. We must, Bifo writes, abjure an "anthropology of the essence" and forge instead an outlook that "does not anticipate any restoration of humanity, does not proclaim any human universality, and bases its understanding of humanity on class conflict."[23] Bifo's concept of "estrangement" is therefore meant to capture the "positive" attempt on the part of the laboring classes to create an alternative set of social relations separate from the capitalist mode of production, through the *refusal* of work. Hence, workers *want* to be estranged from the labor-process, not "realize" themselves in some ostensibly "liberated" version of it.

Bifo has similar doubts regarding Marcuse's repression hypothesis. Although influenced strongly by Gilles Deleuze and Felix Guattari, Bifo rejects their premise that desire per se is innately subversive and resists domination, a position he believes Marcuse shares. For Bifo, desire is not a force, essence or tendency, but rather an unstable field or network constituted dynamically by shifting and opposing sets of political, economic, and social interests. Insofar as desire is not "natural" but a social construct, it can be subsumed and constantly repurposed by very different ideologies, institutions, and practices. Contra Marcuse, for whom the *content* of erotic-creative fantasy is far less consequential than its inherently emancipatory *function*, Bifo is considerably more ambivalent, arguing that "desire is not a good boy, nor the positive force of history," and noting that, for example, "there is a Nazi form of desire."[24] As already intimated, even a cursory examination of such apparently dissimilar phenomena as advertising, politics, and production in contemporary society would seem to demonstrate that in recent decades, desire, both individual and collective, has been very successfully "hijacked" by capital. What we have today is a constant introjection of desire into a "neo-baroque" superexpressivity of signs, virtualities, and simulations. As Mark Fisher notes, "capitalist realism" avoids the identification with the stern, killjoy Father who forbids enjoyment, which was the defining feature of Max Weber's ascetic Protestantism. Rather, post-Fordism is akin to the hip uncle imploring us to "just do it," seek endless new ways to be titillated and entertained in both work and consumption. For Fisher, this leads to a perpetual state of "hedonic lassitude," the inability to seek anything *but* an immediacy of pleasure, in a context of generalized anomie and fractalized time. Reclaiming a sense of political agency, he writes, "means first of all accepting our insertion *at the level of desire* in the remorseless meat-grinder of Capital."[25] For Bifo, although Marcuse is certainly aware of the blandishments of consumer culture, he did not grasp fully the conformist and, more importantly, *self-integrating* properties of the commodification of desire.

To put the matter bluntly: the hypothetical liberation of instinctual desires would not necessarily operate in a space-time "outside" extant systems of power and domination. Marcuse sometimes seems to argue precisely this, as when he suggests there is a "biological" basis for socialism or that the "pacification of existence" must represent the *attenuation* of power, insofar as Eros and power are always "opposites."[26] For the poststructuralist-inflected tradition that Bifo represents, by contrast, desire and power are inextricably intertwined. The pursuit of the pleasure principle does not interrupt, and even enhances in myriad ways, the increasingly frictionless accumulation of capital. And, insofar as we (for the most part) "voluntarily" integrate ourselves into the social order, instances of direct repression by the state apparatus or its surrogates pale in comparison to the narcotic and atomizing effects of informational and neural overload and the endless propagation of "lifestyle choices." The fascism and Stalinism of the 1930s and 1940s relied extensively on direct juridico-military subjugation, censorship, the silencing of dissenting opinion, and the fundamental opacity of the ruling apparatus. But the "postmodern totalitarianism" of which Bifo speaks positively *mandates* hyperexpressivity with regard to our thoughts, feelings, and desires, through which all is revealed and communicated effortlessly, as witnessed by today's endless accumulation of blogs, twitter feeds, and social networking sites. If we do not maintain an active Facebook page, psychologists now tell us, we are dangerously inhibited and antisocial. For Bifo, such a superfluity of expression manifests itself as a kind of obscene hypervisibility and empty chatter, undermining human empathy and solidarity and rendering "thought, dissent and critique banal and ridiculous."[27]

If we take this argument seriously, the cultivation of a critical subjectivity in contemporary life might have less to do with the full realization of the pleasure principle than a self-conscious diminution of excess, an "unplugging" or psychic disinvestment that accepts the inevitability of the aging process and the libidinal and temporal slowdown it entails. Arguably, there is a cult of youth at work in Marcuse's thought, and certainly more than a surfeit of Romanticism, as Michael Löwy has effectively demonstrated.[28] For

Bifo—who, after all, was a young militant in the Autonomist movement and forced to flee his homeland during an anti-Leftist crackdown of savage brutality and dubious legality in 1977—to make a fetish of youthfulness and aggressive militancy (even if formally anticapitalist) might be construed as all-consuming traps for desire that we ourselves construct. According to Bifo, it is immaterial whether repression is understood as a permanent and universal feature of human social relations (Freud) or a historically shaped phenomenon (Marcuse); neither position gets us beyond the repression/expression binary and both ultimately surrender to the "narrative machine of power."[29] The transformed conditions of the twenty-first century demand both a different diagnosis of the social ills we are now subject to and commensurately appropriate strategies of opposition: specifically, we need to disentangle energy from desire, for to conflate them is to elide violence and force.

An Autonomist Marcuse?

Bifo presents us with a provocative and challenging riposte to Marcuse's alienation/repression problematic, one focusing on the capturing and redeployment of human desires for freedom and self-actualization by mechanisms of semiocapitalist valorization. What might blunt this critique, however, is the overly sweeping nature of Bifo's claims and his inattention to many of the specificities and nuances of Marcuse's position. Of course, there *is* considerable merit in what Bifo says about Marcuse, especially the former's assertion that we need to track closely transformations in the capitalist mode of production as well as concomitant changes in the technical and political composition of labor. It is equally clear that Bifo is respectful of Marcuse's stalwart contribution to critical social theory and his status as a consummate public intellectual. Nonetheless, the weaknesses of Bifo's reading of Marcuse have to be addressed for reasons both scholarly and political, which has the additional virtue of identifying certain intriguing and hitherto unexpected convergences between these thinkers.

Our comments here will begin with Marcuse's concept of repressive desublimation as it relates to Bifo's rejection of the alienation/repression dyad, before moving to a consideration of Marcuse's use of Marx's *Grundrisse* so as to analyze key technosocial changes in late capitalism, which seem to anticipate many Autonomist insights. As to the former, it is clear that Bifo relies on key poststructuralist arguments regarding the nexus that links agency, subjectivity, and power, such as Michel Foucault's assertion that power is not a purely "negative" force that blocks, constrains, or (at most) sublimates what are usually taken to be "natural" drives or desires rooted in the biological makeup of the human organism, but rather a "positive" phenomenon that produces particular kinds of subjects endowed with characteristic bodily and psychological dispositions.[30] Foucault's chief intent is to demonstrate that moral codes, particularly those concerning sexuality, are always-already intertwined with prevailing structures of power, and thereby subject us to normalizing pressures. As part of institutionalized procedures of normative categorization and evaluation, modern individuals are compelled to reveal a "true" or "authentic" self through techniques of rational scrutiny and control, in tandem with the demands of governmentality. Although he is not mentioned explicitly in *History of Sexuality Vol. 1*, elsewhere Foucault identifies Marcuse as a "Freudian-Marxist" along with Wilhelm Reich, Max Horkheimer, and others.[31] In such texts, Marcuse is held to adhere to an essentialist line of thinking with regard to the connection between repression and human freedom, which, for Foucault, has been a political and theoretical dead end.

Yet perhaps neither Foucault nor Bifo fully appreciate the originality of Marcuse's concept of repressive desublimation as formulated in *One-Dimensional Man*. Here, Marcuse argues that, with the decline of the father figure's authority and concomitant waning effectiveness of the external imposition of naked disciplinary power, together with heightened social fragmentation and possessive individualism, repressive desublimation in advanced industrial society becomes an effective and insidious tool of domination. It allows for a reconstitution of the "innermost drives" of the population through the controlled redirection of libidinal energies into intensified work routines and hyperacquisitive consumerism. Although repressive desublimation operates differently than the "surplus repression" Marcuse discusses in *Eros and Civilization*, because the former seems to allow for the realization of immediate sensual gratifications of every kind (as summed up by Fisher's "hedonic lassitude"), it remains a process bound tightly to the reality principle. Repressive desublimations, writes Marcuse, "contain more deviation, more freedom, and more refusal to heed the social taboos; [they operate] as the by-product of the social controls of technological reality, which extend liberty while intensifying domination."[32] Libidinal forces are not thereby blocked or contained for Marcuse, but rather released in ways that both reflect and reproduce the essential features of an "alienated" society, thereby effecting the relatively smooth integration of their bodies, desires, and affects into extant systems of technocratic surveillance and control.

Bifo is highly critical of what he takes to be Marcuse's neo-Freudian concept of repression. According to the former, quasi-instinctual desires have no necessary emancipatory quality, at least under the transformed conditions of semiocapitalism, but are indeed integral to its seeming resilience and vitality. Yet in articulating the concept of repressive desublimation, it is apparent that Marcuse does not subscribe entirely to what Finn Bowering describes as an "instinctual or essentialist conception of liberated desire."[33] This point can be illustrated by reference to a fascinating (if highly compressed) discussion in *One-Dimensional Man*, wherein Marcuse ruminates on a strikingly new phenomenon in the workplace of technologically advanced societies. Riffing on Hegelian terminology, he identifies the emergence of a "Happy Consciousness," wherein corporate strategies are suffused with a sense of everyday "fun." By stressing the value of both individual enrichment and interpersonal team work, albeit dedicated to maximum profitability, the challenges of the workplace are cast in a "creative," even playful, light.[34] In his book *Authenticity and the Cultural Politics of Work*, Peter Fleming suggests that, for Marcuse, qualities of playfulness and pleasurability are antithetical to the organization of work under capitalism because the latter requires a slavish devotion to instrumental reason and the abnegation of desire. Drawing on the work of French sociologists Luc Boltanski and Eve Chiapello,[35] as well as various Autonomist sources, Fleming argues instead that twenty-first century capitalism has very successfully fused productive efficacy and lifestyle, work and leisure, thereby co-opting many aspects of the 1960s youth movements' criticisms of the corporate environment. And yet, in this passage at least, Marcuse seems to anticipate precisely what Fleming describes as the "corporatization of 'fun' as a managerial technique of power."[36] Marcuse asserts that these are tokens of a pseudoindividualism so alienated that such un-self-consciousness as to *being* alienated calls into question the theoretical viability of the category itself: a Baudrillardian conclusion he considers briefly but then steps back from, regarding it as a "higher order" manifestation of alienation.[37] But it does imply that productivist values are now so successfully introjected into the human organism and human social relations that most behavior becomes effectively "automatic," performed without mediation by conscious intent or critical reflection. As Marcuse says, "the medium of experience imposed by the established society ... coagulat[es] into a self-sufficient, closed, 'automatic' system [marked by] immediate, almost physical reactions in which comprehending consciousness, thought, and even one's own feelings play a very small role."[38] This suggests further that in its most "advanced" form, "domination functions as administration."[39] What is interesting is that Bifo cites this very passage, acknowledging that in many ways it prefigures his own idea that exploitation under semiocapitalism generally assumes the mode not of overt, violent repression or censorship, but that of the far more insidious and effective internalization and routinized enactment of technosocial automatisms. Indeed, Bifo concedes that it would be profitable to "re-read" the works of Marcuse today with respect to this crucial insight.

We now turn to Marcuse's comments on the *Grundrisse*. It has been argued that Marcuse's analysis of "one-dimensional society" reflects both his theoretical understanding of the postwar corporatist welfare state, as filtered through the paradigm of critical theory, as well as his direct historical experience thereof. Yet there are also hints in his post-1950s writings that we might be on the threshold of a very different form of capitalism and that its full instantiation could unleash wholly unanticipated social forces, as well as raise different possibilities for human freedom and autonomy. A useful way to characterize this idea might be through addressing Bifo's contention that there are three main tendencies in Marxist thought: (1) the Hegelian-humanistic variant, which looks to Marx's early *Economic and Philosophical Manuscripts of 1844*; (2) structuralism, emphasizing the late work of *Capital*, and the alleged epistemological break it represents vis-à-vis the *1844 Manuscripts*; and (3) Autonomism, which conjoins a materialist phenomenology to a preoccupation with the *Grundrisse* and, more specifically, the remarkable passage in the latter titled "Fragment on Machines."[40] It is in the "Fragment," part of a series of drafts and notebooks from 1857, which were never published in his lifetime, that Marx first outlines the concept of the "general intellect." With the automation of production and the increasingly central role played by scientific knowledge, Marx argues that "living labor" would be displaced in favor of the "dead labor" invested in machines and technical systems. Once this advanced productive infrastructure was in place, workers would be freed from harsh and demanding physical labor and the transition to a sort of "high-tech" communism would be all but assured. Thinkers like Bifo and Virno counter that Marx's optimism here is somewhat misplaced because in post-Fordism, the general intellect is not exclusively correlated with machines and so forth, but is instead reflected in the skills, knowledges, and communicative resources of living labor: that is to say, workers themselves. Although it is living labor that now creates the bulk of profit for capital, the time freed up by mechanization (and now computerization) does not lead to increasing leisure time and personal freedom for all, as Marx believed, but rather to the growth of structural unemployment and precariousness, as well as the ever more intensive modes of exploitation and subjectivation. Nevertheless, for Bifo, the last best hope for humankind lies in the collective intelligence of the *entire* cognitariat rather than a self-appointed revolutionary elite of the

Leninist variety, even if cognitive workers only understand this imperfectly at the present conjuncture.

Marcuse is generally identified with the Hegelian-humanist wing of Marxist thought: the central role of the *1844 Manuscripts* in his thinking is well documented, and Marcuse even wrote a long review article on this text in 1932, just as it was initially made available to a readership outside specialists in the Soviet Union.[41] It may therefore come as a surprise that Marcuse quotes extensively from the *Grundrisse* in several writings and develops a number of insights that anticipate, or at least parallel, the Autonomist fixation with this work. Marcuse suggests that integral to the process of technical development in industry, especially in an intensely competitive environment marked by a falling rate of profit, is a pronounced tendency toward ever more complete automation. Such quantitative changes harbor the potential for qualitative transformations in the productive forces themselves, and hence the overarching social totality itself. Marcuse proffers the commonsensical proposition that increasing automation could reduce progressively socially necessary labor time to an absolute minimum, making possible a realm of genuinely "free time" through which Eros, friendship, and critical reflection could be fostered. But Marcuse also asserts that the technological organization of production, because it increasingly relies on abstract scientific knowledge and the "mental energy" of technical labor, results in both a "dematerialization" of work and a growing awareness on the part of the cognitariat as to the collective understanding and control it wields over the productive process. The "degree to which the share of [manual] labor in the material process of production declines," writes Marcuse, "*intellectual* skills and capabilities become social and political factors."[42] As the productive forces become technologically saturated, workers might be on the verge of realizing that the private expropriation of the fruits of their collective labor is technically and historically redundant, that they do not have to be the "principal agents" of production under the thumb of capital, but could step back and become its autonomous overseers, its "supervisors and regulators."[43] What is important here is not so much the "hardware" of the technological apparatus, but the "software" of the social brain of technical and cognitive workers. Of course, prevailing modes of exploitation, subjectification, and class privilege demand that these emancipatory promises are forever denied or deferred. Additionally, there are countervailing tendencies at play here as well: full automation is extremely costly, and it is now often cheaper to either outsource production to less-developed regions of the globe or "liberalize" immigration to keep labor costs down in the metropole itself (without, needless to say, extending full citizenship rights to so-called guest workers), tendencies that are all part of the deterritorializing effects of capital.

Some Autonomists, such as Michael Hardt and Antonio Negri, suggest that the immaterial quality of labor as it is taken up and utilized by the general intellect (cum "multitude") is the Achilles' heel of capitalism.[44] As intimated, Bifo is less sanguine on this point, insofar as the digitalization of production also tends to undermine the traditional bases of workers' solidarity, such as their physical copresence in factory and neighborhood settings, and capacity for empathy and mutual identification through shared experiences, affects, and communicative acts—which also makes possible ever more nefarious (if largely self-actualizing) modes of social control. Although he did not live to see the full effects of computerization vis-à-vis the productive apparatus, or society generally, Marcuse was equally aware of the contradictions here. Automation carries with it the potential for human emancipation, but it also threatens to perfect the apparatus of domination itself, and not necessarily in a transparently top-down, authoritarian way, but through the transmutation of desire, which is effected through the process of repressive desublimation.

Conclusion

Throughout this chapter, we have mostly highlighted the conceptual and political differences between Marcuse and Bifo. However, as demonstrated in the section immediately preceding this one, there are deeper resonances vis-à-vis their respective projects that deserve further investigation, thus raising the possibility of some measure of rapprochement between Marcusean critical theory and Bifo's version of Autonomist thought. Indeed, in reading them side by side, one is struck by the similarities in their rhetorical and writerly approach: both develop sweeping diagnoses of our contemporary malaise and are motivated to theorize about what possibilities exist for the realization of more autonomous personalities and social relations, even if they might have different views as to the nature and scope of any such potential transformation. Marcuse and Bifo even share a terse, highly compressed, sometimes epigrammatic style of writing.

However, the resemblances are not merely stylistic. Bifo, like Marcuse, continually evokes the desirability of Eros, of intimacy and friendship, and stresses the role of the aesthetic, the latter of which they equally understand in terms of embodied human sensibility and the unfettered poetic imagination. Each of them suggests capitalism annihilates a qualitatively experienced sense of *time* and erases the distinctions between work and leisure, public and private, which they view as grave threats to human flourishing and well-being. As such, in their own way, they seek to foment a differential sense of temporality, what Bifo calls a "slow affectivity" and Marcuse terms "pleasurable time," understood as occasions for unhurried rest, repose, and contemplation. Both regard as hollow the claims of liberal democracy to be able to vouchsafe genuine freedom and self-determination and each maintains that, although they might adduce different reasons for this, our society is becoming increasingly "totalitarian" in nature, to the point where the viability of "civilization" per se is under serious threat. Finally, each subscribes to what we might call "utopian pessimism," an outlook tinged with intimations of profound sadness over the scale of human suffering and lost opportunities for progressive change, but not wholly dismissive of potentialities for freedom and autonomy, however fragile and constrained these might be.

However, perhaps the most promising occasion for substantive dialogue between Marcuse and Bifo and the intellectual traditions they represent concerns the one briefly touched on earlier: namely, that Marcuse sees considerable promise in the growth of the "general intellect," although he does not directly use the term, and the radically democratic forms of control over the productive process this might ultimately bring. If so, there is considerable potential for updating Marcuse's original insights on "contemporary industrial society" with reference to Bifo's resolutely up-to-the-minute perspectives on semiocapitalism and its discontents.

Notes

1. Herbert Marcuse, *Five Lectures: Psychoanalysis, Politics, and Utopia*, trans. Jeremy J. Shapiro and Shierry M. Weber (London: Penguin Press, 1970), 44.

2. See Steve Wright, *Storming Heaven: Class Composition and Struggle in Italian Autonomist Marxism* (London: Pluto Press, 2002); Sylvère Lotringer and Christian Marazzi, eds., *Autonomia: Post-Political Politics* (Los Angeles: Semiotext(e), 2007).

3. An Autonomist reading of the 2008 crisis can be found in Christian Marazzi, *The Violence of Financial Capital*, trans. Kristina Lebedeva and Jason Francis McGimsey (Los Angeles: Semiotext(e), 2011).

4. Herbert Marcuse, *Eros and Civilization: A Philosophical Inquiry into Freud* (Boston: Beacon Press, 1966).

5. Wide-ranging questions of automation are addressed in Adam Greenfield, "Automation: The Annihilation of Work," in *Radical Technologies: The Design of Everyday Life* (London and New York: Verso, 2017), 183–207.

6. Anthony Elliott, *Social Theory and Psychoanalysis in Transition: Self and Society from Freud to Kristeva* (Oxford: Blackwell, 1992), 88.

7. Herbert Marcuse, *One-Dimensional Man: Studies in the Ideology of Advanced Industrial Society* (Boston: Beacon Press, 1964), 3.

8. See Maurizio Lazzarato, "Immaterial Labor," in *Radical Thought in Italy: A Potential Politics*, ed. Paolo Virno and Michael Hardt (Minneapolis: University of

Minnesota Press, 1996), 133–147; Wolfgang F. Haug, "Immaterial Labour," *Historical Materialism: Research in Critical Marxist Theory* 18 (2010): 209–216.

9. See Nicholas Thoburn, "The Social Factory: Machines, Work, Control," in *Deleuze, Marx and Politics* (London and New York: Routledge, 2003), 69–102.

10. Franco "Bifo" Berardi, *The Soul at Work: From Alienation to Autonomy*, trans. Francesca Cadel and Giuseppina Mecchia (Los Angeles: Semiotext(e), 2009), 21–22.

11. For more on this transition, see Nick Dyer-Witheford, *Cyber-Marx: Cycles and Circuits of Struggle in High Technology Capitalism* (Champaign: University of Illinois Press, 1999); Max Henninger and Giuseppina Mecchia, "Introduction," in *Substance: A Review of Theory and Literary Criticism*, Special Issue: Italian Post-Workerist Thought, ed. Max Henninger et al., 112, 36, 1 (2007): 3–7.

12. See Wolfgang Streeck, *How Will Capitalism End? Essays on a Failing System* (London: Verso, 2016).

13. See Paolo Virno, "Notes on the 'General Intellect,'" in *Marxism beyond Marxism*, ed. Saree Makdisi, Cesare Casarino, and Rebecca Karl (London: Routledge, 1996), 265–272.

14. Franco "Bifo" Berardi, *Precarious Rhapsody: Semiocapitalism and the Pathologies of the Post-Alpha Generation*, trans. Arianna Bove, Erik Empson, Michael Goddard, Giuseppina Mecchia, Antonella Schintu, and Steve Wright (London: Minor Compositions, 2009), 149.

15. Bifo, *The Soul at Work*, 78.

16. Bifo, *The Soul at Work*, 87.

17. Bifo, *The Soul at Work*, 91.

18. Bifo, *The Soul at Work*, 88.

19. Bifo, *The Soul at Work*, 77.

20. Bifo, "Technology and Knowledge in a Universe of Indetermination," *Substance: A Review of Theory and Literary Criticism*, Special Issue: Italian Post-Workerist Thought, 56–74, 83.

21. Bifo, *The Soul at Work*, 41.

22. Bifo, *The Soul at Work*, 43.

23. Bifo, *The Soul at Work*, 45.

24. Bifo, *The Soul at Work*, 118; see also Elliott, *Social Theory and Psychoanalysis*, 95.

25. Mark Fisher, *Capitalist Realism: Is There No Alternative?* (Winchester, UK: Zero Books, 2009), 15.

26. Marcuse, *One-Dimensional Man*, 235.

27. Franco "Bifo" Berardi, *After the Future*, trans. Arianna Bove, Melinda Cooper, Erik Empson, Enrico, Giuseppina Mecchia, and Tiziana Terranova (Edinburgh: AK Press, 2011), 109; see also Jodi Dean, *Democracy and Other Neoliberal Fantasies: Communicative Capitalism and Left Politics* (Durham, NC: Duke University Press, 2009), 19–48.

28. Michael Löwy, "Marcuse and Benjamin: The Romantic Dimension," in *On Changing the World: Essays in Political Philosophy, from Karl Marx to Walter Benjamin* (Chicago: Haymarket Books, 2013), 133–142.

29. Bifo, *Precarious Rhapsody*, 106.

30. See Michel Foucault, *The History of Sexuality, Vol. 1: An Introduction*, trans. Robert Hurley (New York: Vintage, 1990), especially 95–96.

31. For example, see Michel Foucault, "Adorno, Horkheimer, and Marcuse: Who Is a 'Negator of History'?," in *Remarks on Marx: Conversations with Duccio Trombadori*, trans. R. James Goldstein and James Cascaito (New York: Semiotext(e), 1991), 115–130.

32. Marcuse, *One-Dimensional Man*, 72.

33. Finn Bowering, "Repressive Desublimation and Consumer Culture: Re-Evaluating Herbert Marcuse," *New Formations* 75, 1 (2012): 8–24, 14.

34. Marcuse, *One-Dimensional Man*, 80.

35. Luc Boltanski and Eve Chiapello, *The New Spirit of Capitalism*, trans. Gregory Elliott (London: Verso, 2005).

36. Peter Fleming, *Authenticity and the Cultural Politics of Work: New Forms of Informal Control* (Oxford: Oxford University Press, 2009), 59.

37. Marcuse, *One-Dimensional Man*, 11.

38. Marcuse, *An Essay on Liberation* (Boston: Beacon Press, 1969), 39; *Five Lectures*, 14.

39. Marcuse, *One-Dimensional Man*, 251.

40. Bifo, *The Soul at Work*, 35. See also Karl Marx, "Fragment on Machines," *#Accelerate: The Accelerationist Reader*, ed. Robin Mackay and Armen Avanessian (Falmouth, UK: Urbanomic Media), 51–66.

41. See Douglas Kellner and Clayton Pierce, "Introduction: Marcuse's Adventures in Marxism," in Herbert Marcuse, *Marxism, Revolution and Utopia: Collected Papers of Herbert Marcuse, Vol. Six*, ed. Douglas Kellner (London: Routledge, 2014), 23–29.

42. Marcuse, *Eros and Civilization*, xxv.

43. Marcuse, *An Essay on Liberation*, 49.

44. Michael Hardt and Antonio Negri, *Empire* (Cambridge, MA: Harvard University Press, 2000), 294.

9

Engaging Contemporary Ideology with Mario Perniola, Slavoj Žižek, and Robert Pfaller

Erik M. Vogt

Mario Perniola's intervention into the history of Western philosophy occurs in the form of an aesthetic thinking that is not reducible to an aesthetic conception of art, but that is rather tasked with surveying the collective means by which our sensible world has been construed, partitioned, distributed, and challenged. In other words, his aesthetic thinking analyzes the distribution of collective forms structuring contemporary sentient experience and defines it as "sensology." Sensology refers to a social configuration of sensibility marked by extreme reification that has not only reduced feeling to something already-felt, but has also, together with mass communication, produced a world that might no longer be recognizable in terms of a symbolic order. In order to retrieve the possibility of a public-symbolic order, Perniola suggests that the aesthetic conception of the symbolic character of sentient experience may have to take recourse to the ritual dimensions of sentient experience. This appeal to the ritual dimensions of feeling reveals some surprising affinities to the concept of interpassivity introduced by Slavoj Žižek and further elaborated by Robert Pfaller.

The Enigma of Sensological Society

According to Perniola, the relation between contemporary thinking and contemporary society is that of a profound complicity, of "essential reciprocal belonging,"[1] that he renders into the following image: "Thinkers take to society like ducks to water. And this is so from the moment that philosophy ceases to be metaphysical and boldly declares for historical reality, phenomena, things, or rather from the moment that philosophy is itself a historical reality, a phenomenon, a thing" (*E* 40–41). More precisely, Perniola's account of contemporary thinking does not simply present a type of thinking that would be characterized or mediated abstractly by history, but rather conceives of contemporary thinking in terms of a "philosophy of the present and of presence" (*E* 41) corresponding to a social reality "that no longer has any recollections, but memories that are constantly available, that has no hopes, but only consolations: its emotional tonality is characterized by a trustful and active calm, shot through with sudden flashes and raptures" (*E* 41). The focus of this "philosophy of the present and of presence" is, however, not only on the present and on that which is present, but it also attempts to meditate "on the contemporary social and cultural situation," thereby accepting modernity's inheritance in that "modernity, over the two centuries and through the scientific, economic and political revolutions, has maintained [the link] between philosophy and society and between knowledge and power: the relationship between thought and reality that the Enlightenment, idealism and Marxism have embodied must not be broken" (*E* 43).

Although Perniola insists that the philosophy of the present and of presence represents an heir to modernity, it is at the same time characterized by a collapse of the traditional linear and/or dialectical temporal framework constitutive of modernity: a collapse that has not only rendered the social and cultural present "enigmatic," but also requires, in turn, the elaboration of enigmatic philosophy and thought. The relation of mutual belonging between enigmatic reality and enigmatic thought furthermore indicates that the present must no longer be understood as the object of thought, but rather as its subject. One of the consequences of this shift regarding the status of the present for philosophy consists in the need to reconceptualize the task of the philosopher. For the philosopher must become "someone who turns him- or herself into nothing in order to listen to the present and all its enigmas" and must transform him- or herself into an "intermediary, a transit zone, a gateway for phenomena that because they present themselves in an unexpected and unpredictable way, surprise, disturb and astonish" (*E* 43). Thus, "a philosophy of the enigma exists because, in the first place, socio-historical reality is enigmatic and, secondly, because the contemporary philosopher . . . has, when faced with history, become meek and modest" (*E* 43–44).

How does Perniola explain the matrix of the contemporary society of enigma? He claims that, formally speaking, the enigmatic matrix is best rendered as "the coincidence of antagonists, the concatenation of opposites, the contact of things that are divergent, and even the antagonism of things that coincide, the opposition of the concatenated, and the divergence of things that are in contact with one another" (*E* 18). For this reason, it "is capable of simultaneous explanation of many different registers of meaning, all of which are equally valid, and it is thus able to open up an intermediate space that is not necessarily bound to be filled" (*E* 10). Correspondingly, enigmatic thinking presents a mode of thinking that not only joins "intellectual, emotional and practical life in a single manner of being wakeful" (*E* 18), but it also entails "a transit, a process that travels from same to same" in such a manner that the "points of departure and arrival are at once identical and radically different" (*E* 12). Consequently, enigmatic thinking must no longer be grasped as activity originating, or issuing forth, from some self-identical subject, but rather as a complex process of simultaneous mediation and indeterminacy; that is, as a thinking of differences in the transit from same to same that, furthermore, is opposed to "banality" whose "pre-eminent site" is "the society of integrated spectacle, with its processes of reduction, standardization and leveling" (*E* 12). Perniola explains, "The principal instrument that it uses is de-historicization, the removal of things from the flow of historical becoming and of incessant change and their immobilization on a kind of stupefying idiocy that renders any questioning superfluous" (*E* 12).

But precisely what kind of experience lies at the heart of contemporary enigmatic society? According to Perniola, it is a "process of reciprocal osmosis between man and things, with the result that the former has become similar to the latter, while the latter have assumed increasingly human characteristics" (*E* 44). Thus, Perniola points to an inversion in the relation between humans and things, between the organic and the inorganic world. This inversion has not only affected knowledge, belief, and action, but above all "feeling [*sentire*] across the entire range of meanings of that term, from sensibility to emotivity, from listening to affectivity" (*E* 45). He continues: "On the one hand, things are now able to feel in our stead; on the other, we are being subjected to a process of reification more radical and profound than anything we have known in the past, for it strikes at the most immediate and intimate aspect of existence" (*E* 45). This radical and profound experience of reification marks a shift with regard to sensibility in that the latter is no longer accountable in terms of some interior experience of the (modern) subject, but rather must be grasped in its utter externality and passivity. Moreover, this delegation of sensibility from the human to things indicates that the traditional distinction between organic and inorganic existence has collapsed, and that the human being has become a "thing that feels" (*E* 29). In short, contemporary enigmatic sociohistorical reality—its "Egyptian" dimension—could be understood as the ultimate manifestation of the process of alienation described by Marx. However, what renders this alienation most profound is not only the fact that alienation has encroached upon feeling, that is, "the whole field of sensibility and emotion" (*E* 29), but that it has even led to the establishment of a "sensory horizon that is both collective and socialized" (*E* 28).

Perniola locates the emergence of this collective and socialized sensory horizon in the context of the video and audio culture characterizing the late 1960s and specifies that, due to this alienating sensory horizon, feeling is encountered as something already-felt, which figures as "the a-priori formal condition of post-1968 video and audio experience" (*E* 28). The already-felt as a priori formal condition of sentient experience functions at the same time as the new site of contemporary transsubjective and impersonal power. This amalgamation of structures of power and feeling has transformed objects, individuals, and events into figures of the already-felt taking possession of humans with its already determined sensorial, emotional, and even spiritual totality.[2] Furthermore, while that which was to be felt previously could either be felt or not, the already-felt can only be "caulked" or "traced," and it represents a significant historical turn that seems to release the human being from both feeling and nonfeeling, "from sensibility of non-sensibility, from effort, exertion, responsibility, attentiveness, decision, participation" (*DS* 4). That is to say: "Feeling has assumed a dimension that is to be caulked in an anonymous, impersonal, and socialized manner" (*DS* 4–5).

Perniola defines the quasi-transcendental-schematic status of the already-felt as "sensology" (*DS* 5). Indeed, the term "sensology" seems to entertain analogies with the term "ideology" insofar as ideology could be conceived in terms of an "already-thought." In this respect, sensology is constituted after the traditional pattern of ideology, and it is similarly addressed to all like an immediate imperative to caulk that which everybody has already tried and approved. However, while ideology has usually been associated with false consciousness that, once grasped in its illusory nature, could still hold the promise of making us aware of the actual, true situation, sensology is characterized by a tendency toward identification with a "false feeling" that can no longer be criticized as false because "it no longer claims to be the bearer of some truth. It constitutes itself as sheer reality of the already-felt" (*DS* 6). Moreover, sensology does not only exhibit a family resemblance to ideology, but also to bureaucracy defined as the "already-done," that is, as totality of prefabricated patterns of behavior "as efficient as political activities and as irrevocable as rituals" (*DS* 7). More precisely, the already-felt can be understood as a kind of "mediacracy" designating not only the transition of the mediating activity of thought to feeling and the transfer of the rule of feeling, sensibility, and affectivity from human beings to impersonal devices and apparatuses, but also a "continuous process of negotiation and action in form of opinion polls and audience ratings" (*DS* 8–9). Perniola comments: "These polls and ratings are the already-felt, the already-tasted anticipating, rushing ahead and downright replacing facts" (*DS* 9). In addition to mediacracy, sensology finally also enters into a constellation with "specularism" (*DS* 10). Reiterating his earlier assertion that today's intimate experiences have to be grasped as already-felt experiences, Perniola points to an omnipresent specular structure that does not only underlie already preformed experiences, but also substantially differs from all merely imitative and conformist strategies aimed at adapting oneself to either one's environment or the expectation of others by opening up the possibility of sensing oneself as a site in which "the exterior is mirrored" and sentient experience is transposed "into what we let mirror, touch, and echo," while a "surrogate and subsequent feeling" would pass into our possession "as reflection, reworking and echo of the first one" (*DS* 11). In light of this constellation of sensology, mediacracy, and specularism conditioning the impossibility/possibility of sentient experience today, Perniola observes not only the current subordination of thinking and acting under feeling, but also the presence of a radically externalized, delegated, independent, social, and collective (structure of) feeling that, moreover, can no longer be transmitted but merely be caulked or reflected back. Contemporary sociohistorical reality has thus taken on the guise of an integrated totality that contains not only all possible already-felt sensibilities and emotions that, ultimately, can merely be accepted and repeated, but also the figure of the "thing-man," a result of an unheard-of transformation of the relation of humans to the inorganic world (*DS* 18).

Sensological Styles

In order to render intelligible the figure of the thing-man, Perniola brilliantly elaborates a comprehensive phenomenology of the multiple contemporary styles, cultures, and behaviors sharing the condition of the already-felt, thereby traversing not only culture, but also politics, economics, aesthetics, and art. Initially, he distinguishes between "warm" types of figures of the already-felt—such as the feeling of counterculture and of fundamentalism— and "cold" types of figures of the already-felt that include neocynicism and performativity (*DS* 20–21). Although these styles of feeling have issued forth under different conditions and circumstances—counterculture emerged in a primarily political context and fundamentalism in a religious context, whereas neocynicism appeared in a moral context and performativity in a technological context—Perniola insists nonetheless that not only do these different sentient styles share family resemblances and, moreover, belong to the same time frame, which allows them to tendentially pass into each other, but that they are also constitutive of the very form of aesthetic socialization to be designated as sensology. In short, these figures of the contemporary already-felt point to an experience that, "in the exchange with all historical manifestations of the already-felt, wants to assume the role of their general equivalent" (*DS* 24). In other words, the figures or styles of the already-felt have the status of commodities. As such, they are parts of a "world market of feeling" that is precisely characterized by "the emancipation from each and every internal dimension or from the unrepeatable singularity of individual experience: this market can offer everything, but only in the form of the already-felt" (*DS* 25).

However, counterculture, fundamentalism, neocynicism, and performativity do not exhaust the current possibilities of figures of the already-felt; rather, the cultural and media phenomena of political correctness and neo-Faustianism,[3] as well as the more specifically aesthetic and artistic phenomena of neoclassicism and primitivism are equally dependent on sensology (D 116). To begin with, neo-Faustianism is characterized by a will to transgress traditional limits by means of technological inventions or through extraordinary and extreme physical, intellectual, or psychic performances, ranging from cyberpunk and science fiction to the para-athletic world of extreme performances and "no limits" allowing even for the risk of self-destruction (D 22). The neo-Faustian attitude is marked by a claim to absolute difference from one's opponent and by the concomitant sentiment of triumphalism at all costs. Political correctness, on the other hand, articulates its claim to absolute difference and denial of equality by assuming victimhood in a paradoxical fashion; that is, political correctness employs the strategy of complaint in order to succeed by claiming one's own "difference" as one consisting in suffering. Consequently, political correctness not only lacks any genuine political and emancipatory dimension, but it is also caught in a kind of "melancholic war" that recodes weakness as force and transforms complaint into a weapon (D 23).

Although political correctness and neo-Faustianism appear to be in utter opposition to each other, they should be understood in terms of their speculative identity—a speculative identity consisting in their respective attitudes of violence and intolerance.[4] The same can be said about the two figures of the already-felt that Perniola identifies in the aesthetic and artistic realms: neoclassicism and primitivism. While neoclassicism subscribes to a solemn ideal of beauty and decrees the imitation of prescriptions that supposedly possess metaphysical validity, primitivism decrees forms that allegedly express elementary, simple but nonetheless profound vital energies shared by all human beings (D 117). Once again, Perniola attempts to unearth the very forms of aggression and intolerance that are constitutive of neoclassicism and primitivism. The aggression of neoclassicism consists in its will to universally impose its supposedly trans-historical notion of beauty. The violent character of primitivism reveals itself in its ethnocentric insistence on the reproduction of only those forms that render some authentic artistic activity that must itself be rooted in, and expressive of, some profound lived experience (D 117). What is more, both neoclassicism and primitivism are to be deciphered as modes of misrecognition concerning their respective reference worlds. That is to say: Neoclassicism misrecognizes the ancient worlds by ascribing to them the metaphysical values of "noble simplicity, pacific greatness, and harmonious symmetry" (D 118); primitivism, on the other hand, renders primary cultures in the deceptive images of "simplicity, interiority and affective over-excitation" (D 118). Perniola concludes that "neoclassicism and primitivism are artificial and deceptive constructions" not only presenting obstacles for the analysis of the ancient world and of primary cultures, but also preventing the recognition of the affinities and the differences that are operative between them and our own present (D 118).

Finally, the "postmodern movement" and the "neo-ethnic movement" constitute problematic "updated" versions of neoclassicism and primitivism that have further expanded the reach of sensology. The postmodern and the neoethnic seem, again, opposed to each other with regard to the ways in which they address the question of identity. While the postmodern delights in the dissolution of all (cultural) identities and advocates the playful approach to all images of identity, the neoethnic proclaims the necessity of returning to uniform and homogeneous communal cultural identities that, moreover, have to be reclaimed in an identitarian fashion. Paradoxically, their seeming opposition terminates once more in their identity or, at least, confluence for both obtain the same effect, that is, "the flattening and assimilation of all cultural manifestations in one and the same register" (*D* 125). Ultimately, the postmodern and the neoethnic represent but two sides of the same coin: "The postmodern and the neo-ethnic have progressed on opposite paths toward a simplification and banalization of private and collective life; both are solidly united in rigidifying the climate of spectacular neo-obscurantism in which we are immersed" (*D* 126).

But these cultures and behaviors of the already-felt still fail to fully account for the repertoire of sensology. Rather, the more recent return to realism, especially in the guises of "extreme realism" and "psychotic realism" (in art), has to be grasped as one of the latest sensological styles.[5] Extreme realism represents a type of contemporary (artistic) sensibility that "has taken shape as a veritable irruption of the real in the rarefied and highly symbolic world of art" (AS 3). Its typical focus lies "on the most violent and raw aspects of reality," and it is often fixated on the themes of death and sex (AS 4). Moreover, it attempts to expose raw and violent events without (almost) any recourse to symbolic mediation, thereby eliciting an experience "where repulsion and attraction, fear and desire, pain and pleasure, refusal and complicity are mixed and mingled" (AS 4). The encounter with this real devoid of any theoretical and symbolic mediation leads not only to a mortification of the existent, but also generates at the same time "the ambivalent and ambiguous experience of disgust" that, elevated to the central category of extreme realism, betrays a problematic proximity to vitalism (AS 6, 8).

What is more, this extreme realism of much contemporary art can even exhibit a properly psychotic dimension that is not only indicative of the collapse of any structure of mediation between art and the real, but also often accompanied by a shift toward bodies "engaged in dangerous experiments, directed toward the discovery of perception and feeling" (AS 23). Examples of extreme body art can be found in movies and videos that have brought "the poetics of reproduction of a real phenomenon caught in the moment in which it occurs . . . to its extreme consequences" (AS 23). But the very cinematic versions of psychotic realism also expose the latter's limitations. Perniola explains: "In the first place, it is difficult to consider the *business* of brute reproduction of the crudest realities (sex, extreme violence, death) a manifestation of difference. One can hardly deny that *gore, splatter, trash* constitute a banal version of experiences that are actually known by only a few" (AS 23); on the other hand, they also no longer provide "any guarantee that what we are witnessing is true. In fact, the possibility exists of manipulating any visual document electronically. Thus, the reality effect that constituted the main cause of excitement of this type of product is lacking" (AS 23). The most problematic aspect of psychotic realism consists, however, in its idolization of abjection; for abjection must be seen not only as symptom of the inability to think difference, but even of some "absolute hostility toward the world and the human body considered as evil. In other words, feeling the difference cannot mean insisting on the most crude and repellent facts" (AS 24). Ultimately, psychotic realism as experience of abjection "restore[s] indirectly precisely what the thinking of difference is fighting against. If the human being is just garbage, this means that the only one to shine is the transcendental" (AS 24)!

Communication as the Reverse and Privatistic Side of Sensological Society

The extreme realism of some contemporary art can, however, not be fully captured by the negative categories of disgust and abjection. Rather, one can identify another trend in extreme realism and its attempt to completely dissolve art in living reality by rendering art indistinguishable from fashion, information, and mass communication. In this case, art does not only lose its specificity, but it also adopts the primacy of the (vitalistic) imaginary over the symbolic and the real that is characteristic of fashion, information, and mass communication and deprives art, having been reduced to a mere communicative operation, of any possibility of resistance. What is more, this functional version of extreme realism and its mimicry of mass communication point to certain crucial questions regarding the precise relation between sensology and communication. Is communication to be subsumed under sensology? Is it to be grasped as a type of ideology analogous to sensology? Or does communication constitute a rather "different phenomenon that cannot be grasped as a definite and relatively fixed message, as a . . . relatively stable mode of feeling"?[6]

Communication is characterized, first, by its sheer ubiquity in the contemporary world; it has not only permeated art, culture, and education, but also science and politics. Perniola describes its omnipresence in the following manner: "It is the magic wand that transforms weak factors such as incoherence, revocation, and chaos into proofs of strength and it replaces education and instruction with *edutainment*, politics and information with *infotainment*, and art and culture with *entertainment*" (CC 5–6). Moreover, it pretends to address its audience in an immediate and direct manner and gives itself a democratic veneer that is best rendered as *"democratainment"* (CC 6). In contrast to sensological identities still granting a certain degree of consistency and certainty, communication operates in such a way that it both evokes oppositions, antagonisms, and conflicts and simultaneously dissolves these very oppositions, antagonisms, and conflicts, thereby eluding any identification and definition. It entails a kind to triumphalism that, in its very violence, exhibits an affinity with the culture of performance and its constant generation of *highs* and addictive experiences (CC 14–15).[7] What is more, the type of violence constitutive both of communication and the culture of performance is no longer that of functional violence inscribed into the continuum of means and ends; rather, it pursues the sole purpose of "inserting the individual into the image of the world. This violent action elevates . . . the individual onto the public scene and attempts to keep her/

him there as long as possible" (CC 15–16), thereby subjecting the public to the private.

Although communication represents a contemporary phenomenon, it must not be seen as a representative of what is often called "new economy." While in the "new economy" the source for the creation of value occurs via mediation, through the paradigms of "network, conjunction, and transit" articulating differences, communication constitutes a reactionary force, a remainder of the "old economy," and attempts to submerge everything in immediacy, spontaneity, and instantaneity (CC 23–24). In short, it transports a "totalitarian" vitalism that does not register any differences, lacks the experience of antagonism, and is therefore incapable of thinking and feeling antagonism and difference. In other words, communication is the captive of imaginary fixations and, more precisely, the psychotic effect of the foreclosure of the symbolic realm (CC 34). This fact may also explain the catastrophe of meaning occurring in communication, for the communicative universe presents itself as inaccessible, impenetrable, and non-decipherable self-enclosed totality, and it is resistant to a "dialectical or post-dialectical mobilization" (CC 35).

Finally, although contemporary sensology and communication seem to be largely accounted for by Perniola with reference to recently emerged cultural, artistic, sociohistorical, and political phenomena, he nonetheless insists that the ultimate roots of sensology (and even communication) are to be sought in ancient Greek metaphysics and its claim regarding the primacy of "action over potentiality, action over passion, form over matter, being over nature, soul over body, intellectual faculties over affective faculties" (*DS* 81–82). That is to say, "Emotional life is conceived as state of inactivity and subordination under intellectual, active and insensible life" (CC 82). In other words, (ancient Greek) metaphysics accords an ontological minority status to inactivity and this decision implies a project aimed at the subjugation of sentient and affective experience that, moreover, is perceived as "pathological, feminine, servile" (CC 82). Consequently, sensology must be understood as full realization of metaphysical activism because metaphysical insensibility has become social reality in the figure of the already-felt; that is, it has become the sole prescribed access to social reality: "The spectrality of the one who has been able to make of himself living money and the specularity of the one who has become thing-man are both aspects of the same exclusion of feeling that the metaphysical project has pursued for millennia" (CC 82). However, this metaphysical abolition of the sentient experience sounded at the same time the demise of metaphysics, for "the destruction of feeling went hand in hand with the destruction of the autonomous intellectual activity in which metaphysics sees the primordial ground for all movement" (CC 82–83).

How is one, then, to engage the contemporary "ideologies" of sensology and communication, especially when one considers that sensology and communication share, with metaphysics (in demise), a striving for totality? What could constitute possible exit routes from sensology and communication? In the face of their quasitotalitarian character, would one not have to surmise that the only possible exit routes are either disalienation in humanist terms or some flight into foreign, non-Western styles of experience? As to the possibility of non-Western alternatives, Perniola notices that those sentient experiences can become forms of resistance to sensology and communication only if they are inscribed into the history of Western feeling and sensibility; otherwise, they would remain mere ineffective enclaves. Against humanist strategies of disalienation that insist on the task of reappropriating experiences of alienation and reification for the sake of reestablishing the integrity of the subject, he suggests "homoeopathic remedies to alienation which, as it were, would treat the wound by means of the weapon that caused it" (E 30). Instead of reclaiming the possibility of a return to subjective interiority and authenticity, he maintains that "the battle therefore has to be waged at the level of the external" (E 30). In other words, invocations of forms of subjective feeling do not present genuine alternatives because they belong not only essentially to the past epoch of bourgeois society, but they also necessarily miss the very externality and reification constitutive of the impersonal, postsubjective feeling of current capitalist sensology.

On the other hand, contemporary culture contains an arsenal of counterstrategies subverting or displacing the grip of sensology. For instance, both "new apathy," "whose fundamental tonality consist in a deliberate cult of indifference," and "new paganism," "whose tonality consists in a deliberate cult of possession" (E 47), present promising avenues of displacement in that they both effect a certain devitalization of images of the human body. Regarding the phenomenon of the "look," Perniola comments: "Through the look an Egyptian effect is achieved: an image is turned into a thing. This annuls not only nudity, but also clothing. . . . The look teaches us to see the human body not as that vitalistic *Leib* . . . but as a *Körper*, similar to a uniform" (E 51).[8] Although the resurgence of "paganism" is certainly not linked to apathy, but rather to different emotional tonalities such as "possession, delirium and trance" (E 52), these emotional tonalities should not be misrecognized as vitalistic expressions. On the contrary, they have to be seen "in terms of the problem of becoming a thing. . . . The premiss of possession is the dispossession, the transformation of the self into nothingness in order to provide a corporeal receptacle for something arriving from outside" (E 53). Ultimately, the reemergence of paganism and polytheism manifested in these contemporary ecstatic states represents not only "the response to the need for a practical philosophy capable of escaping from the universal standardization that Western culture seeks to impose" (*E* 55) but, even more, a consequence "of the extreme ambiguity, indeterminacy and multiple meaning of every event, fact or thing" (*E* 57).[9]

"Neoancient" sensibility presents another form of sensibility setting itself apart from both sensological neoclassicism and sensological primitivism in that it neither simplistically reduces the ancient worlds to a mere foundational origin of the modern world, nor generates fantasies that identify non-European cultures with some originary and primordial vitality (*D* 118). The centrality of the haptic sense and of rhythm in neoancient sensibility accounts, moreover, for the fact that it might be capable of freeing artworks from aesthetic-contemplative and vitalistic-empathetic frameworks of interpretation (*D* 124).[10] Perniola sees the distinctive feature of neoancient sensibility in its emphasis on "the links, connections and fetters binding [artworks] to their environment and context" (*D* 124). The underlying idea of neoancient sensibility amounts to the recognition that "the things of the world are interconnected and that there is no void between them. . . . What is important in this idea of the world is . . . the monistic idea of reality that is conceived of as coherent, compact, and continuous and . . . the fact that this idea does not exclude the reception and admixture of bodies" (*D* 124). In other words, neoancient sensibility maintains not an immobile monism, but rather a monism "permeated by a continuous movement devoid of leaps and ruptures," and its rhythm represents "a fluid form, a transit, a transition without leaps" (*D* 124). In contrast to both the postmodern update of neoclassicism and the neo-ethnic update of primitivism, neoancient sensibility not only stresses moments of difference in ancient Western cultures, it also revokes the metaphysical distinction between thinking and feeling; that is, it grasps thinking and feeling in their inseparability. What is more, it seeks affinities and correspondences in other, non-Western cultures and civilizations, and its approach is characterized by the capacity for astonishment, "both about itself and the other," which thereby makes it able to recognize "the other and distant" (*D* 127). Ultimately, neoancient sensibility practices neither closure characteristic of the neoethnic nor the "uncritical and apologetic acceptance of foreign cultures . . . the fanatical glorification of Oriental religions" (*D* 127).

Neoancient sensibility can thus be grasped as heir to those moments in ancient (Greek and Roman) philosophy that already suggested an alternative conception of the relationship between feeling and thinking. Perniola demonstrates that there existed semantic fields in ancient philosophy that did not separate sensibility and emotionality from thinking and acting. For instance, *aísthēsis* comprises "both perception and intelligence," whereas *ménos* comprises both "affective fervor and the principle of the will to act" (*DS* 85). Ultimately, Perniola's unearthing of alternative forms of presubjective feeling receives its most condensed form in the syntagm "*farsi sentire* (making/letting oneself be felt/heard)"—a syntagm that unites in itself "the operative, receptive, and reflexive dimension" (*DS* 86), and that allows for the possibility of sketching a different conception of feeling/thinking. For it can be shown that, one the one hand, feeling implies "a wanting-to-feel: sensibility, affectivity, emotionality are not comparable to some inactive matter that would be shaped by some ideal and immaterial form. They are born from a decision, they consolidate through praxis, they call for working on oneself, for an ascesis in the literal and etymological sense of the term that means precisely exercise" (*DS* 86). If, therefore, the affective dimension already implies an intellectual operation, an affective reception resides, in turn, in the intellectual dimension:[11] "Thinking means to receive that which comes from the outside; it means to admit, to host what presents itself as different and enigmatic" (*DS* 87). Moreover, "to make oneself feel means to offer oneself so that something in us can find a possibility of being-in-the-world. In this way, we posit ourselves as the conditions of manifesting that which is outside, impersonal, trans-individual. It is not that we as subjects feel something, but rather that we offer ourselves to a feeling that is located elsewhere" (*DS* 87). To make oneself feel is thus the very condition of experiencing difference that manifests itself as/in the world, as/in the movement of things, as/in history. That difference not only makes palpable that neither the world nor history can be reduced to human projects and the human will, but also sensing and feeling difference becomes possible only if subjectivity is submitted to a kind of *epoché* bringing about an indifference toward the identity of subjectivity: an indifference that is, at the same time, a transit receptive to that which comes from the outside.

"Feeling the difference" (*AS* 14)! This exhortation encapsulates Perniola's historical anthropology of feeling that is directed against sensology and its different styles of the already-felt. He seeks to articulate a notion of feeling that can no longer be subsumed under the metaphysics of the subject and modern aesthetic thought with its "tendency toward ideals of harmony, regularity, and organic unity" (*AS* 14). It is equally opposed to a conception of aesthetics as *Vorschein* of reconciliation, "of peace to come, of an irenic moment when suffering and struggle are, if not definitively eliminated, at least temporarily suspended" (*AS* 14). Finally, it also remains suspicious of an aesthetics of the sublime that often presents the sublime as irruption, as traumatic or miraculous event. Moreover, aesthetics can constitute a strong alternative even to communication, but only if some of its central concepts are submitted to deconstructive operations that introduce a distance between them and the privatizing tendency of communicative society.

Ritual Feeling and the Interpassive Retrieval of the Symbolic Realm

It is, above all, disinterestedness—a central category of aesthetics since the eighteenth century—that must be detached from its traditional ideological interpretation in terms of mere public ineffectiveness. For a genealogical account of the notion of disinterestedness reveals that disinterested actions constituted the public rule in traditional societies and that they were part of a "gift-based economy" (CC 71). More important, as Pierre Bourdieu has shown, aesthetic disinterestedness itself was never completely without any public interest and it could therefore be seen as a type of symbolic economy that is not only equipped "with its own autonomous rationality," but also different from capitalist economy (CC 72). This economy of symbolic goods is, according to Bourdieu, not only found in traditional societies, but also in the "world of bureaucracy, of the educated profession, of research, and of teaching" (CC 73). In other words, "'interested disinterestedness,' whose most radical formulation is aesthetics, would be the dispositif on which the modern public world is constructed" (CC 73). That is, the deconstruction of aesthetics in terms of "interested disinterestedness" not only reveals aesthetics as *the* matrix of symbolic economy, but it also suggests that the different realms of science, morality, education, economy (that is, the "new economy" that is distinguished by its post-industrial and cultural-capitalist status), and politics should be treated as significant components of this alternative symbolic economy.

If aesthetics is to restore the symbolic order against imaginary communication, it has to oppose the communicative society of constant "*spin*" (CC 108). It has already been mentioned that communicative society is not only marked by systematic practices of disinformation and messaging, but that it also does not function according to the rules of traditional ideology because it no longer interpellates its individuals into subjects with stable identities, but rather with merely instantaneous identities subject to permanent revision and self-fashioning according to the imperatives of communicative society. That is, it dissolves every kind of certainty and transforms its audience into a "kind of *tabula rasa* that is extremely sensitive and receptive but incapable of keeping its inscriptions beyond the instant of reception and transmission" (CC 108). If the audience is to be released from its imprisonment in the here and now, from transmitting and receiving without memory and unconscious, aesthetics has to side with "*habitus*, forms, rituals that, in their exteriority, continue to exist as something fixed and accepted, even if their meaning has been lost or has lapsed into the unconscious or has never existed in the first place" (CC 109). Perniola insists that the possibility of the symbolic public realm is founded on these "dimensions that represent an inorganic corporeality" (CC 109). In short, one has to protect these inorganic public forms and ritual behaviors from the privatizing, expressionist prejudice constitutive of communicative society.

Against the false communicative claim that ritual behaviors can ultimately be reduced to mere expressions of subjective emotions, it has to be asserted that they constitute something like a "medium forming individual subjectivities" (CC 111). By insisting that the ritual is simultaneously an action, a thinking, and a feeling, Perniola provides a different interpretation of rituals. That is to say, contrary to the mythological appropriation of rituals and behaviors characteristic of communicative society, one has to reassert "the autonomy of modes of behavior, of gestures, and of rituals with respect to beliefs, explanations, myths."[12] In short, ritual experience is not only a suspension of purposeful activities and a tarrying with inorganic corporeality, but its iterative structure also deactivates the opposition between tradition and innovation generating the same as difference in repetition. Ultimately, only rituals "with their relative opacity and inexpressiveness can defy the obscure flow of communication" (CC 111) and open up a symbolic space for modes of feelings and behaviors that are no longer overwritten by the psychosis of intimate subjectivity.

Perniola's basic thesis, according to which the contemporary world is fundamentally structured by the delegation of feeling from humans to things, entertains a profound affinity to the conception of interpassivity that was first introduced by Slavoj Žižek and elaborated further by Robert Pfaller.[13] Taking as his point of departure Jacques Lacan's famous account of the chorus in ancient Greek tragedy, according to which the chorus "can take over from us and experience for us our innermost and most spontaneous feelings and attitudes, inclusive of crying and laughing" (HRL 22–23), Žižek mentions phenomena such as the "so-called 'weepers' (women hired to cry at funerals)," the Tibetan prayer wheel, "canned laughter" accompanying TV sitcoms, and the "compulsive recording" of movies by "VCR aficionados" (HRL 23–24), in order to illustrate that the symbolic order (also) functions as an interpassive medium by means of which "the object itself takes from me, deprives me of, my own passive reaction of satisfaction (or mourning or laughter), so that it is the object itself which 'enjoys the show' instead of me" (PF 112). Thus, interpassivity clearly demonstrates that feelings and enjoyment can be delegated on to something else. What is more, contemporary society is permeated by a multiplicity of interpassive media ranging from cultural-capitalist commodities serving as representative lifestyle props that must no longer be practically lived, to literature and artworks. Commenting on the tendency toward self-referentiality that has characterized (meta-)literature since the second half of the nineteenth century, Perniola interprets this transformation of "poems and novels into self-referential things" as acquiring "a kind of autonomous sensibility with respect to the writer and the reader," that is, as a "kind of sentient book which receives and makes room for all languages, enters into them and bends them by making them reflect themselves" (SI 124; 126).[14] Pfaller, on the other hand, repeatedly points to artworks that, as interpassive media, relieve the observer or spectator of any receptive or consumptive effort (AI 30); in short, they are bearers of delegated reception, consumption, or enjoyment.

It is interesting that Pfaller claims that interpassivity as externalization of supposedly intimate feelings, as surrender of emotions and affects to interpassive media, contains a liberating potential that becomes visible once one has understood that interpassivity consists of ritual actions. That is to say: "The interpassive person and her medium are connected . . . through a symbolic representation. The interpassive person delegates her enjoyment to a medium by ritually prompting this medium to offer a figurative, symbolic representation of consumption" (AI 150–151). What is more, this interpassive delegation is grounded in an "*anonymous illusion,*" an "*illusion without subject,*" which must be seen as "objective" (AI 154, 155). This anonymous illusion that allows us not only *not to enjoy or feel*, but also *not to believe*, is generated by the exercise of rituals.[15] Additionally, "interpassivity does not only rest on rituals, but, in turn, the ritual itself is based on interpassivity" (AI 156). Pfaller, like Perniola, affirms therefore the possibility of "rituals without myth" because ritual as objective belief "emerges historically before any subjective disposition ('myth')" (AI 161). That is, he insists that the interpassive dimension of rituals not only makes it clear that rituals precede subjectivation, but that they also potentially liberate the individual from subjectivation. In other words, interpassivity can be grasped as "defense against interpellation; by fleeing their enjoyment, these individuals attempt to elude the very ideological interpellation contained in enjoyment" (AI 181). Moreover, its resistance to the ubiquitous social imperative of constant subjectivation evoked by the current ideology of hyperproductivity, hyperactivity, participation, and performativity is equally directed against the communicative imperative and its tendency to subordinate the public realm under private interests, to destroy the public realm of appearances through enforced processes of intimization. Against communication's disenchantment of the world, by opening up the possibility of delight in the very distance from the current hegemony of intimate subjectivation, interpassivity and anonymous, impersonal feeling could even be understood as practices of "civil disobedience" (*AI* 257) that are attempting, moreover, to reenchant the world in its objective materiality by insisting on a culture of public appearance that allows for "exchange, confrontation, and productive dissensus" (*AI* 295). It is in this very context that, more recently, Perniola has attempted to elaborate a reinterpretation of "catholic feeling" as a worldly feeling that, with its different relation to exteriority, things, and the world, presents an experience that contains the potential for universalization.[16] That is, catholic feeling contains a mode of universality or universalization that is no longer grounded in some rigid identity, but rather in a common world that, as difference, is not the product of subjective will and thus cannot be reduced to subjectivity or to a collective of subjectivities. This common world is one of inorganic corporeality and thus cannot be rendered as idea, notion, thought, or meaning (*DSC* 62). Rather, it is a world that, precisely because it is without any ground or reason, remains constitutively unpredictable and provokes astonishment and amazement (*DSC* 17).

The political import of both interpassivity and anonymous, impersonal feeling consists in their respective pleas for the public realm understood as an utterly nonpsychological symbolic order. Both subscribe to a culture of appearance that is opposed to the neoliberal communicative culture of privatized, individualized sentiment.[17] They also encourage aesthetic-cultural attitudes marked by distance toward sensology, as well as toward communicative ascriptions and impositions. While they certainly do not purport to be ideology critiques of cultural capitalism but rather accept that the latter presently constitutes something like an unsurpassable horizon, they nonetheless engage in the renunciation of the very styles of subjectivation and self-subjectivation that sensology and communication continue to prescribe violently in order to perpetuate a totalitarian world of immediacy, of "authentic" individualist expressivity and enjoyment, impervious to thinking or feeling differently.

Notes

1. Mario Perniola, *Enigmas: The Egyptian Moment in Society and Art*, trans. Christopher Woodall (London, New York: Verso, 1995), 40; hereafter referred to as E.

2. Mario Perniola, *Del sentire* (Turin: Einaudi, 2002), 4; hereafter referred to as DS (all translations from the Italian are mine).

3. Mario Perniola, *Disgusti. Le nuovo tendenze estetiche* (Ancona-Milan: Costa & Nolan, 1999), 2; hereafter referred to as D.

4. Their difference is ultimately only a minor one. Whereas neo-Faustianism openly affirms violence and intolerance, political correctness does so in the form of

disavowal. For a more detailed account, see Erik Vogt, "Vrnitev Realnega v popularno kulturo in (abjektno) umetnost," trans. M. Puncer, *Borec* 57 (2005): 276–293.

5. Mario Perniola, *Art and Its Shadow*, trans. Massimo Verdicchio, with a foreword by Hugh J. Silverman (New York, London: Continuum, 2004), 5, 21; hereafter referred to as.

6. Mario Perniola, *Contro la comunicazione* (Turin: Einaudi, 2004), 8; hereafter referred to as CC.

7. In another text, Perniola specifies the addictive qualities of communication in terms of the phenomena of miracles and traumas; see Mario Perniola, "Impossible, Yet Real!," trans. Giulia Borghese, *Cultura. International Journal of Philosophy of Culture and Axiology* 8, 1 (2011): 187–212. Communication represents a new regime of historicity that is characterized by the end of action. That is, communication produces real effects without belonging to the category of historical actions (195). Furthermore, communication is a fixation on events and the eventful; the two modalities of the event recognized by communication are miracles and traumas, although there is ultimately not only an alternation between miracles and traumas, but even an equivalence (195). In addition to discrediting action, communication also dissolves facts into news, reduces knowledge to mere opinion, and gives hegemony to the present in terms of immediacy and simultaneity (208–209).

8. In Mario Perniola, *Sex Appeal of the Inorganic*, trans. Massimo Verdicchio (New York-London: Continuum 2004), hereafter referred to as SI, Perniola returns to the phenomenon of the "look" and renders it in more ambiguous terms. While he continues to maintain that the look represents the emancipation both from "the conformism of *haute couture* and from the subjectivity of anti-fashion," it still may remain subject to "an ethico-aesthetic ideal of the human figure" (SI 46, 47). At the same time, the look can also be understood as manifestation of reification in its full autonomy, "without being obliged to imitate the natural models of beauty, to make the old look young, to smooth away wrinkles from worn faces, and to redesign figures made heavy by cellulite" (SI 7). Examples would be "punk," the "hairdos of unnatural colors," the "neo-baroque taste for the funerary," or "the torn clothes where cloth and skin alternate," and they all belong "to the "sex appeal of the inorganic" (SI 47). Of course, the "sex appeal of the inorganic" represents a pivotal point in Perniola's endeavor to elaborate a "neural and impersonal sexuality" that is emancipated from both instrumentalist and organic or vitalistic accounts of sexuality (SI 61).

9. Another counterstrategy can be identified in information technology. Information technology contains the contours of "an alternative cultural model" in which "the processes of simultaneous reception and leveling give way to the accumulation, conservation and ordering of data" and replace the "actual" with the "virtual," the "instant" with "memory," the "appearance" with the "thing itself," the "ephemeral" with the "available," "consumption" with "preservation," and so on (E 61). Regarding memory, Perniola claims that it no longer signifies "the integral self-preservation of the spirit and the preservation and obstinate survival therein of all the spirit's actions and affections, all its manifestations and modes of being"

(*E* 65), but rather something that "is external to humans and in relation to which they indeed find themselves in a state of listening and reception. What is essential does not issue from the inwardness of the soul, but from the outwardness of writing, of the book, of the computer" (*E* 66). Consequently, information society suggests "a model of consciousness that regards it not so much as an activity undertaken by a subject, but as a mania, a state of possession" (*E* 66). Furthermore, under the condition of information society, whose "basic tonality consists in the parcellization and spatialization of psychological experience," contemporary spirit represents no longer "a stream, but an archive, a media resource, a library" (*E* 66).

10. Perniola identifies the emergence of this new sensibility concerning the ancient worlds in the Vienna School, particularly in the work of Alois Riegl (*D* 119). At the same time, more recent research on non-Western cultures exhibits a type of aesthetic thinking that has freed itself successfully from primitivism (*D* 121).

11. A particularly telling example of this coimplication of the affective and the intellectual is the theory of knowledge developed in the context of Stoic philosophy: a theory of knowledge that is simultaneously "radically sensualist and radically logical" (*D* 96); moreover, elements of the Stoic account of knowledge can be found in Alain, Maurice Merleau-Ponty, and Gilles Deleuze (*D* 97–98).

12. Mario Perniola, *Ritual Thinking: Sexuality, Death, World*, foreword by Hugh J. Silverman; translated with an introduction by Massimo Verdicchio (Amherst, New York: Humanity Books, 2001), 47.

13. Some of the texts relevant to the conception of interpassivity are Slavoj Žižek, *The Plague of Fantasies* (London: Verso, 1997), 86–122, hereafter referred to as *PF*; Slavoj Žižek, *How to Read Lacan* (London: Granta Books, 2006), 22–39, hereafter referred to as *HRL*; and Robert Pfaller, *Aesthetik der Interpassivität* (Hamburg: Philo Fine Arts, 2008), hereafter referred to as *AI* (all translations from the German are mine). Also, it would not be too difficult to point to additional affinities between Perniola's thought and that of Žižek (and Pfaller). After all, as Paolo Bartoloni states, Perniola's more recent thought "gravitates around Lacan's psychoanalysis"; see Paolo Bartoloni, "Thinking Thingness: Agamben and Perniola," *Annali d'Italianistica* 29 (2011): 142, 141–162. However, it is not possible here to either elaborate on these affinities or give a more systematic account of interpassivity itself; instead, the focus will be on some moments of proximity between Perniola and Pfaller. Although Perniola articulates his notion of anonymous, impersonal feeling primarily within the context of a thinking of difference and Pfaller develops his take on interpassivity primarily within the context of ideology critique, both share a strong suspicion regarding the notion of the subject; that is, both seem to identify the problematic of the subject with the question of subjectivation. In this respect, they strongly differ from Žižek, who insists on the constitutive nonidentity of subject and subjectivation, that is, on the necessity of thinking the subject "beyond" subjectivation. This difference has also consequences regarding the evaluation of interpassivity; see, for instance, *PF* 121–122.

14. In another text, Perniola identifies this transformation in Roland Barthes' shift from work to text. He writes: "The text is autonomous and independent of

the subjectivity of those who speak and those who listen, those who read and those who write. . . . The whole range of emotions and sensibilities is displaced in the neutral space of the text" (AS 17).

15. As the example of the Tibetan prayer wheel shows, the prayer wheel produces an objective illusion by means of which the believer can establish a distance from his/her religion. One finds of course similar ritual practices in other religions. The crucial point here is that the objective belief/illusion that is at work in the ritual "renders superfluous the 'subjective,' personal belief of the religious believer" (AI 157).

16. Mario Perniola, *Del sentire cattolico. La forma culturale di una religione universale* (Bologna: Il Mulino, 2001); hereafter referred to as *DSC*.

17. Robert Pfaller,"Figuren der Erleichterung. Interpassivität heute," in *Wir sind nie aktiv gewesen. Interpassivität zwischen Kunst- und Gesellschaftskritik*, ed. Robert Feustel, Nico Koppo, and Hagen Schölzel (Berlin: Kadmos Verlag, 2011), 22, 17–26.

Part Four

Community, Apocalypse, the Political

10

Between the Inoperative and the Coming Community

Jean-Luc Nancy and Giorgio Agamben on the Task of Ontology

María del Rosario Acosta López

The following chapter is an attempt to put Jean-Luc Nancy and Giorgio Agamben's work on community in dialogue with one another.[1] I would like to stress the role the concept of community plays in both Nancy and Agamben and how, in each case, it demarcates a step from politics to ontology. Moreover, I would like to show why ontology—as an ontology of being singular plural for Nancy, as the ontology of "whatever being" for Agamben—becomes a necessary moment—and perhaps the most essential moment—of philosophical-political critique. The question of being-in-common is therefore tied, and not only in Nancy's and Agamben's work, to a critique of ontology but also to a new critical ontology and even to *ontology as critique*.

If ontology is, as Nancy explicitly claims and Agamben's work tacitly suggests, the stumbling block of metaphysics, this is precisely because ontology leads to the affirmation of the irreducibility of "community." Both authors present a critical conception of ontology that, by exposing the violence of metaphysics' grounding gesture, can simultaneously interrupt and open from within the ineradicable character of being in common conceived both as resistance and as a task. As such, ontology opens the possibility of a radical interruption of metaphysics' totalitarian, sovereign gesture: the possibility of an unworking of metaphysics' violence from within.

This interruption is understood and conceived, in both Nancy and Agamben, as *inoperativity*. For both, inoperativity is tied to an exploration on community and, more specifically, to the constitutive gesture of community (and ontology) to come. Even though they employ different sources—Nancy thinks of the inoperative in conversation with Blanchot's notion of *désœuvrement* and therefore, in the lineage of a French interpretation of Hegel via Kojève and Bataille, whereas Agamben's conception of inoperativity results mostly from a rereading of *(im)potentiality* inspired by Aristotle and profoundly indebted to Heidegger—the critical task of both Nancy and Agamben is that of *rendering community inoperative* by taking a step back from the political to ontology, and from politics to critique.[2]

In what follows, I want to go over these steps from community to ontology, and from ontology to inoperativity and critique, by following, first and very briefly, Nancy's opening remarks in *The Inoperative Community* and then Agamben's project of an ontology of potentiality as "whatever being" in *The Coming Community*. I propose to understand both these works as seminal in Nancy's and Agamben's trajectories, that is, as points of departure for a reflection on the connection—its limits and possibilities—between ontology and political philosophy, which serve as conceptual frameworks for much of their later work. My intention in pointing to the continuities between Nancy and Agamben's projects is not to obliterate the differences that distinguish their philosophical undertakings. I would rather like to bring to light a connection that, precisely because of these differences, is rarely brought to the fore and explore the possible fruitful consequences of this dialogue for our current understanding of their projects.[3]

Thinking Community Anew:
Nancy's Inoperative Community as an *Ontological* Task

When, in 1983, Jean-Luc Nancy published the first version of "The Inoperative Community,"[4] accepting J. C. Bailly's invitation to take part in a special issue of the journal *Aléa* titled "The Community, the Number," the subject of community was off limits for philosophical debate. Talking about "community" meant, at the time, as Nancy recalls elsewhere, a reference either to communism (especially its Soviet, Stalinist version) or to *Volksgemeinschaft*, a term connected to the experience of National Socialism in Germany.[5] In fact, as Nancy himself asserts at the beginning of *The Inoperative Community*, in creating the myth of a *human community*, Western thought tends to translate the notion of "the common" into an essence to be actualized and a guiding principle for every political project, thus conceiving community exclusively as a project: "There is no form of communist opposition—or let us say rather 'communitarian' opposition in order to emphasize that the word should not be restricted in this context to strictly political references—that has not been or is not still profoundly subjugated to the goal of achieving a community of beings producing in essence their own essence as their work, and furthermore producing precisely this essence as community."[6] This is, according to Nancy, what serves as the grounds for any form of historical totalitarianism. The project of community, understood as a project and a work to be fulfilled, was associated in the minds of Nancy's contemporaries with the history of twentieth-century totalitarianisms.

But one should not limit this history to specific regimes and societies at particular points in modern history, and certainly not exclusively to our most recent political experiences. Community conceived as a project and a work belongs, according to Nancy, to "the general horizon of our times."[7] Furthermore, it belongs in a way to the entire history of Western thought as the history of metaphysics, which, in Nancy's terms, is grounded on a logic of "immanentism" that serves as the general framework for any totalitarian account of the common.[8] It is not just totalitarianism, therefore, but also immanentism (as a process of self-foundation and appropriation) that need to be addressed and radically questioned by contemporary philosophical critique. The question of community is traversed by a thought of the immanent logic of the "absolute," a mode of "being without relation," conceived of as "detached, distinct and closed," which transforms any discussion of community into the quest for a *common being*.[9]

Thinking *community* anew requires that philosophy revise the very way in which thought unfolds and understands itself *as* thought. It entails, in the first place, destructuring and deconstructing the categories that have reduced any thinking of community to a totalitarian, immanent account of the common. However, and this is as clear in Nancy as it is in Agamben, to renew a philosophical approach to community (and, in the process, to renew philosophy's own task) is not just a matter of *deconstruction*. If philosophy wants to turn into an effective critique of the present, it must do more than expose the emptiness, the danger, and arbitrariness at the core of our philosophical categories. It must do more than interrupt by exposing, and expose by interrupting, the operativity of our political structures. It must also *render them inoperative* through the exposure of an ontology of being-in-common that can accompany the destructive side of critique with a mode of thought, and a *mode of being*, that offers a way of resisting any attempt to secure the exhaustion of being in any fixed meaning, identity, or work.[10]

A renewal of the question of community is therefore closely tied to a renewal of philosophy altogether. And in Nancy, as it will also be the case with Agamben, this means a critical approach to, and a renewal of, ontology. If philosophy does not want to fall back into a precritical and totalitarian account of the common, if it does not want to renounce the possibility of being more than "mere" deconstruction and critique, the question and the task of community for philosophy become also, and simultaneously, the renewal of the question of being: the task of ontology.

"In Bailly's invitation," Nancy writes, "I immediately heard: 'What *about* community?' as a question that was silently substituted by another one, namely, 'What is the *being* of community?' Is there an ontology that can account for a well-known—i.e., 'common'—word, the concept of which, however, has possibly become very uncertain?"[11] The urgent demand behind the question of community, behind the claim of thinking it anew, is a "reconsideration of the very meaning . . . of 'philosophy' in light of the originary situation: the bare exposition of singular origins."[12]

As Nancy states at the beginning of *Being Singular Plural*, "being cannot be anything but being-with-one-another, circulating in the *with* of this singularly plural coexistence."[13] *Inoperative* community is the name—and only the first name—that this reflection on being-in-common attains in Nancy's work,[14] as that which resists and unworks (renders inoperative) community from within.[15] Community, Nancy stresses, "cannot arise from the domain of *work* [*œuvre*]. One does not produce it, one experiences or one is constituted by it as the experience of finitude."[16] Thus, he continues, "community necessarily takes place in what Blanchot has called 'unworking' [or inoperative, *désœuvrement*], referring to that which, before or beyond the work, withdraws from the work, no longer having to do either with production or with completion, encounters interruption, fragmentation, suspension. Community is made of the interruption of singularities, or of the suspension that singular beings *are*."[17] In order to understand what singularity *means*, in order to interrupt the order of identity, of community as a production of work, and to think of community as "inoperative," one has thus to confront oneself with an ontology of being-in-common, which is nothing but an ontology of the singular that is always plural, a being that is always *in* common, and that can never be reduced to a common being, an identity, a closure, and an already realized essence.[18] Or, in Nancy's own words, it is not a matter of choosing to confront ourselves with such an ontology. It is, rather, that it inevitably comes to the fore to resist every single time the appropriative movement of the absolute, and to expose the radical impossibility, the contradictory character, of its immanent logic: "To be absolutely alone, it is not enough that I be so; I must also be alone being alone—and this of course is contradictory. The logic of the absolute violates the absolute. It implicates it in a relation that it refuses and precludes by its essence. This relation tears and forces open, from within and from without at the same time, . . . the 'without relation' from which the absolute would constitute itself."[19] The contradiction at the heart of immanentism, which Nancy describes also as the "relation" (or the very same logic of relationality) that forces open the self-enclosing logic of the absolute, is the "critical, suspended, inoperative point at the heart of the dialectic."[20] Community is that which resists and interrupts, "from within and from without," the logic of immanentism and the sovereign operation that it both presupposes and grounds in the history of metaphysics.

In this way, Nancy's reflections on community, starting with *The Inoperative Community* and continuing with his further and more definitive developments of this subject in works such as *Being Singular Plural* and, more recently, in *The Disavowed Community*, not only open again in very interesting ways a debate around the notion of community for contemporary philosophy and political thought; a debate Agamben is engaging in his own way in *The Coming Community*. They also succeed in showing that the question of community is the question of philosophy in general, the question of being itself because being is always "being-in-common," being exposed in our singularity to an irreducible plurality.

This move toward ontology also allows for ontology to present itself as a more radical form of critique. In pointing to the need for a reconsideration of the question of being-in-common—a question that is at the center of the political and, as Nancy will propose, serves as a reminder of its limits—Nancy's deviation through ontology also preserves the fruitfulness of a shift from a strictly political theoretical critique to an essentially philosophical one. And this is precisely what gives it the potential for being structurally interruptive rather than merely normatively critical.[21]

Community, Inoperativeness, and Impotentiality: Agamben's Coming Community

It is following a similar line of thought that Agamben, in *The Coming Community*, decides to stress the ontological rather than "immediately political" character of his work. As he puts it to Badiou in response to a conversation about this book, in addressing the question of "whatever singularity," *The Coming Community* is "primordially and purely ontological."[22] In his attempts to think singularity through "whatever being" and through what he, in other places, describes as *form-of-life*, Agamben actively takes part in the "exchange (a *communication*, a *commercium*, a *commentarium*)"[23] about the philosophy and politics of community that Nancy had inaugurated in 1983.

Furthermore, as Agamben himself will continuously remark, the ontology of "whatever singularity" in *The Coming Community* responds to the very same challenge as Nancy's ontology of the singular plural. As Agamben makes clear in *Homo Sacer*, only the inoperative, understood in connection to "a new and coherent ontology of potentiality," can free any political theory "from the aporias of sovereignty."[24] This potentiality that cannot be exhausted in the act, this form of understanding being that radically interrupts and diagonally crosses the traditional relation between potentiality and act, frames Agamben's approach to ontology and, with it, Agamben's reflections on community.

Everything depends, however, as Agamben also remarks in *Homo Sacer*, "on what is meant by 'inoperativeness.'" He continues: "It can be neither the simple absence of work nor (as in Bataille) a sovereign and useless form of negativity. The only coherent way to understand inoperativeness is to think of it as a generic mode of potentiality that is not exhausted . . . in a *transitus de potentia ad actum* (a transit from potentiality to act)."[25] The inoperative shows up in Agamben's work as a gesture that seems, at least to a certain extent, to refer back to Nancy. The references are, however, always sufficiently oblique to leave open the question of how closely he situates his own thought in relation to Nancy's project. A closer look at what "inoperative" means for Agamben, and how it connects to what he describes as the need for a new ontology, not only will allow us to explore the nuances of his own approach, but will also help us bring to light the points where his political ontology continues, without touching, Nancy's inoperative community.[26]

"The Gift of a Supplemental Possibility": Toward an Ontology of Pure Potentiality

To think the kind of inoperativity that could give place to what Agamben describes as a coming community of inessential singularities calls for an ontology of "a being of pure potentiality," that is, an ontology of a mode of being "which no identity and no work could exhaust."[27] According to Agamben, only such an ontology can interrupt the logic behind sovereign power, since the latter depends entirely, in order to remain operative, on a traditional interpretation of "the primacy of actuality in its relation to potentiality."[28] This is the reason why Agamben's analysis of potentiality is central not only to his diagnosis of sovereignty, but also to his conceptions of both community and politics. "The modern (or rather postmodern) problem of a fulfilled realization of human work and thus of a possible *désœuvrement* of man at the end of history," he writes, finds in the thought of "an inessential inactivity of man . . . its logical metaphysical foundation."[29]

However, what do "pure potentiality" and "inessential inactivity" even mean? To explain these concepts, in *The Coming Community* Agamben takes us back to Aristotle's analysis of "impotence" or the "potentiality to not-be."[30] It is in these passages from Aristotle, according to Agamben, that one finds the key to reinterpreting the notion of potentiality, one that the history of philosophy has overlooked and that he then proposes to read attentively. "Everything rests here," Agamben writes, "on the mode in which the passage from potentiality to act comes about."[31] If one pays attention to this passage, one discovers that the symmetry between the potentiality to-be and the potentiality to-not-be—one that the tradition has, according to Agamben, taken for granted—is only apparent.[32] Whereas the passage from potentiality to-be to its act has always been interpreted teleologically, that is, as a transition from potentiality to act in which potentiality exists only "for the sake" of its ultimate fulfillment and realization in the act, something entirely different happens in the case of the potentiality not-to-be: "as for the potentiality to-not-be the act can never consist of a simple transition *de potentia ad actum*."[33] The potentiality to not-be is not exhausted in the passage to actuality. It is rather "conserved and exercised in the act,"[34] generating a relation to actuality that is different from one that "affirms the superiority of the positive potentiality over the act."[35]

Agamben's interpretation of Aristotle reveals that impotentiality is not only essential to the notion of potentiality as such (in Aristotle's definition, "what is potential can both be and not be"), but it is also precisely what makes it possible to consider potentiality in itself, autonomously, no longer as a merely logical modality, but in its *effective mode of existence*. "If potentiality is to have its own consistency and not always disappear immediately into actuality," Agamben writes, "it is necessary that potentiality be able not to pass over into actuality, that potentiality constitutively be the potentiality not-to (do or be) or, as Aristotle says, that potentiality be also impotentiality (*adynamia*)."[36] All these passages, both in *The Coming Community* and in *Homo Sacer*, are the result of an argument that Agamben developed in much greater detail some years before in "On Potentiality," a paper originally delivered in 1986, parallel to the publication of Nancy's *The Inoperative Community*.[37] "On Potentiality" is also directly connected to the question of a kind of "unworking" or "inoperative" praxis, or work, resulting from the specific mode of impotentiality that comes to light in Aristotle's analysis. If followed attentively, Agamben suggests, Aristotle's analysis of the question of impotentiality (*adynamia*) leads to a form of *existing* potentiality that not only does not exhaust itself in actuality, but also maintains an essential relation to its own lack. *Existing* potentiality means simultaneously to be capable of making or "not making a work."[38] "To be potential" in this context thus means "to be one's own lack, to be in relation to one's own incapacity."[39] In other words, to be potential is to be properly improper, to "recognize" impropriety as one's own potentiality.

Put now in the terms Agamben will use in *Homo Sacer*, the analysis of the potentiality to-not-be reveals a potentiality "sovereignly capable of its own impotentiality (*impotenza*)."[40] By being capable of the act in not realizing it, potentiality "maintains itself in relation to actuality in the form of its suspension."[41] Thus, this form of potentiality opens a realm (a zone, says Agamben in *The Coming Community*)[42] where possibility and reality, potentiality and act, become indistinguishable. This is the origin, for Agamben, of what in *Homo Sacer* is presented as the logic of sovereignty but also of what, already in *The Coming Community*, becomes the possibility of its interruption, of its *inoperatività*.

In order to understand what community really means in Agamben, as an interruption and an instance of rendering inoperative the logic of sovereignty, one needs first to understand what this exact and somewhat enigmatic connection between impotentiality and sovereignty is. Only then can one clearly draw the line that goes from the latter to the former via inoperativity and community. As becomes clear in *Homo Sacer*, it is precisely a logic that presupposes pure potentiality (instead of denying it) that makes sovereignty possible. "The sovereign is precisely this zone of indistinction"[43] between possibility and reality. This is also the ambiguity coming out of Aristotle's account, since pure potentiality and pure actuality are just two facets of sovereign being: "Sovereignty is always double because Being, as potentiality, suspends itself, maintaining itself in a relation of ban (or abandonment) with itself in order to realize itself as absolute actuality (which thus presupposes nothing other than its own potentiality)."[44] Potentiality can only be transformed into *absolute actuality* (which is the movement of sovereign power itself, of the sovereign act and, therefore, its constitutive paradox) when it sets aside its potential not-to-be. This "setting aside" is what Agamben, following Nancy, calls a relation of ban: "Taking up Jean-Luc Nancy's suggestion, we shall give the name ban (from the old Germanic term that designates both exclusion from the community and the command and insignia of the sovereign) to this potentiality (in the proper sense of the Aristotelian *dynamis*, which is always also *dynamis mē energein*, the potentiality not to pass into actuality) of the law to maintain itself in its own privation, to apply in no longer applying. The relation of exception is a relation of ban."⁴⁵ "To abandon," writes Nancy, "is to remit, entrust, or turn over to such a sovereign power, and to remit, entrust, or turn over to its ban. . . . Turned over to the absolute of the law, the banished one is thereby abandoned completely outside its jurisdiction. The law of abandonment requires that the law should be applied through its withdrawal."⁴⁶ What is "applied through its withdrawal" in the case of sovereign power or, to put it in Agamben's terms, what is *included by exclusion* is what gives way to *homo sacer*, to the inclusion by exclusion of bare life.

However, it is also the thinking of this pure potentiality that can interrupt and escape the relation of ban and the logic set in play by sovereignty itself. The task is, as Agamben suggests in *Homo Sacer*, "to think the existence of potentiality even without any relation to being, in the form of the gift of the self and of letting be. This, however, implies nothing less than thinking ontology and politics beyond every figure of relation, beyond even the limit relation that is the sovereign ban."⁴⁷ *The Coming Community* is the first step toward the ontology to which this passage from *Homo Sacer* refers. The ultimate problem, which *The Coming Community* seems to grapple with, is for Agamben the fact that, instead of properly assuming our potentiality *as* potentiality, we understand this incapacity (this being "devoid of foundation") as a *guilt*, a *debt*. "The only evil," Agamben writes, consists in the decision "to regard potentiality itself, which is the most proper mode of human existence, as a fault that must always be repressed."⁴⁸ Very much in the same line as Nancy, therefore, Agamben understands the problem of community in its traditional philosophical setting as the problem of compensating for a lack—what Nancy calls our finitude—by setting a task, a work, and an essence to be accomplished. He writes: "There is no essence, no historical or spiritual vocation, no biological destiny that humans must enact or realize. This is the only reason why something like ethics can exist, because it is clear that if humans were or had to be this or that substance, this or that destiny, no ethical experience would be possible—there would be only tasks to be done."⁴⁹ If there is something that humans "have to be," Agamben insists, "this something is not an essence, nor properly a thing: *It is the simple fact of one's own existence as possibility or potentiality.*"⁵⁰ This is the only way of interrupting the process by which a constitutive potentiality that should become the only point of departure for ethics becomes the *fault* (the original sin) that humanity has to repair.

These passages from *The Coming Community* explain the ethical (and, as one can already see, political) consequences of what Agamben, in "On Potentiality," had shown to be a misinterpretation of Aristotle's theory on potentiality. And it is the argument that gives rise, in Agamben's work, to an "ontology of pure potentiality"—the need and call for this ontology as a task—which he will put in motion both in *The Coming Community* under the name of "whatever being" and in other works, such as *Means Without End* and *Homo Sacer*, by introducing the concept of "form-of-life." To think of pure potentiality, Agamben will insist, in order to interrupt instead of reproducing the logic of sovereignty is to think of the possibility of a potentiality that "gives itself to itself."[51] There is still something coming in that which has already reached its end and exhausted all of its possibilities. It is the gift of an always "supplemental possibility in what is given," a gift that we may still be able to collect, Agamben writes, "from the empty hands of humanity."[52]

The Threshold that We Are: Inessential Commonality

At the beginning of "Form-of-Life," an essay written between *The Coming Community* and *Homo Sacer*, Agamben asks: "Is today something like a *form-of-life*, a life for which living itself would be at stake in its own living, possible? Is today a *life of potentiality* available?"[53] *The Coming Community* was one of the first attempts to answer this question in Agamben's work. A form-of-life, a life of potentiality, is a life that not only understands potentiality (and not actuality) as "the specific characteristic of man,"[54] but also, and perhaps more importantly, a life that, as pure potentiality, understands itself as always held in common. What this community is and how it looks like is something that Agamben develops in very close proximity to Nancy's inoperative community. Agamben writes: "If humans were to succeed in belonging to this impropriety as such, in making of the proper being-thus . . . a common and absolutely exposed singularity, . . . then they would for the first time enter into a community without presuppositions and without subjects."[55] Thus, as it is also the case with Nancy's inoperative community, Agamben's coming community cannot be understood through a property predicated in common, nor as an identity that encloses within its limits a shared form of life. Community cannot be translated into the notion of a *common being* that exhausts and realizes itself in the fact of *being common* as such. There is, Agamben writes, a "necessarily potential character of any community," since community can only take place among beings who are "not always and solely enacted," who are not "always already this or that thing, this or that identity," but "rather delivered to a possibility and a power" in which "living and intending and apprehending are at stake each time."[56] The special mode of being that is brought to light in the event of community is intelligible only, Agamben explains, as "whatever singularity" (from the Latin *quodlibet*), that is, not as "the intelligence of some thing, of this or that quality or essence, but only [as] the intelligence of an intelligibility."[57] As is the case with the *"libet"* (the lovable) of "whatever singularities" (the *"libet"* preserved in the Latin),[58] singularity here is taken *as such* not because of "this or that property of the loved one," nor because of an abstract, indifferent generality, but because of "all of its predicates, its being such as it is."[59]

Borrowing Badiou's description of Agamben's project, the question of community is thus a question not of *inclusion* but of *belonging*. While inclusion is always related to the logic of sovereignty and is still trapped in the framework of a sovereign decision and a sovereign ban, belonging is rather the sign, in Badiou's words, of a "multiple exposure," of that "being-in-pure-donation" that Agamben's "whatever singularity" seems to be attempting to capture.[60] *Ek-stasis*, Agamben writes, is the gift of singularity,[61] the gift that singularity gathers at the threshold of being. These limits are neither the means to delineate a determined common realm, nor the framework for a particular community of identities. They are rather the very site in which community can ever take place: "The threshold is not, in this sense, another thing with respect to the limit; it is, so to speak, the experience of the limit itself, the experience of being-within an outside."[62] And this, Agamben would insist, is the threshold that *we are*: to be expropriated of all identity is to appropriate belonging, and only belonging, by itself.[63]

That is the only community that remains to be thought if one is to think of a community of "whatever singularity": namely, a community that cannot be mediated by anything (neither by conditions, nor by the absolute absence of conditions) other than belonging.[64] It is not, therefore, Agamben writes, Blanchot's negative community.[65] Nor is it its impossibility, as has been thought, perhaps, by Derrida.[66] It would seem to be much closer to Nancy's inoperative community and to his notion of "compearing": an *inessential commonality*,[67] Agamben writes, whereby *"the communication of singularities . . . does not unite them in essence, but scatters them in existence."*[68] In Nancy's own words, "Communication [of singularities] consists before all else in this sharing and in this compearance of finitude: that is, in the dislocation and in the interpellation that reveals themselves to be constitutive of being-in-common . . . finitude compears, that is to say it is exposed: such is the essence of community."[69] Community thus understood as the dispersion of singularities into existence is, as it is also the case with Nancy's inoperative community, an experience of pure and radical exposure. This is the only way in which one can think of "singularities forming a community without affirming an identity."[70] And wherever there is such community, wherever such experience takes place (*if* it has, *if* it could), there is a form of potentiality that no State, no sovereign power can tolerate: "Wherever these singularities peacefully demonstrate their being in common," writes Agamben, "there will be a Tiananmen and, sooner or later, the tanks will appear."[71] The risk that such radical exposure entails is simultaneously the form of resistance that only community—inoperative, inessential, a community of whatever beings—can exhibit in its existence. What kind of critique this is, and how can it be both the gift of existence and a community *to come*, is the question to which I devote the last section of this chapter. In this ambiguity between the stubbornness of being-in-common and the promise of community, both Nancy's and Agamben's ontologies are put to the test.

Between a Given and a Coming Community: "A Tiny Displacement of the World"

For Nancy too, community is that which resists—undermines, interrupts, and renders inoperative—the sovereign gesture. And, for the very same reasons Agamben suggests at the end of *The Coming Community*, its existence is always at risk of being the target of an attempt to its elimination. In *The Inoperative Community*, Nancy writes: "Only the fascist masses tend to annihilate community in the delirium of an incarnated communion. Symmetrically, the concentration camp—and the extermination camp, the camp of exterminating concentration—is in essence the will to destroy community. But even in the camp itself, undoubtedly, community never entirely ceases to resist this will."[72] The force of this resistance seems to be guaranteed, at least in the case of Nancy, by a sort of *stubbornness* of being, that is, by the ineradicability of being-in-common, of our shared existence, and of the fact that, as Nancy clarifies, community is always already "given to us with being and as being. . . . At bottom, it is impossible for us to lose community. . . . We cannot not compear."[73]

The question that arises, however, as in the case of Agamben, is the issue of what the status of this resistance is, and what it means for critique. How can Nancy argue for the irreducibility and inexorability of community while sustaining nonetheless that community is also a "struggle and a task"?[74] Community, Nancy argues, is "the ontological responsibility of *being*-in-common."[75] It is "given to us," indeed, but "as a gift to be renewed. . . . It is not a work to be done or produced. But it is a task, which is different—an *infinite task at the heart of finitude*."[76]

The same question lies also in the "coming" (or "to come," "*che viene*" in Italian) announced in Agamben's title, which Nancy often uses too ("*à venir*") to describe the temporal character of his ontological project.[77] Is the coming community that which is *already* taking place (as a form of resistance, perhaps, anywhere and everywhere against the state and against any sovereign attempt to obliterate being-in-common) or are Agamben and Nancy arguing for an "event" and a task that are *not yet* here, but the imminence of which is there to be thought of within the very same conditions that attempt to preclude it? Is there perhaps something like a "negative dialectic" playing a role in these authors?[78] Or are they inviting us to do something else with what is already there but which has no meaning until we give it one?

One should try to address these questions, however, under the scope of the ontology of potentiality and inoperativity that has been shown to be central to Nancy's and Agamben's thinking of community. If the framework of this ontology disrupts our traditional understanding of both potency and act, the notion of a coming/inoperative community cannot be thought of within such dialectics of possibility and reality, promise and fact. This returns us to the question of inoperativity, to the kind of critical gesture that is entailed by this "operation," and to the essential connection that seems to be at stake in these two authors between ontology and critique.

To render inoperative, according to Nancy, is the critical task that comes along with the stubbornness, and thus the imperative, of *being*-in-common, with its refusal to be turned into a project, a work, and an essence. To "destitute," as the key interruptive—and perhaps only effective—gesture, Agamben points out, is the possibility of a thinking of the "inessential inoperativity of man" not "as the cessation of all activity, but as an activity that consists in making human works and productions inoperative, opening them to a new possible use."[79] "But," Nancy asks, "where and how does the destitute subsist?"[80] Whereas, for Agamben, the main question seems to be how to prepare us for the possibility of "an otherwise" and thus the main gesture related to the inoperative is that of a radical interruption of sovereignty, one that requires a thinking beyond *relation as such* (as quoted before, "thinking an ontology and politics *beyond every figure of relation*, beyond even the limit relation that is the sovereign ban"),[81] Nancy's project seems to be much more committed to the affirmation of the inexorability of *relation* at the heart of any attempt to preclude it. The inoperative is the task that arrives at radical exposure and describes, therefore, the where and how of that which, in Agamben's project, has been "destituted." Perhaps this is the difference between potentiality and plurality, between "whatever being" and "being singular plural"; the difference between Agamben's reference to the coming community as "an imperceptible trembling of the finite"[82] and Nancy's call for the inoperative community as "the trembling of existence as exposure."[83]

One of the final chapters of *The Coming Community* starts with a parable that, according to Agamben, Benjamin told Bloch as he had heard it once from Scholem: "The *Hassidim* tells a story about the world to come that says everything there will be just as it is here. Just as our room is now, so it will be in the world to come; where our baby sleeps now, there too it will sleep in the other world. And the clothes we wear in this world, those too we will wear there. Everything will be as it is now, just a little different."[84] The parable, writes Agamben, "introduces a possibility there where everything is perfect, an 'otherwise' where everything is finished forever,"[85] a "tiny displacement" that does not seem to refer to the state of things "but to their sense and their limits."[86] Perhaps Nancy's and Agamben's invitations would be better described by the idea conveyed in the parable. To interrupt sovereignty, to unwork politics, bringing back an ontology that puts our whole understanding of being toward actuality on hold, is not an event that will take place in a possible—maybe even imminent—future, if we let it come. What ought to happen, if it happens or if, perhaps, it is already taking place, here and now, once and again, Agamben writes, is "to fall properly in love with the improper . . . if it is true that, according to Jean-Luc Nancy's beautiful phrase, love is that of which we are not masters, that which we never reach but which is always happening to us."[87]

Notes

1. A shorter version of this text, in which I focused almost exclusively on Agamben, was published as an article in a special issue of the philosophical journal *Epoché* devoted to the work of Giorgio Agamben and edited by Alejandro Vallega. See María del Rosario Acosta López, "A Tiny Displacement of the World: On Giorgio Agamben's Coming Community," *Epoché: A Journal for the History of Philosophy* 16, 1 (2011): 93–112. I thank Silvia Benso for inviting me to expand, in my contribution to this volume, what were initially just a very few suggestions about the possible relations between Agamben and Jean-Luc Nancy's work on the question of community. I thank also Colin McQuillan at Saint Mary's University (San Antonio) for having gone through several versions of this essay and helped me make it more concise, clear, and conceptually sound.

2. I acknowledge that it is precisely this move that has been criticized in some secondary literature as an ultimate renunciation of the political and of the possibility of critique altogether, both in Nancy and in Agamben's work. See, among the more recent ones, Brian Elliot, "Community and Resistance in Heidegger, Nancy and Agamben," *Philosophy and Social Criticism* 37, 3 (2011): 259–271; and Bruno Bosteels's publications on the impolitical as antipolitical and his upcoming work on *The Jargon of Finitude*. For a more classical and very clear articulation of this

problem, see Andrew Norris, "Jean Luc Nancy and the Myth of the Common," *Constellations* 7, 2 (2000), 272–295; and "The Exemplary Exception: Philosophical and Political Decisions in Giorgio Agamben," in *Politics, Metaphysics, and Death: Essays on Giorgio Agamben's Homo Sacer*, ed. Andrew Norris (Durham, NC: Duke University Press, 2005), 262–283. See also William Rasch, "From Sovereign Ban to Banning Sovereignty," in *Giorgio Agamben: Sovereignty and Life*, ed. Matthew Calarco and Steven DeCaroli (Stanford, CA: Stanford University Press, 2007), 92–108. I expect to show throughout this chapter that, even though these are the risks at place when moving from political philosophy to ontology, the move itself can be understood as a radicalization rather than a renunciation of critique. For a more explicit discussion of the implications of this move, and the risks it involves, see María del Rosario Acosta López, "Ontology as Critique: Jean-Luc Nancy's Inoperative Community," *Research in Phenomenology* 47 (2017): 108–123.

3. The literature devoted to an explicit comparison between Nancy and Agamben is scarce, and it is mostly developed around their indebtedness to, and critique of, Heidegger's work. One of the most complete and in-depth analyses following this line, and precisely around the question of community, is Greg Bird, *Containing Community: From Political Economy to Ontology in Agamben, Esposito, and Nancy* (Albany: State University of New York Press, 2016). In continuity with Bird's work, I would like to point to the relation, in both Nancy and Agamben's case, between ontology and community, but this time, however, stressing the connection between inoperativity and critique, and the way these relations and connections take shape in both Nancy and Agamben's work in their reflections on being as being-in-common. I must also thank Greg Bird for our conversations on these subjects, which go all the way back to the special issue on Esposito's *Communitas* he organized for *Angelaki* in 2015; see *Angelaki: Journal of the Theoretical Humanities* 18, 3 (2013); and *Community, Immunity and the Proper: Roberto Esposito*, ed. Greg Bird and Jon Short (London: Routledge, 2015).

4. Published first as an essay and only in 1986, after publication of Blanchot's *The Unavowable Community*, as a book.

5. In fact, as Nancy himself recalls, his first edition of *The Inoperative Community*, which was translated into German in 1988, was described as "Nazi" in a Berlin journal. See Jean-Luc Nancy, *La comunidad enfrentada*, trans. Juan Manuel Garrido (Buenos Aires: La cebra, 2007), 19. All the translations from this text are mine. See also, for a similar discussion of this context, what Nancy says in Robert Esposito and Jean-Luc Nancy, "Dialogue on the Philosophy to Come," *Minnesota Review* 75 (2010): 80–81.

6. Jean-Luc Nancy, *The Inoperative Community*, trans. Peter Connor (Minneapolis: University of Minnesota Press, 1991), 2.

7. Nancy, *The Inoperative Community*, 3.

8. Nancy will be followed on this point both by Agamben and Esposito, contra Foucault: the history of sovereignty, of community as a work to be set out, cannot be reduced to a modern history of the subject; it finds its grounds and tradition in the entire history of Western thought and politics. The modern subject,

and the individual as translated into political terms, is simply the "residue of the experience of the dissolution of community" (Nancy, *The Inoperative Community*, 3) and, therefore, it belongs to the same logic of immanence that has given place, since the beginning, to the myth of community as a common *work*. In Agamben's words, "biopolitics is at least as old as the sovereign exception" since "the production of biopolitical body is the originary activity of sovereign power"; see Giorgio Agamben, *Homo Sacer: Sovereign Power and Bare Life*, trans. Daniel Heller-Roazen (Stanford, CA: Stanford University Press, 1998), 6. For Foucault, on the contrary, biopolitics emerges in the eighteenth century with the emergence of "the problem of population" and, with it, of techniques of governance. See Michel Foucault, "Governmentality," in *Power*, ed. Paul Rabinow, *The Essential Works of Michel Foucault: 1954–1984* (New York: The New Press, 1997), 3: 215, 201–222.

9. Nancy, *The Inoperative Community*, 4.

10. The expression is Agamben's. See "The Work of Man," trans. Kevin Attell, in *Giorgio Agamben: Sovereignty and Life*, ed. Matthew Calarco and Steven DeCaroli (Stanford, CA: Stanford University Press, 2007), 2. Also see Agamben's well known critique of the *limits* of deconstruction as an infinite form of deferment; see Giorgio Agamben, *The Time That Remains: A Commentary on the Letter to the Romans*, trans. Patricia Dailey (Stanford, CA: Stanford University Press, 2005), 101–104. Agamben's insistence on a messianic "fulfillment" or *pleroma* of the law, or on preserving "another use" of the law, its "deactivation" rather than its "erasure" (see Giorgio Agamben, *State of Exception*, trans. Kevin Attell [Chicago: University of Chicago Press, 2005], 64), are all related to the task of rendering sovereignty inoperative as distinct from offering a deconstructive account of its conceptual foundations. Nancy's insistence on community and his refusal to renounce ontology are tied up to the same dissatisfaction with deconstruction and the risks that this kind of critique entails: "A law without ontology," he writes, "reabsorbs Being and its meaning in the empty truth of the Law" (Jean-Luc Nancy, *Being Singular Plural*, trans. Robert Richardson and Anne O'Byrne [Stanford, CA: Stanford University Press, 2000], 48).

11. Nancy, *Comunidad Enfrentada*, 19.

12. Nancy, *Being Singular Plural*, 25.

13. Nancy, *Being Singular Plural*, 3.

14. "With the definition of an 'inoperative community' I wanted precisely to speak of a community that does not put into effect any community. This is why I have continued to let the lexicon that I had been using slide from 'being-in-common,' 'being-together,' and 'separation,' arriving at 'being-with' or the pure and simple 'with,' as one will see in *Being Singular Plural*" (Nancy, in Esposito and Nancy, "Dialogue on the Philosophy to Come," 81).

15. One of the difficulties of the translation of *désœuvrement* into English is that in French this word works both as an adjective and as a conjugated verb. "*La communauté désœuvrée*" means both the "unworking" of/by community and an "inoperative" community, namely, one that is and has been "unworked," that is, one that is and has been constantly undergoing the process of being rendered inoperative.

16. Nancy, *The Inoperative Community*, 31.
17. Nancy, *The Inoperative Community*, 31.
18. I cannot explain here how this interruption takes place in Nancy's work and in what sense it is made possible precisely by the ineradicability of relation, of being in common, that ontology is able to find even at the heart of the dialectics of the absolute and immanence as its conceptual and existential presupposition. For a much more detailed exposition of Nancy's argument, see María del Rosario Acosta López, "Ontology as Critique."
19. Nancy, *The Inoperative Community*, 4.
20. Nancy, *Being Singular Plural*, 91.
21. I am following here the distinction proposed by Catherine Kellog, "Freedom after the Law: Arendt and Nancy's Concept of 'The Political,'" in *After Sovereignty*, ed. Charles Barbour and George Pavlich (New York: Routledge, 2010), 68–82.
22. Giorgio Agamben in Alan Badiou, "Intervention dans le cadre du Collège international de philosophie sur le livre de Giorgio Agamben: *La communauté qui vient, théorie de la singularité quelconque*," accessed January 2017, http://www.entre-temps.asso.fr/Badiou/Agamben.htm: "Mon livre n'est pas du tout conçu comme immédiatement politique, il relève de l'ontologie, à savoir penser la singularité quelconque en tant que pure ontologie" (the translations of all English quotations of this text are mine).
23. Jean-Luc Nancy in Roberto Esposito, *Communitas: Origen y destino de la comunidad*, trans. Carlos Rodolfo Molinari (Buenos Aires: Amorrortu, 2007), 9.
24. Agamben, *Homo Sacer*, 44.
25. Agamben, *Homo Sacer*, 62.
26. The question of the inoperative also plays a key role in Agamben's more recent works. In *The Use of Bodies*, for instance, Agamben speaks of *inoperativity* as the main theoretical context within which his own conception of use needs to be understood: "In the course of this study of the use of bodies, a term has never stopped appearing: inoperativity. . . . The concept of use that we have attempted to define can be correctly understood only if it is situated in the context of this theory. Use is constitutively an inoperative praxis, which can happen only on the bases of a deactivation of the Aristotelian apparatus potential/act. . . . The inoperative work, which results from this suspension of potential, exposes in the act the potential that has brought it into being. . . . Rendering inoperative the works of language, the arts, politics and economy, it shows what a human body can do, opens it to a new possible use" (Giorgio Agamben, *The Use of Bodies*, trans. Adam Kotsko [Stanford University Press, 2015], 93–94). "Use" may be, therefore, the concept that helps to bridge, in Agamben's most recent work and as part of the completion of the *Homo Sacer* project, an ontology of pure potentiality and its consequences for a conception of politics outside of the paradigm of sovereignty. As he puts forward starting at the beginning of this work, "One of the hypothesis of the current study is, by calling into question the centrality of action and making for the political"—and thus, by stressing the importance of the inoperative as a "specific form of human praxis"—"that of attempting to think use as a fundamental

political category" (*The Use of Bodies*, 23). In this context, the comparison and contrast with Nancy's work becomes even more relevant.

27. Giorgio Agamben, "The Work of Man," 2.
28. Agamben, *Homo Sacer*, 44. The logic and paradoxes behind sovereign power are, of course, more complicated than just this primacy of actuality over potentiality. I will develop this issue further on in this section.
29. Agamben, "The Work of Man," 2.
30. Agamben, *Coming Community*, 34.
31. Agamben, *Coming Community*, 34.
32. See Agamben, *Coming Community*, 35.
33. Agamben, *Coming Community*, 34.
34. Agamben, *Coming Community*, 35.
35. Agamben, *Coming Community*, 35.
36. Agamben, *Homo Sacer*, 45.
37. See Giorgio Agamben, "On Potentiality," in *Potentialities: Collected Essays in Philosophy*, ed. and trans. Daniel Heller-Roazen (Stanford, CA: Stanford University Press, 1999), 177–184.
38. Agamben, "On Potentiality," 179.
39. Agamben, "On Potentiality," 182.
40. Agamben, *Homo Sacer*, 45.
41. Agamben, *Homo Sacer*, 45.
42. Agamben, *Coming Community*, 56.
43. Agamben, *Homo Sacer*, 47.
44. Agamben, *Homo Sacer*, 47.
45. Agamben, *Homo Sacer*, 28.
46. Jean-Luc Nancy, *The Birth to Presence*, trans. Brian Holmes (Stanford, CA: Stanford University Press, 1993), 44.
47. Agamben, *Homo Sacer*, 48.
48. Agamben, *Coming Community*, 44.
49. Agamben, *Coming Community*, 42.
50. Agamben, *Coming Community*, 42.
51. Agamben, "On Potentiality," 184.
52. Agamben, "On Potentiality," 68.
53. Giorgio Agamben, *Means without End: Notes on Politics*, trans. Vincenzo Benetti and Cesare Casarino (Minneapolis: University of Minnesota Press, 2000), 9. The translation says "life of power," but I would like to maintain the notion of potentiality here. The word in Italian remains the same.
54. Agamben, "The Work of Man," 7.
55. Agamben, *Coming Community*, 64.
56. Agamben, *Means without End*, 9, 10.
57. Agamben, *Coming Community*, 2.
58. This is something that is definitely lost in the translation into English: the Latin *quodlibet*, and even the Spanish "*cualquiera*," still remind us of the idea

of a being that is not being whatever, indifferently, but a being "as likable," "as lovable." *Libet* refers to desire, to love. It is not indifference (the usual interpretation of "whatever") but singularity that is at play here.

59. Agamben, *Coming Community*, 2.

60. Badiou, "Intervention": "L'inclusion est le signe de la prise étatique, l'appartenance est le signe de l'exposition multiple, ie le signe même de l'être en tant qu'être dans sa pure donation en multiplicités indifférentes."

61. Agamben, *Coming Community*, 68.

62. Agamben, *Coming Community*, 68.

63. Agamben, *Coming Community*, 11.

64. Agamben, *Coming Community*, 85.

65. Agamben, *Coming Community*, 85.

66. It is an impossibility defined by the fact that its conditions of possibility coincide with the conditions of its impossibility. Although Derrida's thinking of the impossible could be closely read in relation to Agamben's ontology of potentiality, I think that Agamben would still be part of those "discourses on community," too close still to the notion of fraternity, that Derrida explicitly rejects in his *Politics of Friendship*; see Jacques Derrida, *The Politics of Friendship*, trans. George Collins (London: Verso, 1997), especially 296–300.

67. Agamben, *Coming Community*, 18.

68. Agamben, *Coming Community*, 19.

69. Nancy, *The Inoperative Community*, 29.

70. Agamben, *Coming Community*, 86.

71. Agamben, *Coming Community*, 87.

72. Nancy, *The Inoperative Community*, 35.

73. Nancy, *The Inoperative Community*, 35.

74. Nancy, *The Inoperative Community*, 36.

75. Jean-Luc Nancy, "The Compearance: From the Existence of 'Communism' to the Community of 'Existence,'" trans. Tracy B. Strong, *Political Theory* 20, 3 (1992): 396, 371–398.

76. Nancy, *The Inoperative Community*, 35. For this notion of task as different from "work" or "project," Nancy refers in *The Inoperative Community* in a footnote to his essay "Dies irae," in *La Faculté de Juger* (Paris: Editions de Minuit, 1985), an essay devoted to Kant's faculty of reflective judgment. The reference to an "infinite task at the heart of finitude" is also connected to Nancy's reading of Kant's categorical imperative; see Jean-Luc Nancy, *L'impératif catégorique* (Paris: Flammarion, 1983). I cannot explain here Nancy's main argument in these essays. What is important to have in mind is that, for Nancy, the conception of community as an "imperative" and a "task" is connected to a realm of action that is conceptually separated, as it is in Kant, from the realm of means and ends that constitutes the framework of action understood as "project" and "work" (*ergon*). See María del Rosario Acosta López, "'An infinite *task* at the *heart* of finitude': Jean Luc Nancy on Community and History," *New Centennial Review* 17, 3 (2017): 21–42.

77. Nancy sometimes speaks of "the to come of the ontology of being-in-common" (Jean-Luc Nancy, "The Compearance," 388).

78. See Antonio Negri, "Giorgio Agamben: The Discreet Taste of the Dialectic," in *Giorgio Agamben: Sovereignty and Life*, ed. Matthew Calarco and Steven DeCaroli (Stanford, CA: Stanford University Press, 2007), 109–125.

79. Giorgio Agamben, "What Is a Destituent Power?," *Environment and Planning D: Society and Space*, 32 (2014): 69, 65–74.

80. Jean-Luc Nancy, "Restitution," lecture given in the context of a conference in honor of Agamben, unpublished, accessed July 14, 2020, https://www.youtube.com/watch?v=XhAeKx46638.

81. Agamben, *Homo Sacer*, 48.

82. Agamben, *Coming Community*, 56.

83. "D'abord d'un être ou d'un esprit attentif à sa propre stase, à la pulsation et au tremblement de son exposition" (Nancy, "Restitution").

84. Agamben, *Coming Community*, 53.

85. Agamben, *Coming Community*, 54.

86. Agamben, *Coming Community*, 54.

87. Giorgio Agamben, "The Passion of Facticity," in *Potentialities: Collected Essays in Philosophy*, ed. and trans. Daniel Heller-Roazen (Stanford, CA: Stanford University Press, 1999), 204, 185–204.

11

Who Can Hold the Apocalypse?
Massimo Cacciari, Carl Schmitt, and the *Katechon*

Pietro Pirani

In a passage of the Second Epistle to the Thessalonians (2, 1–12), Paul introduces a new concept, the importance of which political philosophy has yet to fathom. The notion is that of the *katechon*, the restrainer. In his letter to the Christian community of Thessalonica, Paul warns his Christian brothers and sisters against believing in false oracles and fanatics who predict the imminent second coming of Christ (*parousia*) to seal history once and for all. As Paul explains, as long as the *katechon* will hold back the Enemy, Christ will not be able to return. However, this phase will not last forever; eventually the *katechon* will cease to restrain and, as soon as the "wicked One" reveals himself, God will destroy him, marking the beginning of the second return of Christ.

As such, the *ketachon* appears as a paradoxical concept: on the one hand, it prepares the way for the imminent coming of Jesus Christ by holding back (*to katechon*) the Enemy, the son of perdition; on the other hand, the *parousia* can only happen when the *katechon* will be removed (*ho katechon*) so that the "wicked One" may fully appear and, only at that time, be destroyed by God. The interesting aspect of this dense passage is that it has not only inspired a long exegesis since the second century AD,[1] but it has also become foundational for the understanding of the modern state and its role in our age.[2]

In this chapter, I will delve into the latter literature by comparing the readings provided respectively by Carl Schmitt and Massimo Cacciari on the subject matter. Both scholars share the notion that a full comprehension of our historicity cannot leave theological considerations aside, and both identify in the concept of the *katechon* a fundamental aspect of political power, namely, its intrinsic contradiction determined by its capacity to hide and nurture supreme evil in itself, while fighting it.

However, Schmitt and Cacciari also deeply disagree. Schmitt argues for the possible coexistence and compatibility of political and religious powers since both powers aim to contain evil; on the contrary, Cacciari refuses this thesis, claiming the fundamental unsustainability of such a "*compromesso storico* [historical compromise]." For the Italian philosopher, political and religious powers are indeed inseparable, but contrary to the German jurist's interpretation, they are in constant tension, given that the necessity of fulfilling their respective mandates impinge on their prerogatives. As these concepts will be elucidated later on in this chapter, it will become clear how the writings of Schmitt and Cacciari, despite their differences, can be considered as apocalyptic since they try to uncover, unveil, and reveal "all those contradictions that, maturing during Modernity, end up exploding in the Globality."[3]

Carl Schmitt and the Notion of the *Katechon*

The concept of the *katechon* emerges for the first time in Schmitt's writings in 1942, when he introduces the term to explicate the role played by the Carolingian Empire in containing Islam in Europe in the eighth century.[4] However, it is in his *Nomos of the Earth* that he provides new details on the nature of the *katechon*. Schmitt highlights two major elements. First, he identifies in the empire of the Christian Middle Ages the historical concretization of the *katechon* of the Pauline tradition. Second, he highlights how the political unity of Europe was not obtained through the centralization of power in one person; rather, it was consolidated in the delicate equilibrium between two equal entities represented by *imperium* (the empire or secular leaders) and *sacerdotium* (the priesthood or ecclesiastical hierarchy), reflecting the unique Western distinction between *potestas* (power) and *auctoritas* (authority). In Schmitt's view, the famous passage from Matthew's Gospel, "Render unto Caesar the things that are Caesar's, and unto God the things that are God's,"[5] establishes two separate spheres of influence in which church and empire are forced to operate. For Schmitt, therefore, the clash between the German emperors and the papacy during the Middle Ages cannot be compared to the struggle that characterized the relationship of church and state during the nineteenth century because, in the Middle Ages, "the antitheses of emperor and pope were not absolute, but rather *diversi ordines* [different orders], in which the order of the *respublica Christiana* [the Christian republic] resided."[6]

The peculiar nature of the relation between church and state during the Middle Ages brings Schmitt to reach three conclusions. First, since the empire does not hold absolute power, it does not represent a perfect and overreaching community; rather, the empire has to be conceived merely "as a transcendent unity that effects peace and justice" among political entities that had gradually emerged within its borders. Moreover, the cohabitation and collaboration between church and state is intrinsically possible: there is no conflict a priori between the two entities as "the essence [of theology] is defined by its relationship with God and not with Caesar."[7] Finally, any political form that wants to have *katechontic* ambitions must include in its form both *potestas* and *auctoritas*, that is to say, the prerogatives of church and empire. Indeed, it is in this perspective that we should read Schmitt's most famous concept of political theology. As the *respublica Christiana* starts waning away in the fifteenth century and the empire is replaced by the modern state as the central unit of the international system, the *katechon* reconfigures the relation between *potestas* and *auctoritas*. It does not renounce them.

Contrary to the dualistic canonical reading of the relation between state and church, Schmitt draws a different picture in which theology is not excluded from the political; rather, it is included by becoming the instrument through which the state legitimizes its newly found immanence. Like Max Weber, Schmitt believes in the irreversibility of the process of secularization; however, unlike Weber, Schmitt does not believe that secularization is part of the process of disenchantment of the modern world. Contrary to thinkers of the Enlightenment, he argues against the proposition that science alone can generate order. Schmitt clearly outlines this process in his 1929 lecture, "The Age of Neutralizations and Depoliticizations," in which he points out how modern Western history has been always characterized by the constant search for a neutral sphere, that is to say, an intellectual theme that could end all conflicts. Schmitt identifies five moments in this process—the sixteenth, seventeenth, eighteenth, nineteenth, and twentieth century—each of which was marked by a different central sphere (theology, metaphysics, humanitarian ethics, economics, and technology, respectively) and expressed the intellectual paradigm of its age. At the core of this progression from one stage to another, Schmitt places the concept of neutralization. As a central sphere becomes controversial, a new sphere emerges, which becomes domineering as it appears able to neutralize the source of the arisen conflict in the previous stage.

Schmitt pays special attention to technology because, as humanity left behind the nineteenth century and entered the twentieth century, the belief in technology has supplemented economics as "the absolute and ultimate neutral ground."[8] Schmitt disagrees with these conclusions. He contends that the belief that technology may represent a new central sphere is misplaced since "technology is always only an instrument and weapon; precisely because it serves all, it is not neutral. No single decision can be derived from the immanence of technology, least of all for neutrality."[9] For Schmitt, technology is ultimately "*culturally blind*. . . . No conclusions which usually can be drawn for the central spheres can be derived from technology as such and nothing but technology—neither a concept of cultural progress, . . . nor a specific political system."[10] Since technology lacks objectivity, not only "not everyone will see in it the very same thing and use it in the same way, rendering [technology] a source of universal commonality, [but also] everyone will see . . . something subjectively different to be employed in a different way, and [technology] will become instead the ultimate means of conflict. . . . Every strong politics will make use of it."[11]

If science cannot provide a meaningful solution to the phenomenon of crisis, how can the erosion of state sovereignty caused by the process of modern secularization be contained? For Schmitt, the solution lies in political theology, that is to say, in the instrumental use of the theological for the creation of "a new transcendence, different from the ecclesial one, [but] able to justify the meta-juridical superiority of the decision on the polity."[12] This ideological reading of Schmitt's political theology is most forcefully advanced by Massimo Borghesi, who sees in Schmitt's embracement of the Catholic philosophy of the Restoration a theoretical framework, stripped of its religious meaning, and offered analogically to the state as "a mere cultural paradigm,"[13] as a way to contain the process of secularization. For Borghesi, therefore, political theology becomes in Schmitt's hands an ideological tool, "a barrier and, at the same time, a product of secularization."[14] To clarify his interpretation, Borghesi quotes *in extenso* a critical passage from Schmitt's *Political Theology*:

> The idea of the modern constitutional state triumphed together with deism, a theology and metaphysics that banished the miracle from the world. This theology and metaphysics rejected not only the transgressions of the laws of nature through the exception brought about by direct intervention, as is found in the idea of the miracle, but also the sovereign's direct intervention in a valid legal order. The rationalism of the Enlightenment rejected the exception of every form. Conservative authors of the counter-revolution who were theists could thus attempt to support the

personal sovereignty of the monarch ideologically, with the aid of analogies from the theistic theology.[15]

In Borghesi's eyes, this reference to the authors of the counterrevolution is the ultimate proof of the instrumental usage that Schmitt makes of the theological. As Borghesi points out, "The political, in the modern sense, can only subsist by secularizing the theological."[16] Thus, the circle is finally closed; the link between *potestas* and *auctoritas* is finally reestablished. Contrary to the *respublica Christiana* where *potestas* and *auctoritas* were held by two separate entities, reflecting two different forms of power, in the new modern state they are an appanage of the one sovereign. The *katechon* requires such an order, as Schmitt famously formulated in his definition of sovereignty: "Sovereign is he who decides on the exception."[17]

At the same time, the end of the *respublica Christiana* also requires a new equilibrium, a new form of legitimacy that manifests itself through the absorption of one order into the other. *Auctoritas* becomes instrumental to *potestas*; it cannot be the other way around since, for Schmitt, the Christian eschatological reserve prevents the full participation of the church in the mundane world, though it does not totally exclude it. The church is of this world; it operates *in saeculum* (within time); it has a physical existence, and these aspects cannot be simply discharged a priori. Schmitt refuses Erik Peterson's belief in "the theological impossibility of a political theology" and rejects the accusations of his alleged resistance toward the differentiation of spiritual and political power.[18] To those who accuse him of paganism ("Whoever renounces the 'Jewish-Christian' division of political unity, ceases to be a Christian and has chosen paganism"),[19] Schmitt replies by stressing how Providence and "the finger of God" operate in the world and this, in turn, prevents the creation of any fictitious dichotomy between the purity of theology and the impurity of the political.[20]

Whether it is possible, or not, to trace a genealogical link between divine and mundane monarchy is ultimately irrelevant for the German scholar since, from a theoretical point of view, the central issue of political theology is the theme of political unity, that is to say, which categorical structure, both symbolic and institutional, may be used to represent sovereignty, even in its democratic form.[21] The fact that it is possible to conceive a political monarchy that derives from the dogma of the Trinity—as Eusebius of Caesarea does with the Roman emperor Constantine the Great in his *Life of Constantine*[22]—shows to Schmitt the permeability of the eschatological reserve of the political such that the "ubiquity of the political extends into the theological realm and becomes the public space of the Church; . . . the mere fact that a theological argument extends into the realm of praxis makes it political."[23]

In a world that has officially banned the miracle, Schmitt claims the opposite. The modern state must take possession of both *auctoritas* and *potestas*, since the *katechon* cannot contain evil without having absolute power, namely, without containing in itself the totality of all citizens. As on the famous frontispiece of Hobbes's *Leviathan*, in which a giant crowned figure emerges from the landscape, clutching a sword and a crosier, while the torso and arms of the figure are composed of persons all facing inwards such that any political entities with *katechontic* ambitions must project transcendence. However, this can occur only if some form of religious experience is included in the state organization: God may not exist, but the state cannot control its own citizens without myths and legends. The outcome of this process is what William Cavanaugh has recently defined as "migrations of the holy,"[24] that is to say, the process by which the state has increasingly displaced the church and replaced it by becoming the place for a transcendent experience. Given these premises, it does come as a surprise that Schmitt reaches the conclusion that, from an institutional point of view, when *auctoritas* is instrumental to *potestas*, dictatorship is the only logical conclusion to any political order with *katechontic* ambitions: "It is the solution that Hobbes also reached by the same kind of decisionist thinking, though mixed with mathematical relativism. *Auctoritas, non veritas facit legem* [it is authority, not the truth, that makes the law]."[25]

Massimo Cacciari and the Eschatological Reading of the *Katechon*

For Massimo Cacciari, as for Schmitt, any serious thought on the *katechon* must start with a reflection on the relation between *potestas* and *auctoritas* illumined by Christian eschatology. Cacciari acknowledges the existence of an indissoluble bond between theology and the political, whose understanding is of the utmost importance for any serious consideration of the modern state. To those, like Peterson, who deny an affinity between conceptions of sovereignty and government, and metaphysical and theological doctrines of the unity of being, Cacciari simply replies that the mere existence of such concepts legitimates any speculation on their relationship ("If these ideas have experienced a process of secularization, it means they could be secularized").[26] Yet Cacciari's philosophical thinking radically diverges from that of Schmitt insofar as he does not see the compatibility between the mandate of the church and that of the empire. What stands between the two powers, and this is particular to Cacciari's thought, is the existence of a political impetus in religious life, which prevents any possible form of peaceful coexistence between political and religious power. This impetus originates from the belief that the end of time, the *eschaton*, does not make reference to a future event but is already happening or, at least, has just started.[27]

From this interpretation, three consequences follow. First, Christians are constantly forced to decide between good and evil, between friend and enemy, since the *parousia* is happening, as Paul's exhortation to the Thessalonians recounts, in order to resist the devious machinations of the Antichrist.[28] Second, decision not only means resistance in the face of evil but also generates a sense of responsibility toward those individuals who have not yet heard the word of Christ. Therefore, the eschatological message must be announced to the rest of the world; it must be universalized.[29] The *katechon* must be removed so that the coming of Christ may happen and, yet, it must be resisted, even at the risk of inhibiting the *parousia*. Every human being must have the opportunity to be saved. Finally, although the message of salvation is addressed to humanity, there is a dichotomy between those individuals who have the Kingdom in themselves, as Martin Luther says, and who therefore can recognize the beginning of the eschatological time, and those who do not have it.

This contraposition between those who can understand and those who ignore it is pivotal in Cacciari's view because it creates a "dissymmetry" of *auctoritas*, which stands at the very core of his argument on the impracticability of Schmitt's understanding of political theology. Cacciari writes, "There is indeed an evident dissymmetry between those who anticipate *civitas dei* and those who represent the mundane time, the state, the political power. A dissymmetry of *auctoritas* absolutely insurmountable, which *de facto* 'destines' the temporal authority to a subordinate position. The modern state tries to escape from this implicit subordination, but from the point of view of *auctoritas*, not of *imperium*, not of *potestas*. . . . In the eschatological time, an unsustainable dissymmetry arises: you [state] *potestas*, I [church] *auctoritas*."[30]

Thus, contrary to Schmitt and Peterson, for whom political theology is respectively a tool for political order in a secular society and an oxymoron, Cacciari maintains that a statement of faith reveals a public dimension that relates to every individual as well as to the entire society and the globalized world at large. The eschatological reserve consists of eschatological promises present in Christian theology and conceptualized in reference to the historical present. Eschatology does not lead to a relationship of identification, as in Schmitt, nor rejection, as in Peterson; rather, in Cacciari's thought, eschatology is actualized as a *critical reserve* of the historical present. The Kingdom of God will be fully realized at the end of time, and yet, it is already among us and aims to build, despite our insurmountable human limitations, a society already tending toward justice and peace. To exercise a critical reserve means to refuse those who are opposed to these values in history.

The peculiar aspects of the eschatological conceptualization of history, which is both being and yet from being, explain its contradictions; but it also pushes the believers to oppose those who object to Christian values and those who work for the coming of the Kingdom. Although Cacciari seems to draw from a long tradition that can be traced back to the 1930s with the writings of the French philosopher Jacques Maritain, and later to the 1960s with the work of the German theologian Johann Baptist Metz, Cacciari's reflections clearly depart from those of his predecessors. Unlike Maritain, Cacciari's interpretation of the historical role of the eschatological reserve does not become a way to legitimize the modern world, nor can his emphasis on the critical role of the church in history be associated with that of Metz. In Metz, "the *critique* to society becomes *self-criticism* of that Church that legitimizes the world instead of refusing it"[31] and historical moments, such as modernity, come to be opportunities for a Christian emancipation "from the residues of paganism that pollutes the Mediaeval world."[32] In Cacciari, instead, the relationship between time and church is not inherently instrumental; rather, time should be better understood as a background in which church and empire compete to express their *katechontic* prerogatives.

Christianity does not run away from the political power, nor can it condemn it in its totality. As Paul writes in his letter to the Romans, since "there is no authority except that which is from God" (13:1), the political power is also a work of God and as such, it cannot be understood only in negative terms. The empire as an institution is important. We need protection and an efficient administration because we live *in saeculum*; but these are the only roles that the patristic exegesis bestows to the empire. Ambrose, Bishop of Milan, expresses the radical conception of the Christian understanding of the relation between spiritual and political power in his commentary to the Gospel passage, "Render unto Caesar the things that are Caesar's, and unto God the things that are God's," when he claims that if the coin belongs to Caesar, everything else, namely, body, soul, and will, belongs to God.[33] However, political power does not respect such a division of labour; the Roman empire—the *katechon* par excellence—does not act within these limits. Tertullian reminds the Roman emperor that "It is not the power of the empire that restrains but rather the prayers of Christians. . . . The true *katechontic* power is the Christian seed, and all empires work unaware that they soon will be annihilated."[34] Likewise, Augustine condemns Rome because it cannot liberate itself from its civil religion (*religio civilis*), that is to say, "all the citizens on whose harmony the *civitas* originates and is founded must recognize themselves as members of this community, belong to its future destiny, and assert the power of Rome as their supreme good."[35] Yet the empire refuses such subordination. The church recognizes the legitimacy of the empire within such limits, but the empire cannot accept them. Every *katechontic* power has never been satisfied by such a role. The empire cannot be a mere administrative body since each *katechontic* power has strategies, a desire to expand its boundaries.[36] "The empire," Cacciari writes, "must demand *auctoritas*, from *augeo* [to expand]: its *civitas* is either *augenscens* [in expansion], or it is not. It contains in itself the same *katechon*, but as a minister at the service of its most authentic mission: the universalization of its own kingdom, to make of its world its own system."[37] The church recognizes a *potestas* in the empire that is limited to techno-administrative functions. However, the empire cannot fulfil its role within these narrow boundaries and, therefore, yearns for a spiritual *auctoritas* that necessarily forces the empire to enter in conflict with the church. It is from this desire that "the modern state is borne, . . . to fill this dissymmetry; my power is also *auctoritas*, this is the great vindication which, through the Mediaeval treatises, . . . reaches the modern theorizations [of the state] which claim *auctoritas* for *potestas*."[38]

Cacciari's investigation on the meaning of the *katechon* ultimately highlights an indissoluble yet conflictual bond between the empire and the church, which characterizes the history of Western political thought; nonetheless, it is ineluctable and necessary. The empire aspires to acquire a spiritual *auctoritas* so that its subordination to the church may be removed and its *katechontic* ambitions fulfilled. However, the church also is not alien to the function expressed by the *katechon* and refuses any assimilation in the political structure of the empire. The church cannot accelerate the return of Christ and believers should not be discouraged from this event. Yet the church has to contain the rampant spirit of the Antichrist; it must hold back the wicked One by being vigilant and praying as it waits for the return of the Son of Man so that when He comes back, He will find faith in the world.

These *katechontic* properties that distinguish both church and empire create a common ground in which Cacciari detects the seeds for a new alliance between the administrative *potestas* and spiritual *auctoritas*. Cacciari recognizes the presence of many issues in the process of concretization of such an alliance, *in primis* the innate imperial ambitions of every administrative *auctoritas*. Nonetheless, there are no other solutions since, when the political power wants to rule through the mere exercise of its administrative capabilities, the empire is powerless before evil. The political is two-faced, always ambiguous. "There is a reassuring side and unsettling side" in the political: on the one hand, it promises security and peace; on the other, it claims that such objectives must be achieved no matter what, at the prize of any sacrifice.[39] A power that provides only administration and security cannot recognize the evil that it generates in the exercise of its prerogatives. Administration and security are indispensable attributes of political power but their employment must be grounded in the eschatological reserve.

Conclusion

In the forward to his *Nomos of the Earth*, Schmitt writes, "The earth has been promised to the peacemakers. The idea of a new *nomos* of the earth belongs only to them."[40] The question raised by Schmitt, more than sixty years ago, on the nature of the new international order, still appears extremely relevant today. In a world which, at the crossroad between statehood and globality, claims the possibility to end all conflicts by banning the unpredictable, Schmitt and Cacciari claim the opposite. Contrary to those who advance the notion that it is possible to conceive the political without contradictions, without conflicts, Schmitt and Cacciari respond negatively. For both scholars, the political can only be understood in a *katechontic* manner, namely, as a power that withholds the evil of the world. However, although they share the same theoretical framework (that is, political theology) and make reference to the same theological concept, the *katechon*, Schmitt and Cacciari reach conflicting conclusions. Whereas for Schmitt the restraining power of the *katechon* is a stabilizing force which aims at repelling the external foe, for Cacciari the *katechon*—an expression of the Christian eschatological view—is inherently characterized by a tension between *potestas* and *auctoritas*, which jeopardizes the stability of the *polis* from within. These contradictory judgments of the *katechon*, nonetheless, highlight a common understanding of the nature of our time: we live in an apocalyptic age and, as such, we are forced to act.

Notes

1. For a detailed list of excerpts on the subject, see Massimo Cacciari, *Il potere che frena* (Milan: Adelphi, 2013), 143–211.

2. The literature on the *katechon* addressed by Italian philosophers is staggeringly vast and diverse. Among the most notable, on a Girardian reading of the *katechon*, see Giuseppe Fornari, *Da Dionisio a Cristo. Conoscenza e sacrificio nel mondo greco e nella civiltà occidentale* (Genoa: Marietti, 2006), and *Catastrofi della politica. Dopo Carl Schmitt* (Rome: Gangemi Editore, 2014). On messianism and the *katechon*, see Giorgio Agamben, *Il tempo che resta. Commento alla lettera ai Romani* (Turin: Bollari Boringhieri, 2000). On the *katechon* in relation to the concept of immunity, see Roberto Esposito, *Due. La macchina della teologia politica e il posto del pensiero* (Turin: Enaudi, 2013), and *Politica e Negazione. Per una filosofia affermativa* (Turin: Enaudi, 2018). On the *katechon* as the prevention of all-out wars and totalitarianism, see Paolo Virno, *Multitude between Innovation and Negation* (Los Angeles, CA: Semiotext(e), 2008).

3. Antonio Cerella, "Until the End of the World: Girard, Schmitt and the Origins of Violence," *Journal of International Political Philosophy* 11 (2015): 44.

4. Carl Schmitt, *Terra e mare* (Milan: Adelphi, 2006), 10.

5. Matthew, 22:21.

6. Carl Schmitt, *Nomos of the Earth in the International Law of the* Jus Publicum Europaeum (New York: Telos Press Publishing, 2006), 61.

7. Massimo Borghesi, *Critica della teologia politica. Da Agostino a Peterson: la fine dell'era costantiniana* (Genoa-Milan: Marietti, 2013), 171.

8. Schmitt, "The Age of Neutralizations and Depoliticizations," *Télos* 96 (1929, 1993): 138.

9. Schmitt, "The Age of Neutralizations and Depoliticizations," 139.

10. Schmitt, "The Age of Neutralizations and Depoliticizations," 139 (emphasis added).

11. John E. McCormick, *Carl Schmitt's Critique of Liberalism: Against Politics as Technology* (Cambridge: Cambridge University Press, 1997), 102.

12. Borghesi, *Critica della teologia politica*, 172 (translations of cited passages are mine).

13. Borghesi, *Critica della teologia politica*, 171.

14. Borghesi, *Critica della teologia politica*, 172.

15. Carl Schmitt, *Political Theology: Four Chapters on the Concept of Sovereignty* (Chicago: University of Chicago Press, 2005), 36–37.

16. Borghesi, *Critica della teologia politica*, 172.

17. Schmitt, *Political Theology*, 5.

18. Erik Peterson, "Monotheism as a Political Problem: A Contribution to the History of Political Theology in the Roman Empire," in *Theological Tractates* (Stanford, CA: Stanford University Press, 2011), 68.

19. Erik Peterson cited in Jürgen Moltmann, "Covenant or Leviathan? Political Theology for Modern Times," *Scottish Journal of Theology* 47 (1994): 37.

20. Borghesi, *Critica della teologia politica*, 166.

21. Vincenzo Rosito, *La teologia politica contemporanea. Paradigmi, autori, prospettive* (Rome: Edizioni Studium, 2015), 49.

22. Eusebius, Life of Constantine (Oxford: Clarendon Press, 1999).
23. Peter U. Hohendahl, "Political Theology Revisited: Carl Schmitt's Postwar Reassessment" *Konturen* 1 (2008): 10.
24. William T. Cavanaugh, *Migrations of the Holy: God, State, and the Political Meaning of the Church* (Grand Rapids, MI: William B. Eerdmans Publishing, 2011).
25. Schmitt, *Political Theology*, 52.
26. Massimo Cacciari and Mario Tronti, *Teologia e politica al crocevia della storia* (Milan: Edizioni Albo Versorio, 2015), 34.
27. Cacciari and Tronti, *Teologia e politica*, 35–36.
28. Bruno Morroncini, "Il potere che frena e il potere che governa. Walter Benjamin e la teologia politica," in *Il potere che frena. Saggi di teologia politica in dialogo con Massimo Cacciari*, ed. Tommaso Gazzolo et al. (Ariccia: Aracne Editrice, 2015), 275.
29. Cacciari and Tronti, *Teologia e politica*, 36–39.
30. Cacciari and Tronti, *Teologia e politica*, 43–44 (the translation of the cited passage is mine).
31. Borghesi, *Critica della teologia politica*, 213.
32. Borghesi, *Critica della teologia politica*, 205.
33. Cacciari, *Il potere che frena*, 54–55.
34. Massimo Cacciari, *Europe and Empire: On the Political Forms of Globalization* (New York: Fordham University Press, 2016), 148.
35. Cacciari, *Europe and Empire*, 117.
36. Cacciari, *Europe and Empire*, 148.
37. Cacciari, *Il potere che frena*, 107 (translations of cited passages are mine).
38. Cacciari and Tronti, *Teologia e politica*, 44.
39. Massimo Cacciari, "Agonia di un trattino," *Pantarei*, April 14, 2014, accessed August 27, 2016, http://tuttoscorre.org/massimo-cacciari-agonia-di-un-trattino/.
40. Schmitt, *Nomos of the Earth*, 39.

12

Movements or Events?
Antonio Negri versus Alain Badiou on Politics

Christian Lotz

> Do not say that social movement excludes political movement. There is never a political movement which is not at the same time social.
>
> —Karl Marx, *The Poverty of Philosophy*

> Constituent power constitutes society and identifies the social and the political in an ontological nexus.
>
> —Antonio Negri, *Insurgencies: Constituent Power and the Modern State*

Introduction

This essay was written while, in Hamburg, Germany, the leading politicians of the Group of 20 (G20) nations were meeting for an international summit in order to discuss political and economic policies for the future (with no effective results, with the exception of policies related to the "war on terror").

Whereas the leaders were meeting in the city of Hamburg in the name of democracy, public discussion, and global justice, the event was one of the most secured political meetings ever. More than 20,000 police officers were charged with controlling and securing two minor areas of the city. They were controlling antiglobalization and anticapitalist protestors who turned Hamburg into a place where the political conflict lines of today's world emerged most visibly. Outdoor camps for sleep and food, that is, for basic necessities for the reproduction of life, based on human rights, were at first forbidden by the German police, whose decision not to allow protestors to stay outside and overnight had to be challenged in the German constitutional courts. Protest marches, one with more than 70,000 people, were fenced in and surrounded by the means of violence that are available to the police today. Helicopters controlled the scene from the air. Politicians warned of the "violent potential" of a few hundred "radical" protestors," and this turned into a general antileft outcry after the event was over.

Despite the pervasive range, the police and party officials rarely mentioned the visible violence originating in the state in the form of a police force that, from day one, followed an *escalation* and confrontational strategy toward the protestors. Quasi-feudal politicians such as Putin, Trump, and Erdogan, who were residing in the most luxurious places and are the representatives and deciders of today's most devastating global economic and ecological policies, stand for a global wealth class which, when viewed from the perspective of the protesting activists, is the enemy of a just and free global order. Indeed, the deep divisions between the state, the activists, and the spectators in front of their television sets could not be more visible than during this "event" in Hamburg.

Democracy, as it exists today in most countries that the G20 leaders represent, is characterized by a deep gulf about which Marx had already worried more than 150 years ago, namely, the gulf between the political system and a civil society separated from it and structured by capital. This gulf depoliticizes civil society because it tends to establish a total barrier between the political system and its constituting power, that is, the people. As a consequence, democratic participants are turned into spectators. The protest marches and the public resistance are the consequence of this dividing line of our societies. Ironically, those who claim to stand for democracy must be protected against democracy.

In the meantime, the German national press, including *Der Spiegel* and *Die Zeit*, bemoaned that these protests were not a sign of a "democratic culture." Even if the abstract argument that the destructive negativity brought about by the "Black Bloc(k)" (which turned Hamburg's *Schanzenviertel* into a war-like zone) does not lead anywhere is correct, the targets of the outrage of the most radical protestors such as private property, the hypocritical attitude of most citizens, global wealth divisions, and the militarized state are rarely really analyzed and named. Instead, the protests are dismissed as "violent" without a clear understanding that the G20 leaders stand for a global military imperialism, a security and control system, as well as a global dynamics of wealth accumulation involving by far some of the most violent arrangements that ever existed; this is the case even though this is not always visible on our media screens. Instead, the centrist media, think tanks, and public relations spokespersons tend to depict the protestors' violence as the main problem, even when many first-person accounts pointed out that it was the police that provoked the violence by overextending the already massive security measures and limitations of constitutional rights of German and non-German citizens alike.

As a consequence, a member of the right-wing party *AfD* (Alternative for Germany), herself a representative of a state parliament, called for shooting radical left activists and the police union organization announced via Twitter that limiting constitutional rights is constitutive of democracy. In addition, the police compiled a secret blacklist of journalists and more than thirty lost their accreditation: a practice that we have seen in states such as Russia and Turkey. Given this "hatred of democracy" (Rancière) and these authoritarian reactions, signs of discontent could be detected in the German media, but overall, the attention had shifted away from the connection between capital, power, and police violence to focus instead on those few who were attacking the connection with pavement bricks.[1]

Given this overall situation, should we read these events as a sign of hope in times at which the "post-Marxist" intellectual left is still struggling to redefine itself in the face of its twentieth-century defeats, or should we read them as a sign of further failure and defeat?

Contemporary post-Marxist ideas ranging from Foucault and Laclau/Mouffe to Butler and Žižek are rooted, to a large extent, in political and social experiences after 1945 and 1968 in Europe, such as the failure of the French and Italian Communist parties, the exhaustion of the East European socialist project, the downfall of the Soviet Union and the German Democratic Republic, the development of welfare states, the stabilization of representative democracies in Europe, the development of the European Union as well as the events in Hungary, Prague, and May 1968 in Paris. Moreover, contemporary left thought is also rooted in the development of the neoliberal era, which began with the Thatcher and Reagan administrations in Great Britain and the United States and was extended then by social-democratic governments under Tony Blair, Gerhard Schröder, and Bill Clinton. These in turn led to a destruction of traditional labor organizations and, through the embracement of global capital, to the hastened arrival of postindustrial social structures in Europe and the United States. Faced with these defeats and in accord with the overall liberal-democratic and centrist turn in most Western countries, most post-Marxists, such as Axel Honneth and Chantal Mouffe, gave up the idea that a fully liberated society could ever exist. As a consequence, thinking about political movements in a pluralistic and "antagonistic" context is, for most post-Marxists, more central than thinking about the possibility of a different world.

There are two exceptions to this generalized conceptual situation, namely, Antonio Negri and Alain Badiou: neither has given up on the idea of communism and on strong visions of a postcapitalist society even though their thinking represents two contrasting positions on the left political spectrum. On the one hand, we have Badiou's contemporary Maoist thinking, and on the other, Negri and Hardt's "postmodern" version of linking together topics concerning cognitive capitalism, biopolitics, and empire.

Although Negri and Hardt are usually described as offering a "non-dogmatic" version of post-Marxism, their position can be identified with the attempt to deliver a *contemporary* vision of Marxist thought that, at least to some extent, remains true to its core, namely, the connection between Marxist social theory and political philosophy. Accordingly, for them political thought can only be defined in connection with a theory of subjectivity and labor defined by recent developments in global capitalism.

In contradistinction to this and in relation to the question of how to combine social theory, political economy, and political thought, Badiou is furthest away from a Marxian base (broadly defined), insofar as one of his central claims is that politics needs to be rethought as "true" politics, which he conceives of as being independent from questions of social form and social-economic structure. Seen in this light, Badiou represents a political thinking that positions itself against Marx since it rejects any dialectical relation between the social-economic and the political.

Dissimilarly, Negri's thinking is, on a close reading, one of the few exceptions in contemporary post-Marxist thought, insofar as it remains, perhaps surprisingly for some readers, *closest* to the attempt to read the social and the political as *coconstitutive* of subjects. Consequently, the premise of this essay is different from the position of some commentators who, in a recent critique of Negri and Hardt, write that Negri and Hardt succumb "to the relativistic left-liberal point that truth has a diversity of different meanings and interpretations. For us, Hardt and Negri are indeed representatives of those left-liberal thinkers who we believe disavow the Real of capitalism."[2] It may be true that Negri and Hardt fail properly to understand contemporary capitalism; nevertheless, their thinking of politics cannot be disconnected from their thinking about contemporary forms of labor and productivity. As such, I argue, they have a far superior position in comparison to Badiou's outdated Maoist thinking in the form of an *"all or nothing,"* which falls back, especially once one understands the concrete aspects of his ideas, not only on idealism but also on what Adorno once called "regressive romanticism."

The differences between Negri and Badiou can be schematically presented in the following way:

	Negri	Badiou
The political agent	creative laborer/multitude	militant soldier/masses
Relation between the social-economic and the political	dialectical relation	primacy of politics
Marxism	theory and praxis	praxis
Form of the revolution	movements and transitions	events and ruptures
Communism	reappropriation of the common	absolute egalitarianism
Ethos	Joy	discipline

In what follows, I will side with Negri and suggest that, due to its abstractions, Badiou's political thinking should be rejected and, instead, Negri's model of thinking about the political in connection with the social should be favored. Badiou's thinking is still oriented along old Maoist (and Sartrean)[3] claims that the political can be conceived of as external to the social structure and the social form. As Balibar puts it, "the central materialist category for Badiou is not that of *social relations*, and even less that of *production*, but in the Maoist tradition, that of the *masses*."[4] Knowledge, technology, education, transportation and communication, military and police, geographical condition, ecological conditions, gender and race relations are all secondary for Badiou. Even if one might disagree with their analysis of contemporary forms of labor and subjectivity,[5] Negri's (and Hardt's) concept of the political in connection with the social is far superior to Badiou's notion, insofar as it takes the social into account as constitutive of the political and it does not lead to the consequence that we need to wait for some truth-event that can only be defined retroactively. As Negri pointed out, waiting for the revolutionary moment in Badiou's sense seems to be an extension of Heidegger's rather apolitical concept of *Gelassenheit*.[6]

Negri: Society Exists

Negri's basic position regarding the problem of how to think about left politics, revolution, and social struggles is not very difficult to understand.

Though he no longer puts it in words that stem directly from Marx, Negri does still argue that a proper analysis of the political openings and political resistance to the given system must be based on a thorough examination of where we currently are in general social and economic terms. Accordingly, we are asked to analyze the "changes taking place in the ontology of the present."[7] By "the ontology of the present," Negri has primarily four aspects in mind: (1) the changes in terms of labor productivity under the conditions of what others have called "cognitive capitalism"; (2) the emerging new "subjectivities" that are connected to new forms of labor and productivity; (3) the specific contemporary domination and control that capital forces upon us; and (4) the global structures related to the state and its system of material apparatuses. As Negri puts it, "materialism today means the biopolitical context."[8] He writes that one goal of his philosophizing is

> to understand how a new materialist analysis, applied politically in a class sense, could create a proposition for social struggles against capitalist command—and for how critique should work; not by seeking to impose (sometimes heroically; too often in vain) a past onto a present that had by now been thoroughly reshaped by the reforms and transformations taking place in command and in capitalist exploitation, but by shaking up this present, breaking it from the inside, and making possible the expression, in a rough and constituent manner, of the subjectivities that had been produced in it and were enclosed in it.[9]

The base theorem regarding the relation between the social-economic and the political is clearly formulated in the quote above insofar as Negri points out that the possibility of struggles *against* capital can only be defined, and are structured by, the *specific* form that the capital-labor relation has taken on in our times. To repeat the point: Even if one does not agree with all aspects of Negri's and Hardt's "ontology of the present," the fundamental claim about the substantial intertwinement of the social and the political remains intact and, in this regard, Negri differs from most other "post-Marxist" philosophers who prioritize the political over the social and end up with totally different ontologies (such as Badiou's).

It is clear, then, that for Negri, any political struggle can only be defined in terms of how such struggles relate to capital, whereas Badiou's position disconnects the political from capital. Negri writes: "If this is the situation, it becomes logical and essential that the rupture—every rupture—should take place within this framework."[10] Put differently, the possibility of rupture and the *form* that it can take depend upon the contemporary social-economic situation, which, according to Negri, has significantly changed during the twentieth and twenty-first centuries. Badiou claims exactly the opposite, namely: the situation of capitalism has not changed a bit. Consequently, for Negri, the struggle to overcome a society determined by capital can only come from *within* a society organized by capital and must be built upon the openings provided by the dialectics of labor power and exploitation. In contrast, Badiou argues that *any* attempt to think about the political from within the system is helpless and meaningless insofar as it simply reproduces the dynamics of capital itself. Consequently, he also does not seem to take seriously Marx's own position that is of importance for Negri; namely, the idea that capital has the tendency to "socialize" itself.

As Marx already understands in volume 3 of *Capital*, with the growing public nature of capital (through public investments, stock markets, public stakeholders, and so on) capital opens up the possibility of what Marx calls, in a letter to Engels, the "communism of capital," the idea of which is decisive for Negri.[11] Stated in Negri's own words, "Under these conditions, subjected to this dynamic, capital strips itself of any 'individuality'; it becomes *social capital*. But even more important is the fact that the 'productive forces' immediately become 'social.'"[12]

Given these specific social forms of capital and labor, the political struggle cannot be understood, for Negri, without a precise comprehension of the political subjects (multitude) and the productive capacities (cognitive and affective labor) by which these subjects are determined. Put differently, according to Negri, political struggle has a social *form* whereas for Badiou political struggle is socially formless. Instead, as Badiou argues, the political subject is constituted by an "idea" (I will return to this in the next section). As a consequence, all social-economic mediators, such as labor, communication, transport, exchange, technologies, and so on, have no importance for Badiou.[13]

We can already see at this point how abstract Badiou's position remains in the end, insofar as he does not take seriously Marx's advice, in the introduction to the *Grundrisse*, that one cannot rob a "stockjobbing nation" in the same way as one would rob a society that is determined by "cow shepherds," given that the plane of the relations of production and distribution is decisive. Put in contemporary terms, one cannot beat a highly militarized state that is based on the development of digital technologies and highly educated laborers with pavement bricks and beer bottles. Accordingly, the *entire* trust of Badiou's vision is based on the massification of populations and the "people's war."

In contrast, Negri remains in close proximity to the notion of social experiment; his philosophy is more playful, open, positive, hopeful, and is also in solidarity with the oppressed. Trust in life and joy of life "in the sense of the increasing power of an expansive social subject" are central:[14] "No, the human being is not one dimensional, and the concepts about which we have spoken up to now, which the left, moralizing and pessimistic, claims as its own—these concepts must be categorically rejected. In the first place, because they are not true; in the second place, because they produce ethical impotence and political defeatism."[15] Where Badiou remains in safe philosophical distance and sees only limitations, Negri sees possibilities and potentialities. Constituent power "always refers to the future."[16]

The concepts of movement politics and reform are far more important for Negri than they are for Badiou. As Negri jokingly puts this, "ensuring the recognition of these common rights is the only right way out of the crisis. One last joke on this subject: there will be some (Rancière, Žižek, and Badiou have already said as much) who see these 'reforms' as completely useless, indeed as damaging for workers—well, why not try them? Why don't we suggest them to Wall Street?"[17] What Negri calls "dispositifs of *exodus*"[18] refers to revolutionary openings *because* the contemporary developments of cognitive labor has led to a situation in which labor is totally subsumed under capital. Therefore, at least if we accept Negri's premises about the nature of the contemporary productive subject, the subject remains outside of capital accumulation since cognitive and affective labor, in the form of what Marx called "the general intellect," create forms of expression that are difficult for capital to dominate and subject to its power: "When labor is recognized as immaterial, highly scientific, affective, and cooperative (when, in other words, its relationship to existence and to forms of life is revealed and when it is defined as a social function of the community), we can see that from the laboring processes (follow the elaboration of networks of social valorization) and the production of alternative subjectivities."[19]

The intellectualization of the labor process leads to a different form of the class struggle as a "political recomposition of antagonism"; in addition, the old Marxist distinction between intellectual and manual labor no longer holds, for Negri, insofar as nowadays, in cognitive capitalism, almost all labor is intellectual.[20] "Today the intellectual can speak as a common individual."[21] The contemporary conflict lines that surround biopiracy, patent rights, and intellectual property are probably a good example for what Negri has in mind: capital is unable to discipline and command intellectual and creative laborers insofar as the "networks of cooperation"[22] and the well-educated laboring subjects can only unfold their creativity if they are not totally commanded by capital: "immaterial labor does not require command."[23] All capital can do is to establish legal barriers and parasitically take surplus value from a system of labor that, as such, could also exist without capital.

One could just think of academic publishing corporations as an example: they do not educate their laborers, they get their laborers for free, they do not control and command the productive subjects; instead, they steal the access rights from academic authors, sell the latter's products for a lot of money, create ideologies of "status" and "hierarchy" as well as legally fence in and rent out (via online fees and library access) the products of academics who—at least in principle—no longer need the publishing industries for their labor. As Negri sums up, "what happens on the web, and the way in which public and private rights enter into conflict with common practices, is now a daily phenomenon."[24] The commons *could* exist (via free and open online libraries and cooperative publishing platforms). The exodus of the multitude[25] becomes possible *because* of contemporary social and economic realities, which *could* provide a common ground, provide new subjective desires, and be built upon "subjects' capacity of expression."[26] Labor becomes increasingly autonomous from capital and, via networks and cooperative nature, we see a new "figure of the *common potentiality* of labor"[27] as the "*potenza* of the general intellect"[28] emerging: "Capital is, rather, always a relationship of power, and machinery itself (subsumed by social capital) is itself a relationship. This relationship cannot be defined deterministically. It is struggle and conflict, it is a historical assemblage—and hence open-ended—of victories and defeats: this is where politics lives; and the changes, the effects of struggle, the workers' bodies' being 'within or beyond' are variables, dynamics, ontologically defined with the passing of time."[29]

Since life in its entirety has been subjected to capital accumulation, biopolitics, which now contains entire populations, is the new field of class struggle, even though the new forms of class conflict can no longer be arranged along the lines of factories and factory workers. It is clear, then, that for Negri the potential struggle lines can *only* be defined from within capital and labor. "Living labor is the internal force that constantly poses not only the subversion of the capitalist process of production but also the construction of an alternative."[30]

Given the intellectualization of labor, communication itself becomes productive,[31] and it is therefore absolutely coherent to assume that the political subjects are determined and defined by these communicative capacities that, in turn, are the result of the general intellect, science, and common production. "But communication is life. In advanced capitalism, therefore, conflict, struggle and diversity are focused on communication, with capital, by means of communication, trying to preconstitute the determinants of life."[32]

As we will see in the next section, Badiou does not pay *any* attention to what, from a Marxist point of view, is the *fundamental* connection among forms of labor, forms of subjectivity, and forms of political struggle. Seen from this point of view, Badiou is an anti-Marxist thinker insofar as he claims that the "true" political subject is defined from *outside* the system. In contradistinction, Negri has it in the following way: "But this is not the case: capitalism is fought both *within* and *against*; it does not permit an 'outside,' and this is because the adversary of living labour is not simply the abstract figure of exploitation reshaped in the continuity of the circuits of the labour process, but the concrete figure of the capitalist who sucks out surplus labour."[33]

Badiou: Society Does Not Exist

In contradistinction to Negri, Badiou's ontology—which excludes the social as irrelevant to truth—is characterized by the central concept of "the event." Events are truth-related occurrences that restructure the entire reality. Badiou assumes that there are four such events that constitute truth, namely, politics, art, science, and love. Events cannot be foreseen strategically and they bring about a "truth procedure" that carries with itself a radical restructuring of everything that exists within historical situations, which, as such, remain singular. Events cannot be planned or instrumentally brought about; yet if they occur, the reality of a singular situation changes in its relations and its utterances, as well as with respect to the things that make up this singular situation itself. Truths establish themselves retroactively.

As we can already notice here, the social does not appear on Badiou's list of truth-relevant events; instead, it is treated, particularly in relation to politics, as a secondary area, given that for Badiou political events are ultimately constituted *outside* of existing social-economic frameworks. Accordingly, politics is an event that functions as the ultimate ground of the social, indeed as *external* to the social insofar as social organization is always rooted in historically relevant (re)organizations of the social reality through "true" thought as politics. As such, events and, in particular, political events are characterized as being beyond any historical transitions. The new is described in terms such as "rupture," "sudden emergence," or "explosion."[34] These are clear indicators of Badiou's extreme thesis that politics can be thought of as being *outside* of, and *external* to, any social determination.[35] Truth-events, we might say, seem to come from *nowhere*. The possibility of truth in politics or of a true politics is, accordingly, *always* possible, even if a given situation makes such an event of reorganization unlikely or improbable.

It comes as no surprise, then, that for Badiou Marxism is neither a philosophy nor a theory but *only* a political praxis that is constituted through "truth." Marxism is a politics that is thought of in name of the idea of equality: "Genuine Marxism, which is identified with rational political struggle for an egalitarian organization of society, doubtless began around 1848."[36] Badiou's extremely reductive position is nicely visible in the following passage: "Marxism . . . is neither a branch of economics (theory of the relations of production), nor a branch of sociology (objective description of 'social reality'), nor a philosophy (a dialectical conceptualization of contradictions). It is, let us reiterate, the organized knowledge of the political means required to undo society and finally realize an egalitarian, rational figure of collective organization for which the name is 'communism.'"[37]

Regardless of the question of how, in the previous statement, we are supposed to understand "collective organization," this extreme view of Marxism as praxis, even when it is no longer thought of within the party paradigm, reduces the entire theoretical and scientific side of Marxism to a political project instead of understanding it as a dialectics of praxis *and* theory, as Marx did.[38] Consequently, the critique of political economy, labor, contemporary forms of capitalism, and so on disappear from Badiou's radar screen. In short, for Badiou, society has no reality and does not belong to reality because, in all of its aspects, society is the *effect* of politics, which brings about social organization. In this vision, we might add, society is *only* political organization. Consequently, Marxism must be taken as a movement that—independent from all socially determining factors—either reorganizes the entire reality or is meaningless.

This reduction of Marxism to politics, consequently, comes along with Badiou's rejection of social theory and his ahistorical and reductive version of capitalism, which is especially visible in Badiou's reduction of capital, capitalism, and other categories of society to something that is irrelevant for ontology.[39] According to Badiou, capitalism, for example, is a "regime of gangsters," driven by profit and greed and characterized by privatization.[40] Capital is simply defined as a "nihilistic" principle through which the market expands globally, formalizes communication, and leads to the hegemony of the United States[41] Instead of analyzing capitalism as a system of social organization that is characterized by a specific set of social-economic categories, as well as by the central category of life, Badiou offers only general platitudes for understanding it. Reflections on the specific social form of social reproduction and the subjectivities that it brings about are missing since, for Badiou, political subjects are not constituted within the system but come from the outside.

The coming social formation, a postcapitalist world, need not be thought of as a different social organization of labor and society, according to Badiou; rather, it purely reorganizes itself in political terms, which are based on the "force of an idea,"[42] namely, communism. This idea constitutes and addresses individuals, according to Badiou, as political subjects who project the egalitarian idea onto a nonexisting history and thereby militantly reorganize reality.[43] Indeed, according to Badiou, the political subject is "a militant of this truth" through the "incorporation" of the idea.[44] Faith and conviction are its central elements: "A politics is," as he puts it, "an active and organized conviction, a thought in action that indicates unseen possibilities."[45] The individual goes through a process of "subjectivation."[46] Indeed, "the communist idea," as Badiou has it, "is what constitutes the becoming-political Subject of the individual as also and at the same time his or her projection into history."[47] According to Badiou's idealism, through this political baptism and renewal of isolated and "animalistic" bodies, these bodies now belong to a new order. As Badiou phrases it, "without the idea, the only thing left is an animalized humanity. Capitalism thereby is the animalization of the human beast, who no longer lives except in terms of its interests and what it deems to be its due. This animalization is extremely dangerous because it is devoid of values and laws."[48]

Badiou's view of capitalism as "animalization," its reduction to an apocalyptic nihilist system, and its definition as a life without idea should remind us of a mix of Christian theology, extreme speciesism, Heideggerian views of modernity, and Platonic essentialism. "The idea," as Badiou puts it elsewhere, "is that which makes the life of an individual, a human animal, orient itself according to the True" and capitalism is portrayed as a system in which people live without the idea (of the True).[49] Capitalism is here characterized by a spiritual downfall onto our own flesh and meaningless life, which only the baptism by *the* idea can redeem. Moreover, the subjection to "the" idea of communism is here introduced as a form of "possession." Adrien Johnston properly calls this a figure of grace.[50] The subjection of the body to an idea is nothing else than the *total* control of that body. In reality, however, even if we imagine a situation in which the current political system becomes unstable, it will not be simply the idea that will rule over bodies; instead, we will need to take into account the idea's *social* form, that is, its *mediation* by leaders, different levels of organizations (even if not the party), political technologies, embodied practices, and communication technologies (which, in turn, presuppose a social system of knowledge, knowledge production, productive forces at a specific historical level, and so on). Moreover, without some kind of knowledge about how to reorganize the *social* world, all political ideas will remain empty.[51] Even if we believed that Badiou's abstract notion of "the" communist idea injected into bodies makes *any* sense, we would however still need to take into account that this idea would need to go through an entire system of relations of production and its accompanying social relations before it could enter and steer bodies toward the golden land. As a consequence of his a-subjective concept of the subject, Badiou's political subject is at its base, in contrast to Negri's, neither productive nor creative.

Badiou wants us to become reborn communists in the hope that the idea of communism will turn our meaningless lives into spiritualized subjects who overcome their animalized individuality by turning into fighters for the truth. This image of "church soldiers" is very central to Badiou's "visions" insofar as the Badiouan communist soldiers do not simply liberate us from the dynamics of capital domination but, instead, free us from the downfall of civilization, turn us around spiritually, and save us from our "animalization." Needless to say, all of these terms are also used on the far right. Moreover, all stages of Badiou's political thinking are structured by hierarchies. Everything is conceived top-down: first the idea, then the political axiom, then the concrete directive, then the procedures, then the consequences, and so on. All this reminds one more of machine-like party politics and its total discipline than of what contemporary social organizations in all their pluralistic expressions are and can be about.

The underlying authoritarian tone in Badiou's theorizing is more than disturbing. Social communication, plural forms of resistance, and a nonhierarchical organization of social movements are absent. As he put it in a recent interview, "the people have nothing except their discipline."[52] This might be true for the poorest populations on earth, and it might have had some ramifications during the anticolonial wars, but it is very unlikely that a Maoist revolution would lead anywhere in advanced technological societies. One needs more than political "discipline" to move toward a socialist society, which includes technical experts, educated individuals, ethical visions, and knowledge. Put differently, it requires *more* than empty and abstract political agents; namely, it needs historically specific *social individuals*. In sum, Badiou's collectivist vision of a mass that marches behind a leading idea, that is, a "collective life under the sway of the idea"[53] is, given the experiences of the twentieth century, truly frightening insofar as one wonders what would happen to those who may not want to subject themselves to Badiou's collectivist idea. We should note that it is only a small step from Badiou's talk about "animalization" to the logic of political cleansing given that, as a consequence of their status as "beasts" and "bodies without truth," those who do not want to subject themselves to the communist idea in a communist future could easily be called "pest" and insects."

The frightening aspect of Badiou's thinking is further evidenced by his claim that communism "will gradually reduce all the 'big differences' in terms of social organization: differences between the city and the country, rich and poor, manual and intellectual labor, women and men."[54] In addition, Badiou claims that labor division[55] will be overcome.[56] If one imagines a world without any of these differences, then one must come to the conclusion that it is modeled after small religious (agrarian) communities that are held together both by unified labor and by religious faith in what constitutes the spirituality of this community. The (communist) religion must be one-dimensional. In this vein, the idea that overcoming class division also overcomes labor division is highly doubtful, as our complex societies require at least a minimum of socially necessary labor time, which will, I submit, be characterized by *extreme* labor division (and time *off* for voluntary labor).[57] As Adorno put it in 1968, the call for an abolishment of labor division is "regressive romanticism."[58] Badiou's call for abolishing labor division echoes attempts by the early Soviets to eradicate all specialists for the sake of collectivization and, I submit, is naïve and destructive, given the current level of labor division and sociological analysis in our contemporary societies. In addition, Marx himself argues, in his critique of the *Gotha Program*, that labor division and unequal distributions are necessary for a socialist society.

What Badiou pushes aside in what he presents as a self-evident interpretation of Marxism as a primarily political project is Marx's critique, in his *Critique of the Gotha Program*, of a simple-minded egalitarian position and the idea of communist social organization as a form of radical *individualism*, in which the individual does *not* become identical with the collective. As Negri puts it, political expressions of the multitude can be multifarious: "The multitude's unity of action is the multiplicity of expressions it is capable of."[59] Negri is much closer to Marx's position than Badiou is. According to Negri, total egalitarianism is less central; communism is defined as "radical economic-political democracy and a search for freedom."[60] This is because "labor is defined ontologically as freedom through the common: labor is productive when it is free, otherwise it is dead, and it is free only when it is common."[61]

In addition, Badiou claims "that human societies do not need to be governed by the principle of private interest."[62] This claim is also highly doubtful, as its underlying assumption is that the individual interests and the collective interests become *one and the same*, that the individual is *totally* absorbed by the whole, that rights are no longer needed, and that all conflicts can be solved without the intrusion of law and institutions that are positioned *between* the individual and the collective. The individual no longer counts, if we take into account that individuals express themselves by individual desires, wants, and *interests*. Badiou's claim that all of this ultimately leads to a "healthy" society seems to follow a dangerous *logic of eradication* that we have seen in action during the twentieth century but, as Andreas Arndt has pointed out, this position has nothing to do with Marx.[63] Finally, Badiou is a legal positivist, if not even—as others of the radical left before him have been—a *legal nihilist*, for the law is reduced to an instrument of the *status quo* and an instrument of the state[64]; and any normative elements and rights of *individuals* that could point toward the *transcendence* of the given social organization and to the expression of freedom are reduced to what Althusser called the repressive state apparatuses. For example, Badiou states that the establishment of international law might have "some demonstrable merit," but that this does not "represent *any* progress in terms of political intelligibility."[65]

Badiou on Negri on Badiou

Given Badiou's political projections, we can easily see why and how Badiou positions himself in opposition to Negri on almost all levels of thinking about society and the political. To Badiou's mind, the question of the political is not a question about classes, movements, and other agents; rather, as he argues against Negri, it is a question of how to organize a mass under the heading of an idea. The antiglobalization movement, for example, is rejected as operating within the system. Thus, protesting at a G20 meeting does not make sense, according to this position, because it requires one to remain too close to the operations of capital. If we follow this position all the way to its end, then we need to conclude that any attempt to develop alternatives to the current economic system, such as degrowth, steady state economy, new climate technologies, and so on, all remain within the system and, hence, they are considered by Badiou as *meaningless*, that is, spiritless, since this is only a reconfiguration of the same:[66] "And it is not the sympathetic and unavoidable language of movementist democracy that will save us. 'Down with this or that,' 'all together we will win,' 'get out,' 'resistance!,' 'it is right to rebel.' . . . All of this is capable of momentarily summoning forth collective affects, and, tactically, this is all very useful—but it leaves the question of a legible strategy entirely unresolved. This is too poor a language for a situated discussion of the future of emancipatory actions."[67] As he puts it even more forcefully, "Politics is the real of communism, in all of its forms. *Everything else* is a matter of the state, of managing things."[68]

> What kind of politics is *really* heterogeneous to what capital demands?—that is today's question. Our politics is situated at the heart of things, in the factories, in a direct relation with employers and with capital. But it remains a matter of politics—that is

to say, of thought, of statements, of practices. All the efforts to construct an alternative economy strike me as pure and simple abstractions, if not simply driven by the unconscious vector of capital's own reorganization. We can see, for example—and will see more and more—how so many environmentalist demands simply provide capital with new fields of investment, new inflections and new deployments. Why? Because every proposition that directly concerns the economy can be assimilated by capital. This is so by definition, since capital is indifferent to the qualitative configuration of things. So long as it can be transformed or aligned in terms of market value, everything's fine. The only strategy worth the name is a political struggle—that is to say, a singular, active subjectivity, a thought-praxis.[69]

It comes as no surprise, then, that Badiou rejects Negri's dialectical position in its entirety:

We have on the one side the definition of democracy as a form of the state, and on the other, democracy as an immanent determination of the collective movement. But I think the classical opposition of state and movement is saturated. We cannot simply oppose state oppression or the oppressive system with, on the other side, the creativity of the movement. That's an old concept, not a new one. We have to find a new concept of democracy, one that is outside the opposition of formal democracy (which is democracy as form of state) and concrete democracy (which is the democracy of the popular movement). Negri remains inside this classical opposition, while using other names: Empire for state, multitude for movement. But new names are not new things.[70]

For Negri, social ontology is primary and, as a consequence, communism and its possibility cannot be thought of without understanding *from where* and *in what social form* they are possible.[71] Communism is a *potentiality*. Badiou's thinking of the event is opposed to this idea that the future must be grounded in the present for the event comes from nowhere. However, an ecologically sustainable society or a society that organizes the commons without private property cannot be reduced to a merely political organization, as Badiou seems to assume, since it requires well-educated subjects, certain institutions that form it, administrative institutions, and specific organizations of labor and technologies that cannot be brought about through politics alone. Since Badiou reduces the political subject to an embodied idea, all social aspects are removed from it.

In contradistinction, Negri argues that "without historical ontology there is no communism."[72] Contra Badiou, Negri poses the following:

> We have to understand, then, whether and to what extent, within this variation of different positions, there sometimes emerge positions that, in the name of the universality of the proposed political project, oppose ontological praxis—for example by denying the historicity of categories such as "primitive accumulation" and consequently by proposing the hypothesis of communism as a pure and immediate restoration of the commons; or by devaluing the productive transformations that configure in various ways the "technical composition" of labor power (which is real and actual production of materialist subjectivity in the relationship between relations of production and forces of production) and by asserting that the root of communist protest is simply human nature (always the same, *sub forma arithmetica*)—and so forth: this is clearly an ambiguous repackaging of idealism in its transcendental aspect.[73]

Negri argues against abstract definitions of egalitarianism or communism: "the universal is an abstraction from subjects isolated from each other, whereas the commons is that which each subject can build"; that is, the difference between individual and collective has to be maintained.[74] "The foundation of democracy (and, without contradiction, the foundation of communism) is not the development of equality, but the freedom of the individual, as a positive, cooperative action."[75]

Conclusion

To return to the events described at the beginning of this essay, we can see that Negri's philosophy allows us to see the positive, the new, the creative, and the *potentiality* in the G20 protests, whereas in Badiou's world protest marches are nothing more than a perverted affirmation of the world of capital and therefore should be dismissed.[76] We should note, though, that Badiou would classify the destructive riots that occurred in connection with the G20 and the Black Bloc(k) as an "immediate riot," that is, as one with limited spatial extent and without concept (idea).[77] In contrast,

Negri argues that "constituent power is defined here: where the multitude seeks to construct itself anew through subjectivity, and the virtual thus presents itself as more real than the real. Constituent power is not something that is prefigured. . . . It is the efficacy of the struggle, of the claims of the multitude, of the *Potenza* of its movements—this is what invents and constitutes new reality."[78] Negri is here close to Marx's famous claim that "mankind . . . inevitably sets itself only such tasks as it is able to solve, since closer examination will always show that the problem itself arises only when the material conditions for its solution are already present or at least in the course of formation."[79] However, this view requires us to see and lay open the *potentialities* within the given; that is, it requires a return to a dialectical theory of social reality and a dialectical theory of the relation between theory and praxis. This is to say that we need *critical* concepts of technology, postgrowth, money, and sustainable economic visions. Badiou's political philosophy remains disappointing in this regard. Accordingly, we do not need to wait for the big rupture. Communism is, as Marx told us, the real movement of history: whether we know it or not.

Notes

1. One week after the meeting, Germany and France announced that they would build a new "European" fighter jet with increased military budgets and the German government approved new multibillion-dollar military technology sales (boats, trucks, armor) to Saudi Arabia and a U-Boat deal with Egypt. In the meantime, the Turkish government—with the help of more than 8,500 police officers—carried out further overnight repressive actions against around 1,000 critical journalists, academics, and artists. By now (as of this writing), Turkey has put more than 40,000 people in prison and laid off more than 120,000 people as a result of the military coup against the Turkish government in July 2016, primarily in the academic and legal systems. In most cases, all this took place without any legal protection for the victims.

2. Colin Cremin and John Michael Roberts, "Postmodern Left-Liberalism: Hardt and Negri and the Disavowal of Critique," *Critical Sociology* 37, 2 (2011): 180.

3. For Sartre's dismissal of social-economic considerations and his focus on political strategy, see the very enlightening interview in Jean-Paul Sartre, *Between Existentialism and Marxism*, trans. John Mathews (New York: Pantheon Books, 1974), 118–140.

4. Quoted in Gavin Walker, "On Marxism's Field of Operations: Badiou and the Critique of Political Economy," *Historical Materialism* 20, 2 (2012): 46; see also Alain Badiou, *Metapolitics*, trans. J. Barker (London: Verso, 2006), 73.

5. For more on this, see Christian Lotz, *The Capitalist Schema: Time, Money, and the Culture of Abstraction* (Lanham. MD: Lexington Books, 2014), and "Marx contra Negri: Value, Abstract Labor, and Money," in *Contemporary Political Italian Philosophy*, ed. Antonio Calcagno (Albany: State University of New York Press, 2015).

6. Antonio Negri, *Marx and Foucault*, trans. Ed Emery (London: Polity Press, 2017), 32.

7. Negri, *Marx and Foucault*, 4.

8. Negri, *Marx and Foucault*, 37.

9. Negri, *Marx and Foucault*, 2.

10. Negri, *Marx and Foucault*, 30.

11. For more on this, see Christian Lotz, *Christian Lotz zu Karl Marx: Das Maschinenfragment* (Hamburg: Laika Verlag, 2014).

12. Negri, *Marx and Foucault*, 44.

13. In contrast, Negri writes: "If we want to describe the political transitions taking place in the age of communication technologies and socialized knowledge, in the age of the postmodern biopolitical, we have to remember that the fundamental element traversing this reality is living labor as it places its hegemony in intellectual and affective, cooperative and excedent action" (Antonio Negri, *Empire and Beyond*, trans. Ed Emery [London: Polity Press, 2010], 164).

14. Antonio Negri and Michael Hardt, *Labor of Dionysus: A Critique of the State Form* (Minneapolis: University of Minnesota Press, 1994), 1; for this, see also Negri, *Insurgencies*, 323.

15. Antonio Negri, *The Winter is Over: Writings on Transformation Denied, 1989–1995*, trans. Isabella Bertoletti, James Cascaito, and Andrea Casson, ed. Giuseppe Caccia (Los Angeles: Semiotext(e), 2013), 137.

16. Negri, *Insurgencies*, 11.

17. Negri, *Marx and Foucault*, 31.

18. Negri, *Marx and Foucault*, 39.

19. Negri and Hardt, *Labor of Dionysus*, 13.

20. Negri and Hardt, *Labor of Dionysus*, 21.

21. Negri, *The Winter Is Over*, 117. On a side note, this position also has consequences for the Marxist theory of the state since the state is no longer, as for example Poulantzas claimed, the proper center of intellectual labor (see Negri, *The Winter Is Over*, 116); rather, it expands over the entire society.

22. Antonio Negri, *Reflections on Empire*, trans. Ed Emery (London: Polity Press, 2008), 107.

23. Negri, *Reflections on Empire*, 106.

24. Antonio Negri, *The Porcelain Workshop: For A New Grammar of Politics*, trans. Noura Wedell (Los Angeles: Semiotext(e), 2008), 69.

25. Negri, *Marx and Foucault*, 40.

26. Negri, *Marx and Foucault*, 41.

27. Negri, *Marx and Foucault*, 52.

28. Negri, *Reflections on Empire*, 112.

29. Negri, *Marx and Foucault*, 46.
30. Negri and Hardt, *Labor of Dionysus*, 6.
31. Negri, *The Winter Is Over*, 133.
32. Antonio Negri, *The Politics of Subversion: A Manifesto for the Twenty-First Century*, trans. James Newell (London: Polity Press, 2005), 118.
33. Negri, *Marx and Foucault*, 53.
34. For this, see Adrian Johnston, *Badiou, Žižek, and Political Transformations* (Evanston, IL: Northwestern University Press, 2009), 6.
35. Johnston, *Badiou, Žižek, and Political Transformations*, 7.
36. Badiou, *The Rebirth of History*, trans. Gregory Elliott (London: Verso, 2012), 8.
37. Badiou, *The Rebirth of History*, 8.
38. Badiou rejects that the idea of communism is dialectical; see Alain Badiou, *Philosophie und die Idee des Kommunismus. Im Gespräch mit Peter Engelmann* (Vienna: Passagen Verlag, 2014), 45; thereby, he rejects the ideas presented in Marx's and Engel's *Manifesto*.
39. Badiou, *The Rebirth of History*, 12.
40. Badiou, *The Rebirth of History*, 13.
41. Alain Badiou, *Infinite Thought*, trans. Oliver Feltham and Justin Clemens (New York: Continuum, 2005), 120.
42. Badiou, *The Rebirth of History*, 15,
43. Alain Badiou, "The Idea of Communism," in *The Idea of Communism*, ed. Costas Douzinas and Slavoj Žižek (London: Verso, 2010), 3–5.
44. Badiou, "The Idea of Communism," 3.
45. Alain Badiou, "Our Contemporary Impotence," *Radical Philosophy* 181 (September–October 2013): 45.
46. Badiou, "The Idea of Communism," 3.
47. Badiou, "The Idea of Communism," 4.
48. Alain Badiou, *Philosophy and the Event*, trans. Louise Burchill (London: Polity Press, 2013), 35.
49. Alain Badiou, *Second Manifesto for Philosophy*, trans. Louise Burchill (London: Polity Press, 2011), 105.
50. Johnston, *Badiou, Žižek, and Political Transformations*, 18.
51. Astonishingly, despite his dismissive gesture toward Arendt (see Alain Badiou, "The Saturated Generic Identity of the Working Class," 2006, http://interactivist.autonomedia.org/node/5400, chap. 1), Badiou comes very close to Arendt's preference for the political as the true realm of freedom over the social understood as the realm of necessities and the reproduction of life. In contrast, for Negri, freedom must be *part of* the labor process (see Negri, *Empire and Beyond*, 164–166).
52. Badiou, *Philosophie und die Idee des Kommunismus*, 82.
53. Alain Badiou, *Controversies: A Dialogue on the Politics and Philosophy of Our Time*, trans. Susan Spitzer (London: Polity Press, 2014), 12, 157.
54. Alain Badiou, *Confrontation: Alain Badiou Alain Finkielkraut*, trans. Susan Spitzer (London: Polity Press, 2014), 116.

55. Badiou, *Confrontation*, 97.

56. Badiou seems to have shifted his position in recent publications. In Alain Badiou, *Bedingungen und Unendlichkeit. Ein Gespräch mit Gernot Kamecke*, trans. Gernot Kamecke (Berlin: Merve, 2015), 126, he states that the idea of communism is based on (1) a form of politics that cannot be transformed into a state, (2) an idea of egalitarianism as the overcoming of class division, and (3) resistance to the view that the entire world is controlled by private property. All these points sound more reasonable than some of the earlier definitions. However, given these shifts, we can see how the concept of "idea" remains an empty placeholder for many things and Badiou nowhere explains why "the" idea must be the idea of communism and not, for example, the libertarian or fascist idea.

57. "'Communism' signifies the *historical hypothesis* according to which *it is not necessary* that freedom be ruled by property, and human societies be directed by a strict oligarchy of powerful businessmen and their servants in politics, the police, the military and the media. A society is possible in which what Marx calls 'free association' predominates, where productive labour is collectivized, where the disappearance of the great non-egalitarian contradictions (between intellectual and manual labour, between town and country, between men and women, between management and labour, etc. . . . .) is under way, and where decisions that concern everyone are really everyone's business. We should treat this egalitarian possibility as a principle of thought and action, and not let go of it" (Badiou, "Our Contemporary Impotence," 46).

58. Theodor W. Adorno, "Frankfurter Adorno Blätter VI," ed. Rolf Tiedemann (Frankfurt: Edition Text & Kritik, 2000), 146.

59. Negri, *The Porcelain Workshop*, 67.

60. Negri, *The Winter Is Over*, 199.

61. Negri, *Reflections on Empire*, 107; see also 166.

62. Badiou, *Confrontation*, 112.

63. For this, see Andreas Arndt, *Geschichte und Freiheitsbewusstsein: Zur Dialektik der Freiheit bei Hegel und Marx* (Berlin: Eule der Minerva, 2015), 154.

64. Badiou, *Bedingungen und Unendlichkeit*, 75.

65. Badiou, *Controversies*, 55; emphasis added.

66. Badiou, "Our Contemporary Impotence," 4.

67. Badiou, "Our Contemporary Impotence," 45.

68. Badiou 2014, *Controversies*, 23; emphasis added. In a recent article, Gavin Walker provides a reconstruction of Badiou's political and intellectual background in French radical politics in the 1960s, namely, the *Groupe Yenan-economie*: "By what miracle today is technology able to avoid capitalism by developing social relations in labour of an entirely different nature, of a socialist nature? This miracle only exists in the heads of the revisionists. Today, automation does nothing but prolong the essential tendencies studied by Marx. It does not make any point as a decisive rupture" (quoted in Walker, "On Marxism's Field of Operations," 59).

69. Alain Badiou, *Ethics*, trans. Peter Hallward (London: Verso, 2002), 106.

70. Alain Badiou, "The Saturated Generic Identity of the Working Class."

71. "First off, the systematic recourse to constitutional reforms that are proposed at the European level certainly plays the role of an obstacle here. What interests the movements, by contrast, is to ask what political actions can be put to work to favor the processes of subjectivization that are adapted to a new subversive and communist project" (Antonio Negri, "From the End of National Lefts to Subversive Movements for Europe," *Radical Philosophy 181* [September–October 2013]: 31).

72. Negri, *Marx and Foucault*, 73.

73. Negri, *Marx and Foucault*, 75.

74. Negri, *Marx and Foucault*, 73.

75. Negri, *The Winter Is Over*, 149.

76. Negri sees this point clearly: "For him [Badiou], indeed, every mass movement is a petty bourgeois performance and every immediate struggle, whether of material or cognitive labour, of the class or of 'social labour' [*lavoro sociale*'] is something that will never touch the substance of power—every enlargement of the collective productive capacity of proletarian subjectivity will be merely an extension of their subjection to the logic of the system; thus the object is unattainable, the subject is undefineable—unless theory produces it, to discipline it, to adapt it to truth and to raise it to the level of event, beyond political practice, beyond history" (Negri, *Marx and Foucault*, 76).

77. Badiou, *The Rebirth of History*, 21.

78. Negri, *Reflections on Empire*, 110.

79. Marx and Engels, *Werke*, 13:9.

Part Five

Voices of Difference

13

A Critique of the Forms of Political Action
Carla Lonzi and G. W. F. Hegel

Maria Luisa Boccia

The Originary Differentiation of the Sexes

In what is undoubtedly her most famous writing, *Let's Spit on Hegel*, Carla Lonzi argues in favor of consciousness-raising (*pratica dell'autocoscienza*) as the only possible practice because it is personal and not "political." This claim is true even when we need to engage in operations that directly affect politics such as a radical transformation or revolution in the existing order. The necessity of challenging "all that has been done and thought" in human history, while nevertheless always starting from and remaining anchored in the person, is clearly announced at the beginning of the essay: "The woman problem signifies a relation between *each woman*, who is without power, history, culture, and roles, and *each man* with his power, history, culture, and absolute role."[1]

For "each woman," the problem of her being a woman and of her relation with men is grounded on a common foundation; yet each woman is marked by an irrepressible diversity such that no woman is completely identifiable with that common foundation, nor is it easy to abstract and separate out from concrete specific exigencies a single essence or a commonality that represents the problem of *all* women. The nonindividualistic and particular dimension of the "woman problem" takes shape in the relation of similarity and difference that connects the single woman to sexual gender and not to a collective sexual identity. Furthermore, the woman who wonders about her own being and posits herself as a different subject challenges for "each man" his own self-positing as consciousness and absolute subject. Therefore, she opposes herself to history, culture, and power, which are "what has been done and thought" by such absolutes. One should note that, here, even the forms of patriarchy refer back to the concreteness of each single man instead of being grasped only in their objective reality and power.

The relation between "each woman" and "each man" is the *logical* form that enables us to tap into the woman problem. To abdicate this logical form in favor of the abstract logic of politics as it is expressed in the relation between "women" (in the plural sense) and the institutions of patriarchy amounts to renouncing a plumbing of the depths of the problem.

Hence, Lonzi's choice to emphasize a "personal" form and practice is not based on empirical considerations. The confutation of political action is a consequence of the necessity not to submit to the distinction between the "private" and "public" domains. On the basis of such a distinction, the woman problem becomes evident in the private sphere alone as the problem of "each woman" and "each man." In the "public" domain, whereas each woman is more often than not reduced to a social group identity, each man disappears behind the abstraction of forms and structures wherein the preeminence and uniqueness of the male protagonist has expressed and deposited itself. By contrast, each woman concretely experiences in herself the fact of belonging to a gender that has been conquered in the "dark times of origins." The millennial roots of the originary defeat of their sex push women to think of themselves as "second."

Carla Lonzi does not focus her polemic on the extreme societal structural forms used to justify female inferiority; likewise, she does not posit them as the foundation for the oppression and subordination of women. Her target are the ideas of thinkers who, worthy of "humankind's esteem," have pushed women to favor other objectives and goals ahead of their own autonomy and freedom.

If the title of Lonzi's pamphlet takes aim at Hegel, nevertheless the principles of patriarchy are also retraced and refuted in the revolutionary ideologies of thinkers like Marx, Engels, and Lenin. In fact, it is class struggle that, at the time when the text was written, is found by "almost all feminists" to be the major source of women's oppression.[2]

Hegel is not a screen destined to muffle the critique of Marxism. Hegel represents the culmination of male thinking in the West precisely because he attributes to woman "all possible meaning," giving philosophical and ethical dignity to sexual difference and subtracting it from mere nature in order to insert it into the unfolding of Spirit. Carla Lonzi sharply and unequivocally anticipates what, in more recent years, has become a widespread conviction among feminist thinkers, that is, the conviction that the site of the actual denial of difference is precisely the place where it has been noticed and "thought."

Lonzi clearly saw what today has become a widely accepted argument in feminism. Thought, affirms Lonzi, assumes as its base the subordination of one sex to the other. This represented a "practical solution" to the problem of the relation between the sexes. According to recent reflections carried out by the women's collective *Diotima*, Western thought avoids "the problem of the human subject that is not one but two."[3] "The originary sexual differentiation that, like living and dying, each person carries within her- or himself, in her or his flesh" is understood by thought, unlike birth and death, as a "trivial event."[4] Difference is not registered as an originary feature of the subject, but as a secondary accident that is to be rediscovered "afterwards," subsequently to the constitution of the subject that "speaks himself and speaks the world from his own self."[5] Feminist reflections on the neutralization of sexual difference in thought have followed many paths of development. What we want to stress here is that through sexual difference one can see the essential core of the problem of the feminine, that is, the sexuation of the subject and its relevant effects on the relation between logical form and the historicity of sexual difference.

The philosophical passion with which Lonzi refuted Hegel spread widely following her reflections; this expansion was strictly connected to the way in which the problem of the feminine was discussed. According to this kind of analysis, the institution of a relation of domination belongs to the prehistory of the relations between the sexes, for the very first definitions of the subject that have been handed down to us by the Western cultural tradition, and which we employ routinely, already record the erasure of sexual difference.

The word "Man," writes Adriana Cavarero, works "as a masculine sexed neuter; precisely for this reason, though, it also functions as the universal neuter for the male and female sex." Whereas the "I" "supports and grasps sexuation indifferently," nevertheless it is "in welcoming male sexuation" that it ultimately reaches "its intimate completeness."[6] The history of the two sexes unfolds based on the premise of the completion of the most powerful form of feminine inferiorization, for which woman is said and says herself in the language and thought of the other. Woman is always "a surplus [*un di più*]," that is, a specification of the universal, neutral subject (as is the case for man also) and she is "something less [*un di meno*]," because she does not intimately correspond with such a universal.[7]

Consequently, if woman pauses to consider the history that has emerged from the erasure of the "originary differentiation" of the sexes, she ends up mistaking the "practical solution," borrowing Lonzi's phrase, for the problem, ultimately finding herself faced with the logical and historical insignificance of being a woman. Concretely, woman ends up living her very own "being-woman" as an accident, as a particular and secondary determination. Her relation to subjectivity will be marked by that "surplus/something less," regardless of the forms in which she historically experiences it. Hence, the logical form of sexual difference, that is, the way in which thought has neutralized it, marking the asymmetry between the two sexes, also represents the form of the historicity of sexual difference insofar as it is the only interpretative key to understand the difference between the sexes that is not deducible from the historical and political context.

If we closely examine *Let's Spit on Hegel*, we note that at the center of Lonzi's critique lies the totality of Logic and History created by Hegel, totality in which sexual difference finds a relevant but subordinated place. In Hegel, in order for the subject's freedom and self-determination "to become a world," that is, in order to adequate sensible reality to themselves, thereby transforming and freeing reality from nature, all of the subject's determinations, including sexual determination, must be comprehended within the process and become part of the *objective* development of Spirit. The way in which sexual difference participates in the life of Spirit is such that it will never progress toward the universal, thus losing significance with respect to the very forms of freedom and will.

Lonzi's questioning and rejection of Hegel starts at the foregoing point. She asks, why must the dialectic of Spirit fix "in essence" the hierarchy that distinguished and opposed sexes as superior and inferior?[8] The male vision of the world finds the justifications concerning the limits of its own unilateral experience. For woman, however, "the origin of the opposition between the sexes remains unexplained and she seeks in the reasons for her initial defeat the confirmation of the crisis of male spirit."[9] The man-woman relationship cannot be grasped within a conception of history that has as its center Struggle and Work, as in the master-slave dialectic. If, on the contrary, one accepts the dialectic between the feminine "divine" principle and the "human," virile principle, then woman is placed on the other side of history, civic community, and self-consciousness.

This argument is one of the most important points of Lonzi's critique. Let us examine more closely Lonzi's text. "Hegel's master-slave relation is a relation *internal to the male, human world*, which, in turn, is matched by a dialectic of terms precisely deduced from the presuppositions of the seizing of power. The conflict woman-man, however, is not a dilemma: there is no solution to it insofar as this conflict is not posited by patriarchal culture as a *human problem*."[10] "To understand the woman problem within the conceptual terms of the master-slave struggle" means two things.[11] First, for woman, it means borrowing the terms of her own inferiority "from a type of servitude that is different from her own"; this constitutes the "most convincing testimony of its misrecognition."[12] Second, it means buying into a conception of history that excludes "the essential point of discrimination within society, namely, the absolute privilege of man over woman."[13] Hence, such a conception of history cannot offer "humanity any perspectives" except in terms of masculine problems, of the redefinition of "power relations among men," and of a male community. Women are aware of the political link that exists between the development of such power relations and the "imbalance between the sexes understood as the need for power of each man over each woman";[14] nevertheless, they cannot adhere to "the project of historical or power alternatives," which is "the stronghold of male pre-eminence"; "they cannot accept the struggle approach and a perspective that are imposed upon them."[15] The fact that the woman's perspective is situated at another level is argued in depth by Lonzi because the forms of historical dialectic and of the social and political struggle are the "most convincing testimony" of the misrecognition of the woman problem as a "human problem."

Struggle and Power in the Master-Slave Dialectic

In Hegel, Lonzi observes, being-woman is not posited as a *human condition*: since it depends on a divine principle, it incarnates itself in an unchangeable metaphysical essence. "By recognizing herself in her relatives and blood kinship, woman remains *immediately universal*. Woman lacks the premises that would allow her to separate herself from the ethos of the family and reach the self-conscious force of universality through which man becomes a citizen. The feminine condition that is the product of oppression is indicated by Hegel as the motivation of oppression itself: the difference of the sexes comes to constitute the natural, metaphysical foundation both of the opposition and of the reunification of the sexes."[16]

Grounding sexual difference on the splitting of spiritual "substance" between the sexes allows Hegel not to recognize "the human origin of the oppression of women." The figure of the slave, as condition and not as an "immutable principle" or "essence," causes the dialectic of superior and inferior to become history; with this becoming history, the entire social dynamic comes to be grounded on Struggle whose central figures are Work and Power. If Hegel had had to apply the master-slave dialectic to the man-woman relationship and their opposition as superior and inferior, he "would have encountered a serious obstacle" because "at the level of woman-man there is no solution that eliminates the other. Hence, *the goal of the seizure of power is nullified*."[17]

The foregoing claim is one of the most famous points in Lonzi's text and it was taken up in various ways by feminism. It has been mostly stressed that feminism opened itself up to a polymorphic conception of power void of any one center. This reading does not properly apply to Lonzi's texts though, for she speaks of "man's absolute privilege," and identifies the double-sided structure of the universal-male subject as the "center" from which privilege radiates out to the entirety of history and human forms.

What Lonzi questions is the foundation and legitimization of a historical dialectic grounded on power and the destruction of the enemy, and hence its realization first and foremost as political history. To assign to the inferiority of woman the status of "human condition" would have implied the impossibility of referring the entire dimension of dominance back to the master-slave dialectic. It is only the erasure of the inferiority of woman from the scene of human history that allows both the foundation of the dialectic to be based on the seizing of power and the making of this seizure of power the heart of political theory. If there is no form of political struggle that does not have at its core a seizure of power, then there is no way to reduce the relation between the sexes to this schema because, as has often been stated, "Woman does not reject man as subject, but she rejects him as absolute."[18]

Around this theme of power and the relation between superior and inferior, understood in terms of the dialectic between servitude and lordship, Lonzi constructs a complex argument that is not always intelligible in a linear manner, for she proceeds in a spiralling mode, returning on various passages in the text. Lonzi states that "the constitution of Work as Struggle marks the move to the supremacy of male culture"[19] because "war and the *aut-aut* [either-or] of violence" appear, from the beginning, as connected to man's possibility "of identifying himself and being identified as a sex, thereby overcoming, through some external test, his internal anxiety over the failure of his own virility."[20] In many passages, we repeatedly find reference to "emotions," "to instincts," to man's "psychological mechanism," to the pathologies and disorders that afflict him, all in terms of a dimension of dominance and history that has been ignored.

This approach helps to clarify how the relation between Work and Struggle is to be viewed. When Work and Struggle become "the actions from which the human world starts as male history,"[21] war turns from being "a specific male profession" to becoming the engine of history and of culture itself. As conflict, violence, struggle, either-or, war avoids the stasis, fixedness, and "perpetual peace" that is death. Carla Lonzi characterizes the male unconscious as "a receptacle of blood and fear" and regards male thought as the ratification of a mechanism that wants to defeat "blood and fear," that is, death, by killing, by negating the negation. She cites a passage by Hegel in which the "ethical sanity" of war is referred to the need that "what, as man, is negative-or-negating by his own nature, be made to remain negative-negating."[22]

Drawing from psychoanalysis, Lonzi establishes a direct relation between man, understood as male human being (and, in particular his unconscious), "the disorderly course of things" that he achieves in history, and the dialectic with which thought defeats the stasis of death by negating, that is, enacting, the negation. The supremacy of Struggle, which also becomes the form of Work insofar as Work is an action that produces while destroying, is indicated by Lonzi as the source of the spreading, in the form of a "mental illness of humanity," of man's psychological mechanism whose first and essential manifestation is the subjugation of women and the need to objectify them through possession.

Confronted with this deadly path that man has impressed on history and thought, "woman's consciousness turns spontaneously backwards to the origins of life, and wonders."[23] In doing so, woman's consciousness "sees the world as an alien product" because her consciousness does not share the reasons "that brought man to institutionalize war as the security valve of his interior conflicts."[24] Woman is unable to recognize herself in this *primum* of the human condition constituted by the virile identity. "Albeit in the passivity of *pietas*,[25] she separates her role from that of man."[26] *Passivity* and *pietas* are nothing other than "the feminine principle" Hegel mentions in which "the evidence of male dominance is annihilated" and the distribution of the sexes into superior and inferior becomes, as we have seen, a distribution of metaphysical substance.

Sexual difference would seem here to be confirmed as a polarity between two "essences." Two significant passages of Lonzi's text emerge in this context and both have maternity as their theme. In the first text, Lonzi affirms that maternity is woman's "journey" because, while she is experiencing "the initial stages of life in symbiosis with her son," woman becomes deacculturated (*disaccultura*).[27] In the second text, we read, "The male species has continuously challenged life and today it challenges survival; woman has remained a slave for her non-acceptance; she has remained inferior, incapable, impotent. Woman claims survival as a value."[28] In the figure of the mother, and no longer in that of the sister, the law of Antigone understood as the law of the species seems to reemerge in an irreconcilable opposition to the law of community.[29] However, what remains undemonstrated is how that which rendered woman "inferior, incapable, and impotent" may turn into the lever for her own autonomy, giving start to her "journey" of deacculturation, which, for Lonzi, is the content of feminism.

This is not, though, the greatest perplexity that is raised by Lonzi's texts we have here quoted. The greatest dissonance with the overall structure of Lonzi's text has to do with the implicit recovery of an essentialist conception of the difference between the sexes. It matters little whether the male and female "essences" come to play themselves out primarily at the psychological level. The consequence of referring sexual difference back to essence would constitute, in any event, a theoretical legitimation of something that, for Lonzi herself, is instead the result of a relation of domination. Her critique of Hegel and Western philosophy is precisely that they have derived the originary and metaphysical being of man and woman from the "efficacy of facts." Nothing other than "facts" and, first of all, "the institution of power" enable the recognition of man's transcendence while denying it to woman.[30] The aforementioned aspect, which is the strongest and most radical part of Lonzi's critique, would require, however, that we leave open the question of sexual difference and do not derive the content of the "originary differentiation" of the sexes from history and from sexual identities. In many other parts of Lonzi's writings in addition to the passages we are examining here, we find this inclination she has to situate herself radically on the side of the unthought. As an example, one can think of her reflections on culture, which attest precisely to the exigency to remain loyal to the void, to invent the mediations through which thought can account for the subject's sexed being without affirming the essence of the "feminine" and the "masculine."

The Idolization of Facts

To remain within the logic of power, of struggle, is to continue to define oneself on the basis of the other, even if it is to impede the other from defining us. The critique of political action becomes here radical. Not only does woman not aspire to participate in power, but she also sees in it "a particularly effective form of alienation."[31] Through an instrumental orientation, namely, that in order to achieve one's own goals one must have a power objective, man has become accustomed to find in the external world the reasons for his own anguish, and to insert them within a hostile structure against which he himself must fight. Action, which is not *a cast's specialty*, by directing itself toward power, becomes such a specialty. Culture is the rational "justification" of this mechanism. Additionally, power produces an "*idolization* (mitizzazione) of facts," for the only facts recognized as such are those that correspond to an action directed to and confirmed by power.

The action "we opt for," Lonzi affirms with reference to women, is *deacculturation*. Woman has nothing to oppose to "man's constructions except her existential dimension: she has never had leaders, thinkers, scientists; rather, she has had energy, courage, attention, sense, madness."[32] The significance of the foregoing claim becomes clearer, if we consider the preceding sentence in Lonzi's essay: "The split between structure and superstructure has sanctioned a law according to which the changes of humanity have always been and will be structural changes: the superstructure has mirrored these changes back and will always do so." Deacculturation, however, is "not a cultural revolution that follows and integrates the structural revolution."[33] Deacculturation is the action that belongs to a "revolution" whose core is not objectivized power, "facts," structures, and superstructures, but the subject itself. Deacculturation is the action through which one assaults the logic of the subject. In so doing, one also wishes to transform the world in which the subject has objectivized itself.

One must not underestimate the aforementioned distinction. Instead of opposing man and his "constructions" with other "facts," with another specular mechanism of idolization, woman wants to bring man to the precipice of his consciousness. This would reveal that the problem lies in him, "in the historical continuity of the protagonist: . . . this is the transformation that we will to happen."[34] This transformation must not be confused with the "self-critique" and "crisis" of roles and identity through which man periodically deludes himself into thinking that he can redeem himself of his very history soaked with oppressions and atrocities. In our contemporary epoch, this crisis seems to have become final because the development of human history "has reached the limits of certainty of survival."[35] Nevertheless, as we have seen, male spirit constitutes and maintains itself only in the struggle to death; therefore, man's crisis renounces neither the axiom of the rationality of the real nor the negation of the negation.

To realize "subjective operations" is for woman, therefore, the way to question the foregoing axiom. She does not limit herself to opposing "the facts" produced by man, that is, the objectivity of the world; rather, by judging culture and human history, she judges the male transcendence that culture and history presuppose. Woman "sees where man no longer sees" because "life has yet to begin for her on the planet."[36] "The one who is not part of the master-slave dialectic becomes conscious and introduces the Unforeseen Subject into the world."[37] This is a subject whose actions do not submit to that element of continuity in male thought and action that is power.

Existence and Politics: An Irreconcilable Opposition?

Political action seems, therefore, wholly irreconcilable with free woman's thinking and acting. *Let's Spit on Hegel* may be understood as one single statement of self-distancing from the thought and action through which the male subject has objectivized himself in the world. If we, however, consider carefully the structure of Lonzi's essay, this self-distancing is less easy to interpret.

In the beginning of the text, Lonzi defines the principles of equality and difference. "Equality," she affirms, "is a juridical principle: it is the common denominator present in every human being to whom justice is owed. Difference is an existential principle that concerns the ways of being human, the particularities of human experiences, finalities, possibilities, the sense of one's existence in a given situation and in the situation one may want to create for oneself. The difference between man and woman is the fundamental human difference."[38] This passage lends itself to an initial interpretation that deserves a pause for consideration.

The distinction between the two principles seems to be configured as a sharp opposition between politics and existence. Equality and difference seem to delineate two spheres, two forms of the subject and action that are situated as contrasting alternatives. Hence, the self-distancing from politics, in the name of difference, comes to be sanctioned as pure and simple *extraneousness*.

If we examine the text more carefully, this extraneousness does not seem to imply, for women, a full and total irrelevance of equality and the political sphere. The "existential" principle of difference does not exclude, in fact, the recognition of "equal rights" for women, nor does it exclude the insertion of women into society and the state as equals. On the contrary, being somehow placed in opposition, the principle of difference presupposes both equal rights and women's insertion into society and the state. If equality is, in fact, the principle that aims to give justice to the "common denominator" proper to every human being, it is only by obtaining this very justice (that is, by conquering political-juridical equality) that woman is able to manifest her own difference within existence. The sharp distinction of the principles of equality and difference and their two concomitant dimensions, that is, politics and existence, does not seem to mark the irrelevance, therefore, of the woman problem of political equality. On the contrary, political equality is vindicated in its proper function, which is revealed in the emancipatory tradition.

The *extraneousness* of the *principle* of sexual difference to the political sphere does not imply but rather excludes that women may remain *extran-*

eous to law and politics. If this were the case, women, on account of their difference, would suffer the negation of that "common denominator" that defines human beings. Sexual difference would present itself as a quality that inhibits the female human being from achieving full subjectivity and being recognized, through equality, as possessing the status of "being human" de jure and not only de facto. If difference is instead connected to the "multiplicity of life," to the "meaning of existence," it refers more to the empirical differentiation among single individuals than to the form and status of the juridical and political subject. Even though she claims that there is a fundamental difference between man and woman, in the aforementioned passage Carla Lonzi seems to understand sexual belonging as one of the many specific determinations of an individual. As such, sexual belonging does not seem to modify the universalistic foundation of individuality insofar as individuality is based on that "common denominator," of which Lonzi speaks, and not on the "multiplicity of life."

Sexual difference, therefore, does not seem to present *a formal status different from other differences*: man and woman can recognize themselves as different from each other on the basis of a common equality they have reached with each other insofar as they are both "human beings." This reading of the relation between equality and sexual difference does not imply a radical questioning of Lonzi's critique of political action; rather, we have here a reconceptualization of it. The autonomous status of sexual difference indicates, then, the resistance, on the side of this specific aspect of the "multiplicity of life," to being disciplined and reduced to a unifying, synthetic formal logic. Concerning equality, a domain in which the "juridical principle" can operate must be delineated, its boundaries must be redefined, and the principle itself must be reformulated to make it compatible with the "autonomous" development of differences.[39] Equality can eliminate discrimination against women, but it neither adds nor reveals anything with respect to their subjectivity. Within politics, women can obtain justice as equals insofar as they are part of the human universal, but they cannot define themselves as different subjects. This implies both a strong delimitation of the relation between women and juridical-political equality and a subtraction of a large part of human activities and relations from political action and juridical formalization.

It is undoubtedly possible to grasp in Lonzi's reflections an openness to the aforementioned line of thinking. The opposition between politics and existence, and between equality and sexual difference, when understood in these terms, does not, however, cohere with the overall structure of Lonzi's thought. For one thing, her entire way of reasoning tends to emphasize the strong interdependence of the universal forms of thought and action with the originary defeat of the female sex. Moreover, the moment woman refuses the "absolute role" of man, she cannot but deeply assail the forms in which this absolute role has been expressed and sedimented.

Let us consider another passage focused on the principles of equality and difference: "Equality is what is offered to the colonized at the level of laws and rights; it is what is imposed on them at the level of culture. Equality is the principle through which the hegemonic continues to condition the non-hegemonic." Consequently, Lonzi writes, "Let us take advantage of difference: Were woman to be successfully inserted into the framework of difference, who could say how many years it would take to lift this yoke?"[40] This passage moves in a different direction from the first one examined earlier. How could the "juridical principle" of equality, which is supposed to render justice to what is common to every human being, turn into a "new yoke"? What is the nature of the yoke? "The world of equality," Lonzi affirms, "is the world of legalized subjugation, the world of the unidimensional. . . . Equality between the sexes is the clothing that today masks the inferiority of woman."[41]

Here, equality is viewed as the form through which man reasserts his supremacy over woman, imposing his laws on her and defining her rights according to his culture, according to his principles that order life and the world. Woman's inferiority is reestablished through the insertion of woman into society and the state "under the parameters of equality" because that very society and state, with their principles, do not see her as a subject, except within the terms already prescribed by man.

"Positing the different" is not to strive for insertion; on the contrary, it is to "*carry out a global change of the civilization that has excluded it.*"[42] The principle of difference refers here to human subjectivity and, as such, cannot remain extraneous to the forms of political and juridical subjectivity. The relation between difference and equality, then, does not seem definable on the basis of a distinction of spheres that are potentially irreconcilable and autonomously regulated. Difference questions "the common denominator" of the human being to which the principle of equality refers.

Lonzi's critique of Hegel clearly demonstrates how the differentiation of the sexes, if understood as a quality of the subject, questions the human universal upon which equality is founded. Sexual difference, Lonzi affirms, is not seen by Hegel as a "human problem" because difference is not separated from the ethos of the family in order "to achieve the self-conscious force of universality through which a human being becomes a citizen."[43] The figure of the citizen presupposes, therefore, a neutral human being, who has left difference behind in the family. For Hegel, in blood and family relations, both of which belong to the family, each individual experiences directly in the other his or her own participation in a unity.[44] Sexual difference does not find a place outside of this unity of part and whole, singularity and universality, which the family realizes. It cannot be rediscovered without mining the universalistic foundation, not even were it to be thought in the form of "plurality" or the "multiplicity of life." Hence, sexual difference is given a position of eccentricity with respect to political equality and subjectivity.

Political Subjectivity and the Human Subject

As we have seen, in order for equality to operate, it must presuppose the recognition of a common human condition. The affirmation that "all men have equal rights" is preceded logically by the claim that "all men are equal." Only the identification of a common measure enables the many and the different to recognize one another, to make agreements, and live together. Political subjectivity presupposes and also produces the paradigm of modern subjectivity. Those who can fully recognize themselves as protagonists of the social and political contract will be recognized as "Man." Furthermore, only those who are and can be assimilated to the human condition that makes them equal to others may participate in the social and political community. As is well known, the figure that enables the establishment of the continuity between political subjectivity and human subjectivity is the individual.

Human/Man (*Uomo*)-individual-citizen are forms of subjectivity that come to be in a strict logical relation, and hence, each is constitutive of the other. Outside this relationship, no subjectivity is possible. There is no way of establishing a relation with one's individual being that is not merely contingent. This renders the possession of citizenship a decisive feature, because citizenship determines who can fully posit himself as a subject. Insofar as it regulates the receiving and exclusion from citizenship, equality becomes the means, for the one who is excluded, to see oneself recognized as a subject. To obtain citizenship, the excluded individual must emphasize that which communalizes her with the figure of the individual-citizen while neutralizing that which differentiates her. "Equal," in this sense, indicates that which we can abstract from the "multiplicity of life" and reduce to a shared condition. The individual is the pivotal figure in this delicate passage. The individual is in fact capable of bearing all specific determinations while concomitantly transcending them, thereby rendering them partial and contingent *in the same way*. Through this process of abstraction, equality relegates differences to the world of real experiences while subjecting them to itself on the level of forms. One of such differences is sexual difference.

To maintain unchanged "the juridical principle" of equality means, therefore, the acceptance of the formal irrelevance of sexual difference with respect not only to citizenship but also to the subject. This has two important consequences. First, woman can recognize herself in the human condition presupposed by equality. Second, sexual difference becomes assimilated with other differences, first of all with social difference. Let us briefly consider these two consequences.

To affirm that women have *equal rights*, that is, to enact the principle of equality as such in relation to woman, means that one must accept also the formulation "All men are equal"; that is, one must erase sexual difference from the human condition that lies at the foundation of political subjectivity. From a situation of exclusion from citizenship on account of their sex, women move to a situation in which their sex becomes absolutely irrelevant. The postulate "All men are equal" literally means, then, either that the social and political contract exists only between male individuals or that woman is assimilated to man. In relation to citizenship, woman finds herself between two opposite poles: either she becomes part of the pact as a *male citizen* [cittadino] or she remains excluded from it. She is unable to participate in the social contract as a *woman citizen* [cittadina]. Her sex either counts too much and so she is placed outside of equality and deprived of the very "common denominator" that is common to all human beings or her sex disappears, rendering her entirely similar to a man. The foregoing move of difference, which goes from being the foundation of an exclusion to difference being fully neutralized, reveals that equality can in no way account for the eccentric position of woman with respect to the social and political contract.

To solve the problem of the impotence of the principle of equality to account for sexual difference, the latter has been assimilated with the social condition. Negated on the political plane, sexual difference acquires significance and value on the social plane as the common condition of women and as women's "specific interest." The eccentric position in which sex places women in relation to the "common denominator proper to every human being" is corrected by turning a quality of being, which pertains to universality, into a determination produced by the social relation. We here face that very overlapping of the relation of domination between the two sexes and their originary differentiation, of which we have already spoken. When one cannot give an account of difference in terms of the duality of the human being, one of the two sexes ends up being reduced to a specific function, a social condition, or a role; that is, it is reduced to determinations that never reach but rather presuppose universality.

Woman's "moving at a different level" from the male world cannot be understood, therefore, as the definition of a dimension that is wholly other. Lonzi affirms that woman does not posit herself as the *antithesis* of the male world. The asymmetry of which she speaks comes to take shape between the woman subject and *all forms* of male thought and action. The asymmetry, therefore, certainly operates on the forms of politics, but not only on them, and certainly not by favoring one specific form (or dimension), namely the form that would be most proper to woman, over others. Here, Lonzi's appeal to "take advantage of difference" becomes clear.[45]

The invitation to women is not necessarily one of placing themselves outside; rather, Lonzi wants women to assume an extraneous and dissonant (*estraneo e dissonante*) *point of view* based on a subjective difference. Extraneousness does not refer to diverse domains of experience and presence between the two sexes, nor does it refer to a distinction between an unchanged plane of equality and a plane of difference yet to be invented. The woman problem is neither comprehendible nor resolvable within the logic of politics and social conflict; yet "moving at a different level" means to escape the alternative between exclusion and a "neutral" insertion into the world that man has constructed. In relation to politics, free woman action cannot thus coincide with pure and simple extraneousness. Only if we avoid identifying extraneousness with an elsewhere in which woman would find her own proper place, will such an extraneousness present itself as it truly is: that is, as the absence of a place that can be defined by woman as truly *appropriate* because autonomously chosen.

There is a passage in *Vai pure* (*Now You Can Go*) that clearly indicates how between the private and the public, social-political spheres, there exists no qualitative diversity with respect to woman's free and autonomous action. "Once you have sacrificed yourself in the private sphere, you wish to do so also in the social sphere."[46] The sacrifice is the sacrifice of one's authenticity, of one's will *to be recognized for oneself*, and not for an experience, a function, a role, a value defined by what is proper to a female existence or world. Woman can experience self-sacrifice in motherhood or in her devotion to a man such as when, for example, she inspires and supports great male undertakings like revolutions or art. Woman fails, if she accepts the traditional roles of mother and wife. Likewise, she fails if she "accepts the way out" that men offer, which is to remain always at his side and share his "external" world. In both cases, woman renounces herself, she renounces asking the question "Who am I?" and "What lies behind this or that situation, this or that relation?" Briefly, she forsakes investigating and finding answers about the world and the mechanisms that govern it. If the risk of failure exists, no matter the sphere of presence chosen by woman, there evidently can be no advantage in remaining external in one domain as opposed to another.

What significance, then, can we attribute to the definition of difference as an "existential principle"? I believe that the principle is to be understood as the position from which one observes and evaluates the sphere of politics, its specific forms of actions, and the principles that regulate it. This position is the stand of the human being understood in its singularity and in its entirety. Sexual difference, as it refers to the singular individual, comes to situate itself in an asymmetrical position vis-à-vis both the universal and the particular. On the one hand, sexual difference escapes the naturalization inherent in the concept of the individual and, on the other hand, it also escapes being assimilated to other differences understood as specific and contingent qualities that individuals adopt within concrete existence. Sex is a strong trait that qualifies the human being, for it defines the human being in his or her *gender* at the same that it allows the singular individual to attain his or her own identity. The inseparable connection between singularity and gender renders one's belonging to a sex incomparable with any other kind of belonging, above all, social belonging. Sex distinguishes each human being from others and, as such, it structures the very form of alterity. Hence, sexual difference challenges "Man" as the universal subject and, consequently, all figures in which this universality has found expression, including the notion of the citizen-individual.

When speaking of an "existential principle," Carla Lonzi, in my view, is referring to the differentiation of the sexes as to a reality that cannot be suppressed or neutralized either in logic or in the forms of politics precisely because sexual difference pertains to the universal and not to the particular. Lonzi's constant reference to "woman" and not to "women" thus displays its full value and meaning. The critique of politics from the viewpoint of difference, understood as existential principle, is the critique of the logic and forms that were instead constructed upon the insignificance of difference. The goal of Lonzi's critique of politics, then, is neither the insertion of new contents into politics (for example, new rights of political and juridical equality) nor the safeguarding from the influence of politics of a sphere where difference may come to its expression. Sexual difference pertains to the human being, understood both as individual and as species. To take on sexual difference is, therefore, to produce a new formal order, a new logical and symbolic configuration of reality. This will affect also the political sphere.

The presupposition underlying this different formal order is, first of all, a change in the subject. "Dualizing consciousness": this is the true essential change that, for Lonzi, women must realize. Up to this point in time, the existence of the two sexes has manifested itself as a distribution of functions and roles; from now on, this existence must be brought back to its real dimension, namely, the duality of the subject.

To introduce sexual difference into the formal order of politics implies, in this context, the overcoming of the opposition/distinction between the universalistic and abstract logic of political forms and the differential logic of existence, of the personalization of forms. Thanks to this distinction, existence and personalization can be applied with more or less efficacy. The "existential principle" of difference, positing itself as a new measure, a new formal criterion, lends itself to overcoming the aforementioned opposition/distinction and its functionality. It is evident that, in the relation between woman's existence and politics, what is in questions is not only the contents and the efficacy of the means of politics but also, and primarily, its principles and forms.

Not all the aspects discussed in this chapter are explicitly present in the work of Carla Lonzi. In analyzing her passages, I also meant to draw the reader's attention to various possible contradictions and difficulties of interpretation within her thought. If, however, we pay tribute to the core themes in her work rather than the strict development of her argumentation, we find in Lonzi a fundamental coherence of thought sustaining all of her diverse approaches, insights, and intuitions. It could be said, then, that Carla Lonzi's thought revolves around one central insight: the woman I. Her thought, which revolves around her attempt to know her own "I" or to define the forms of the I as a sexed subject of thought and action, has only one center.

Carla Lonzi is interested in grasping the manifestation of a woman I, who finds within herself the principle and sense of her own being, understood as sexed being. Here, we find an I that is turned to the world in order to redefine its codes, forms, and relations. Carla Lonzi remains always loyal to this thematic core and does so in forms and ways that are rarely to be found in other feminist thinkers. On the basis of this perspective, she also analyzes and evaluates politics. It could be said, then, that Carla Lonzi is extremely eccentric as a thinker precisely because she does not assume the point of view of objectivation. She never frames the woman problem within an objectivized framework, as if woman were a reality definable from outside herself. There is, for Lonzi, no "woman problem" as such; rather, there exists the problem that belongs to this and/or that specific woman of thinking of herself as "a woman Self" and positing herself as such in the world. Lonzi's thought and her practice, which is inseparable from her thinking, are faithful to the demand to elaborate forms in which the woman subject can speak and posit herself as an "I." Here lies the powerfulness of her critique of the abstract and universal forms of politics. Here too, however, we also find the risks and limits of hypersubjectism, of the difficulty of and resistance to self-alienation" in the world, of placing the conditions of one's own self-realization outside oneself.

Translated by Antonio Calcagno

Notes

1. Carla Lonzi, *Sputiamo su Hegel. La donna clitoridea e la donna vaginale e altri scritti* (Milan: Scritti di Rivolta Femminile, 1978), 19; Boccia's emphasis.
2. Lonzi, *Sputiamo su Hegel*, 8.
3. *Diotima. Il pensiero della differenza sessuale* (Milan: La Tartaruga, 2003), 10.
4. Adriana Cavarero, "Per una teoria della differenza sessuale," in *Diotima. Il pensiero della differenza sessuale*, 48.
5. Cavarero, "Per una teoria della differenza sessuale," 45.
6. Cavarero, 44.
7. Cavarero, 44.
8. Lonzi, *Sputiamo su Hegel*, 23.
9. Lonzi, 23–24.
10. Lonzi, 23; Boccia's emphasis.
11. Lonzi, 24.
12. Lonzi, 24.
13. Lonzi, 24.
14. Lonzi, 22.
15. Lonzi, 23.
16. Lonzi, 25.
17. Lonzi, 27; emphasis in original text.
18. *Manifesto di Rivolta Femminile*. Translator's note: This is a manifesto that was written primarily by Carla Lonzi on behalf of the Roman collective "Rivolta Femminile" and was posted on the walls of Rome in July 1970. It constitutes one of the fundamental texts in Italian feminism.
19. Lonzi, *Sputiamo su Hegel*, 51.
20. Lonzi, 50.
21. Lonzi. 50.
22. Lonzi, 49.
23. Lonzi, 48.
24. Lonzi, 51.
25. Translator's note: *Pietas* is often translated as pity or mercy (sometimes piety) and understood as a form of love.
26. Lonzi, *Sputiamo su Hegel*, 51.
27. Lonzi, 51.
28. Lonzi, 48.

29. G. W. F. Hegel, *Fenomenologia dello spirito*, 2nd ed. (Florence: La Nuova Italia, 1972), 2:11–13; *Lineamneti di filosofia del diritto* (Bari: Laterza, 1971), 156.
30. Lonzi, *Sputiamo su Hegel*, 59.
31. Lonzi, 20.
32. Lonzi, 47.
33. Lonzi, 47.
34. Lonzi, 56.
35. Lonzi, 57.
36. Lonzi, 57.
37. Lonzi, 60.
38. Lonzi, 20.
39. Recent studies have appeared that define equality in terms of cognitive paradigms of complexity. See Michael Walzer, *Spheres of Justice: A Defense of Pluralism and Equality* (New York: Basic Books, 1984); Ota de Leonardis, "I diritti difficili," *Democrazia e diritto* 2–3 (1988); and Carlo Donolo and Franco Fichera, *Le vie dell'innovazione* (Milan: Feltrinelli, 1988). For a feminist critique of equality that takes into consideration the complexity of society, see Ida Dominijanni, "Donne si nasce, differenti si diventa. L'uguaglianza ed il percorso femminista," *Il bimestrale* 1 (January 1989); Maria Luisa Boccia, "L'uguaglianza impermeabile. Il corpo femminile ridisegna l'orizzonte dei diritti uguali," *Il bimestrale* 1 (January 1989).
40. Lonzi, *Sputiamo su Hegel*, 21.
41. Lonzi, 21.
42. Lonzi, 21; Boccia's emphasis.
43. Lonzi, 25.
44. "If the *ethical being* of the family determines itself as an *immediate being*, it still remains within the terms of its ethical existence, not *insofar* as this family remains the *natural* comportment of its own members or insofar as the relation between family members remains the *immediate* relation of *real, individual* members. The ethical element is in itself universal and this comportment of nature is itself essentially a spirit, and it is ethical only as a spiritual substance." This ethicality is a response "in the comportment of the *individual* member of the family to the *whole* family, understood as substance, such that the acting of the single member and its efficaciousness have as its end and content only the family" (G. W. F. Hegel, *Fenomenologia dello spirito*, 9–10, emphasis in original text).
45. Lonzi, *Sputiamo su Hegel*, 21.
46. Carla Lonzi, *Vai pure. Dialogo con Pietro Consagra* (Milan: Scritti di Rivolta femminile, 1980), 34.

14

C'è Altro

Luisa Muraro on the Symbolic of Sexual Difference along and beyond Luce Irigaray

Elvira Roncalli

> Knowing how to love the mother is the basis of our liberation.
>
> —Luisa Muraro, "Female Genealogies"

Depending on how familiar we are with the work of Luisa Muraro, we may be surprised to find that a good portion of it is devoted to women mystics.[1] Over the course of twenty years, starting with the 1995 publication of *Lingua Materna Scienza Divina. Scritti sulla filosofia mistica di Margherita Porete* (*Mother Tongue Divine Science: Essays on the Mystical Philosophy of Margherita Porete*), Muraro has studied, reflected, and written about the experience of women mystics. If we include her earlier work published in 1985 and titled *Guglielma e Maifreda. Storia di un'eresia femminista* (*Guglielma and Maifreda: The History of a Feminist Heresy*)—a book on the religious community of Guglielma that flourished in Milan in the thirteenth century—along with other numerous articles and books on related topics, it seems fair to say that the religious order and the divine are Muraro's central preoccupation. This prompts a question: How does her passion for the religious fit in with her political activism and her philosophical work?

Luisa Muraro is indisputably among the most prominent Italian feminists,[2] one of the founders, together with other women, of the Milan Women's Bookstore, *Libreria delle donne*, the author and coauthor of many articles and books dealing with sexual difference, women's authority, and the symbolic order. She is by formation a philosopher, but one who, very early, understood that women's freedom cannot exist unless the specificity of being woman is acknowledged first. Carla Lonzi's famous words, "The difference between woman and man is the basic difference of humankind" are echoed, in one form or another, in Muraro's many writings.[3] Like Lonzi, she rejects that equality leads to women's freedom. In presuming a standard of measurement, equality promotes assimilation: becoming equal to "x" is tantamount to becoming the same as "x," leaving such a standard and the systemic structures that keep it in place unquestioned. But, to borrow again from Carla Lonzi, this keeps women "colonized,"[4] entrenched in the obliteration of their specific distinctiveness. Muraro argues instead that only by affirming sexual difference—naming it, making it visible, and giving it value—does women's freedom come into being.

Since its inception in 1975, the Milan Women's Bookstore has been a place for thinking sexual difference and for practicing relationships among women who, in so doing, create meaning and establish women's authority. Similarly, the philosophical community of Diotima, created by Muraro together with other women (Adriana Cavarero, among them) in 1983, at the University of Verona, exemplifies the practice of thinking starting from the undeniable fact of being a woman.

There is no question that Muraro has played a crucial role in making the thought of sexual difference what it is in Italy today. At the same time, it has not been without criticism. Italian feminism is anything but univocal and even though, from the outside, this aspect may be perceived as a sign of weakness, from the inside, it is a shared struggle, manifesting a wide spectrum of voices, out of which tensions, conflicts, and even divisions may arise. It is not surprising, therefore, that Muraro's writings are genuinely debated and, at times, contested.

Two aspects among others stand out as somewhat controversial: the emphasis on separateness and the acknowledgment of the disparity among women. With regard to separateness, Muraro insists that women must find by themselves, separately from men, the language that expresses and manifests their difference, thus developing an independence from the dominating male order. She is not interested, as other women may be, in engaging in a dialogue with the mainstream and patriarchal philosophical tradition; she insists that such an interaction is neither necessary nor fruitful to women's freedom. As a philosopher, she knows this tradition well and makes use of it to show all that it leaves out, referring to this or that philosopher as needed. However, such a tradition is not her main focus of attention. With regard to the disparity among women, it originates in a discovery made at the Milan Women's Bookstore, namely, as she puts it, there is disparity among women and it is the recognition of an asymmetry in women's relations that grounds feminine authority.[5] I will say more about this asymmetry in the later part of this chapter; this point is also where Irigaray and Muraro diverge.

Sexual difference, as Muraro understands it, is the main focus of this chapter. How it stands in relation to Luce Irigaray's thought of sexual difference, specifically how it cannot be reduced to it, is also considered. What then brings together Muraro's persistent passion for the religious, the divine, and feminism? Why does she keep going back to a time and place that seem so far removed from the present world and not immediately tied to Muraro's most pressing concerns? What does she find in women mystics and their experience of God that is so valuable to her political and philosophical work? The short answer (perhaps a little too obvious, but perhaps not) is: "she is inspired." Luce Irigaray's thought about sexual difference and the political practice born out of the Milan Women's Bookstore Collective certainly play an important part in Muraro's work. Nevertheless, I would like to suggest that what she learns from the mystics nourishes her work, both politically and philosophically, at a more fundamental, *origin*-al, level.

Nothing in Between

"*Niente di mezzo*"—"nothing in between"—this is what women mystics teach us, writes Muraro. Nothing stands in between us and God. If God is to be found, they exhort, we should open the way, do away with everything that may inhibit and obstruct such an encounter. All this begins in language: the concepts, the structure, the logic, the method necessary in speaking about God. Words have the power to reveal and allow us to understand, yet not when they are not our own words, when they are given to us as a given set, those and no others, when they have produced a knowledge about God with principles and doctrines against which everything needs to be measured. Then language becomes constraining, an obstacle; rather than giving us the power to speak, it silences us.[6] Unless we choose to speak anyway, telling and saying of God in other words, our own words, defying the given conceptual order by daring to speak otherwise. This is what the women mystics do, risking their lives as Marguerite Porete did. After being put on trial for writing *The Mirror of the Simple Souls*, which tells of God in unheard ways, she is condemned and burned at the stake in 1310, along with her book. Muraro tells us that during her trial, Marguerite Porete never uttered a word. What she had to say, she had already said; it was all written down in her book. Not wanting to rebuke any of what she had written, she did not speak.

In telling us about Marguerite Porete, Muraro turns our attention to Porete's text, letting it speak for itself. She refers to scholars and experts in the field, but they are mentioned mostly as background to contextualize the prevailing knowledge of the time and not because they have revealing knowledge of the mystics. According to Muraro, they more often obscure and take away rather than shed light, with the exception of a few, and they too, like Marguerite Porete, get in trouble.[7] Above all, Muraro is particularly attentive to the words and ways women mystics speak about God: what they say, what words and images they use, how they name their experience with God. This language is revealing. They have something to say that is "unheard," and only those who can "hear" will grasp the significance of their words and deeds.

In her effort to help us along in hearing and grasping what the women mystics reveal, Muraro chooses examples that are, as she writes, "*terra-terra* [down to earth]," not academic works, not a knowledge that has already made us deaf to their words. Muraro knows that to be able to feel the living language women mystics speak requires something other. Resorting to fairy tales and memories from her childhood, she strikes a chord with the reader. Who, as a child, has not believed that the world is an incredible reality in which the most extraordinary things happen, that there is more than what we hear and see? Referencing a fairy tale evokes something that is immediately with us, it is part of us and, strangely enough, we feel as if we are transported to another dimension, somewhere else, or even somewhere better. We discover that there is more than what the words can say or, even, that words intimate something other.

As an example, when speaking about the God of love according to the ancients, it is said that love is the child of "need" (*Penia*) and "resourcefulness" (*Poros*). Muraro ponders over the name of love's father, *Poros*, a name that defies all translation and about which, she tells us, there is no agreement among scholars. After listing a number of different translations, she writes: "Although all of these interpretations are approximately acceptable, none is as fitting as we would wish";[8] and then she draws a connection with Cinderella's prince: "and—speaking of fitting and shoes—it is as the prince of Cinderella wished as well when he was going around town with a shoe in his hand, looking for a foot."[9] She concludes by saying: "Here, we have a foot and we are looking for the shoe."[10]

I know of no scholar who moves so freely from theological and philosophical disquisitions to fairy tales. The effect is both liberating and exhilarating, even humorous. The image is vivid and speaks to us instantly. Literally, it makes sense; consistent with Muraro's overall approach, it creates meaning, shifting away from speaking of God in the usual theological and philosophical language, with its apparatus of theorems and rules, to a more immediate and unusual, novel, yet familiar language. Should anyone think that this "diminishes" the value of what is at stake, one would have missed the relevance of moving freely in and out of preconceived ways of speaking. The point Muraro is conveying is that "being displaced," being put out of place, is key to being. In the teachings of the women mystics, God is where nothing is, where recognizing our being in need puts us out, decenters us, in Italian "*ci spiazza* (displaces us)." A shift must happen for there to be being, a shift that radically transforms us so that we are, in a way, other or at least open to that possibility. As Muraro writes, "Love belongs to an economy of exchange between nothing and being. Exchange, not elevation, not ascent, not dialectic. Being turns itself into nothing to become passage, nothing calls being to give of itself endlessly."[11] Thus, the name of the God *Poros*, writes Muraro, is "passage," understood not in the sense of transcendence, as it has been understood ever since Plato, as a movement beyond this world into the realm of the contemplation of being. Rather, this name of God signifies a passage that lets being into the world, a being that gives of itself freely as if it were the beginning of the world.[12] Indeed, it seems that only there and then, where spirit moves, being and world begin.

By privileging the use of concrete examples taken from lived experience, Muraro is doing what women mystics have done before her: undoing and removing what stands in the way in order to say, name, and give voice to their experience. Muraro likes to speak of this activity also in terms of "undoing what has been knit [*disfare la maglia*]"; a preeminent women's art, taken from everyday life, it undoes what has been done.[13] That same operation is at work in the women mystics when they talk about the art of undoing the world as it has been construed. They "undo," not in order to provide new thought conceptions; rather, they wish to be closer to God. They talk about "the absolute" in terms of that which "liberates the potentialities of being and makes the passage to the infinite possible." They talk about making themselves open to the passage into what is other. They tell us about God in their own terms, as God passes through them and dwells within them. They are not afraid to be "*origin*-al," to remain with the origins of their being, and name it with the words that best reveal it. Consider the way Marguerite Porete refers to God, "*il lungiprossimo* [the far-near]."[14] It defies all logic, and in hearing this, we know instantly we are no longer in the world of transcendence understood as contemplation of being. Marguerite Porete clears the way of what inhibits our seeing and our hearing.

This is no small matter: rather, it is symbolic work. It consists in giving meaning to things and the world in light of one's own experience, being able to see oneself in that world: finding oneself. In other words, being able to be, live, and breathe. Women, whose words and meanings do not find circulation in the sociocultural space, live this condition as an ongoing struggle. Muraro writes: "It is a struggle for the originary significance of women's experience against its being entirely reduced to being signified—being made meaning—by the other, the other in small letter, which historically is represented as the other sex, men, and their discourses."[15]

In talking about this ongoing struggle, Muraro writes that it gives rise to a feeling of "estrangement [*estraneità*],"[16] of being outside, of being stuck: how to give words to that which has no words? However, realizing this *impasse* (literally, a place without a passage) becomes a turning point or, as she calls it, a "source of intelligence of reality [*una fonte d'intelligenza della realtà*]," a way of understanding and conceiving reality anew. Such has been the case for Muraro, whose feminism, she writes, is born out of this "contrast" and the practice of relationships with other women, relationships founded on authority and trust. She observes, "I have become one who thinks better and has original thoughts—of whose value, obviously, I am not the judge." This, she writes, has happened to many other women.[17] In the women mystics, Muraro has found her teachers; teachers (*maestre*) like no others, they teach her to be free, and they teach her a new language. They show a way of being. They inspire.

In the Mother Tongue

In the women mystics, Muraro has found teachers like no others. What do they teach her? They teach her to be free, free from constrained ways, free from a given language, free to be. In Marguerite Porete's own words, to be free is "knowing how to be [*un saper essere*]."[18] To be other and more is a matter of creating emptiness (*fare il vuoto*). Only where there is openness, where there is room, does God come in. *Comprendere*, to comprehend, means precisely that: to be able to take in, into oneself, and hold within.

This discovery, however small it may seem, is one of great proportions for a woman: it recognizes the value of women's experience in all its manifestations, even if it escapes language, even if it exceeds the given words, even if it is not visible or remains unspoken. It is there. It is real. This realization is comparable to a "revolution of being" or, to borrow from Hannah Arendt, a "natality of being," of being born and coming into existence as a woman fully aware that being a woman is not irrelevant. Why?

If a woman has found herself in that place—not a physical place per se, yet a very real place nonetheless—that lacks words that "fit" her experience properly, now she is able to see there is a way through, a passage, there is a way of being, there is a way of naming it. It is a turning point, a point of new departure that urges her to get closer to the origins of her being and save it, by way of putting it into words and giving it a language. Save it, not absolutize it, as Muraro never tires of pointing out. There is much to be gained here, and a deep sense of freedom. The disproportion between what is visible and what remains invisible, what is said and what remains unsaid, is the "normal" condition under which her life as a woman has been given to her.

The women mystics' new language is the language of new beginnings, of releasing, letting go of the given that obstructs, and of being able to reconnect with a more primordial way of being. Their language is neither Latin nor philosophy nor logic. It is the living tongue of being with God, "*la lingua vivente.*"[19] What the women mystics make apparent is that when a woman gives up the logic of explaining everything, when she lets go of the given language, she does not thereby lose the ability to speak. On the contrary, she recovers the language of beginnings and gains the capacity to speak again.[20]

Muraro calls the way women mystics speak about God a "theology in the mother tongue," and in that expression is hidden, but present, the relationship with what is living, what gives life and words.[21] The mother tongue comes from the mother, literally and figuratively: she gives life and a promising world, where the possible is still possible. Above all, the mother exemplifies a way of being: being able to bear emptiness and yet, thanks to that, being able to bear more. What does this "theology in the mother tongue" reveal? That lacking is more, not less. In Marguerite Porete's words, it is a "leaning out towards the other [*sporgersi all'altro*]."[22] By being outside themselves, by being decentered, far from the center of gravity of their being, women are closer to what is other and more. Thus, in what sense is to be free "knowing how to be"? The answer: In the sense of "knowing how to be lacking without being any less [*sapere essere mancanti senza essere da meno*]."[23]

It is a distinctive feminine (*femminile*) way of being, not to be understood in a biological sense as given, but symbolically, through practices and a language rooted in an experience of the self that is not full, not self-sufficient, not absolute. Muraro writes: "To be born a woman means to be predisposed to a displacement of the center of gravity, which moves toward something other, outside herself. It is not a metaphysical or physiological predisposition; it comes from the relationship with the mother."[24] In the relationship with the mother, a woman finds herself to be closer to the mother than the male counterpart; like her, she is a woman, but she does not identify with her fully. By giving her life, the mother as mother is always more, and she, the daughter, is less. Yet as a woman, she is always potentially a mother, whether she will become one or not; she is the possibility of being more and other. Hence, she is at the same time less, lacking, yet more. This is the feminine (*femminile*) condition or experience, according to Muraro, which nevertheless does not belong exclusively to women: "an experience whose distinctiveness is not to exclude the other—because it discloses a sense of being that is always being able to be other, without separation, as it is in the woman's relationship with her mother and with her own potential for becoming mother."[25]

The women mystics give words to this way of being, open to the other without being any less. They "symbolically make a hole [*quello che fanno, simbolicamente, è un buco*]," a hole that opens a passage to what is hidden or latent.[26] To them, freedom is rooted in a relationship with something lying beyond the sayable and the possible, but nonetheless they seek relentlessly to name and bring it to light. There is a sense of something that cannot be fully grasped by words, that exceeds and spills over. Yet recovering it is precisely what needs to be done: only in the possibility of saving what is unseen and unsaid, without either destroying or absolutizing it, lies the possibility of being.[27]

To say and name what is, yet may not be visible; to say what is present though unsayable: this is symbolic work. The given symbolic order ignores and dismisses the fact that one is a woman and not a man; it has constructed the feminine (*femminile*) from the outside, as if in itself the feminine had no value. Only in and through the masculine does it acquire value. Sexual difference as "feminine" does not count, it is literally "dis-counted." What counts is the universal, which speaks for everyone. But the universal is a construction: by assuming to say everything, it reduces the possibility of thinking and saying what is. In this sense, the universal is meager and reductive: in pretending to say all there is to say, in speaking for the universal human, abstracted and removed from concrete life, it says very little. Moreover, even though the symbolic order is presented as "neutral," it is rooted in a father-son genealogy, after which all social relationships are molded: all meaningful exchange, all that has value goes through a relation with man. Women "are" insofar as they conform to such a symbolic order, speaking its language, adopting its ways of thinking. While they may acquire some degree of visibility and value in so doing, it is an order they experience as foreign. Women are not, for the most part, in and through their association with men, and this necessarily thanks to what they desire for themselves. Their relationships with other women and, more important, the mother-daughter relationship, find no place in the given symbolic order. They are not.

There is much work to be done in thinking and naming that which is not named, that which is not seen, yet is there. In the women mystics, Muraro finds something she finds nowhere else: a way of creating a symbolic order, producing meaning out of what does not have any, forging words that say what is left unsaid and is unsayable. These women speak of God freely and boldly. They speak of God in their own words, through their own experience, free from any given constraints, yet with authority. The women mystics show Muraro how to create a symbolic order that gives value to one's feminine experience by naming it and giving it voice so that such experience is not swallowed up by a universal/neutral framework of thinking. After all, if we find no words that can say it, if the language we speak is not our own, if this language remains foreign to us, and if there is no "passage" from me here, in this concrete embodied and sexed being, to a symbolic that acknowledges my way of being as a woman, what possibility of being is there? Am I alive? Am I able to speak? Am I?

The Symbolic of Sexual Difference

In her seminal work *An Ethics of Sexual Difference*, Belgian born philosopher Luce Irigaray writes: "Sexual difference is one of the major philosophical issues, if not the issue, of our age. . . . Sexual difference is probably the issue in our time which could be our 'salvation' if we thought it through."[28] Irigaray's entire work is a thorough examination and critique, an indictment, no doubt, of the dominant symbolic order of the West, centered around "god-the-father" and the ensuing culture where "preference is given to the male lines of descent and the society of men-among-themselves [*la société de l'entre-hommes*], in which women are not regarded as adults, but as men's property: family property, domestic property, sexual property, cultural property."[29] Irigaray's work is dense, philosophical and poetic, unrelenting and provocative. In order to break out of the given structures of discourse that govern her language and constrain her speaking and her writing, she experiments with new styles, new modes, bringing new dimensions of life out of the shadows and making thinking the unthought possible.

She has been as controversial as influential, but her proposal of an ethics and politics of sexual difference for a more just and life-giving world cannot be ignored when it comes to fundamental issues of our time. On the side of controversy, her thought has been criticized, particularly by a portion of Anglo-American feminism, as a form of essentialism, whether biological or psychic, and therefore dismissed as a nonviable position.[30] There is no doubt that Irigaray has had an enormous impact everywhere on philosophy, psychoanalytical thought, literary and critical theory studies, and beyond. Her work has been translated into many languages, but perhaps nowhere has the reception of her thought been stronger than in Italy. In the context of this chapter, my focus is limited to her influence specifically on the work of Luisa Muraro, who does not hesitate to acknowledge it. As a feminist, Muraro is always quick in specifying that by feminism she means not the feminism of social equality, but that of symbolic difference, thus situating herself close to Irigaray.[31]

In the footsteps of Irigaray, Muraro places the erasure of sexual difference at the heart of her project, that is, feminine (*femminile*) sexual difference. The dominant symbolic order being "of the father," woman is left with no symbolic home, one that originates from her own desire and not from what the male counterpart desires of her. Irigaray's work provides ample evidence of the way in which the dominant symbolic order (myths, imaginary, conception of god, the law, organization and structure of society down to the family, and so on) is actually an expression of male desire, a desire to be the sole and universal lord of the world. As Irigaray writes, "Language is one of the primary tools for producing meaning. . . . If language does not give both sexes equivalent opportunities to increase their self-esteem, it functions as a means of enabling one sex to subjugate the other."[32]

Thinking the difference, specifically thinking the symbolic of "feminine [*femminile*]" difference, is for both Irigaray and Muraro the way forward. They call it a "symbolic revolution," and they mean precisely that: a radical cultural transformation and, as Irigaray writes, "a revolution in thought and ethics" that "reinterprets everything concerning the relations between the subject and discourse, the subject and the world, the subject and the cosmic, the microcosmic and the macrocosmic."[33] They acknowledge that this transformation will take time, but it is "a peaceful revolution," to put it in terms of the subtitle of Irigaray's *thinking the difference*. It does not destroy, but rather leads to "salvation," if we seriously commit to it. Needless to say, having both Irigaray and Muraro devoted their life and work to bringing about such a symbolic revolution, the work of the one evokes the other in many respects. It would be erroneous, however, to think of Muraro's work as a transposition of Irigaray's thought into the Italian context. There is a distinctiveness and specificity to Muraro's symbolic of sexual difference that resists being reduced to any one theoretical framework. But there is more.

In the introduction to *Sexual Difference*, a reference is made to Virginia Woolf's *A Room of One's Own*, in which Woolf argues that a woman needs a space if she desires to write and do intellectual work. However, it is pointed out that such a physical space would remain paralyzing, if it were governed by texts and words coming from outside, through which the mind cannot find its way. "The room of one's own must be understood differently, then, as a symbolic placement, a space-time furnished with female gendered references, where one goes for meaningful preparation before work, and confirmation after."[34] In other words, unless such a *locus* is there, as a collocation in a time and space that *inspires* women to be and speak freely, then their work is difficult, obstructed, and scattered. It remains in pieces. Unless a woman sees herself in that *locus* as connected to other women whose words nourish her own, then she will struggle to find words. She will struggle to be.

Picture this: A woman college student in her early twenties is in the office of a woman professor. She holds Virginia Woolf's *A Room of One's Own* in her hands. She has just finished reading the book as part of the professor's course assignment and she wants to talk about it. Her voice trembles when she says: "This is my story." Tears flow down her cheeks. It is a deeply felt moment, followed by silence. What words could convey that precise instant, so full that it cannot be contained? Yet one tries to hold on to it tightly, to dwell in it and feel every bit of it! It is a moment of realization that enables the student to find words and say the unsaid: the book names, makes visible and explicit what she has not been able to name herself, while *hearing-feeling* it (in the Italian sense of "*sentire*") all along. Thanks to what Woolf writes, the young woman sees herself connected to other women who have gone before her, who are in a different time and in a different place, on the surface very distant from her, yet so close. They speak her language, they give voice to their experience, and this helps her find sense in her own. She sees herself as part of them, they are part of her, despite their lives and world being so far apart. They are struggling to find their voice, while the dominant symbolic discourse silences them. Only in seeing them connected, and recognizing their struggle similar to her own, is the young woman student able to see herself as part of a genealogy of women. They are related and connected with one another. In looking harder, in hearing more closely, she will find some more unheard new senses. Why could she not see them? Where were they? There. Yet not as a matter of course.

It is not a coincidence that Ulysses, the ancient hero of the *Iliad*, comes to mind. He too cries when he hears his life-story being told by a poet; it is only then that he fully grasps the meaning of his life and, overwhelmed by it all, he cannot help but cry. What has happened to the woman student has happened before. To Ulysses. The dynamic at work is the same. It shows how significant it is for anyone to be able to find oneself and meaning in what one does. For this to happen, others outside of us are key. They present us with possibilities for us to be, not in the sense of prescribing to us the content of our being, but in the sense that they give us the language and words so that we can give meaning and sense to what we do and think about who to be, making it possible for us to think beyond. The dynamic is the same for Ulysses as for the young woman student, but how far apart![35] For where does the woman student turn to find women's words that give her a language to put hers into life? Where does she find a genealogy of women as a framework for a way of thinking that shows her who to be? Where does she find relationships among women, between mother-daughter, as source of meaning and creative of symbolic authority? This is why Irigaray never tires of writing about the urgency of affirming sexual difference: "Not accepting and respecting this permanent duality between the two human subjects, the feminine one and the masculine one, amounts to preventing one of the two—historically the feminine—from attaining its own Being, and thus from taking charge of the becoming of what it already is and of the world to which it belongs, including as made up of other humans, similar or different."[36] Affirming sexual difference means therefore reestablishing a female genealogy, beginning with the mother-daughter relationship, which "is always erased, even in places where a mother-daughter couple is honored." Irigaray gives the example of Lourdes, a place that attracts many pilgrims and tourists, and which is about "the relationship of a daughter to a so-called divine mother."[37] Nowhere, however, are they represented together; only the mother without the daughter.

The need for a female genealogy is therefore crucial for a feminine symbolic: "To make an ethics of sexual difference possible once again, the bond of female ancestries must be renewed."[38] This will have two ethical dimensions: a vertical one, the relationship between mother-daughter, and a horizontal one, the relationship among women or sisters.[39] In restoring female genealogy, the original matricide is unmasked as the foundational act of the symbolic order of god-father-son. As Irigaray writes: "If we are not to be accomplices in the murder of the mother, we also need to assert that there is a genealogy of women. Each of us has a female family tree: we have a mother, a maternal grandmother and great-grandmothers, we have daughters. . . . Let us try to situate ourselves within that female genealogy so that we can win and hold on to our identity."[40]

It is here, in the context of recovering and asserting female genealogies that Irigaray's and Muraro's projects appear to diverge. In an essay titled "Female Genealogies,"[41] Muraro goes straight to the heart of the matter; she detects a change in Irigaray's position toward female genealogies and writes: "It is not a question of inconsistency on Irigaray's part but of the progression of her thought."[42] How has Irigaray's thought progressed, we may ask? According to Muraro, even though the politics of women is said to continue to nourish Irigaray's thought and work, now Irigaray sees both sexes involved in a mediation to set up "an ethical world, of men and women together, whereas before it concerned the world of women-among-themselves."[43]

The change in Irigaray's thought is signaled by a change in her interpretation of ancient myths presenting the mother-daughter relationship. Muraro points out that earlier, in a 1980 lecture given in Montreal, "Body against Body: In Relation to the Mother," in talking about the *Oresteia*, Irigaray spoke of the original matricide, the murder of Clytemnestra by her son Orestes as the founding event of our society and culture: "Orestes kills his mother because the empire of the God-Father, who has taken for his own the ancient powers [*puissances*], of the earth-mother, demands it."[44] With the murder of the mother, any relationship to the mother is buried with her and replaced with the order and language of the father. Anything that intimates our bond with the mother, our being *corps-à-corps* with her, is cut and erased. Irigaray then spoke of the need "to give life back to that mother, to the mother who lives within us and among us. We must refuse to allow her desire to be swallowed up in the law of the father," and this means also "to invent the words, the sentences that speak of the most ancient and most current relationship we know—the relationship to the mother's body, to our body—sentences that translate the bond between our body, the body of our daughter."[45]

Muraro contrasts Irigaray's early position with Irigaray's later talks given in southern Italy in 1989 and collected under the title "The Forgotten Mystery of Female Ancestry," in which she returns to ancient myths and to the erasure of the mother-daughter relationship by the rising patriarchal culture. In speaking about this erasure, Irigaray states: "This culture erased—*perhaps out of ignorance, perhaps unwittingly*—the traces of an earlier or contemporaneous culture."[46] Muraro, an attentive reader of Irigaray's work, does not miss the shift that may otherwise go easily unnoticed to a less acquainted reader, and writes: "This hypothesis of ignorance or lack of awareness is incompatible with what Irigaray herself had said in Montreal, in 1980, to the effect that an unpunished matricide lay at the foundation of our present civilization."[47] This change is expressed also in other notable ways, Muraro tells us: for example, in the change in the way Irigaray reads the figure of Antigone and her preference for talking about the myth of Demeter-Kore/Persephone over other myths, especially in her later lectures. Concerning Antigone, Muraro points out Irigaray's shift from seeing her as "the antiwoman, still the production of a culture that has been written by men alone,"[48] to later praising her "unreservedly." Antigone is then seen as a heroine who "defended the community [*la convivenza civile*] on several fundamental counts, including respect for the cosmic order and respect for maternal genealogy."[49] With regard to the preference given to the Demeter-Kore/Persephone's myth, Muraro writes that in that myth, although different readings are possible, Irigaray emphasizes "natural harmony and spiritual fruitfulness" in the mother-daughter relationship at the price of letting go of "the enigma of hate and ingratitude" present in earlier readings.[50]

What is at stake, here, exactly? Why does it matter? Although Muraro plays down this shift by stating, "This change does not directly concern either the theme of female genealogies or the political practices of relations among women," she also calls it "a radical reinterpretation,"[51] and a "turning point."[52] If Muraro is right in calling it a "turning point," and I take her word for it, then it cannot be brushed aside so easily. In drawing our attention to it, Muraro is telling us, though not in so many words, that the change is symptomatic of a fundamental difference between the thought of sexual difference as practiced in the Italian context—specifically as exemplified in Muraro's work and as found in the work of the women at the Milan's Women Bookstore—and Irigaray's thought on sexual difference. It appears now that, for Irigaray, female genealogy, although still relevant, is not the fulcrum around which women's identity revolves. For Muraro instead, female genealogy is the condition for women's freedom and comes to life in and through women's mediation. What is at stake here is of a "political" nature: the issue is precisely the recovery of female genealogies so as to give life to a feminine symbolic in a way that is "effective," that is, transforms a woman's life, is a revolution of her entire being as a woman. This is a turning point indeed.

The Practice of Women's Relations

Muraro acknowledges that "the change in Irigaray's view [of Antigone] is *obviously* a sign of a change that has to do with politics."[53] But why does she use the adverb "obviously"? If anything, far from being obvious, it is unclear and in need of some further explanation. The same essay "Female Genealogies" in which Muraro presents the change in Irigaray's thought offers some clues. There, we read that the theme of female genealogies "appears and develops through Luce Irigaray's direct encounter with women's politics."[54] However, when Irigaray addresses an audience of men and women, the shift with regard to female genealogies is undeniable to the point that Muraro raises the following question: "Why does Irigaray's assessment of Antigone change when we pass from the first context, the ethical order among women, to the second one, the ethical order of men and women together?"⁵⁵ Muraro's answer is straightforward: "It seems as though feminine mediation is not an adequate politics within the horizon of the universal, where women's politics would become witnessing; efficacy at the universal level, then, would be something either produced by the power of men or by men and women together." What follows is, however, more revealing. After exposing this shift in Irigaray's thought and calling it a "turning-point," Muraro then tries to downplay it by stating that it is "less important from her point of view than from mine." Why? In what sense? She continues: "When she turns from the politics of women-among-themselves to a politics of men and women together, she is not abandoning an effectiveness that she has actually experienced; whereas *I have experienced the power for change of the practice of the genealogical relation*. I must not underestimate this difference."⁵⁶

Politics; effectiveness; the genealogical relation: in these, we find the solution to the riddle of the difference between Irigaray's and Muraro's thought on sexual difference. As Muraro writes, it is not a difference to be underestimated. At stake is the mother-daughter relationship, the genealogical relationship, and what Irigaray calls the "vertical relationship." Muraro points to the "paradoxical fact" that "in a patriarchal society, sons have a far better relationship with their mothers than do daughters."⁵⁷ This, she writes, "is a flaw at the very roots of our cause."⁵⁸ Unless this flaw is confronted, then the mother-daughter relationship remains out of the realm of possibilities—it is not a reality; perhaps it is a vision, but what does a vision do, if it does not affect change in the present? Muraro states that she has experienced change through the practice of women's relations as conceived and lived out by the women of the Milan Bookstore.⁵⁹ In presenting how such practice developed out of events and ideas in the years 1966–1986, the Milan Women's Bookstore Collective writes: "They commonly go under the name of feminism. But in reassessing them retrospectively, in rewriting its history, the book renames it *genealogy*."⁶⁰

What does this practice entail? What does Muraro mean by change? It is a political practice that does not remove the given of feminine sexual difference from the concrete material reality. On the contrary, it starts precisely there: it is about "doing justice starting with oneself,"⁶¹ putting oneself at the center, and "saying by ourselves what we want, think, desire within ourselves, and not in imitation of, or in reaction to, what others say."⁶² However, this does not go far enough. Since women find it difficult to express their desire, they experience a disproportion between such desire and the words to name it unless some way of legitimizing feminine desire is found. From this difficulty comes the idea of a feminine mediation, the idea that it is only through the relationship with another woman that women are able to legitimize their own freedom and signify it in the world. Why is this necessary? "Attributing authority and value to another woman with regard to the world was the means of giving authority and value to oneself, to one's own experience, to one's own desires."[63] It is here that the practice of women's relationships comes upon the discovery, which is there from the start but not fully acknowledged, of a disparity among women: "We were not equal, we had never been equal, and we immediately discovered that we had no reason to think we were."[64]

Disparity means that rather than seeing themselves as "sisters," women acknowledge that some among them are more like "mothers," women who display authority as women. There is a *symbolic mother*, an origin that gives value to what women do and say, and in relying on her through a "relationship of entrustment [*rapporto di affidamento*]," women are able to rely on themselves and give voice to their desire. This relationship of entrustment must be acknowledged as a debt, a symbolic debt that each woman has toward other women, "to the one who brought her into the world, to those who have loved her, those who have taught her something, those who have spent their energies to make the world more comfortable for her."[65] It must be acknowledged with gratitude and publicly, "simple gratitude in the relation between women is what female freedom is practically founded on. Everything else, in theory as in practice, is either a consequence of that or has nothing to do with freedom."[66]

In other words, there is a "plus" of female difference that consists in being irreducible and is unerasable: "Sexual difference is an originary human difference," and this means that it cannot be assimilated in the world of men, except by being neutralized, turned null, silenced.[67] Hence, it is not about a better world or about improving society. These may come as consequences of shifting the balance from the given symbolic order to the practice of women's relations. It is about "freeing women and their choices—that is freeing them from the obligation of justifying their difference," it is a "liberating transgression," an "inevitable passage" that is very difficult. It requires making female sexual difference the point of departure for being a woman. "Sexual difference is partiality, it is a sign of finiteness, the most powerful sign marking thought as corporeal. Its value can come only from what the fact of being a woman makes possible when this limit is recognized, accepted, not denied but changed into a pathway."[68] The chance of having been born a woman becomes "grace" when acknowledged and made one's own, "a woman is free when she chooses to signify her belonging to the female sex, well knowing it is not an object of choice."[69]

This is a revolution of the symbolic order that does not destroy. It saves. Instead of forcefully introducing the new into the social order by severing the ties with the past, it releases women from their subjugation to the given symbolic order, opening the possibility of establishing new relations with other women and, specifically, with the symbolic mother, whose authority enables her to find words and meaning for her existence. It is about saving and giving meaning to female freedom, in and through female entrustment, and this means, at its source and origin, feminine difference. This alone is the measure of feminine experience: to realize "that to become great or to grow, in every sense of the word, she needs a woman greater than she is."[70]

The practice of women's relations is the practice of putting the relationship with the mother at the center, indeed "a genealogy." It is in acknowledging the authority of the mother that women gain their freedom. It is in acknowledging sexual difference as irreducible, in seeing that "fidelity to what is, to what one is, comes before everything else"[71] that a revolution of the symbolic order happens. For Muraro, this reality is not something yet to come, whether it be in a near or distant future. It is already here. It is this practice of women's relationships grounded in the authority of the mother that makes possible what the given symbolic order has made "unthinkable."[72] This practice is the source of the change that draws Muraro and Irigaray apart. If thought is always contextual, as Muraro writes, her context of reference is the practice of women's relationships and what she has learned thanks to them, namely, that freedom for women does not happen without acknowledging the relationship with the mother, which itself is fidelity to sexual difference. Feminine freedom is both the end and the means to feminine freedom; everything else that comes with it, such as a better world, improved relationships with the other sex, and so on, may all be desirable and good, but they are not the end. There is no female freedom without female genealogy, without practicing relationships between women who make it visible and tangible.

In Muraro's eyes, Irigaray's emphasis on a "universal mediation," rather than female mediation, shortchanges sexual difference for something else, a better world perhaps, though it is all somewhat uncertain since it lies ahead, yet to come. More important, in Irigaray's later writings, female freedom is neither the end nor the means. From the perspective of the knowledge Muraro has gained through the practice of women's relationships, this change appears to be a loss, a political and a symbolic loss. Without repairing the mother-daughter relationship, even if a better new world is brought about, it is not one where the symbolic order of the mother has gained visibility and authority. In reinterpreting Antigone, Irigaray makes her "the heroine of political demonstration and witnessing," Muraro writes; yet this does not amount to making her action effective.[73] On the contrary, as "witnessing," it hangs there, so to speak; she may be a witness of female ancestry, open to a synthesis perhaps, a synthesis that may resolve many contradictions, but if it does not confront the one at the heart of the mother-daughter relationship, it leaves female genealogy open to question and its effectiveness is lost.

The change that Muraro claims to have experienced in and through the practice of women's relationships is the effectiveness she does not see at work in Irigaray's later writings. What she calls a "turning point" in Irigaray's thought is the absence, perhaps even the negation, of the possibility of Muraro's own personal and political experience and practice of women's relations. Irigaray's later writings do away with the need for feminine mediation, whereas for Muraro women's freedom comes about in and through women's relations. The separateness and the disparity mentioned at the beginning of this essays are two sides of the same practice of sexual difference as experienced and lived by Muraro and other women at Milan Women's Bookstore.

While this divergence does not take anything away from the valuable work of both philosophers, it does leave us with some vital questions. How is Muraro's position and the practice of women's relations the locus for engendering feminine freedom? Does such a practice of women's relationships not remain limited in its ability to give visibility to female authority, beyond the scope of the Women's Bookstore, no matter how wide and far-reaching? If it is based on a disparity among women, how does it avoid turning into a practice of exclusion? In positive terms: How truly effective is it in establishing a symbolic of sexual difference?

Women Mystics Inspire

There is an Italian expression, *"fare largo"* which, literally, means "to make large," or "to enlarge," in the sense of creating space for something or someone to go through. It is usually translated as "to make way" or "to open up." To make way for what? For the possible, the otherwise, and the beyond. How do we do so? By avoiding being trapped, by not letting ourselves be caught, by "swerving,"[74] Muraro suggests; just like animals do when they are being pursued. According to her, women are predisposed to "making way." In what sense? Not in the sense that they are biologically or naturally so constituted; rather, insofar as they are able to grasp the paradox of their being, their symbolic independence is rooted in the interdependence with their mother, the source of their existence, in a far more deeply involved way than it is for men. The mother leans out toward the other, and in so doing she is elsewhere and otherwise. As a potential mother, Muraro writes, a woman lives likewise on a "tilted" plane of existence, "between a sense of self and a sense of lack," a being "on the ridge,"[75] which is a difficult and laborious way of being, treading the struggle between affirming herself and acknowledging her lack. This is precisely the condition that Muraro calls "feminine excellence." Why? It exposes a woman to being more and otherwise, it predisposes her to being decentered, dislodged (*sbilanciamento dell'essere*), and in this leaning out, she is able to free herself from the given, releasing herself from it, making a new point of departure possible, and creating new possibilities for seeing, for hearing, for naming and speaking.

Muraro has experienced this change in herself, a "break" that goes to the roots of her being. It has radically changed the way she relates to the world, it has released her from her customary and expected ways of being, and it has liberated her. It has given her the ability to see what may not be apparent to all and hear what is unheard, to think the unthought, precisely because she is a woman who recognizes the words and gestures of other women as bearing truth; she looks and listens or, as she puts it, "turns the light on."[76] It is without a doubt a personal and political turning point for Muraro, one that enables her to see that there is more, a *surplus*, in the feminine way of being. It is the excellence of being able to lean out toward the other and more. Women, she claims, have something to teach, and at a time when the logic of self-sufficiency seems to have run to the ground, we may be well disposed to hear what women have felt and continue to experience in their everyday existence, namely, that awareness of one's lack of being means to be open to the other and more. To acknowledge one's debt toward the one, the mother, who has brought us into the world and given us life, means to acknowledge one's dependence and need.

Muraro's project is not without risks. In choosing feminine mediation and maternal authority, she is aware that she does not know for sure what it will lead to; she sees it as a "gamble [*una scommessa*]": one, however, that she is willing to take for the sake of female freedom and a feminine symbolic. She is also aware that in thinking the unthought, she risks self-deception and ambiguity; yet these are risks she is willing to take for, in the process, "it happens that we make formidable discoveries, as long as we don't lose our awareness of this exposure."[77] What about the risk that relying on women's relations may become a sectarian, self-enclosed or even ideological practice? In keeping itself open to women's desire and in sustaining women's desire, the practice need not constrain nor absolutize; it is up to the woman to choose according to her desire: what she wants and what she is willing to risk. Neither is it ideological as it is not preconceived, nor is it detached from the real. On the contrary, the real becomes real when I can connect my experience to it through my own words; only then does it become meaningful.

As Muraro never tires of pointing out, this is not a practice exclusive to women. What is crucial is the recognition of female authority, that we acknowledge the debt we owe the mother by naming it and giving it visibility, men and women, publicly and openly. It requires a choice and a decision on our part; it pushes us to confront what we are (or are not) willing to risk in a deeply personal way. Once we choose, we still have to keep choosing and give meaning to what we do in our words and through the words of women who have done so before us; the tendency to wash away sexual difference being the norm, it becomes an ongoing struggle to hold on to it. It is a way of being that does not absolutize it; rather, it saves it from disappearing, from letting it be gone. For Muraro, this is a "great gain [*il grande guadagno*]" in that it makes for justice to be possible here and now. She writes: "To feel/hear inside myself, starting with myself, that women exist in themselves, not as secondary, the same or complementary to men, has changed me and the world; we both have changed, because when it has become true for me, the world has started to be populated by women, not only in my life, but also, surprise, in history: they have started to come out and continue to come out from people's memories, from the attics, from libraries' boxes, from archives, from the basements of museums."[78] Irigaray writes tirelessly about the need for a feminine symbolic and a female genealogy, but she does not seem to see the promising dimension of the feminine condition, she does not talk about the "fortune" or the "privilege" of being born a woman. To her, female ancestry was in the remote past and may be, perhaps, in the distant future. When, in the aftermath of the accident in Chernobyl, she exhorts everyone to make the mother-daughter relationship visible, she does so out of the need to compensate for an absence of feminine authority in history more than out of an assurance of its presence and reality.[79] "A female god is still to come," for Irigaray;[80] and yet without a feminine divine, woman is left to be the other of man, not a subject in her own image, with her own values and her own world. Without a transcendence that is truly her own, she is not. She is not free. Irigaray writes, "Is not God the name and the place that holds the promise of a new chapter in history and that also denies this can happen? Still invisible? Still to be discovered? To be incarnated? Archi-ancient and forever future."[81]

Conversely, for Muraro, a female God has come, is here; it is simply a matter of bringing it to light, a matter of hearing and seeing. Women mystics have spoken of God in feminine ways and in the mother tongue. They have reinterpreted transcendence in an entirely new sense. They show us, Muraro writes, that divine transcendence may be "God's contingence," if we can think and imagine a God that happens in this world, "a point of contact between that which is and that which can be [*un punto di contatto tra quello che è e quello che può essere*]."[82] An opening, a hole, a passage. A way of being that goes back to the origin and saves it. Women have spoken of God in unheard ways; through their words, a "female god" has come into existence, it is not "yet to come." Women mystics inspire, they open the way, go before us, and make it possible for us to see the unseen, hear the unheard. They make way, "*fan largo*," they do not tell us to wait for a better future; rather, they tell us this is the time, this is the world, it is this life, your life.

Think again about the young woman student for a moment. The realization of her life being part of a long genealogy of women who have come before her enables her to see and hear what she could not. She sees the women in her life under a different light, they have given her much, and although they may not make it into history books, she has learned a great deal from them. She closes her eyes and hears their voices. She hears them, all the women in her life, and others she does not recognize. She feels like she has never felt before, as if she has discovered some parts of her own self that she did not know. It is a turning point. The world looks like a different place now: she is able to see the invisible, she can hear the unheard. She is inspired. Now she knows that she has a chance to be, herself, in and through her own words. She realizes it will not be easy, but her freedom is not given, she must choose it every time. The risk is not so much that what she will do and say will not endure in time. The greater risk is, instead, that she will not make way for it.

Notes

1. "C'è altro" may be translated as "there's more," "there's something else," "there's something other." The polyvalence of this expression strikes me as particularly suited for the work of Luisa Muraro.

2. As an example of this, in "The Italian Difference," Antonio Negri claims that Luisa Muraro, together with Antonio Gramsci and Mario Tronti, represents the only true philosophical and political original voice in the twentieth-century Italian context. He attributes to her the genius of a transformative practice, the "creative difference" that breaks domination, "not from the margins, but from the

centre" (Antonio Negri, "The Italian Difference," *Cosmos and History: The Journal of Natural and Social Philosophy* 5, 1 [2009]: 13, 8–15).

3. Carla Lonzi, "Let's Spit on Hegel," in *Italian Feminist Thought*, edited by Paola Bono and Sandra Kemp (Oxford: Basil Blackwell, 1991), 41.

4. The full quotation reads: "Equality is what is offered as legal rights to colonized people. And what is imposed on them as culture. It is the principle through which those with hegemonic power continue to control those without" (Carla Lonzi, "Let's Spit on Hegel," 41).

5. The specific event that Muraro calls a "turning point" is related in Milan Women's Bookstore Collective, *Sexual Difference: A Theory of Social Symbolic Practice* (Bloomington: Indiana University Press, 1990). In an article titled "The Narrow Door," in referring to this same event, Muraro writes: "It was necessary to recognize a disparity among women and to turn this awareness into a new political practice"; Luisa Muraro, "The Narrow Door," in *Gendered Contexts: New Perspectives in Italian Cultural Studies*, ed. Laura Benedetti and Julia Hairston (New York: Peter Lang, 1996), 11. The portion of this chapter in the section "The Practice of Women's Relations" also refers to this specific event.

6. Anyone who speaks a language other than one's own mother tongue knows this all too well. There is always an expression, a way of saying, a word that defies all translation. We may try to convey its meaning with as many different words as we can find, trying to explain what that specific word or expression in our own mother tongue really means. Even when we think we have been successful in translating such word or expression, we are still left with a feeling that something is missing, that something was lost in the process, something does not quite make its way into the other language. Similarly, I propose that this is an existential condition many women, but not only women, find themselves in, an impasse that is felt as tangible and incontrovertible as it is elusive.

7. Dietrich of Freiberg and Meister Eckhart are the most prominent ones. Muraro calls them "friends" of women mystics.

8. In the original: "Si tratta comunque, d'interpretazioni tutte approssimativamente accettabili, ma nessuna calzante come vorremmo" (Luisa Muraro, *Il dio delle donne* [Milan: Mondadori, 2003], 137). Unless otherwise indicated, the English translation of Muraro's texts is mine.

9. In the original: "e come voleva anche il Principe della favola di Cenerentola—a proposito di calzante e calzature—quando girava per la città con una scarpa in mano, alla ricerca d'un piede" (Muraro, *Il dio delle donne*, 137).

10. In the original: "Qui, abbiamo un piede e cerchiamo la scarpa" (Muraro, *Il dio delle donne*, 137).

11. In the original: "L'amore appartiene a un'economia di scambio fra il niente e l'essere. Scambio, non elevazione, non ascesi, non dialettica. L'essere si fa niente per farsi passaggio, il niente chiama l'essere a darsi senza fine" (Muraro, *Il dio delle donne*, 136).

12. Muraro, *Il dio delle donne*, 138.

13. Muraro, "Introduzione: In vacanza per sempre," *Il dio delle donne*, 18.

14. My translation.

15. In the original: "È una lotta per la significanza originaria dell'esperienza—femminile—contro il suo trovarsi ad essere tutta ridotta a essere significata (ad essere significato) ad opera dell'altro, l'altro minuscolo che storicamente si rappresenta come l'altro sesso, gli uomini e i loro discorsi" (Luisa Muraro, *Le amiche di Dio* [Naples: D'Auria Editore, 2001], 111).

16. Muraro, *Le amiche di Dio*, 126.

17. In the original: "io sono diventata una che pensa meglio e che ha pensieri originali (del cui valore, ovviamente, non sono io la giudice). La stessa cosa posso dire di molte altre" (Muraro, *Le amiche di Dio*, 127).

18. Muraro, *Il dio delle donne*, 16.

19. Muraro, *Le amiche di Dio*, 110.

20. Muraro, *Il dio delle donne*, 61.

21. Muraro, *Il dio delle donne*, 132.

22. Muraro, *Il dio delle donne*, 20.

23. Muraro, *Il dio delle donne*, 16.

24. In the original: "Nascere donna vuol dire nascere predisposta allo sbilanciamento del centro di gravità che si sposta in altro, fuori di sé. Non è una predisposizione di natura metafisica o fisiologica; proviene dal rapporto con la madre" (Muraro, *Il dio delle donne*, 130).

25. In the original: "la chiamo esperienza femminile—senza considerarla esclusiva delle donne, il proprio della differenza femminile essendo di non escludere l'altro—perché dischiude un senso dell'essere che è sempre poter essere altro, senza separazione, così com'è nella relazione di una donna con sua madre e con il suo poter essere madre" (Muraro, *Il dio delle donne*, 112).

26. Muraro, *Il dio delle donne*, 94.

27. It is interesting to note that in Italian, the word "*sentire*" means both "to hear" and "to feel," conveying that grasping something entails at the same time both "hearing" and "feeling" it in and through our own whole being. To put it differently, without "hearing-feeling" it in us, it remains at a distance, outside, removed from us.

28. Luce Irigaray, *An Ethics of Sexual Difference*, trans. Carolyn Burke and Gillian C. Gill (Ithaca: Cornell University Press, 1993), 5.

29. Luce Irigaray, *thinking the difference*, trans. Karin Montin (New York: Routledge, 1994), xiv.

30. For a short but thorough analysis of these charges and how they are mostly misconceived, see Margaret Whitford, "Rereading Irigaray," in *Between Feminism and Psychoanalysis*, ed. Teresa Brennan (London: Routledge, 1990), 106–126. See also Naomi Schor, "This Essentialism Which Is not One," in *Engaging with Irigaray*, ed. Carolyn Burke, Naomi Schor, and Margaret Whitford (New York: Columbia University Press, 1994), 57–78. As the title indicates, this book is a rich and diverse collection on Irigaray's work.

31. Luisa Muraro is also the translator of several works by Irigaray from French into Italian.

32. Irigaray, *thinking the difference*, xv.
33. Irigaray, *An Ethics of Sexual Difference*, 6.
34. Milan Women's Bookstore Collective, *Sexual Difference: A Theory of Social-Symbolic Practice*, trans. Patricia Cicogna and Teresa de Lauretis (Bloomington: Indiana University Press, 1990), 26. The title has been translated with the English-American readers in mind, less so in keeping with the original. In Italian the title of the volume reads: *Non credere di avere dei diritti. La generazione della libertà femminile nell'idea e nelle vicende di un gruppo di donne* (Turin: Rosenberg and Sellier, 1987). A more literal translation would be: "Don't believe you have any rights. The engendering of feminine freedom in the idea and in the events of a group of women." The first part of the title, "don't believe (or don't think) you have any rights" is a quote taken from Simone Weil's *Notebook II*. It is regretful that "the engendering of feminine freedom" has been lost in the English title as this is precisely what is at stake.
35. In *An Ethics of Sexual Difference*, Irigaray refers to Ulysses in the chapter titled "Love of Self" and states that the maternal-feminine sheds tears not for herself, but for him. She has no "nostalgia for herself—her *odyssey*." And she adds: "That might happen if woman also went in quest of 'her own' love. Successfully accomplishing her journey" (Irigaray, *An Ethics of Sexual Difference*, 71). It appears that woman does shed tears for herself too, as the woman student shows.
36. Luce Irigaray, *The Way of Love*, trans. Heidi Bostic and Stephen Pluhácek (London: Continuum: 2002), 110.
37. Irigaray, *thinking the difference*, 10.
38. Irigaray, *thinking the difference*, 109.
39. Irigaray, *An Ethics of Sexual Difference*, 108.
40. Luce Irigaray, *Sexes and Genealogies*, trans. Gillian C. Gill (New York: Columbia University Press, 1993), 19.
41. Luisa Muraro, "Female Genealogies," in *Engaging with Irigaray*, 317–333.
42. Muraro, "Female Genealogies," 321.
43. Muraro, "Female Genealogies," 326.
44. Luce Irigaray, "Body against Body: In Relation to the Mother," in *Sexes and Genealogies*, 12.
45. Irigaray, "Body against Body: In Relation to the Mother," 18–19.
46. Luce Irigaray, "The Forgotten Mystery of Female Ancestry," in *thinking the difference*, 101; emphasis mine.
47. Muraro, "Female Genealogies," 321.
48. Muraro, "Female Genealogies," 328. The quote from Irigaray is taken from *An Ethics of Sexual Difference*, 118–119.
49. Muraro, "Female Genealogies," 328.
50. Muraro, "Female Genealogies," 330–331.
51. Muraro, "Female Genealogies," 329.
52. Muraro, "Female Genealogies," 328.
53. Muraro, "Female Genealogies," 329; emphasis mine.
54. Muraro, "Female Genealogies," 320.

55. Muraro, "Female Genealogies," 329.
56. Muraro, "Female Genealogies," 330; emphasis mine.
57. Muraro, "Female Genealogies," 321, 327.
58. Muraro, "Female Genealogies," 327.

59. It is important to point out that the practice of women's relationships may not be identified with lesbianism. Simonetta Spinelli, among others, has criticized the Milan Women's Bookstore Collective in her essay entitled "Silence is Loss," claiming that lesbian desire has remained the unsaid of the movement. In addressing questions in this regard posed by Teresa de Lauretis, Muraro states that "we are working exclusively toward human freedom, which is the only thing that can constitute a goal common to all women, and hence the reason for a politics of women. . . . From the way you speak of lesbianism, it almost seems as if you are making sexual choice a principle or a cause or a foundation of freedom. If that were what you thought, I would say to you: no, the principle of female freedom is of symbolic nature . . . that in order for us to enter the symbolic order we must start from silence, we must clear everything out—the place of the other must be empty" (Teresa de Lauretis, "The Practice of Sexual Difference and Feminist Thought in Italy: An Introductory Essay," in Milan Women's Bookstore Collective, *Sexual Difference: A Theory of Social-Symbolic Practice*, 18). More on this issue can be found in the same introductory essay by Teresa de Lauretis.

60. Milan Women's Bookstore Collective, *Sexual Difference: A Theory of Social-Symbolic Practice*, 2.
61. Milan Women's Bookstore Collective, *Sexual Difference: A Theory of Social-Symbolic Practice*, 134.
62. Milan Women's Bookstore Collective, *Sexual Difference: A Theory of Social-Symbolic Practice*, 52.
63. Milan Women's Bookstore Collective, *Sexual Difference: A Theory of Social-Symbolic Practice*, 112.
64. Milan Women's Bookstore Collective, *Sexual Difference: A Theory of Social-Symbolic Practice*, 111.
65. Milan Women's Bookstore Collective, *Sexual Difference: A Theory of Social-Symbolic Practice*, 129.
66. Milan Women's Bookstore Collective, *Sexual Difference: A Theory of Social-Symbolic Practice*, 130.
67. Milan Women's Bookstore Collective, *Sexual Difference: A Theory of Social-Symbolic Practice*, 125.
68. Milan Women's Bookstore Collective, *Sexual Difference: A Theory of Social-Symbolic Practice*, 149.
69. Milan Women's Bookstore Collective, *Sexual Difference: A Theory of Social-Symbolic Practice*, 138.
70. Milan Women's Bookstore Collective, *Sexual Difference: A Theory of Social-Symbolic Practice*, 119.
71. Milan Women's Bookstore Collective, *Sexual Difference: A Theory of Social-Symbolic Practice*, 132.

72. "The relationship of one woman to another is unthinkable in human culture" (Milan Women's Bookstore Collective, *Sexual Difference: A Theory of Social-Symbolic Practice*, 48). In the original Italian text: "il rapporto della donna con l'altra donna è l'impensato della cultura umana" (*Non credere di avere dei diritti*, 43). In Italian, *"l'impensato"* means both "the unthought," what has not yet been thought and also what is not "thinkable" in that there are no ways for thought to conceive it, given that the concepts of thought are as they are.

73. Muraro, "Female Genealogies," 329.

74. Luisa Muraro employs this image of the "swerve," in Italian *"schivata,"* in an essay about the philosophy of Iris Murdoch titled: "Conclusion: A Meditation in Swerves," in *Iris Murdoch and the Moral Imagination: Essays*, ed. M. F. Simone Roberts and Alison Scott-Baumann (Jefferson, NC: McFarland, 2010). It appears also, among others, in Luisa Muraro, *Non è da tutti. L'indicibile fortuna di nascere donna* (Rome: Carocci Editore, 2011), 95.

75. In the original: "essere in bilico tra senso di sé e un sentimento di mancanza, a restare su questo crinale" (Muraro, *Non è da tutti*, 67).

76. Muraro, *Non è da tutti*, 34.

77. Luisa Muraro, "The Symbolic Independence from Power," *Cosmos and History: The Journal of Natural and Social Philosophy* 5, 1 (2009): 63.

78. In the original: "Sentire dentro di me, a partire da me, che le donne esistono per sé stesse, non come seconde, pari o complementari degli uomini, ha cambiato me e il mondo; siamo cambiati entrambi, perché, quando è stato vero per me, il mondo ha cominciato a popolarsi di donne, non solo nella mia vita, ma anche, sorpresa, nella storia: uscivano e continuano a uscire dai ricordi delle persone, dalle soffitte, dagli scatoloni delle biblioteche, dagli archivi, dalle cantine dei musei" (Muraro, *Non è da tutti*, 68).

79. "To anyone who cares about social justice today, I suggest putting up posters in all public places with beautiful pictures representing the mother-daughter couple—the couple that illustrates a very special relationship to nature and culture. Such representations are missing from all civil and religious sites" (Irigaray, *thinking the difference*, 9).

80. Irigaray, "Divine Women," in *Sexes and Genealogies*, 67.

81. Irigaray, "Divine Women," 72.

82. Muraro, *Il dio delle donne*, 150.

15

Adriana Cavarero and Hannah Arendt

Singular Voices and Horrifying Narratives

Peg Birmingham

Adriana Cavarero is forthright in acknowledging her debt to the thought of Hannah Arendt. In a 2008 interview, she states, "My point of reference is neither Heidegger nor Nancy, but Arendt." She goes on to say, "Therefore, I do not refer to the being-with, which I take from Arendt, as *mit-sein* or being-with, but as in-between, as relationality, as something more material and relational. Arendt-like, I give an ontological and political meaning to this in-between."[1] The first part of this essay will examine the ways in which Cavarero's relational ontology relies on and departs from Arendt's thinking of the in-between, specifically focusing on Cavarero's natal ontology with its insistence on vulnerability and the primacy of voice rather than Arendt's emphasis on speech and action in thinking uniqueness and plurality. In the second part of the essay, I give what I take to be the Arendtian response to Cavarero's critique. The third part of the essay turns to Cavarero's thinking of vulnerability and violence, focusing on her reading of Arendt's notion of superfluousness and the role it plays in Cavarero's account of horror. Cavarero argues that, for Arendt, superfluousness is a condition created by totalitarian violence; she suggests that a relational ontology rooted in bodily vulnerability offers a way to address the totalitarian creation of superfluity, which she argues continues to be at work in contemporary acts of horror. In the conclusion, I raise the question of whether Cavarero misreads Arendt on the origin of superfluousness, a misreading that would account for the almost complete lack, in her work, of any consideration of Arendt's analysis of the worldlessness of modern capitalism as the "origin" of superfluousness that, in turn is a key element in the rise of totalitarianism. This raises the question of whether a political in-between rooted in an ontology of bodily vulnerability and the unique voice goes far enough in offering a remedy to the horrifying violence of the contemporary world.

Cavarero and the Ontological Event of Natality

Cavarero's account of the event of natality marks her greatest proximity and greatest distance from Arendt. While she agrees with Arendt that natality is the ontological event of appearance, she is highly critical of what she views as Arendt's complete disregard of the vulnerability and exposure of this event. Vulnerability, for Cavarero, is the paradigm of the human and at the very center of the event of natality. She states, "The choice of assuming vulnerability, a paradigm of the human, far from an abstract speculative move, is instead rooted in the analysis of concrete situations and, as Judith Butler would say, of precarious lives that are especially exposed."[2] Going further, Cavarero argues that Arendt's account of natality misses entirely our natal vulnerability, evidenced by the complete lack of the mother in Arendt's account. Such a lack means that there is no account of the initial tenderness for the child and what this might mean for a different account of the ontological and political in-between. Instead, Cavarero argues, the main scene in Arendt is the second birth into politics, where the child is now a political actor among a plurality of others, capable of beginning something new.

Most instructive of Cavarero's criticism of Arendt is her reading of Arendt's well-known reference to the glad tidings announcing "A Child has been born unto us." Arendt's emphasis is on the miracle of action at the very heart of this announcement. Cavarero notes, "The miracle is, in other words, the birth of new men and the new beginning, the action they are capable of by virtue of being born. . . . It is this faith in and hope for the world that found perhaps its most glorious and most succinct expression in the few words with which the Gospels announced their 'glad tidings': A child has been born unto us."[3] Cavarero argues that Arendt errs on two counts when citing the glad tidings. First, the citation is from Isaiah, not the Gospels, and second, the correct citation is "For unto us a child has been born," and not as Arendt puts it, "For a child is born unto us." Cavarero argues that Isaiah's text is messianic whereas the Gospels allow for a more secular reading:

The text of the Gospels . . . is more susceptible to a secular reading and as such places the fewest obstacles in the way of the Arendtian strategy of circumscribing the sense of birth to the ambit of the untranscendable horizon that, in her vocabulary, goes by the name of "the world." Since for Arendt "living" and "being among men" means the same thing, the child—indeed, every newborn, each human being who makes its entrance into the world—is not born *to us* coming from elsewhere, but instead, according to the Arendtian vision appears *among us here*.[4]

For Cavarero, Arendt's incorrect reference to the Gospels reveals her deeply Christian roots, despite her being Jewish, on two matters: the coming of the child and the creation of the world. Further, Arendt's misstating the Isaiah text reveals her misplaced emphasis on plurality to the detriment of a concern with uniqueness.

In emphasizing the coming of the child, Arendt, according to Cavarero, emphasizes the promise of new beginnings inherent in the event of natality. The stress on new beginnings aligns natality with the capacity for action. Lost, for Cavarero, is the helplessness of this beginning. Far from acting, the infant is radically dependent and surrenders herself completely to the caregiver, usually the mother. According to Cavarero, Arendt misses the opportunity for a "phenomenology of natality" that would give us something different, "a relationality marked by deep asymmetry and by originary dependency."[5] Cavarero goes on to argue, "In this way, the free and rational subject's supposed integrity, free from all constraint, allows space for an originary and structural vulnerability, which is emphasized precisely in the fateful moment of beginning when the new creature appears to the world and surrenders to another (who is, normally and in ordinary experience, the mother). In this framework, in other words, birth holds vulnerability and relationality together in an inseparable ontological bond."[6] Contrary to Arendt and deeply critical of her, Cavarero stresses the asymmetrical relationship of birth rather than Arendt's "equal and horizontal equality of action." She asks: "What indeed might we make of Arendt's main thesis—that of a correspondence between the first and second births, between the inaugural theater of birth and the political theater of action—if we introduce a mother into the scene? What might happen to the horizontal relation of reciprocity, which defines politics as the scene of appearance, if it is the unbalanced relationship between the newborn and the mother that serves as a premise for securing the ontological root for action?"[7] Important here is Cavarero's emphasis on the vulnerability and helplessness of the new beginning rather than the plurality of equals that for Arendt is the condition for action. Shifting the primal scene to that of the mother inclining over the child, she argues, "permits a shift of attention from a subject modeled on the idea of autonomy to a subjectivity structurally characterized by dependence and exposure, from the assertions of a self-consistent and partitioned subjectivity to one that is open and relational."[8] I will return to this momentarily.

Cavarero also disagrees with Arendt's account of the creation of world, specifically, the creation of Adam and Eve. She points out that Arendt takes up the Pauline account wherein Adam and Eve are created together, thereby from the outset introducing plurality into the world. Cavarero, however, is critical of Arendt's emphasis on *an inaugural plurality* that excludes the natal scene of *beginning*: "As Arendt of course knows, the truth is that God also creates Eve, but according to her interpretation of this second version of the narrative of Genesis, the passage in question alludes not to the phenomenon of beginning, but to the human condition of plurality."[9] She notes that the emphasis on the plural creation of Adam and Eve "conveys in an elementary form the human condition of plurality and hence too of action. If the beginning starts not with one but two who differ from one another, then already at the origin we have a *plural reality*."[10] Arendt's emphasis on a plural reality is, for Cavarero, "symptomatic" of her complete erasure of the figure of the newborn "since it alludes to an unbalanced and unequal relationship that does not fit with her definition of politics as an interaction on a horizontally shared plane."[11] To go further, Cavarero's embrace of the figure of the newborn whose relation to the mother is unequal and dependent gives us a very different relational in-between than that of Arendt's. The mother and the infant are uniquely situated vis-à-vis each other. Certainly, they are exposed and opened to each other, but they do not yet constitute a plurality in the sense of acting in concert. In other words, Cavarero posits an *ontological relationality of uniqueness* that is the condition for an Arendtian relationship of plurality.

Cavarero's emphasis on ontological uniqueness prior to plurality is of a piece with her earliest work on the voice, which she self-describes as a "vocal ontology of uniqueness," claiming that the "voice manifests the unique being of each human being."[12] Signaling a particular and living body, the voice "communicates the presence of an existent in flesh and bone."[13] Her emphasis on the voice challenges Arendt's exclusive focus on speech as the key aspect of political action: "each unique and 'unrepeatable speaker'" has a "face, a name, and a life story, unrepeatable and different from every other, they communicate the uniqueness of their own personal identity; they communicate reciprocally who they are."[14] The speakers are not political because of what they say, but because "they say it to others who share an interactive space of reciprocal exposure. To speak to one another is to communicate to one another the unrepeatable uniqueness of each speaker."[15] Rather than the Arendtian conception of the political as a plurality acting in concert for the sake of something new, Cavarero understands the political as rooted in an ontological space of unique voices appealing to and communicating their uniqueness. The desire is not for worldly beginnings, but instead for new and unique voices to be heard in the world.

Fundamental to Cavarero's vocal ontology is the unique self's desire for unity between the beginning of its life and all that ensues from this moment, a unity that can only occur through narration. In her reading, Odysseus weeps not because he hears the story of his life but, more fundamentally, because the story reveals to him his desire to join his life with his story. This is a deeply temporal desire of a self that longs to unify himself through the stretch of time that marks his life. Here, Cavarero departs significantly from Arendt's discussion of narration. In Arendt's telling, Odysseus weeps because the muse speaks to his desire for immortality, possible only through the telling of his life-story by another. By contrast, Cavarero argues that Odysseus weeps because his desire for his unique story was not known to him prior to hearing the story: "as the emotional listener, he discovers that his desire for narration is immediate. . . . There is a substantial difference between the desire to leave one's own identity for posterity in the form of an immortal tale, and the desire to hear one's own story in life."[16] The ontological desire for a story is the desire of a unique self who from the moment of birth is never one with itself; its desire for the story is a desire fed by the lack of self-unity, recoverable only through the narration: "The unity that the narratable self asks of the tale is never a question of the text. It is rather the question of her innate desire, which can turn in many directions—to the narration for the thread of the story, or to a single act, or to a summary of the dying one. . . . Ulysses weeps not because the rhapsod faithfully reproduces that identity which the hero himself does not know and does not control. Rather it is because the text that he is unexpectedly given clearly recognizes—or, better, reveals—his desire to him."[17] Given over to the world, fragmented and unstable, the desire for narration is a desire for a stable unity; this desire for stability and unity is set between "a self that always already senses herself to be narratable and the act of narration."[18]

Still further, the self's desire for the lost unity of birth marks an ontological loss incurred when the self is given over to the world. From this moment forward, on Cavarero's telling, the voice and its story are separated, rejoined only by another who recounts the life: "Fragile and continent—and already marked at birth by a unity that makes of herself first a promise, and then a desire—the narratable self is an exposed uniqueness that awaits her narration."[19] Paraphrasing Arendt's reference to Augustine, Cavarero claims that the promise of beginning is a promise of unity, the promise of a unique life that will become a unified self through the joining of its inaugural sense of life with its life-story.

Again, it is not the text of the narration that is at issue here, but instead, the ontological desire of the unique "who" to engender her life through a narration that is irrevocably her own even as narrated by another. The narratable self requires plurality to recover the lost unity of the miraculous and unique beginning and this because the narratable self cannot narrate its own beginning: "If everyone is *who* is born, from the start—and with a promise of unity that the story inherits from that start—then no recounting of a life-story can in fact leave out this beginning with which the story itself began."[20] Rather than the Arendtian desire for endurance through the narration of one's life when one departs, Cavarero emphasizes the desire for the living story: "There is a substantial difference between the desire to leave one's own identity for posterity in the form of an immortal tale. And the desire to hear one's own story *in life*."[21]

Arendt on Natality and Narration

It is instructive to turn to Arendt's accounts of natality and narration respectively as they illuminate the distance between Cavarero and Arendt, a distance that has significant repercussions for how each understands the relation between ontology and politics. Often missed by her readers, Arendt's turn to the ontological event of natality and its promise of a new beginning is not out of concern for the unique newcomer *as such*; instead, from the outset of her reflections on natality she is concerned with the endurance of the world. The promise of a new beginning—a promise with which she concludes *The Origins of Totalitarianism*—is a promise of the renewal and endurance of the world even after the worst has happened. As she puts it in *The Human Condition*, "The miracle that saves the world, the realm of human affairs, from its normal, "natural" ruin is ultimately the fact of natality, in which the faculty of action is ontologically rooted."[22] Important here is her emphasis on the miracle that *saves the world*, the realm of human affairs. The event of the new is a world-saving event insofar as it radically interrupts the world's ruination in time, a ruination that will be its fate if the law of mortality rules.²³ The glad tidings that "a child has been born unto us" are glad tidings for the *world* insofar as the child's birth is an ontological interruption of time. This is the messianic moment (missed by Cavarero) in Arendt's thought because the child comes from "nowhere" in the sense that the miracle of birth interrupts all genealogy.

Here, I pause to note that Cavarero critiques my position, which I affirm in *Hannah Arendt and the Right to Have Rights*, that the event of natality proceeds from "nothingness."²⁴ For Cavarero, this claim forgets the mother as the preoriginal moment from which the infant appears. However, if the stress is on the primacy of the mother, then the event of natality is reduced to the biological *genesis* in which, it seems, far more is lost than gained. I think that Arendt's notion of interruption carries with it the notion of in-fancy as the break, the beginning, the unpredictable moment that cannot be captured in a genealogical history that includes not only the mother, but the father, the grandparents and great-grandparents, and so on and so forth. Whereas this genealogy is not unimportant in defining the situatedness of the infant—the web of relations into which she is born and which Arendt spends several pages discussing—nevertheless, this genealogical history will not account for the break, the interruption, the miracle of the newcomer, "before whom there was nobody." Arendt is not so naïve as to mean by this that infant spring forth like Hobbesian mushrooms, but she does want to emphasis the ontological break that occurs with the event of natality. It is to Arendt's credit, in my view, that she thinks the ontological interruption and not the genealogical continuation between mother and child.²⁵

Still further, Arendt claims that uniqueness is impossible without plurality and is inseparable from it. At the outset of her discussion of action, Arendt argues that distinction, which all living beings have in common, becomes uniqueness *only* through speech and action. While alterity is a quality shared with everything that exists and all beings who are alive are distinct, "distinct uniqueness" belongs only to human beings, and this because of human plurality: "In man otherness, which he shares with everything that is, and distinctness which he shares with everything alive, becomes uniqueness. And human plurality is the paradoxical plurality of unique beings. Speech and action reveal this unique distinctness."²⁶ Again, only through plurality does uniqueness enter the world. Contrary to Cavarero, for Arendt, there is no uniqueness that is not yet plural. Paradoxically, the birth of the unique and mortal newcomer is the condition for the possibility of the immortality of the *world*. Cavarero correctly reads Arendt's "glad tidings" as being more concerned with plurality than with uniqueness. Arendt's response would be that Cavarero stresses too much the unique life of the newcomer to the detriment of a concern for the renewal of the world, which for her is the ontological condition for the unique life. Life is worldly appearance and without the endurance of the world, no unique life can appear.

At the very outset of *The Human Condition*, Arendt makes it clear that her primary concern is with the world-saving capacities of the *vita activa*. I want to emphasize that Arendt insists that all three activities, namely labor, work, and action, are rooted in the ontological event of natality and therefore all three are concerned with preserving the world: "Labor and work, as well as action, are also rooted in natality in so far as they have the task to provide and preserve the world for, to foresee and reckon with, the constant influx of newcomers who are born into the world as strangers."[27] The three activities together comprise the material relational in-between of worldly appearance. Speaking of why she uses the term "*vita activa*," she writes, "My use of the *vita activa* presupposes that the concern underlying all its activities is not the same as and is neither superior nor inferior to the central concern of the *vita contemplativa*."[28] Arendt points to the common concern of the *vita activa* in the section immediately following this claim and titled "Immortality and Eternity." In contrast with the philosopher's concern with eternity, the unifying concern of the *vita activa* is immortality, which she defines as "endurance in time," an endurance of the world as much as an endurance of the finite human being.[29]

Arendt is clear that all three activities of the *vita activa* are rooted in the ontological event of natality. Insofar as she most closely associates labor with embodiment, Arendt does not deny that the ontological event of natality is an embodied event. Indeed, when she argues that political life is a second birth founded on the initial birth of the infant, she is not arguing, as Cavarero claims, that the ontological event of natality is disembodied. Instead, the space of appearance is a physical worldly in-between, which is the condition for the second birth of a political "in-between" constituted by acting and speaking.[30] And she is explicit that the second birth is not "laid over" the first like a "superfluous structure affixed to the useful structure of the building itself," but instead emerges from it.[31] For Arendt, actors (always in the plural) are always interdependent with other actors and, furthermore, the interdependence is such that unique bodily perspectives are established only with and through other embodied perspectives.

Arendt's discussion of the two births should be understood from her discussion in *The Human Condition* of the two senses of the public which, she argues, "are closely inter-related but not altogether identical phenomenon."[32] Arendt then states: "It [the public] means, first, that everything that appears in public can be seen and heard by everybody and has the widest possible publicity. For us, appearance—something that is being seen and heard by others as well as ourselves—constitutes reality."[33] This first sense of publicity as appearance *as such* undergirds or supports the second sense of the public, defined as the common, *political* space that gathers its participants like a table that both brings together and separates.

Arendt develops this first sense of appearance in the first part of *Life of the Mind: Thinking*, titled "Appearance." Repeating her claim that being and appearing are coincident, she now adds that appearance is always appearance *in common*: "all sense-endowed creatures have appearance as such in common, first an appearing world and second, and perhaps even more important, the fact that they themselves are appearing and disappearing creatures, that there always was a world before their arrival and there always will be a world after their departure."[34] In this later work, Arendt extends the "common" beyond a common, political world to the worldliness of appearance as such. At the same time, in this later work she argues that plurality is not merely the *conditio per quam* of political life, as she claims in *The Human Condition*, but is the *conditio per quam* of earthly life: "Nothing and nobody exists in this world whose very being does not presuppose a *spectator*. In other words, nothing that is, insofar as it appears, exists in the singular; everything that is meant to be perceived by somebody"[35] Following from this, she claims that "Plurality is the law of the earth."[36]

Contrary to Cavarero's claim of an ontological desire for self-unity established through joining the unique voice and its narration, Arendt argues that everything that appears is possessed by an ontological urge toward self-display: "It is indeed as though everything that is alive—in addition to the fact that its surface is made for appearance, fit to be seen and meant to appear to others—has an *urge to appear*, to fit itself into the world of appearances by displaying and showing, not its 'inner self' but itself *as an individual*."[37] Here Arendt significantly changes her position on the distinction between animal and human life articulated in *The Human Condition*. In the earlier work, Arendt claims that only human beings are concerned with their uniqueness; only the human being is concerned with a distinct uniqueness that requires acting with a plurality of others. In *Life of the Mind*, Arendt does not change her mind on the fundamental condition of plurality, but now claims that each and every appearing being has the urge to self-display *as an individual* and not merely as a member of the species. Citing the research of the Swiss biologist and zoologist Adolph Portman, Arendt argues that this "desire to appear" cannot be explained in functional terms; instead, she suggests, it is gratuitous, having to do with the sheer pleasure of appearing and self-display.[38] No longer an exclusively human desire, each and every appearing being desires unique distinctness and this because every sentient being appears in a plurality with others.

Critiquing the distinction between depth and surface, as if the surface owed its appearance to something hidden, Arendt argues that the self makes it appearance *on the surface* in its sentient, embodied relation with the world.[39] As Kimberly Curtis points out, for Arendt our capacity to experience a world in common is "utterly dependent upon the aesthetic provocation of multiple, distinct appearing beings. If we can locate the common world at all, therefore, it is paradoxically to be found only where this provocation flourishes."[40] The plurality of perspectives that marks the Arendtian public space is a plurality of embodied and sensual perspectives. Appearing beings, human and animal alike, are living beings enmeshed in an in-between matrix of material, embodied, and interdependent relationships; the human capacity for action is inseparable from this material, embodied in-between wherein one desires to see and be seen, touch and be touched, hear and be heard.[41]

At the same time, Cavarero adds significantly to Arendt's account by developing an ontology of voiced appearance prior to, and inseparable from, the "second appearance" of political speech. While Cavarero's account ties the voice to the ontological event of *human* natality, it seems to me that her account can be extended to include the whole of appearance or, at least, the whole of appearance of sentient beings. Still further, her account of a vocal ontology develops considerably Arendt's claim of an ontological desire or longing for self-display and distinctness, which we have seen through Portman's work to be at work in all appearance. Putting together Cavarero's natal ontology with Arendt's ontology of appearance, it is not too much to claim that all of appearance has the desire to give itself voice. Already implicit in Arendt's later account of appearance, the desire to give voice to one's unique appearance is seemingly more fundamental and precedes the political desire for speech and action with a plurality of other actors.

Further, while Arendt emphasizes the second birth of political action and power, she is not unconcerned with the vulnerability and fragility of the first birth, a fragility that for her is at work in the second birth of the political. The Arendtian distance from Cavarero's account lies in the location of the fragility and vulnerability. As we have seen, Cavarero's account stresses the vulnerability and fragility of the unique newborn and her utter dependence upon the mother. Following Hans Jonas, Cavarero argues that this vulnerability and fragility carry with them an imperative of responsibility of protection and care.[42] While Cavarero is entirely right in pointing out that Arendt has little or no concern with the mother at the natal scene, she overlooks Arendt's concern with the need to protect both the newcomer and the world: each is vulnerable, each needs protection in order to ensure the promise of a new beginning essential to each. While I cannot give a full account here, Arendt's *Crisis in Education* should be read as her fullest account of this double vulnerability and fragility from which emerges a double responsibility: to the child and to the world. Our responsibility to the child is to protect the promise of beginning; our responsibility to the world is to protect its endurance and continuation such that the promise can be enacted.

The child's capacity for a new beginning requires the protection and care of life (which, for Arendt, is the basis of her distinction between the public and the private, the latter being a "non-privative" space where vulnerable aspects of existence can "thrive in concealment" away from "the full light of the public").[43] At the same, the responsibility to the child is to protect its promise of beginning something new. Nothing, she argues, destroys the promise of beginning more than the "dictatorial authority" of adults who decide how the world should look and impose this upon the newcomers. This, she argues, is the mistake of all political utopias and their educational systems, "based upon the absolute superiority of the adult, and the attempt to produce the new as a *fait accompli*, that is, as if the new already existed."[44]

At the same time, the fragile and vulnerable world needs protection against the newcomer. Arendt is clear that by the notion of "endurance" she does not mean the preservation of the status quo. As we saw above, Arendt claims that only the promise of beginning something new saves the world from ruination. Instead, she suggests that the responsibility to the preservation of the world takes the form of introducing the child to the plurality of its histories, to what has happened, in order to set the world anew. Thus, she concludes that education must be conservative, "it must preserve this newness and introduce it as a new thing into an old world."[45]

I want to stress again that, for Arendt, the political birth is not laid over the first birth as "a superstructure on an already existing building." The first birth contains the second birth, as it were, and this because the plurality and publicity of the second birth are already at work in the first. The relational being-in-common of the first birth already contains the capacity for power and action that will characterize the "birth" into the political. Cavarero stresses the absolute dependency and surrender of the newborn in order to make her case that the ontological ground of the political is our shared vulnerability and exposure. She is explicit in not wanting to introduce power into the scene as for her it is too closely aligned with the autonomy and self-possession of the modern subject. But does the child surrender completely to the inclining mother? That seems to claim too much. While certainly the newborn is utterly dependent, she does not "absolutely surrender." From her entry into the world, the child appears in her uniqueness, and that appearance is in part a demand, a crying out for what she needs. At the same time, the infant expresses pleasure and joy in the world and those around her. While certainly there is a dependency on others to meet her needs, there is from the outset a voiced independence or what might be better called a natal capacity for power and action. Cavarero wants it both ways: an ontological uniqueness, an original "*ipse*" located in the voice and, at the same time, an ontological vulnerability and dependency that belies the independence of that voice. In other words, and this is known to every new and sleep-deprived parent, the infant does not totally surrender; her voice is her own, displaying at the natal level the twin characteristics of dependence and independence.

Arendt's claim of an ontological desire for appearance and self-display returns us to the question of biography and narration in her work. For Arendt the appearance of the "who" is always already plural. She does not allow for a transcendental "*ipse*" of a subject prior to this plurality. Thus, there is no lost unity that must be recovered through narration. Instead, self-unity is only achieved through action with others. This is Arendt's disagreement with Heidegger, for whom the unity of the self is achieved in thinking. By contrast, for Arendt, thinking is always the activity of a divided self, the two-in-one of a thinking self in dialogue with itself. Only in acting with others is the self a one, a "who." Thus, Arendt suggests that the desire infusing the ontological event of natality is the desire for worldly appearance. We saw above that, on Arendt's account, all sentient appearance is infused with the ontological desire to give itself voice. Cavarero's vocal ontology adds a great deal to Arendt's claim. However, Arendt adds to Cavarero's account, suggesting that the *distinctive* desire of the human being to give voice to its appearance takes the form of a double desire for immortality: both individual and worldly. The double desire for immortality is the desire for the world to continue in order that the self can appear and endure in it. Accompanying the desire for a story *in life* (Cavarero's claim), Arendt adds that there is the desire that the world will continue so that my life-story is not only told, but also endures. For Arendt, a different desire is at the heart of Odysseus's weeping; the narration reveals to him his longing for a life-story that confers upon him a finite immortality. She would agree with Cavarero that the text of the narration is not as important as the fact that the poet remembers and retells the story, indicating not only his longing for his life-story, but also that his life, through the story, will be remembered after he departs.

Arendt's claim of an originary desire for immortality may have its theoretical roots in her account of "superfluousness," which she defines as the unbearable condition of loneliness in which the capacity of acting with others has become impossible. Superfluousness is the loss of significant speech and action, a loss in which one becomes literally "dead to the world." Such a social and political death, for Arendt, means that there is a sense in which my life-story may not be told and, more radically still, a sense in which my life has no story at all. Here a caution must be inserted: for Arendt, the desire for immortality is not the heroic desire for glory as seen with Achilles who, as Cavarero correctly notes, "desires to define his life in a single moment" of horrifying violence. Arendt insists that the concern for immortality infuses labor, work, and action; as such, the desire for the endurance of the world and the disclosure of the self is as much at work in the daily cleaning of the Aegean stables as in Pericles' speech.[46] The desire for immortality—the desire for the preservation of the world and the endurance of the self—animates all three activities comprising the *vita activa*. I submit that Arendt's thinking of immortality is a rejection of the concept of political glory tied to singular deeds and sacrificial violence. Again, worldly immortality is gained through the daily cleaning that keeps decay at bay, the work of our hands that builds a world in common, and political action that saves the world from ruination. The violence that may erupt with a sense of superfluousness—another name for loss of the possibility of immortality—gives evidence for this originary longing for worldly appearance and endurance that animates each finite human life. I will return to this in my conclusion.

In sum, while each thinker offers an ontology rooted in the event of natality, Arendt and Cavarero differ radically on the nature of this event. Cavarero's natal ontology emphasizes the unique voice of the vulnerable and exposed beginner, always already a "who" and, therefore, from the outset a narratable self who desires unity through her life-story. Her account of the ontological event of natality underwrites her claim that totalitarianism's ontological crime is the destruction of uniqueness by attempting to render it superfluous. By contrast, Arendt's ontology of natality emphasizes the worldly appearance of a plurality whose condition of possibility is an enduring world. Hence, Arendt's claim that totalitarianism's ontological crime is the destruction of plurality without which there is no uniqueness. In what follows, I examine briefly each thinker's respective account of the creation of superfluousness as, in my view, the differing accounts illuminate how their different emphasis on uniqueness and plurality governs their respective analyses of totalitarian violence and our ontological and political response to it.

Superfluous Violence and Horrifying Narratives

Cavarero's account of superfluousness relies heavily on Arendt's account of terror and the death camps in *Origins of Totalitarianism*. She focuses on Arendt's account of the production of "living corpses" and the attempt to eradicate through terror the unpredictability that characterizes the unique individual, claiming that according to Arendt, the "Lager 'fabricated' the superfluity of human beings."[47] Making a distinction between Arendt and Foucault, Cavarero argues that, for Foucault, the "living dead" are fabricated from biopower's "making live and letting die," while for Arendt (in her reading), the living dead are produced on the basis of *an ontological criterion*, namely the annihilation of uniqueness. The ontological annihilation of uniqueness eradicates life *and* death. As Cavarero puts it, the fabrication of living corpses is "an attack on the ontological material, transforming unique beings into a mass of superfluous beings whose 'murder as impersonal as the squashing of a gnat' also takes away from them their own death."[48] From this, Cavarero draws the conclusion that the ontological annihilation of uniqueness moves us from terror to horror. Distinguishing terror in the face of "imminent death from which one flees," Cavarero defines horror as a "repugnant," revulsed paralysis, a "disgust for the violence that . . . aims to destroy the uniqueness of the body, tearing at its constitutive vulnerability. What is at stake is not the end of a human life, but the human condition itself, as incarnated in the singularity of vulnerable bodies."[49]

Horror, unlike terror, aims at disfiguring and dismembering the human body. Again, for Cavarero, this is an ontological crime insofar as it is directed at the vulnerability of the unique body, the constitutive ontological "material" that marks the "fundamental status of the human being."[50] Consistent with her analysis of the unique self's longing for unity, the ontological crime is a dismembering of this unity in which the body has been cut into, torn apart, penetrated in some manner or another. This is a violence that "aims to erase singularity."[51]

Going further, the horror of the disfigurement of the body is one end of the extreme vulnerability that marks the status of being human. At the other extreme lies our shared political and ethical responsibility to care for this vulnerable other. Cavarero gives the example of the young man who places a gauze mask upon a woman wounded in the London bombings as an example of the two extremes of vulnerability: being wounded and being cared for. From this example, among many others, Cavarero finds the basis for community. Following Butler, for whom vulnerability is the basic human condition, she claims that "vulnerability, understood in physical and corporeal terms, configures a human condition in which it is the relation to the other that counts. That allows an ontology of linkage and dependence to come to the fore."[52] Again, vulnerability of the unique bodily being is the ontological ground of being human. Care of the other's vulnerability is the political and ethical responsibility that emerges from this constitutive ground.

Concluding her analysis of Arendt's discussion of the death camps and the fabrication of superfluousness, Cavarero turns to philosophy, arguing that for Arendt, "radical evil is connected . . . to the way in which the philosophical tradition has conceived ontology, not politics . . . the linkage with totalitarian evil is not to be sought on the plane of the history of political philosophy. This linkage is to be sought first and foremost on the plane of ontology."[53] Cavarero cites as evidence Arendt's letter to Jaspers in which she concludes that philosophy is implicated in radical evil because its tradition speaks of "the human being as an individual and only plurality tangentially." Overlooking Arendt's explicit reference to plurality without any reference to uniqueness, Cavarero concludes that "the category of uniqueness—along with the closely connected ones of relation and plurality—performs a decisive function in the Arendtian reading of horror in ontological terms that characterizes the text on totalitarianism."[54] She then cites Simona Forti, who claims that Arendt accuses modern philosophy, specifically Hobbes. in the same letter to Jaspers, "of an unprecedented attack on the ontological dignity of the singular being in favor of the absolutization of the One." Thus, Cavarero concludes, "what philosophy only thought Nazism put into practice, namely, the fabrication of the superfluity of the unique being."[55]

Cavarero's linking of philosophy and Nazism is not surprising given her commitment to the relation between the ontological and the political. Although she criticizes Jean-Luc Nancy for reducing the political to the ontological and despite her endorsement of Arendt's insistence that the two realms speak to one another as if from across mountaintops, Cavarero is much closer to Nancy than she admits. As seen in the close reading offered above, Cavarero is clear that philosophy's forgetting of uniqueness and its embrace of the sovereign One provided the ontological ground for the horrifying effect of the death camps and the production of superfluous living corpses. The remedy, then, is to change the ontology to one in which vulnerability is the ontological ground of the human condition, which, in turn, provides the basis for a community whose shared collective responsibility is to care for this condition.

Cavarero arrives at this conclusion in part through a reading of Arendt's analysis of superfluousness. The problem, however, is that Cavarero begins at the *conclusion* of Arendt's analysis. Arendt's own analysis of superfluousness in *Origins* claims that the horror of the camps and the killing of uniqueness were the *final* step in a genealogy that began with the political emancipation of the bourgeoisie, whose private interests, driven by the imperialism of capitalism, took over and destroyed the public space, a destruction that *produced* millions of superfluous people, many of whom were vulnerable to the ideology of racism which, she claims, is capitalism's driving engine. In other words, Arendt argues that the *economic* creation of worldlessness is the condition for the alliance between the mob—one category of the worldless and superfluous—and capital that eventually led to the death camps. In between the alliance and the camps, Arendt offers a genealogy of murder: first of the juridical person, then of the moral person, and, only at the end, of the unique person. The salient point here is that the genealogy begins with capitalism's production of millions of superfluous people, deprived of a worldly space of significant speech and action. The production of living corpses was the last step. This genealogy actually begins at the very outset of *Origins* where Arendt points to Nazism's attempt to replace worldly reality with a "lying world order," particularly effective in a world where thousands of superfluous people, deprived of worldly reality, were ready to believe that everything is possible and nothing is true.

My point here is that Arendt's genealogy of superfluousness argues against Cavarero's claim that the remedy for horrifying violence is a politics whose foundation is an ontology of human vulnerability. Certainly, neoliberal capitalism (which Arendt suggests is the latest form of nineteenth century imperialism) has rendered lives precarious and vulnerable; however, according to Arendt, capitalism's violence is grounded in a certain conception of unlimited power rooted in unlimited appropriation and accumulation. While Cavarero is correct in pointing out that Arendt faults philosophy for aiding in this violence and certainly Hobbes is, for her, the key figure, nevertheless Arendt's reading of Hobbes leads her to a different political remedy than proposed by Cavarero. To grasp Arendt's political remedy, we must turn not to her brief reference to Hobbes in her letter to Jaspers, but instead to her longer discussion of him in *Origins*.

Hobbes, Arendt argues, is capitalism's philosopher insofar as his conception of power for the sake of power gives capitalism "the expansion of political power without the foundation of a body politic."[56] This is the opening insight of the second part of *Origins*, "Imperialism," an insight from which Arendt never departs in the long analysis that follows, an analysis that ends with the decline of the nation-state and the death of human rights. For Arendt, the decoupling of power from a political space underwrote imperialist politics, a politics whose aim was to destroy the foundation of the political in the name of unlimited power: "The new feature of the imperialist political philosophy is not the prominent place it gave violence nor the discovery that power is one of the basic political realities. . . . But neither had ever before been the conscious aim of the body politic or the ultimate goal of any definite policy. For power left to itself can achieve nothing but more power, and violence administered for power's (and not the law's) sake turns into a destructive principle that will not stop until there is nothing left to violate."[57] Arendt argues that this conception of unlimited power, which eventually brought to the near destruction of any body politic, led to the death camps whose destructive principle was intent on not stopping until "there was nothing left to violate."

Contrary to Cavarero's claim, Arendt does not view Hobbes' ontology as rooted in a conception of the human being as omnipotent and powerful (those characteristics belong only to the sovereign); instead, she argues that Hobbes' individual is solitary and private, "whose membership in any form of community is . . . a temporary and limited affair which essentially does not change the solitary and private character of the individual."[58] Lacking any meaningful participation in public affairs, "the individual loses his rightful place in society and his natural connection with his fellow-men."[59] Arendt suggests that Hobbes philosophically describes the superfluous individuals produced by modern capitalism: solitary and lonely, lacking a public space and the company of others, a "by-product of capitalist production . . . who had become permanently idle [and] were as superfluous to the community as the owners of superfluous wealth."[60] This superfluousness has its ontological condition in a conception of the individual not only as solitary and private, but also as powerless: the individual gains power *only* through the sovereign state. As Arendt points out, however, this power is nothing other than obedience to a sovereign who promises protection in exchange. While the individual gains political subjectivity through the contract, the political subject remains alone. Hence, the Frontispiece of *Leviathan*, in which a multitude of bodies, all singular, are incorporated into the body of the sovereign who now bears their person and acts on their behalf. In the Hobbesian sovereign state, whose aim is unlimited power, the *political* subject as an active participant in public affairs is rendered superfluous.

Arendt's genealogy of superfluousness is the background for her turn to the ontological event of natality and the promise of beginning. As we have seen, the promise of beginning is a promise rooted in the ontological conditions of plurality, power, and action. While Arendt does not deny the human condition of vulnerability in need of protection, she emphasizes the human capacity for power and action that saves the world from ruination. To put it differently, the world can be saved from the horror of superfluous violence (in all its senses) only through a conception of the political in which the ontological desire for worldly appearance can be met. Here

Arendt is answering Hobbes' conception of the human being whose desire for power is actually a desire for security. On the contrary, she argues that the ontological desire of the human being is for worldly appearance, without which one is literally dead to the world: "To be deprived of it [that is, the space of appearance] means to be deprived of reality, which, humanly and politically speaking, is the same as appearance. . . . To men the reality of the world is guaranteed by the presence of others, by its appearing to all . . . and whatever lacks this appearance comes and passes away like a dream, intimately and exclusively our own but without reality."[61] To be superfluous is to be deprived of a space of appearance and therefore deprived of worldly reality. It is for Arendt an unbearable condition because it violates the human condition.

Conclusion

By way of conclusion, I turn to Cavarero's image of the relation of ontology and politics as a relation of distant hilltops in conversation with each other. I suggest that Cavarero and Arendt also stand on different hilltops, not so distant, but in need of conversation with each other. As I have tried to show, Cavarero adds an important correction to Arendt's understanding of the ontological event of natality by emphasizing the vulnerability and exposure of this event and the political responsibility that emerges from it. Moreover, Cavarero's vocal ontology with its emphasis on an originary natal uniqueness offers an important supplement to Arendt's emphasis on plurality from which uniqueness appears. Her account of the narratable self and its longing for its life-story adds an important aspect to Arendt's account of narration that emphasizes a desire for the story's immortality, but neglects the desire for a story in life.

At the same time, Arendt's genealogy of superfluousness adds an important correction to Cavarero's account of horrifying violence and her political remedy for it. Notably, Cavarero's account of the ontological event of natality with its emphasis on vulnerability is emptied of any natal capacity for power; further, power is completely absent from her discussion of our shared political responsibility for this vulnerability. Arendt's genealogy of superfluousness provides a cautionary tale to a politics that does not take into account the ontological desire for power and action, understood by Arendt as the desire for significant speech and action with a plurality of others. The lesson of Arendt's genealogy is that the ontological desire for appearing and acting with others has a tremendous capacity for violence if it is rendered politically superfluous. Without an account of our shared responsibility to ensure the conditions for political appearance and action, only emphasizing our bodily vulnerability and exposure may unwittingly contribute to this horror. As a corrective, Arendt turns to the event of natality and the promise of beginning, a promise that points to the ontological capacity for action. Thus, the political demand is double: protecting vulnerability and providing the political conditions for the possibility of significant speech and action. When lacking a political space of action, vulnerable and exposed beings are very capable of becoming Hobbesian subjects, embracing a sovereign power that will guarantee their protection in exchange for their absolute obedience. This sovereign embrace often includes a (usually racist) ideology whereby vulnerable beings will be complicit in all forms of horrifying violence that substitutes for a space of action. As Cavarero indicates in her reading of Achilles, sacrificial violence also gives vulnerable beings a voice and their life-stories meaning. Arendt's genealogy of superfluousness demonstrates the urgency of bringing together Cavarero's emphasis on the uniqueness of voice and embodied vulnerability with Arendt's emphasis on plurality and action. The superfluousness that begins with the loss of the world and ends in the death camps is addressed only by thinking a relational in-between that is at once a space of bodily vulnerability and a space of power that saves the world and those in it from ruination.

Notes

1. Elisabetta Bertolino, "Beyond Ontology and Sexual Difference: An Interview with Italian Feminist Philosopher Adriana Cavarero" *Differences* 19, 1 (2008): 198.
2. Adriana Cavarero, *Inclinations: A Critique of Rectitude*, trans. Amanda Minervini and Adam Sitze (Stanford, CA: Stanford University Press, 2016), 13.
3. Cavarero, *Inclinations*, 107.
4. Cavarero, *Inclinations*, 108.
5. Cavarero, *Inclinations*, 119.
6. Cavarero, *Inclinations*, 122.
7. Cavarero, *Inclinations*, 120.
8. Cavarero, *Inclinations*, 122.
9. Cavarero, *Inclinations*, 117.
10. Cavarero, *Inclinations*, 117; emphasis mine.
11. Cavarero, *Inclinations*, 118.
12. Adriana Cavarero, *Relating Narratives: Storytelling and Selfhood*, trans. with an introduction by Paul A. Kottman (London: Routledge, 2000), 123.
13. Adriana Cavarero, *For More Than One Voice: Toward a Philosophy of Vocal Expression*, trans. and with an introduction by Paul A. Kottman (Stanford, CA: Stanford University Press, 2005), 177.

14. Cavarero, *For More Than One Voice*, 193.
15. Cavarero, *For More Than One Voice*, 190.
16. Cavarero, *Relating Narratives*, 30.
17. Cavarero, *Relating Narratives*, 44.
18. Cavarero, *Relating Narratives*, 63.
19. Cavarero, *Relating Narratives*, 86.
20. Cavarero, *Relating Narratives*, 39.
21. Cavarero, *Relating Narratives*, 33.
22. Hannah Arendt, *The Human Condition* (Chicago: University of Chicago Press, 1958), 247.
23. Arendt, *The Human Condition*, 242.
24. Peg Birmingham, *Hannah Arendt and the Right to Have Rights: The Predicament of Common Responsibility* (Bloomington: Indiana University Press, 2006).
25. Fanny Söderbäck, for example, misses this aspect of Arendt's account of natality in her article, "Natality or Birth? Arendt and Cavarero on the Human Condition of Being Born," *Hypatia* 33, 2 (2018): 273–288. Söderbäck criticizes Arendt for forgetting the actual birth involved in the event of natality, arguing that Cavarero's contribution is precisely to insist on the primacy of the mother in this event. In my view, this reading reduces natality to the actual birth of the child and thereby replaces the radical rupture of Arendt's event of natality with birth as lineage and nativity.
26. Arendt, *The Human Condition*, 176.
27. Arendt, *The Human Condition*, 9.
28. Arendt, *The Human Condition*, 17.
29. Arendt, *The Human Condition*, 18.
30. In Judith Butler, *Notes toward a Performative Theory of Assembly* (Cambridge. MA: Harvard University Press, 2015), Butler argues that Arendt's account of appearance in the public space lacks an account of materiality and embodiment. In my view, Butler can claim this only by ignoring Arendt's insistence that all appearance in the public space is embodied and rooted in material conditions.
31. Butler, *Notes toward a Performative Theory of Assembly*, 182–188.
32. Butler, *Notes toward a Performative Theory of Assembly*, 50.
33. Butler, *Notes toward a Performative Theory of Assembly*, 50.
34. Hannah Arendt, *Life of the Mind: Thinking* (New York and London: Harcourt Brace Jovanovich, 1971), 20.
35. Arendt, *Life of the Mind: Thinking*, 19.
36. Arendt, *Life of the Mind: Thinking*, 19.
37. Arendt, *Life of the Mind: Thinking*, 13.
38. See Adolph Portman, *Animal Forms and Patterns*, trans. Hella Czech (New York: Faber, 1967), especially 19–34. See also Adolph Portman, *Animals as Social Beings* (New York: Viking Press, 1961). Both texts are cited by Arendt in *Life of the Mind: Thinking*.
39. Kimberley F. Curtis, "Aesthetic Foundations of Democratic Politics in the Work of Hannah Arendt," in *Hannah Arendt and the Meaning of Politics*, ed.

Craig Calhoun and John McGowan (Minneapolis: University of Minnesota Press, 1997), 39.

40. Curtis, "Aesthetic Foundations of Democratic Politics in the Work of Hannah Arendt," 44.

41. For a fuller discussion of this point, see Peg Birmingham, "Rethinking the *Sensus Communis*: Hannah Arendt's Phenomenology of Political Affects," in *Phenomenology and the Political*, ed. West Gurley and Geoff Pfeifer (New York: Rowman and Littlefield, 2016), 3–18.

42. Hans Jonas, *The Imperative of Responsibility: In Search of an Ethics for the Technological Age*, trans. Hans Jonas and David Herr (Chicago: University of Chicago Press, 1984).

43. Arendt, *The Human Condition*, 62. She repeats the "non-privative traits of privacy" on page 70.

44. Hannah Arendt, "The Crisis in Education," in *Between Past and Future* (New York: Penguin, 2006), 173.

45. Arendt, "The Crisis in Education," 189.

46. Arendt, *The Human Condition*, 101.

47. Adriana Cavarero, *Horrorism: Naming Contemporary Violence*, trans. William McCuaig (New York: Columbia University Press, 2009), 45.

48. Cavarero, *Horrorism*, 43. Cavarero is citing Hannah Arendt, *Origins of Totalitarianism* (New York: Harcourt, Brace, Jovanovich, 1951), 457.

49. Cavarero, *Horrorism*, 8.

50. Cavarero, *Horrorism*, 31.

51. Cavarero, *Horrorism*, 20.

52. Cavarero, *Horrorism*, 21.

53. Cavarero, *Horrorism*, 45.

54. Cavarero, *Horrorism*, 44.

55. Cavarero, *Horrorism*, 46.

56. Arendt, *Origins of Totalitarianism*, 135.

57. Arendt, *Origins of Totalitarianism*, 137.

58. Arendt, *Origins of Totalitarianism*, 141.

59. Arendt, *Origins of Totalitarianism*, 141.

60. Arendt, *Origins of Totalitarianism*, 150.

61. Arendt, *The Human Condition*, 199.

Part Six

Topology, New Realism, Biopolitics

16

Topology at Play

Vincenzo Vitiello and the Word of Philosophy

Giulio Goria

Preface

One could easily describe one of the unswerving and defining tasks of philosophy in a few poignant words, namely: to deny all (even philosophy's own) presuppositions and thus never relinquish the need to question while positing everything from out of itself. This undertaking can be easily seen in any of Plato's dialogues and it appears even more explicitly in Aristotle's *Metaphysics* or in Hegel's *Science of Logic*. It is not the case of a linear claim as it may seem at first, though. More specifically, it is not the case of the uncontested assertion of philosophy's control over the things of the world. The question that immediately follows the initial assertion we just mentioned is in fact: When can philosophy speak of itself by saying "I," that is, by eliminating the possibility of doubting its own doubt? Vincenzo Vitiello's topology unfolds as the constant attempt at following up on such a question.

Topology, Religion, Art

In 2012, the Vincenzo Montano Award was bestowed by the jury to Vitiello's volume, *Una filosofia errante* (*An Errant Philosophy*), as an ultimate recognition of the thinker's contributions to philosophy. This volume collects some of Vitiello's reflections from his various works and organizes them according to a progression that deserves attention. The progression moves from topology to religion to art. The sequence describes a sort of movement of absolute spirit, albeit in reverse order, as Carlo Sini has remarked in his introduction to the volume.

The three stages—topology, religion, art—reveal the prevailing concerns of Vitiello's work. They represent something more, though, than three disciplines pursued because of some accident or idiosyncratic interest; rather, one finds here three strata within which Vitiello's thought unfolds toward a unified goal. Before we try to understand what such a goal is, and before we focus on the ways it has presented itself within a path that begins in 1976 (when Vitiello's original monograph on Heidegger was published), it is important to note that the way in which the contents are organized in the abovementioned arrangement does not entail an ascending progression. In other terms, between topology, religion, and art there is neither internal progress nor development. Using an image often employed by Vitiello, we move amid such spheres as if in a castle, entering and exiting the numerous rooms freely, with no preordained order.

Art: Praise of Space

Let us begin with art, with what according to Vitiello is the fundamental question arising between the end of the nineteenth and the beginning of the twentieth centuries, that is, the question of the relation between saying and seeing, language and feeling or sensing (*sentire*). Vitiello's starting point goes against the tendency of much aesthetic thought that, in the twentieth century, finds in philosophy, and especially in Heidegger's philosophy, a fundamental entry point to access artistic experiences. Vitiello's choice of this position pivots indeed on the great interpretations of Rilke and Hölderlin offered by Heidegger. These interpretations are grandiose and fundamental, but they are such only in terms of understanding Heidegger's own thought. All such epochal confrontations, including Heidegger's own thinking "philology," rest on the prominence of the signified. They are carried out on a ground that, on the contrary, Vitiello intends to subvert and suspend. Vitiello's attention to pictorial art and poetical experiences from Andrea Zanzotto to Paul Celan finds its justification in the quest for a language (*lingua*) capable of bringing to words (*linguaggio*) that which is prior to language. In Heidegger, Vitiello finds instead a form of closure with respect to the endeavor to "come close to pure sensation: to retinal color; to the gesture that is not yet figure; to the inarticulate voice that is not sign; to the isolated sound (not yet a 'note') that falls amidst a silence that does not accompany but rather isolates, does not welcome but rather pushes away; and to *kataphýsica* [elemental] matter that cannot even be defined as chaotic or formless because this would already entail having a relation to form."[1]

There is a second element that we should note because, ultimately, it simply constitutes the premise from which we arrive at the claim we made. There is a prevalent trait that characterizes the performance of thinking and the activity of reflection. This feature belongs not only to philosophy (and certainly not only to a specific philosophical "signature"), but also to art, poetry, and writing. Its profile is given to us through the term "reduction," understood as the *epoché* of the natural attitude, of the basic belief in the world as the safe harbor that is simply present in front of our eyes and waits to be known. In short, the task of thought is to induce *askesis* and liberate us from all presuppositions, without exclusions. Twentieth-century philosophy (phenomenology but also, and to no smaller degree, Heidegger's hermeneutics) has certainly been animated by this kind of intention; nevertheless, neither of the abovementioned movements has ever advanced beyond the realms of history, culture, and tradition.[2] In its work of deconstruction, philosophy has not reached what, with reference to Vico, Vitiello calls "iconology of the mind." This expression denotes the ways in which thought orients itself in the world after having already ordained it. It is a matter of that weaving (*tessitura*) that we could generally call "forms of thought" but would be more appropriately described, in Kantian terms, as the intertwining of sensibility and the categories, transcendental aesthetics and transcendental analytics.

According to Vitiello, philosophy (Nietzsche being possibly the only exception) has been too hesitant when challenging the entire assemblage of sensible and reflective categories. Not even Husserl has been successful by the end of his proposed genealogy in *Experience and Judgment*, the work that most takes on itself the task of such an arduous project of challenge. If one considers, however, the method more than the outcomes, then one can appreciate the value of Husserl's endeavor. Briefly, Husserl attempts to reconstruct the world of meanings by expanding the method of reduction from the *cogito* to the precategorial world.[3] Accessing the process of object formation means descending into the lowest strata of experience, the last of which is the sensible realm, where the I is the most passive with respect to worldly stimuli and where it does not carry out any judging activity. In order to access this level of experience, the *epoché* of idealizations and scientific practices is not sufficient. What is also needed is a reduction of the categories of language. Only in this way, that is, only by reducing the field of reality over which the categories extend, can the ultimate goal of genealogy become clear, namely, "the unintentional root of intentionality."[4]

It is still to be demonstrated that this was in fact Husserl's goal, and such a demonstration is not even an essential point. Vitiello's historical gaze is not directed toward historiographic certainties, toward reconstructions that put together pieces of an author's profile or a text. A similar path is avoided not because of a personal idiosyncrasy against coherent and well-structured historiographic profiles. That is not the issue. Rather, we are confronted here with a theoretical consequence of Vitiello's method, namely, topology, which has been his most productive intuition. According to topology, there is history—and, particularly, history of thought—only where there are questions regarding the possibility of thought. There is history only where there is the possibility of an emergent alterity: an alterity that cannot be historicized, made logical, reduced to a meaning; an alterity that confuses the order of history, time, and logic. The task that almost "institutionally" befalls philosophy, that is, the task to distinguish between what is and what is not philosophy, is neither paradoxical nor abstract nor vain. Within this framework, the matter is not that of taking up empty disciplinary partitions; rather, the issue is that of delimiting the horizon of thought in relation to that which is *other* than thought. Thus, if we consider the intentionality of language and the attempts at explaining its origin and form, then we must direct our interrogation to its nonintentional roots. Were we not to do so, we would miss not so much the answer as the radicalness of the procedure, of the method.

This line of thinking entails the possibility that Kandinsky occupies the same topological space as Husserl, while nonetheless animating such space with greater radicalness. Acting within the field of sensibility and not of the logical forms of the philosopher, the painter radically challenges the forms of vision, the logical tools of the craft: shapes and colors, lines and surfaces; in its "historical" relations, space itself is not spared a decomposition that occurs through and in the senses.

Kandinsky's paintings represent for Vitiello the expression of the material power of colors and sounds, of bodily scents and gestures. Briefly, this tendency suspends the distinctions that belong to natural space and its humanized forms, thereby recording an original cobelonging of sounds and figures, colors and scents.

This is not the only direction followed by Kandinsky, as his theoretical writings attest, starting with the most famous of them, *Über das Geistige in der Kunst* (*Concerning the Spiritual in Art*).[5] In this text, what prevails is the inquiry into the elements of the formal structure of composition. Nor is this path followed only by the Russian painter, for it also belongs, albeit in different forms, to Paul Klee and especially to Lucio Fontana.

Vitiello is struck by the 1962 photographs that portray Fontana working at *Concetto spaziale, New York, 10* (*Spatial Concept, New York, 10*)—the man hits an iron piece with a hammer. More precisely, the artist enters into the matter and transforms it, that is, gives it a form that is its own. *Before*, that is, before it is touched, matter is neither iron nor stone nor canvas. It is purely Matter before matter, *prote hyle* (undifferentiated, raw matter), space. The gashes, cuts, and holes on the work that are typical of Fontana are simply references to, localizations of, such an origin. They are certainly physical, rough, pierced, and stony as the matter of the work is as well. Yet they are references (made of a sensibility that has already been made logical and localized) to the element within which we live and perceive the world, both human and nonhuman. The marks and slashes are spaces; yet none of them is Matter any longer, "not even those that allude to astral swirls, to the first formation of space and matter, to the first appearance of light, in the umpteenth instant following the Big Bang; yet they are all spaces because they all make reference to Matter-before-matter, to Space-before-space."[6]

More than with Kandinsky, it is with these "baroque holes [*buchi barocchi*]," as Fontana called them, that Vitiello's topology finds affinities. Here, in this context, one can simply think of the title of Vitiello's important 1994 volume, *Elogio dello spazio* (*Praise of Space*), the subtitle of which is *Ermeneutica e topologia* (*Hermeneutics and Topology*).

Truth: The Critique of Knowledge

In a recent essay, Italian scholar Massimo Adinolfi uses a helpful image to define the central idea, that is, topology, which inspires Vitiello's entire philosophical itinerary. Adinolfi writes, "topology itself could be presented as a divining machine to detect the 'X' that lies underneath Western thought. . . . What else is in fact Vitiello's *Elogio dello spazio* than the idea that space does not resolve itself in time, and that there is no *Aufhebung* of space into time? And what is space, if not the opposite of domestic space, of inhabited place, of a field of experience that has already been practiced?"[7]

Of what space are we speaking? To understand the terms of Vitiello's topology, will it suffice to make reference to what comes to mind most quickly, that is, Kant's pure forms of intuition, which describe the relations of exteriority and succession of phenomena? It is true that Vitiello is a profound (and not very orthodox) reader of Kant, and especially of the *Critique of Pure Reason*. It is also true that, starting with his 1984 volume *Ethos e eros in Hegel e Kant* (*Ethos and Eros in Hegel and Kant*), Vitiello's interpretation of Kantian criticism assumes as its main task the messing up of Hegel's reading of Kant—a reading that, in many ways, has more or less consciously sedimented into a widespread "subjectivistic" understanding of Kant's texts.

All this cannot be doubted. Yet, it is not enough to portray the framework within which the topological praise of space moves. What is at stake in it is not only physical space, or at least not the space that a specific methodological and scientific approach makes objective and considers as the object of its fundamental claims. Rather, what is at stake is a conception of space that belongs to time, with no possibility whatsoever of space being reduced to time. In sum, the matter is that of an atemporal place that is the result of reflection. Vitiello writes, "The spatial dimension of time (the immutable horizon of the totality of time, which remains and does not change, *bleibt und wechselt nicht*) imposes itself in all ways. It is one thing to experience it in a reflective and thematic form, and another to experience it in an immediate and non-thematic one."[8]

Even if we remain within Kant's framework, time—that time that seems to have priority over space—does not exhaust itself entirely in the various finite times that, like all other phenomena, we can describe in terms of birth and death, appearing and fading away. Kant adds that the time that is the condition of all times, of limited and finite times, of historical periods and epochs, such a horizon-time (*tempo-orizzonte*), which endures and does not change, cannot be perceived, grasped, or represented in itself.[9] In truth, we did not even need Kant to make this claim. If we wish to find a time-concept that constitutes the transcendental layer of experience or, in other words, if we want to presuppose an ontological truth, understood as the unavoidable condition of all ontic truth, then it will be enough to consider the history of philosophy from its beginning. It is enough to look, for example, at Plato's *Timaeus*, precisely at the point where it acknowledges that temporal scansions, the "is, was, and will be," can be in a succession only on condition that there is stable time; that is, on condition that time is not only a pure flowing and passing, but also an articulation of present, past, and future within an *order* of time. Hence, the need for an aionic time, which neither arises nor disappears, a present and eternal order that Kant then transposes onto the intertwining of modern sciences and philosophy and that he translates into the modern language of the *mathesis universalis* originally elaborated by Galileo and Descartes.

In short, the change in pace that Kant marks resides neither in the formal structure of the temporal plexus nor in the general centrality that time takes up as cornerstone for the question of truth. Rather, that which, starting with Kant, structures modern and contemporary metaphysics is the ontological status of the order/horizon of time, which concurrently turns judgment and its categories into time's eminent place of manifestation. In transcendental judgment, what is at stake is the judgment's ability to correspond to the need to assign a ground to the relation between concept and object, and between the condition and the conditioned. In other words, given that in this kind of relation one can guarantee nothing—neither sense nor relevance—except by revealing the conditions to which the foundation itself is subjected, then what is here put at stake is the status of possibility of the relation as such. This step back to the conditions that underlie both judgment and the order of time is the outcome of the retreat of reflection, which precisely in Kant is already at work delineating a definition of the *noumenon* as a boundary-concept (*Grenzbegriff*) of sensibility.[10]

Heidegger will devise a comparable operation later with respect to *logos apophantikos* understood as assertion and the way of true-being and false-being. The goal, here, will consist in reaching the prepredicative foundations, thereby disclosing a prior, prelogical appearing.[11] This path, however, is ultimately opened up by the transcendental deduction of the categories as it is expounded in Kant's *Critique of Pure Reason*. In the *Critique*, the question is posed, of course, in terms of conditions of possibility, even when it concerns both the objects and the intellect. To draw attention to the necessary coimplication of the two sides of the deductive project means to open up one of Vitiello's central themes of reflection.

A fundamental feature of the question of truth emerges from this Kantian legacy with respect to the way of posing the question: a question that later is appropriated by hermeneutics, mainly Heidegger's, but not only. That is to say, if one wishes to revitalize the way in which one searches for the ground of truth, one cannot simply attribute to it a different profile, one that, for example, does not repropose the solipsistic solitude of the "transcendental consciousness" or the abstract *Ich denke* (I-think), but rather is intimately tied to the world and its corporeity. All this is not sufficient because a different profile would not, by itself, modify the way in which the ground, albeit under the profile of the *In-der-Welt-Sein*, of being-in-the-world, would carry out its foundational function.[12]

Casting clear light on this element is one of the merits of Vitiello's thinking, a thinking that can hardly be underestimated. Vitiello draws necessary consequences from the aforementioned element. If the question of truth hangs on the *sense* (*senso*) that the ground assumes, then one can only return to it, to its ontologically *possible* character, and have reflection work on it, on possibility, and on the ground as possibility.

Topology: Possibility Higher Than Reality

From *Dasein* to *Ereignis*: Vitiello's path could be briefly summed up in such an expression. *Ereignis* is the guiding word of Heidegger's thinking since the 1930s, a word that is only used in the singular. Before indicating an "event" or a "happening," this word expresses the *place* of the event, the site of all hermeneutic localization (*Er-örterung*).

The sense of such a word is conveyed by a phrase in *Being and Time*, a statement that, for Vitiello, constitutes the fundamental claim of this entire work and of Heidegger's philosophical path, yet a statement that is also a research program still in need of development. The phrase reads: "*Höher als die Wirklichkeit steht die Möglichkeit*, possibility is higher than reality."[13] This sentence overturns the claim of Aristotle's metaphysics, which maintains the primacy of act over potency (*potenza*) or, better stated, the transformation of indeterminate potency into possibility. It is not a matter of denying sensations and their reality or, rather, of denying movement and abandoning oneself to the weakness of that way of thinking that, when confronted with aporias, simply gives up one side of the issue for the other. Aporias must be faced; doing so amounts to determining the indeterminate without eliminating its indeterminacy. Above all, one must acknowledge the ambiguous nature of movement and the fact that it can be placed neither on the side of the potency of beings nor on the side of actuality. From this comes the imperfect nature of this actuality, as Aristotle says in his *Physics*.[14] However, as is well known, Aristotle's solution implies delimiting potency's domain of possibility. All in all, this operation is simple as far as natural potencies are concerned: heat *cannot not* heat because this is its determined destination.

The move is more difficult when it comes to rational potencies, which entail opposites. Yet the two opposites are not on equal footing. The positive has, in fact, the prerogative of expressing the activity belonging to the thing, whereas the negative has an accidental nature. This is the case for medical healing, for example, which only by accident, error, or meanness of the doctor may provoke damage rather than recovery. In sum, even potencies of opposites are possibilities that are determined in themselves; they are determined either to act or to suffer; yet in either case, each potency cannot do or undergo anything whatsoever. Each potency has a domain within which it necessarily unfolds. One thing is the potency of the plant and another is the potency of the human being. What changes is the domain of action, that is, the delimitation of what something properly is, its essence. What ensues is that each potency is determined insofar as it is preceded by actuality.

This is, briefly, what Aristotle says. Heidegger is undoubtedly a profound interpreter of this topic. One could just think of his course on *Metaphysics Theta, 1–3*, which is significantly devoted to "*vom Wesen und Wirklichkeit der Kraft* (the essence and actuality of power)."[15] Heidegger is also convinced, though, that most of the history of metaphysics, especially modern metaphysics, has increasingly wasted the fecundity and authenticity of Greek insight. On this topic, Vitiello is certainly less inclined than Heidegger to build linear canons, whether they are progressive or degenerative. On one point, though, he remains in substantial agreement with Heidegger, namely, the history of metaphysics is not a simple dialogue between present and past philosophers, the ones ready to receive the ball from the others. Deeply rooted under the surface of the various works, their dates, and their different styles, one finds the *topoi*, the places or sites where philosophy's reasons and words keep getting stuck, ever since the beginning and anew. Identity and difference, being and nothing, permanence and becoming: these pairs of opposites constitute the moving plate on which the external surface of the history of thought takes shape.

Therefore, in Vitiello's eyes, the primacy of act over potency is not simply a legacy loaded with its transmission. Rather, it is one of the leading lines of philosophy, at least of that kind of philosophy that has meant to receive Aristotle's metaphysical intent in its entirety and has intended to ground the autonomy of reason on the power of logic and meaning, in the most coherent and robust way possible. A name will suffice here: Hegel, who is the greatest modern Aristotelian because he meant to give full *worldly* manifestation to the Absolute and primarily to its decisive configuration as disclosed through Christianity. For Vitiello, Hegel's work has been a constant topic of confrontation. It has been a constant struggle whose clear goal has been, at least since *Ethos ed eros in Hegel e Kant*, to challenge its central structure, namely, the relation with reason and the world. For Hegel, truth, that is, the logical and historical experience with what we today are used to call truth, has definitely constituted the horizon of our way of being-in-the-world, of human beings' way of being.

In *Ethos ed eros*, Vitiello writes:

> At the bottom of Kant's entire thought there is always the Noumenon, the limit-concept, the last result of the critique of ontology: the void of our not-knowing. Hegel has rejected it as the "entirely abstract," as the "negation of determinate thought." Of course, it is a product of thought, but of a kind of thought that is still capable of preserving the being-other of the other. The most difficult task, for thinking, consists in leaving itself

aside, abstracting itself from itself so as not to reduce the Other to the Same, Difference to Identity. Transcendental philosophy has succeeded where dialectics cannot succeed; it has succeeded in letting possibility be as possibility outside the horizon of reality, which is always a human horizon. It has succeeded in thinking the limit of the human.[16]

This positions Kant *beyond* Hegel, if this may mean something significant for the experience of the possible. Here, the lineage we indicated earlier from transcendental philosophy to Heidegger's hermeneutics becomes clearer. What is in common between the Kantian delimitation of the limits of human knowing and Heidegger's deconstruction of the existential analytics (*Daseinsanalyse*) is the attitude toward the historical world and the domain of being. Human beings' belonging to it, that is, to the principle of non-contradiction that governs all logics and practices, is to be suspended. It has to be suspended in order to give word and meaning to pure possibility, to which human beings belong as to their most proper core.

The affinity with Heidegger is evident, yet it should not be taken for granted. Ever since 1976, Vitiello recognizes that *Being and Time* advances Heidegger's fundamental anti-Aristotelian operation. Two fundamental existential layers comprise *Dasein*'s being: on the one hand, the layer that ultimately corresponds to a possibilizing, enabling possibility which, from the start, is invested in the project and oriented toward the world; on the other hand, one finds a being-possible that is certainly interwoven with the first possibility, yet cannot be reduced to it. This being-possible is the possibility on whose ground all *Dasein*'s being-possible is possible and yet is also beyond such a possibilizing nature.[17]

In *La voce riflessa* (*The Reflected Voice*), Vitiello writes that "in and because of its indeterminacy, the purely possible, properly speaking, is not being: it is not a being, nor is it a place: It is no-being and no-place."[18]

Possibility must earn its primacy over reality: this is *Being and Time*'s fundamental commitment. Possibility remains higher than reality, possibility cannot simply move toward reality; it must be rid of reality. Hence comes the antidejection countermovement that, in the existential analytic, leads from the world with its everyday meanings to the meaninglessness of the world. Now, the move is vertical (from being-in-the-world to its being-possible) and does not at all imply exiting the world in the sense of relinquishing worldly practices. In the anxiety into which one falls, one also experiences that the move from the center of life to meaning, from animal instinct to shouting (which is even prior to speaking), from Earth to World, is a *possible* move, and not one to be taken for granted.

Like for Heidegger, for Vitiello as well, the move to anxiety, to the existential *epoché*, and to the pure possible does not amount to conceding to humanism. Nor does it allow us to throw out the instruments of logic and reflection. This is not the case because it is thanks to reflection that the possible is made to circulate within itself, thus becoming the possibility of the possible as such and, at the same time, the possibility of its impossibility.

Vitiello's attention is oriented to preserving the indeterminacy of such a possibility; this happens in a direction contrary to Aristotle, who had instead asserted the determinate character of potency so as to give it the ontological status of substance. For this reason, metaphysics can become epistemic *first* knowledge whose certification rests on the impossibility that its adversaries/deniers could share the same field of discourse, the one that they wish to subvert; this is what plastically happens in the counterargument that Aristotle's *Metaphysics*, book 4, offers in response to the position that denies the principle of noncontradiction. For that reason, it is not surprising that one of the most relevant advocates for Vitiello's position has been and continues to be Emanuele Severino, who certainly represents the most coherent and radical expression of the Aristotelian "logic of necessity" or, as Vitiello says, the major example of the logic of inherence.[19] The core of this philosophical dialogue is the ontological status of Being and possibility as the main categories that ground a consistent capacity for logical expression and its limits.

In his main work, *La struttura originaria* (*The Originary Structure*), in order to solve the question of the aporia of nothingness, Severino distinguishes the uncontradictory or positive act of meaning (nothingness is nothingness) from the self-contradictory or negative meaning of nothingness, which denies itself in its very mode of self-presentation (nothingness is not). Vitiello criticizes the possibility of this distinction: the power of the principle of noncontradiction, on which Severino's entire philosophy is founded, prevents formulating judgments in which terms are negative, such as: "X is not or does not have Being." Actually, the judgment "nothingness is nothingness" is simply a terminological variation of the judgment "being is being." It is not a judgment, according to Vitiello. It does not mean, because it does not indicate meaning. Nevertheless, it is not removed. The un-meaningfulness proves the limits of thought and of language. It proves the limits of the opposition "being-nothing" and the unavoidability of contradiction.

It is not by lucky accident that, precisely by freeing potency of its intransitivity, topology encounters contradiction. In this sense, according to Vitiello, philosophy has the task of retracing its steps, of re-thinking *dynamis* not as power but as possibility: as *tò aóriston*, the indefinite—from which Aristotle has in fact set off.

As long as we limit ourselves to saying that the possible contains the possibility of being and nonbeing, we bind the possible to the necessity of being possible and nothing else but the possible; that is, we interpret the possible according to necessity: the possible is "necessarily" possible. *The possible cannot be necessarily possible, though; it must be possibly possible.*[20]

Witnessing: The Impotence of Discourse

The title of a chapter in Vitiello's *Topologia del moderno* (*Topology of the Modern*), the volume that inaugurates the topological disposition of philosophy, is "Speaking the contradiction [*Dire la contraddizione*]."[21] If it is true that, starting with this book, the main obsession of topology becomes the modal category of the possible, it is true as well that Vitiello's topology never surrenders the first task of philosophy, namely, *to speak* potency, ultimately the *potency* that belongs to philosophical discourse. This is the precise task that philosophy has given itself since its origins; among them, Vitiello almost certainly situates Plato's *Parmenides*. Also with respect to this aspect, Vitiello absorbs the legacy of Heidegger's thought and enters a dialogue with Gadamer's hermeneutics and Derrida's deconstruction (the occurrences of such interlocutions have been many, in Naples and elsewhere).[22] Yet he also distances himself from these major thinkers.

I would like to address this aspect of autonomy under a rubric coined by Vitiello himself, namely, *from the critique of knowledge to ethics*. Vitiello is too fine a scholar of the history of philosophy not to recognize the ties that link the abovementioned title with Kant and the itinerary leading him from the *Critique of Pure Reason* to moral philosophy. The connection does not mainly rest, however, on a specific unfolding, on Vitiello's side, of Kant's transcendental dialectics or of his categorical imperative. The reason for the reference to Kant lies in the conviction that Vitiello and Kant share regarding the attitude adopted by philosophy toward the world: an attitude, an ethos marked by an originary separation, by philosophy's inability to find satisfaction in the world.

This is, for Kant, the root of freedom; that is, we feel duty, we perceive it as a necessity, and yet the necessity remains impossible to actualize fully. Freedom is a feeling of weakness, of lack, not of strength and power. I would like to translate all this into Vitiello's own words, taken once again from the work with which we began, *L'immagine infranta* (*Broken Image*). Vitiello asks: "Why should philosophy be limited to 'meaning'? On the contrary, shouldn't the most important question of philosophy rather be *Unsinn*, nonsense? Consequently, shouldn't the philosopher be principally concerned with finding/inventing [*invenire*] a possible way of saying *Unsinn*, of sign-ifying it, of sign-aling to it?"[23] Vitiello does not withdraw when faced with this perspective: this is a sign that the question proposed above is not simply a fashionable cliché. On the contrary, bringing the content of thought (*the said*) to its manifestation in words (*the saying*) is a primary need of the philosophical gesture.

We find here, on the one hand, the itineraries that Vitiello follows concerning the most relevant musical, artistic, and poetic experiences of the twentieth century. At the beginning of this chapter, we have briefly spoken of some of these explorations into a "material," "animal," and "sensible" space that is prior to the space delimited by categories, thought, and the relation between subject and object. On the other hand, we find the other side of this itinerary, that is, a position that does not cut any slack to philosophy and its ability to acknowledge the inadequacy of propositional logic and its fundamental element, namely, judgment. The logic and grammar of predicative judgment are incapable of expressing the relation between human beings and the world and things. This logic belongs to philosophy and the sciences, to common knowledge and reality. It is a logic that is expressed through the third person, a logic that, in the copula "is," claims to give us back the objectivity of the world and, even beforehand, the ontological status that inheres in all things. By functioning in this way, this logic does not speak the possible, does not speak the relation between human beings and the world, of which we can say not that it is, but rather that it *is-possible*.

There are illustrious attempts to unhinge this kind of language. Such attempts have often been accompanied by the effort to use alternative expressive modalities. One example is sufficient to signal Vitiello's goal. It is the example of Nietzsche: not simply the author of some specific works, but rather the philosopher who bears witness to the tragic relevance of thought through his own existence.

According to Vitiello in the last part of his philosophical itinerary, witnessing becomes the main burden of philosophy. *Thought itinerary* (*itinerario di pensiero*) becomes the definition of "topology," which, as should be clear by now, means philosophy *tout court*. Its task is witnessing; it is not a matter of a merely subjective and autobiographic profile but rather, on the contrary, the fact that, in philosophy, words neither follow nor anticipate experiences. Simply, the two arise and fall together. Or better, they *may* arise and fall. Witnessing is not even dialogue, at least as long as dialogue is the last landing of the will to power, which, precisely on "meaning" and content, builds a shared belonging to the circle of those who are in dialogue and excludes those who do not use language. As Vitiello writes,

The philosophy of the freedom of freedom witnesses a way of inhabiting time in the present with no frenzy for the future, a way of inhabiting the world as a "thing" among "things" (things, not objects) while being not *alongside* [con] but rather *in proximity to* [accanto] others. Being as a finding oneself among: among human beings and things, trees, animals, stones. Witnessing on the part of a philosophy that, to the ability and merit of questioning, prefers the gift of being questioned by everything and everyone, by anything and any human being. To the merit of giving, it prefers the gratitude of receiving.[24]

Translated by Silvia Benso

Notes

1. Vincenzo Vitiello, *L'immagine infranta* (Milan: Bompiani, 2014), 122.

2. The issue of the relation between transcendental and ontological phenomenology is often described in terms similar to the following: Heidegger admires the realistic Husserl of the *Logical Investigations* but rejects Husserl's "transcendental turn" in *Ideen I*, especially the transcendental reduction, which discloses the activity of consciousness with its noematic correlates. In order to offer a different account, Vitiello argues that it is a mistake to see the transcendental reduction as motivated by epistemological consideration. In particular, he highlights that Heidegger reads the section titled "Considerations Fundamental to Phenomenology" in *Ideen I* as an exercise in ontology; see Martin Heidegger, *History of the Concept of Time: Prolegomena*, trans. Theodore Kiesel (Bloomington: Indiana University Press, 1985), sec. 12–13. On this, see Vincenzo Vitiello, "Alla radice dell'intenzionalità. Husserl e Heidegger," in *Heidegger a Marburgo (1923–1928)*, ed. E. Mazzarella (Genoa: Il Melangolo: 2006), 127–154. See also Steve Crowell, *Husserl, Heidegger and the Space of Meaning* (Chicago: Northwestern University Press, 2001), 182–202.

3. Edmund Husserl, *Erfahrung und Urteil. Untersuchungen zur Geneaologie der Logik* (Hamburg: Classen, 1948), 54.

4. Vitiello, *L'immagine infranta*, 114.

5. See Wassily Kandinsky, *Concerning the Spiritual in Art*, trans. M. T. H. Sadler (Mineola, NY: Dover, 1977).

6. Vitiello, *L'immagine infranta*, 139.

7. Massimo Adinolfi, "La grana sensibile delle parole," in *Trovarsi accanto. Per gli ottant'anni di Vincenzo Vitiello*, ed. M. Adinolfi and M. Donà (Rome: Inschibboleth, 2017), 21.

8. Vincenzo Vitiello, *Elogio dello spazio. Ermeneutica e topologia* (Milan: Bompiani, 1994), 45.

9. Immanuel Kant, *KrV*, A 182, B 225.

10. The passage from Kant's *Critique of Pure Reason* reads: "Der Begriff eines Noumenon ist also bloß ein Grenzebegriff, um die Anmaßung der Sinnlichkeit einzuschränken," *KrV*, A 255, B 311.

11. Martin Heidegger, *Sein und Zeit*, trans. J. Stambaugh (Albany: State University of New York Press, 2010), 62; and Martin Heidegger, *Logic: The Question of Truth*, trans. T. Sheehan (Bloomington: Indiana University Press, 2016), sec. 11–14.

12. On being-in-the world, see Heidegger, *Being and Time*, sec. 28–34, that is, the entire chapter titled "Being-In as Such"; on Heidegger's interpretation of Kant, see also David Carr, "Heidegger on Kant on Transcendence," in *Transcendental Heidegger*, ed. S. Crowell and J. Malpas (Stanford, CA: Stanford University Press, 2007), 28–42.

13. Heidegger, *Being and Time*, 33–34.

14. See Aristotle, *Physics*, bk. 3, 2.201b27–32.

15. Martin Heidegger, *Aristotle's Metaphysik Θ 1–3: On the Essence and Actuality of Force*, trans. W. Brogan and P. Warnek (Bloomington: Indiana University Press, 1995), sec. 9–10.

16. Vincenzo Vitiello, *Ethos ed eros in Hegel e Kant* (Naples: Edizioni Scientifiche Italiane, 1984), 78.

17. The core of Vitiello's interpretation of Heidegger's *Being and Time* is the relation between *Möglichsein* and *Sein-können* as central element for the authentic nihilistic concept of *Sorge* as "*Grundsein einer Nichtigkeit* [Being-the-Ground of a Nullity]," Heidegger, *Being and Time*, 261; see Vincenzo Vitiello, *Heidegger. Il nulla e la fondazione della storicità* (Urbino: Argaia 1976), 405–456.

18. Vincenzo Vitiello, *La voce riflessa. Logica ed etica della contraddizione* (Milan: Lanfranchi, 1994), 158.

19. In this sense, for the Aristotelian legacy in Severino, see Emanuele Severino, *La struttura originaria* (Milan: Adelphi, 1981), chap. 4; see also Emanuele Severino and Vincenzo Vitiello, *Dell'essere e del possibile* (Udine: Mimesis, 2018).

20. Vincenzo Vitiello, *L'ethos della topologia. Un itinerario di pensiero* (Florence: Le Lettere, 2013), 89.

21. Vincenzo Vitiello, *Topologia del moderno* (Genoa: Marietti, 1992), 225–241.

22. Proof of this intense and extended debate on various themes is the volume devoted to religion and edited by Gianni Vattimo and Jacques Derrida, initially in Italy and France, in which Vitiello wrote about Benjamin and Hegel as interpreters of Christianity and Judaism; see Jacques Derrida and Gianni Vattimo, eds., *Religion*, trans. D. Webb (Stanford, CA: Stanford University Press, 1998). In the 1990s, Vitiello had an extended philosophical dialogue in particular with Gianni Vattimo, Massimo Cacciari, and Carlo Sini. The annual philosophical review, *Filosofia*, edited by Gianni Vattimo for the publisher Laterza, was a great occasion for the articulation of this debate.

23. Vitiello, *L'immagine infranta*, 65.

24. Vitiello, *L'ethos della topologia*, 112.

17

On the Question of the Face of Reality
Addressing the "Myths" of the New Realism and Postmodernity

Rita Šerpytytė

The 1979 publication of *The Postmodern Condition*, a tiny book (in its original language, it is only 109 pages long) written by the French philosopher Jean-François Lyotard, marks the entry of postmodernity into philosophy. In this work, Lyotard announces the end of ideologies (such as the Enlightenment, German Idealism, Marxism, etc.), the end of so-called grand narratives. Critics have pointed out that postmodernism brought about a genuine crisis that was however overcome without much tragedy.

> The ease with which the pandemic spread depended not only on what is so obscurely called 'the spirit of the time' but precisely also on the fact that postmodernism was carrying along a cosmopolitical crowd of forefathers: the English historian Arnold Toynbee, who spoke about it in the forties; the German anthropologist Arnold Gehlen, who theorized "post-theory" in the fifties; the American novelist Kurt Vonnegut, who mixed black humour and science fiction in the sixties; the American architect Robert Venturi, who reinstated Las Vegas's Disney style at the beginning of the seventies. At the very beginning, in the thirties, there was even the Spanish literary critic Federico de Onis, who dubbed a poetic trend with that name.[1]

One could certainly doubt and disagree with such an account of the "beginnings" of postmodernity, especially given that Ferraris's description does not convey much about the essential, postmodern attitudes within philosophy. Today, when no one of the leading postmodern philosophers is still alive, except for Gianni Vattimo, one might ask whether these deaths could mark postmodernity's demise as a philosophy. Moreover, is there one book that could act as a "testimony" for postmodern thought, the same way that Lyotard's text functioned as its manifesto? Books of such a testamentary nature are, however, not written deliberately or purposely as such, that is, as explicit testimony to a theoretical legacy for a movement's "heirs"; rather, they take on such a testamentary role when other, new "manifestos" emerge.

The testamentary texts of postmodern thought (sometimes called a "trend," "movement," or "direction") become easily identifiable when considering works expressing an attitude that is critical of postmodernism. These critical attitudes also provoke the creation of testamentary texts. Cases in point are Maurizio Ferraris's (a student of Gianni Vattimo) *Manifesto of New Realism*[2] and Gianni Vattimo's testamentary work, *Of Reality*.[3]

In his *Manifesto*, Ferraris remarks that "postmodernism marks the entry of inverted commas in philosophy: reality becomes 'reality,' truth 'truth,' objectivity 'objectivity,' justice 'justice,' gender 'gender,' and so forth."[4] Scare-quoting, the so-called *virgolettazione* of the world (the term "*virgolettazione*" is coined by Ferraris), helps symbolize and communicate the thesis that the "grand narratives" of modernity are the sources of the worst kind of dogmatism. It is quite easy to see that this "*virgolettazione*" of reality also turns reality into one of the "grand narratives": reality becomes "reality," that is, "reality" (in quotation marks) refers to the fact that we distance ourselves from reality, we see it not as something "given," but rather as reality that has been constructed by others. Consequently, we become deconstructionists and start to look at reality with irony. On multiple occasions, it has been noted that "*virgolettazione*" is a move that can be considered similar or comparable to Husserl's *epoché*, that is, the gesture meant to suspend all unverified judgments and to place the natural occurring attitudes about the existence of objects in brackets so that one may access pure phenomena.[5] According to Ferraris, the best description of the *virgolettazione* of reality, however, can be found in Nietzsche's statement that "there are no facts, only interpretations."

Is it accurate to claim, though, that postmodernity and its move to "bracket reality" do indeed nurture antirealist attitudes? And do the critics of postmodernity, such as the proponents of the Italian new realism or of speculative realism, nurture a truly realist attitude? The very title of Vattimo's book, *Of Reality*, would seem to contradict such a claim. The chapter "*I limiti della derealizzazione* (The Limits of Derealization)," from the new, augmented edition of Vattimo's book *La società trasparente* (*The Transparent*

Society), can also be considered a "testamentary" text and an expression of tendencies that are quite opposite to antirealism.[6]

Therefore, it is justified to claim that the criterion of *reality*, which raises the question of the end of (the thought of) postmodernity, is, in essence, quite problematic. Being an important landmark standing between postmodernism and new realisms, such a criterion leads us to ask: What kind of reality are we talking about? If we bear in mind the recent context within which realist attitudes developed, things become even more complicated. Less than twenty years ago, the vast majority of analytic philosophers were expressly and even vigorously antirealist. The list of those who, at that time, opposed realism included "various members of the Anglo-Saxon philosophical aristocracy such as Dummett, Goodman, Davidson, Kuhn, Feyerabend, Cartwright, Van Fraassen, Hacking, Wright, not to mention the entire Wittgensteinian school *in corpore*, and, of course, Putnam."[7] It needs to be said that, at that time, there were also some voices that opposed the antirealist philosophers, but these were just "voices in the desert." This isolation existed because these realist voices were located in distant Australia. Generally speaking, realism was considered an esoteric matter.[8]

As some contemporary "new realists" note in a somewhat sarcastic manner, in those years, realism was not doing significantly better within the realm of continental philosophy either. For philosophers such as Rorty, Vattimo, and Baudrillard, and, for that matter, the whole "postmodern" movement, such words as "truth," "reality," "objectivity"—that is, everything that, in one way or another, corresponds to or expresses "realism"—were even less welcome and desirable than the writings of analytic philosophers. Today, though, it is precisely the new realists who draw attention to the fact that in spite of this prior situation, some prominent proponents of postmodernism, including Lyotard, Foucault, and Derrida, ended up subsequently revising their positions on realism.

Maurizio Ferraris claims that, after some twenty years, just like in an Alexandre Dumas novel, realism made its return and became fashionable all over the world (from ontological ethics and epistemology to semantics; from aesthetics to philosophy of science). It should be noted, however, that if one still holds to the style of *The Count of Monte Cristo* (which Ferraris mentions in his work), one should also point out the fact that what we are facing here is not just a case of some fresh revision or a new edition of traditional realism. Realism returns in *new* forms, and this novelty of forms is not due purely to the fact that nothing and no one ever returns in their exact previous forms.[9]

Thus, alongside the question of the kind of reality that is in question, we are also compelled to inquire about the forms in which realism returns today. The new realism asks, What does this expression mean? In what ways are these *new realisms* new? It is worth noting that it is the "new realists" themselves that offer accounts of the particular features of contemporary realism. First, there is an emphasis on the assumption that one of the features of new realism is a permanently critical and deconstructive distance, that is, something that the proponents of the antirealist movements regarded as their very own exclusive prerogative.[10] It seems that the new realists, however, wish to restore and reconquer the concepts of *truth* and *reality* that, from the antirealist perspective, are considered as "unthinkable" instruments. The word *criticism* should not be understood here as an adherence to a purely "political realism," which, in fact, has nothing to do with the new realism. We speak here of criticism and deconstruction in terms of a specific philosophical effort to reduce reality to a social construct, but this does not mean that the whole of reality is (held as) socially constructed. Criticism and deconstruction can and must show that the situation is, in fact, quite the opposite. It is argued that when they wrote anything about the constructible character of reality, philosophers of the so-called school of suspicion such as Nietzsche, Freud, and Marx (and then Foucault, Feyerabend, and Rorty as well) did so only because they considered such constructed features real.

A second feature that the new realists tend to emphasize is the fact that they do not consider themselves to be engaging in an antihermeneutic philosophy as, they argue, has been constantly claimed by their opponents. The opponents of the new Italian realism maintain that the new realists allegedly know very well that the most important "chunk" of the world, that is, the part that is the social realm, is impossible without interpretation; interpretation is the search for truth, and it is neither purely an expression of the power of the imagination nor imagination in power. The problem lies not in imagination, but rather in power, in the postmodern obsession—in the "myth"—with the claim that there is no truth, but only conflict, interests, the superiority of the more powerful; according to such a "myth," the act of "interpretation" becomes a kind of war or, at least, a battle. The new realism, however, affirms its rejection of such a use of "interpretation," of such an understanding and practice. It rejects a notion of interpretation that automatically supports the superiority of the more powerful mind and argument. This does not mean, however, that everything is reduced to the imagination and its effects. On the contrary, the "new realists" consider it important to expose the link between interpretation and both truth and reality.[11]

The third claim that the new realists make about themselves is that they do not represent antiscientism (a dominant position in postmodern thought). This claim, they say, is confirmed by the positions of Hilary Putnam and John Searle, who for some time have sought to think about and reflect on the constitutive link between philosophy and science. It is possible that today no one, either the authors we have just mentioned or others, would subscribe to the Australian and, essentially, esoteric notion of the old realism and its claim that philosophy is doomed to surrender itself to science. Contemporary philosophy is granted or has gained its constitutive ontological and methodological power. This does not mean, however, that it should reject scientific achievements.[12]

Finally, the new realism should be viewed as a possible globalized or global philosophy in which both science and interpretation converge. On the one hand, there is the requirement for scientific competence. On the other hand, one finds the public suitability (or applicability) of philosophy. While operating on scientific data, philosophy needs to be able to say something publicly and in an intelligible manner about the problems of body and soul, free will, the ontology of the natural world, the distribution of common goods or, finally, the unconscious.[13]

In his 1994 John Dewey lectures at Columbia University, Putnam announced his realistic turn while making an appeal to perception and praising Austin's work, *Sense and Sensibilia*. Thus, the first turn to realism occurs while appealing to the restoration of the significance of perception. As Maurizio Ferraris, the author of the manifesto of new realism, sees it, this fact, however, does not in any way mean that the turn of new realism coincides with the claim that reality is constituted by the perceptual data of experience. The way or the itinerary that leads from *aesthesis* to realism is more winding and is concerned with aspects that, according to Ferraris, are first explicated and developed by the theoreticians of the new realism.

We should, however, take here a brief pause or, at least, suspend our belief and trust in the "myths" of the new realism about its relation to postmodernity as well as its relation to *realism* and *reality*, and return to the question: What kind of reality are we talking about?

If, based on the texts of postmodern authors, we were to try to describe the relation of postmodernity, or (at least) of one particular postmodern thinker, Gianni Vattimo, to *reality*, and, at the same time, try to answer the question of the kind of reality we are discussing, this project would not be easy. The problem is that even if Vattimo's philosophy is precisely the expression of an openness to reality, the very issue of reality is thematized in it by moving in reverse motion and, for the most part, by using the so-called testamentary regime.

Although Nietzsche's famous adage ("There are no facts, only interpretations") appears repeatedly in every book and almost in every chapter of Vattimo's works, the issue of reality is not addressed directly; it emerges only as a juxtaposition of facts and interpretation. While outlining his philosophical path and, even more, while doing so in order to confront the "myths" of the new realisms and their dangers, Vattimo affirms that his book *On Reality* "presents a long and rather unsystematic work of reflection on the theme of the dissolution of objectivity or of reality itself, which began with the first expressions of 'weak thought' in the early 1980s."[14] Describing not only the direction of his own path, of his own itinerary, but also outlining the structure of his book on reality, Vattimo says that it constitutes a passage from "reality" to reality. What does this mean? On the one hand, there is the recognition that, in Vattimo's philosophy as well as in other postmodern thinkers, reality, as is constructed by common sense, science or metaphysics, becomes "reality" (that is, reality in scare-quotes). Does this then mean that the entire path of "weak thought" is understood and defined as the "others," that is, realities without quotation marks? Is weak thought the path where one finally sets reality free from quotation marks? Vattimo says that the initial attitude, namely, the approach "of taking leave of 'given' reality—by primarily posing the problem of how reality is given (Heidegger: *Es gibt Sein—Es, das Sein, gibt*), in the direction of a consummation of objectivity as the effect of domination—concretized over time into a second form of 'realism,' which recognizes how difficult it is to take such a leave."[15] It is precisely through these considerations that the problematic character of the use of the term "reality" stands out most clearly. What is the meaning of the result of his philosophical itinerary, that is, what is the sense of that reality without quotation marks to which Vattimo refers? Does Vattimo really succeed in removing the quotation marks? When and where does this happen?

As has already been pointed out, Vattimo agrees that the itinerary, which he discusses in the way we just mentioned, is nothing other than the itinerary of the very notion of postmodernity and the path of its elaboration. The starting point of this itinerary coincides with the consequences of Nietzsche's thought, the "Nietzsche effect," as Vattimo remarks. Accepting as a point of departure the opposition and alternative between facts and interpretation and following Nietzsche's logic (entrenching, by the second philosophical move, the attitude "and this too is an interpretation"), Vattimo admits at the same time that "the nihilistic ontology that is announced in Nietzsche, . . . stimulates the need—what I would call neurotic—for a return to 'realism.'"[16] If Nietzsche proposes a phrase like "and this too is an interpretation" in a vague and incomplete manner, this might be the case because Nietzsche could not and did not want to be satisfied by his own perspectivism, which can be understood as a descriptive doctrine of the real state of affairs.[17]

In the case of Vattimo's philosophy, the "Nietzsche effect" of the relation between reality and "reality" emerges, on the one hand, as the dissolution of reality into interpretation, but, on the other hand, and at the same time, as a recognition that this also may be merely an interpretation. This provokes the "effect" that allows us to frame Vattimo's own thought: the very historicity of the interpreter enters into the picture. In this hermeneutical perspective consisting of three degrees, one cannot raise the question of the errors (of thought) of the past, which could become clear only when confronted with knowledge of objective facts. Despite the fact that the Nietzschean relation to reality is seen by Vattimo as neurotic, the "Nietzsche effect" finds its way in Vattimo's work, not as the return to reality, but rather as the passage from "reality" to a second-degree "reality." The quotation marks are here to stay. Reality of the second degree is not just reality but also "reality." Thus, what appears to be most important in this itinerary is not the creation of the theoretical base for some kind of reality or "reality," but the very action of *passage* that creates an effect of double quotation marks. It is precisely this passage that constitutes the sense of the "Nietzsche effect." It should be noted that Vattimo speaks about reality using such terms as "*effettualità*" or "*attualità*" (*Wirklichkeit*). From its very beginning, "weak thought" was taken and treated (from the point of view of reality) as a performative philosophy, with an orientation to reality as actuality. In this case, though, one cannot avoid the question about the relation between second-degree "reality" and reality or, in Vattimo's terms, "*effetualità*" or "*attualità*" (*Wirklichkeit*).

Vattimo's philosophy, his hermeneutical "antirealism," has experienced not only the "Nietzsche effect," but also the "Heidegger effect." Existence is being-in-the-world, and in the world, there are also things. But the idea of the "project-like" nature of our existence means that things are "given" only within the project. This is the source of the essential character of interpretation: the experience and discovery of truth is the articulation of the project, the articulation of that preunderstanding that we, as existing beings, always already are. Heidegger, according to Vattimo, follows in the footsteps of Nietzsche: on the one hand, he is the one who affirms that "there are no facts, only interpretations"; but, on the other hand, Heidegger is the only one who takes seriously Nietzsche's second thesis ("and this too is an interpretation") and unpacks it. Vattimo describes this "Heidegger effect" on the notion of reality in the most striking manner when he writes that "the Kantian *a priori* has become, in Heidegger, the inheritance of mortals and other mortals; what we inherit from it, we can now say, is not the idea (eternal, stable) of Being, but the history of Being."[18]

But here it becomes clear that, in Vattimo's philosophy, there are some problematic issues related to the second-degree "reality" and to reality as "*attualità*" or "*fattualità*." It is obvious that it is not a second-degree "reality" itself that can coincide with reality as *Wirklichkeit*. It is rather the *realistic* interpretation of the experience of the existing being as being-in-the-world (which is always historical) that we can at least link to (when we cannot completely identify it with) the hermeneutic movement, the analytic expression of which is the theoretical emergence of the two degrees of "reality" that create the third degree as *wirken*.

Thus, we ask, What kind of reality, understood as reality "lost" in the "myth" of postmodernity, needs to be restored? Again, Maurizio Ferraris's reference to the devaluation of perception turns out to be a starting point for the announcement of a new realism. Ferraris draws attention to the fact that in the course of the twentieth century, and particularly in the middle of it, the issue of perception became an obsolete philosophical topic. Ferraris considers this as the reverse side of the linguistic turn: the devaluation of perception is linked to the preference given to the concept and conceptual thought. For this reason, the linguistic turn can be renamed and called the "conceptual turn." The preference given to the concept in the construction of experience, as Ferraris sees it, has deep philosophical roots. These roots extend from the thought of modernity, thus, it would seem that one could put an equals sign between modernity and postmodernity. This time, for Ferraris, the classic example of a proponent and representative of such a view is Hegel rather than Kant and his schematism. Ferraris refers to the chapter in Hegel's *Phenomenology of Spirit* in which perceptual certainty is sacrificed while simultaneously providing a criticism of "that" (*Dieses*). To Ferraris's credit, one should draw attention to the fact that he also admits that this Hegelian passage is certainly philosophically excellent.

> One begins with the discussion of perception as a source of knowledge. This source might seem/appear misleading, and, as a result, one considers the necessity of seeking some kind of credibility, looking for the certainty somewhere else. Thus, what appears as the disqualification of perception ultimately brings enormous philosophical benefits, namely, the gigantic potential of the conceptual realm, which is entrusted with the task of defending the immovability of certainty/reality (*il vero*) against the illusions and misrepresentations that the senses entail.[19]

As Ferraris sees it, the essential point of the devaluation of perception is the fact that the senses are assigned purely/essentially epistemological functions, a move that, at the same time, confirms that they have not been assigned any certainty, that they are, from the ontological point of view, unreal. Thus, Kantian constructivism also stems from the devaluation of perception, from its limitation to merely epistemological functions, whereas the Hegelian attitude towards reality (*Wirklichkeit*) is seen by Ferraris as the destruction of reality. Therefore, the claim that "intuitions without concepts are blind" signals the total collapse of ontology.[20]

By making the foregoing claim, Ferraris recalls the origins of the postmodern ontological attitudes: "It is in this horizon that ideas of postmodernity find their origins, those ideas, according to which reality is a social construct, or that there is no Being that is independent of our manipulations."[21] Such a slippery negation of any content that is not conceptual leads, according to Ferraris, to paninterpretationism, and subsequently negationism: one negates nothing else but reality itself.

The arguments of the new realism about the necessity of the restoration of reality are quite simple; in fact, they approach the realm of common sense. Ferraris takes a well-known thesis by Michael Dummett (which has been refuted) on the "inexistence of the past": if there is no past, then the Holocaust did not happen. But since the Holocaust is an obvious fact, this serves to Dummett as an argument for the ontological rehabilitation of perception. Thus, according to Ferraris, the new realism seeks to provide an answer to a simple question: Why does the appeal to perception, a reference to it and, for that matter, to an element which, it seems, one can so easily disqualify from an epistemological point of view, provide such a powerful argument (and, one should add, an ontological argument) in favour of realism? But the epistemological disqualification of perception, according to Ferraris, occurs or, one could say, succeeds since, in principle, one speaks not so much about perceptions, but rather about representation, images. When one speaks about perception, however (and this became feasible after *Sense and Sensibility*), one enters quite a different game.

The "game" of the new realism, for which Ferraris's thought is an introduction, is focused on the restoration of the ontological significance of perception. Ferraris claims that the most interesting aspect of perception is not the fact that it serves as our epistemological resource, but that it performs a certain limiting role in regard to our constructivist ambitions. In a sense, the ontological function of perception is similar to what Popper calls falsification (but, of course, in an epistemological sense). One is confronted with a certain resistant line, a limit, which Ferraris describes as *inemendabilità* (irrevocability, impossibility to amend)—an important aspect of perception. "At this point, we discover the importance of perception and the ontological significance/sense of aesthetics as *aesthesis*. Since the senses do not only amount to the origins of our understanding, they also resist and oppose our theories."[22]

It follows, then, that the ontological importance of the senses lies not in the fact that they confirm and actualize our reality, but in refuting our expectations and understanding by disclosing the existence of something different and separate. "The irrevocable and irreparable [*l'inemendabile*] might be an error, a disillusion, non-sense, but it certainly is."[23]

As Ferraris sees it, perception expresses this particular resistance that is linked to reality, understood in the ontological sense of the term. But, not unexpectedly, if one seeks to qualify something as "real," the negative discourse is the best way to do so. If I say, "This beer is real," I do not say much, I say almost nothing. If I say, however, "This beer is not real," I say quite a lot. It might seem strange, but I think that, here, the Hegel of the first chapter of *The Phenomenology of Spirit*, who was chased out through the door, makes his return, this time, through the window. This appeal Ferraris makes to discourse, to language, and especially to their negativity, brings us back to the concept. This also makes one ask: Is it really true that Hegel was the one who, by limiting our perceptual certainty, did not foresee the resistance and irrevocability of perceptual reality, which, it should be remarked, is accessible only in a negative and indirect way?

In his search for a stronger justification of the new realism as an ontological position, Ferraris discusses certain "traces" (here, by accident, he picks up the postmodernist jargon) that lead *aesthesis* to realism. These traces include: aconceptuality, naïveté, resistance, amazement, opaqueness, and difference. It is not difficult to anticipate what kind of traces these are, and where they are set to lead us. Ferraris, by the way, has been affirming the resistance and aconceptuality of factual reality for quite a while, and he opposes Vattimo's adherence to the Nietzschean thesis by proposing his own thesis according to which "*Non ci sono gatti, solo interpretazioni* [There are no cats, only interpretations]." (As a response to that, Vattimo named his cat "gatto" ("cat" in Italian), demonstrating by this nothing else but the very resistance of the concept we are here discussing).

Let us linger a little longer on the last trace Ferraris mentions, namely, *difference*, which is also taken from the postmodernist vocabulary. In his polemic with postmodernism, Ferraris writes: "Difference, non-identity, all those topics that found such a vast playground in the postmodern philosophical reflection, reveal here, as I see it, their underlying sense which is not the sense of negative ontology or nihilism, but, quite on the contrary, the reference to Being as resistance, which cannot be entirely absorbed in understanding and which makes it real. Being is inherently nonidentical, positive, and is not dissolved in thought."[24] What kind of alchemy would the new realism need to dissolve different, non-identical things into one another? Ferraris assigns different "natures" to perceptually accessible reality and to conceptual thinking, and, in doing so, he attempts to prove something that is not even worth proving, namely, the impossibility of the dissolution/resolution of one into the other.

Do postmodernism and the new realism treat the same reality? The new realism, clearly affected by Nietzschean neurosis, attempts to grasp reality, considering that it provides a new *interpretation* of perception. Whereas, I would argue, the problem of Vattimo, the "last of the Mohicans" of postmodernism, is the problem of the relation between the move towards second-degree "reality" and reality. It is obvious, however, that we are still spiralling within the realm of the distinction between *Realität* and *Wirklichkeit* drawn by Kant and Hegel. Vattimo alone, encouraged by Nietzsche and Heidegger, attempts to take a step forward, whereas Ferraris's "new" realism takes us back to the dispute between Jacobi and his contemporaries.

Let us conclude with a fragment of philosophical theatre offered by Franca D'Agostini:

> Euthydemus claims: "You owe Asclepius a cock." Dionysiodorus replies: "No, I do not." Theaetetus intervenes: "Let us examine the state of affairs (what is the situation concerning these matters). Asclepius, what can you say?" In response, Asclepius offers his own version of facts, whereas Dionysiodorus claims: "No, no, the state of affairs is quite different." Socrates then reconsiders and examines the concepts of "facts" and "interpretations" and replies: "You discuss about facts (about cocks and economic relations between individuals), but, in fact, Theaetetus needs to assess interpretations, so you need to consider the fact, that, for example, Asclepius and Dionysiodorus, while describing reality, have interests, and these interests are part of their reconstruction of facts."

This short theatrical scene, which is historically incorrect (it seems that Socrates owed Asclepius a cock, but no one in Ancient Greece spoke about facts and interpretations), is a text in which the "issue of realism" presents itself.

And the issue immediately resolves itself.[25]

Notes

1. Maurizio Ferraris, *Manifesto of New Realism*, trans. Sarah De Sanctis (Albany: State University of New York Press, 2014), 1–2.
2. Maurizio Ferraris, *Manifesto del nuovo realismo* (Rome: Laterza, 2012).
3. Gianni Vattimo, *Of Reality: The Purposes of Philosophy* (Milan: Garzanti, 2012).
4. See Ferraris, *Manifesto*, 4.
5. See Ferraris, *Manifesto*, 5.
6. Gianni Vattimo, *La società trasparente* (Milan: Garzanti, 2000). Translator's note: the chapter on derealization does not appear in the English translation of the book, which is based on an earlier edition of the volume.
7. Mario de Caro and Maurizio Ferraris, "Nuovo realismo e vecchia realtà," in *Bentornata realtà*, ed. Mario de Caro and Maurizio Ferraris (Turin: Einaudi, 2012), v.
8. See de Caro and Ferraris, v.
9. See de Caro and Ferraris, vi.
10. See de Caro and Ferraris, vii.
11. See de Caro and Ferraris, vii–viii.
12. See de Caro and Ferraris, viii.
13. See de Caro and Ferraris, viii.
14. Vattimo, *Of Reality*, 1.
15. See Vattimo, *Of Reality*, 2.
16. Vattimo, *Of Reality*, 19.
17. See Vattimo, *Of Reality*, 26.
18. Vattimo, *Of Reality*, 45.
19. Maurizio Ferraris, "Esistere è resistere," in *Bentornata realtà*, ed. Mario de Caro and Maurizio Ferraris (Turin: Einaudi, 2012), 144.
20. See Ferraris, "Esistere è resistere, 146.
21. Ferraris, "Esistere è resistere, 147.
22. Ferraris, "Esistere è resistere, 155.
23. Ferraris, "Esistere è resistere, 155.
24. Ferraris, "Esistere è resistere, 165.
25. Franca D'Agostini, *Realismo?* (Turin: Bollati Boringhieri, 2013), 33.

18

Deconstruction or Biopolitics

Roberto Esposito

I

This essay, which summarizes the conclusions of my recent work,[1] focuses on two interrelated questions. First, what is the relation of the Derridean paradigm to the Foucaultian one within French Theory? Second, what is the relation between French Theory and Italian Thought? Contrary to the widely held thesis that maintains both relations as contiguous or continuous, I believe that to understand the specificity of these paradigms we must return them to the originary tension that differentiates them. This move should in no way be read as privileging one paradigm over the other; nor should it be seen, with respect to Derrida and Foucault specifically, as undermining the deep recognition that is due to two of the great philosophical masters of the twentieth century. We must remain faithful to a heterogeneity that both thinkers have never hidden, and it is only by examining this heterogeneity that it becomes possible to recognize the tense relation between French Theory and Italian Thought. Despite all of its undeniable debts and lexical contaminations, Italian Thought is born not from the development of, but from the crisis within French Theory, a crisis that Italian Thought intensifies.

If I were to translate into images that which I am saying, I would refer to a divide that occurs within another divide. The difference between Italian Thought and French Theory originates in the difference between Foucault and Derrida, which retroactively acts on the difference between the two forms of theory, progressively sharpening it. This double divide does not complete the story; rather, it reopens it and makes it more vital:

friction and dissymmetry invigorate philosophies, leading them to the limits of their critical and creative strengths. If we abandon a fashionable form of pacifism, we can see that philosophy has always presented itself as a fight to determine the meaning of words in a given historical moment, a battle of and in concepts. The great philosophers have always known this reality. Could Aristotle's philosophy have arisen without its friction with Plato? And where would Hegel's philosophy be if there were no tension with Kant's philosophy? The indetermination and, sometimes, the inadequacy of expressions like "French Theory" are directly born from the missing awareness of this element, namely, the formative character of conflict. This indetermination arises from the confusion between paradigms that are irreducible to one another and yet have been made to overlap in a unique amalgam that has been repeatedly termed "the postmodern" or "poststructuralism," ultimately obscuring their differentiating traits. In fact, what we clearly have before us is a chasm that separates a post-Heideggerian line of thought, as interpreted by Derrida and his school, from a post-Nietzschean genealogy that is represented foremost by Foucault.

Jean-Luc Nancy admits and upholds the existence of this chasm in a series of collected interviews published in Italian as *Le differenze parallele* (*Parallel Differences*).[2] Here, admittedly, Derrida is contrasted more with Deleuze than with Foucault. In any case, considering the affinities of the two latter philosophers' sources of inspiration, the hermeneutical conclusion does not change, as Nancy suggests when he unites both philosophers under a "French" taxonomy, which he opposes to a German one that is poignantly articulated by Derrida. Nancy sees himself as belonging to this Derridean line. If Nancy places Bergson—or Nietzsche—as the head of the "French" line, which is represented by Deleuze, the "German" genealogical tree, which has Derrida as its head and in which Nancy recognizes himself, takes roots in Heidegger's ontology and Husserl's phenomenology, with all their respective differences. Whereas Derrida's philosophy remains within the horizon of being (an absent being—an empty ontology), Deleuze and Foucault practice a thought of becoming. Not unlike Heidegger's analytics of finitude, Derrida's reflection centers on birth and death. On the contrary, Deleuze and Foucault practice a thought of mutation that unfolds in the flux of a becoming that crosses neither being nor its lack. At this point, Nancy bizarrely affirms, and even provocatively so, that Foucault, in contrast to Derrida and Heidegger, is not a philosopher; rather, he is merely a historian. Even if he immediately softens the blow of his wisecrack by speaking about "two philosophical registers, one metaphysical and ontological, and the other epistemological and ideological,"[3] Nancy still makes explicit the irreconcilable nature of the two lines of thought, which French Theory tends to amalgamate as one.

II

Derrida implicitly maintained the difference between the two registers mentioned above at the time of the harsh polemic that opposed him to Foucault when the latter's *History of Madness* appeared. A philosophical, and even personal, break occurred that was never to be healed.[4] At the center of their tension, covered over by different interpretations of a passage from Descartes's *Meditations* on dreams and madness, lay a dispute over the relation between time and concept, being and becoming, history and philosophy, and also thought and what is external to it. Is there something that is external to thought, as Foucault wants to maintain, or is the outside of thought the differential remainder that cuts thought from within itself, infinitely duplicating it, as Derrida argues? In metapolitical terms, is it possible to decide between folly and madness, power and resistance, identity and difference, or do these notions overlap, resulting in a semantics of the Undecidable? At the heart of philosophy and even life, does one find the neutral, that is, neither one nor the other, as Derrida maintains following Blanchot, or does one find the conflict between opposing forces, as Foucault affirms? In the last analysis, do we have before us Heidegger's ontology or Nietzsche's genealogy? Derrida, of course, does not wish to extract thought from its historicity, thereby rendering it a sort of *philosophia perennis*. *Différance* ultimately coincides with historicity, understood as the eternal deferment of that which appears as present to itself. Yet historicity, as Derrida sees it, seems to have no relation with history and is even constituted in opposition to it. Like in Heidegger's thought, historicity refers to the difference of being, not to the movement of becoming.

By contrast, for Foucault, rather than placing itself within reason, madness situates itself outside the boundaries of reason in a modality that escapes being grasped by reason. In this sense, then, madness is not the transcendental limit that reason carries within itself as an originary mark; rather, it is an event that is historically determined, that produces effects that are also determined and whose genealogy the *History of Madness* seeks to uncover. We have before us, then, a fracture line that separates "a thought of the outside" from a philosophy of difference. Certainly, Foucault's perspective places itself outside the philosophical tradition, as Derrida and Nancy maintain without grasping the full sense of their affirmation. Foucault is not a philosopher in the sense of Heidegger. But it is this difference that gives Foucault's philosophy much theoretical force, a force that is diametrically opposed to that of Derrida's, which remains closed in a circle that he wishes to shatter through the recalling of an archi-origin that coincides with its infinite repetition. From this point of view, so admits Foucault, it is true that Derrida's interpretation of Descartes better adheres to the inherent logic of the Cartesian discourse. Derrida's interpretation repeats the same logic, just as Descartes does when he confronts Plato's texts, excluding the exclusion of madness on the part of reason, which leads madness back to reason's own inside. It is true that writing, as Derrida understands it, is an exteriority with respect to *logos*, but nevertheless it is *its* exteriority. It is the outside *of logos*, the outside of an inside. In Derrida, the circularity of interpretation, which includes exteriority by rendering it the external of an internal, forecloses itself off from the relation with historicity, or at least with history. Ceaselessly reduplicating itself, philosophy refers back more to a form than to a force, which is instead what the post-Nietzschean line does. Here, what disappears together with history, which is reduced to the superficial foaming of an ever-distant origin, is that friction with the outside without which philosophical knowing risks becoming a neutralizing science of the text.

The bifurcation of those who, in the American reading of French Theory, are the two poles of a unique theoretical constellation shines very clearly. Not only do neither Derrida nor Foucault do anything to mask this split, but they also emphasize it with a polemical force that repeatedly displays itself each time the two enter in contact with each other. On the one side, the side of Derrida and his school, Foucault will never be granted the status of the philosopher. On the other side, Derrida is considered the last of the metaphysicians. Far from constituting the head point of a theory capable of pushing philosophy outside its traditional boundaries, Derrida's philosophy appears to Foucault as "a petty pedagogy that is historically determined and that manifests itself in a highly visible manner. This is a pedagogy that teaches the student that there is nothing outside the text, and that in the text, in its interstices, in its silences, and in what remains unsaid in it, one finds the reserve of the origin."[5]

III

In a crescendo of polemical tension, Derrida's response to the foregoing sentences, which are certainly excessive and ungenerous on Foucault's part, is recognizable in the harsh attack that is first directed to Agamben but which also aims at Foucault in the 2001–2002 Paris seminar that was published as *The Beast and the Sovereign*.[6] In those years, the cultural climate had shifted. First Foucault's and then the Italian elaboration of biopolitics began to find a place at the center of the international philosophical debate; the effect was a progressive marginalization of deconstruction. Certainly, scholars continued to deconstruct, but in a form that risked revolving around itself, with the effect more of fatigue than of surprise. To understand these moves, one must keep in mind the entire framework of a philosophy that had become globalized. The first signs of international interest for that which began to be called "Italian Thought" coincided with the weakening of the postmodern paradigm, to which some Italian philosophers had subscribed in the 1970s and 1980s through the proposal by Gianni Vattimo and Pier Aldo Rovatti of what became known as "weak thought (*pensiero debole*)."

Concerning the postmodern cultural climate, the reelaboration of biopolitics provokes a decomposition and restructuration of the continental philosophical panorama; these effects may be connected to a general shifting of interests from the domain of language to the horizon of life. Deconstruction is short of breath, De Man is dead, and Nancy repeats his ontological proposal in an increasingly sophisticated manner. One feels the need for a turn: a return certainly not to the realism of *antan* (yesteryear), but rather to the constituent power of *bios*. In my opinion, this turn to biopolitics explains Derrida's harshness, which is unusual for his style and habitual generosity, in his polemic against Agamben. He writes that Agamben dedicates himself "to a distribution of prizes to the top-ranked students in the class, prizes of excellence and honourable mentions" like a priest "who never gives up the dubious pleasure that is given to him to conduct ceremonies or give lessons."[7] Derrida argues, and this is clearly his hyperinterpretation, that it was Heidegger who first had the intuition about biopolitics, but that Agamben erases Heidegger in his own genealogy. How it could have been Heidegger, who was never interested in living bodies, that invented biopolitics remains a glorious mystery.

But in the background of Derrida's polemic, much like a bull's eye, lies Foucault, whom Derrida chastises in the same way he did forty years earlier when discussing the *History of Madness*. What holds Foucault captive to an outdated line of philosophical thinking is his inadequate use of the category of the event diluted into mere historical succession. In the same year as Derrida's seminar, in a *Note* expressly dedicated to biopolitics,[8] Nancy articulates an analogous critical intention concerning a reflection that, starting with Foucault, has become in the meantime constitutive of the new Italian Thought. The conflict, which sees both Derrida and Nancy take a defensive line with respect to the new philosophical lexicon, is now completely evident. The confusion arises, according to Nancy, from the fact that biopolitics splits between, on the one hand, a historically sharable but general thesis, namely, the displacement of power objectives from the territory to the life of its inhabitants, and, on the other hand, an unusable philosophical thesis that has been superseded by an epochal turn that coincides with a whole array of technological procedures that have deeply modified natural life, leaving behind the biopolitical *dispositif*. For this reason, far from articulating the relation between politics and life, the category of biopolitics can never signify either the former or the latter.

My impression is that Derrida's and Nancy's texts display a symptomatic character that transcends their manifest content. I mean that they both show forth something more than the conceptual dishomogeneity of thinkers belonging to different lines of thought. They express a real allergy of one paradigm to the other, that is, the deconstructive and biopolitical paradigms, which are born in the same period and yet are incompatible because they are anchored in two different modes of contemporary reflection. Whereas deconstruction, which Derrida elaborated within a Heideggerian framework, still belongs to the domain of the so-called linguistic turn, biopolitics refers instead to a regime centered around the emergence of life as the referential point for any other language. Naturally, as always happens in similar cases, it is only possible ex post (that is, retroactively) to establish limits between perspectives that, in their development, have more than one point of intersection: just as language is always a biological function, so too does human life have its own linguistic conformation. But this does not exclude a deep dishomogeneity that impedes the integration of these two folds of contemporary knowledge into the same horizon of meaning or sense.

This dishomogeneity was perceived by thinkers who surely were aware of their own theoretical instruments and was intended to defend them against other competitors. This may explain what seems to be an excessive defensiveness on the part of Derrida toward authors and categories against which he perceives an unbridgeable semantic gap. A theory of language and writing such as Derrida's cannot harmonize with the new thought about *bios* that first Foucault, and then Deleuze, followed by Italian philosophers, pushed ever more intensely to the center of the international debate. Concerning this reconstruction of the difficult relations between deconstruction and biopolitics, some have objected that far from being resistant to the semantics of life, Derrida's entire work has always made reference to it to the point that it becomes what is ultimately at stake in deconstruction.[9] The very same notion of "*gramma*" or "program" may be interpreted in a biological key, as a basic genetic structure. Even logocentrism, understood as the autoaffective presence of *logos*, is basically an articulation of the economy of the living being. Ever since *Writing and Difference*, Derrida has maintained that one "needs to think life as a trace before determining being as presence. This is the only condition that allows us to say that life *is* death."[10]

Already in this affirmation, which attests to the significance of the motive of life in Derrida's work, one sees the specific modality with which it is assumed, namely, as strongly marked by Heidegger's influence. As in Heidegger, in Derrida too life is thought as being more than in itself, always in relation to death and as starting from death. In his seminar on Marx, Nietzsche, and Freud starting in 1975–76 and then in *Otobiographies*, which is dedicated to the logic of living beings, Derrida theorizes that the two terms *life* and *death* are to be pronounced as one single word, namely, *life-death*, precisely in order to signal their indissoluble logic.[11] The use of the one word means that life and death, far from being opposed in a battle over the duration of existence, belong to each other in such a way that it is impossible to undertake any reflection on life that does not presuppose its apparent contrary. This is why the subsequent elaboration of the theme, which occurs amidst a reflection on Freud, focuses on his *Beyond the Pleasure Principle*, that is, it focuses on the text that situates death not only at the end, but also at the origin of life, rendering the "sentinels of life" the "guardians of death."[12] It is not an accident, too, that the category of autoimmunity, theorized by Derrida in his *Faith and Knowledge*, constitutes the intrinsic expression of the presence of death within life. Life protects itself from death by introjecting death into itself, abandoning itself to death's pressure. In no other text as in these on autoimmunity, though they semantically "resonate" with Italian biopolitical thought, does Derrida appear to be situated on the opposite pole of biopolitics, in that Heideggerian horizon that biopolitics wishes to leave behind.

IV

As further proof of this heterogeneity, one need only compare the last three texts by Foucault, Deleuze, and Derrida. Published ten years apart from one another, they all converge on the theme of life, which testifies to the biological turn that is now at the center of contemporary thought, be it continental or analytic, and that follows a path that leads from biopolitics to neuroscience. Foucault's text, titled "La vie: l'expérience et la science (Life: Experience and Science),"[13] was written just before his death and is an homage to Georges Canguilhem. In this work, Foucault underlines the specificity of knowledge on life as opposed to other sciences, such as the physical and chemical sciences. It is from this perspective that he questions the relation between the concept and life: what concepts articulate knowledge about life and how is life itself modified by concepts that continually define it? As Canguilhem maintained, the health of an organism is not measured by the power of self-preservation, but by its capacity to mutate its own norms. The most original element of Foucault's text lies in his grasping the uninterrupted transformation that characterizes life. Unlike what reference to the concept may lead us to imagine, here we are not dealing with the relation of life to truth, but, on the contrary, to error. It is error that causes the living being never to be in its proper place, thereby determining its constitutive errancy. In this sense, then, error is at the root not only of biology but also of human history—the segment along which nature and history forge their own parabolas. Even the traditional opposition between truth and falsehood, with all of the subsequent effects of exclusion, is nothing else than a response to the quantity of errors that are inevitably inherent in a life directly affected by the concept.

One could say, even though Deleuze himself did not directly aim to do this, that his text "L'immanence: une vie (Immanence: A Life)," written just before his own death, responds to Foucault's question about the problematic connection between subjectivity and life.[14] What is clear in this somewhat enigmatic text is that the status of the living being, grasped in its purity, in no way coincides with what the philosophical tradition has defined as "subject" or "person," terms that denote a self-conscious being. This does not mean that the transcendental field that Deleuze mentions does not imply some form of consciousness; it is, however, a prereflexive and impersonal consciousness that excludes the metaphysical dichotomy between subject and object. The immanence that Deleuze discusses is not to be understood as something that affects life, an attribute that makes life the subject of immanence; rather, here we find life itself, subtracted from the excluding thresholds carved into life by the *dispositifs* of the person and the subject. We must not be misled by Deleuze's reference to Dickens's text *Our Mutual Friend* in which the main character, who finds himself at the end of his life, enters into a near-death state that solicits the compassion of those present around him, but only insofar as he remains in that state, and not when he no longer is in that condition. What is important in Deleuze's interpretation of the fleeting overlaying of life over death is that, unlike for Derrida, it is not death that incorporates life within itself, but rather life that includes death, while not ceding to it. Deleuze clearly maintains that "one need not limit life simply to a moment in which the individual life confronts universal death. A *life* is everywhere, in all moments crossed by this or that living subject."[15] Life, in its singular and impersonal being, constitutes both the background and the center of a form of thought that looks upon the emergencies of our age.

It would be difficult to find a text so far removed, in its prevailing tonality, from Foucault's and Deleuze's last works than the last interview given by Derrida before his death, conducted by Jean Birnbaum of the daily newspaper *Le Monde*. This interview was later published in 2005 as *Apprendre a vivre enfin* (*Finally Learning How to Live*).[16] The title draws upon an expression from *Specters of Marx*, which immediately declares the impossibility of learning to live, for "living, by definition, is neither learned nor can be taught, neither from itself nor by life. Living is learned from the other and through death."[17] Like philosophy in Plato's myth, life too is characterized by a meditation on death: death does not arrive at the end of life because it is situated in the midst of life. In this sense, Derrida can declare that, like all mortals, rather than a living being, he is a survivor in the extreme sense of living not only with death, but also in the immanence of death: "Life *is* survival. Survival in the current sense means continuing to live, but it also means living *after* death."[18]

Here, we have to be mindful of the circumstances of Derrida's interview. It has the explicit tone of a living will, which is marked by an awareness of imminent death. This lends a dramatic urgency, which has always been the hallmark of Derrida's thought. It is not an accident that the motifs of the specter, the crypt, and *adieux* are all fundamental elements of his philosophical lexicon. It is true that in the very same interview he denies looking at survival more from the perspective of death and the past than from life and the future. Derrida, right up to his death, effectively never resigned himself to death, he never delivered himself over to death. The decisive element, however, that locates him in a sphere far away from Foucault's and Deleuze's immanent and impersonal domain lies in the circumstance that in any case life, even though coveted, remains thought from the standpoint of death. Writing itself, in its grammar, is an operation of death: "The trace that I leave signifies for me both my death, which is to come or which has already happened, and the hope that the trace survives me."[19]

I would like to end this essay with a tribute to Derrida. Deconstruction was our youth. I recall the impression I had when Derrida welcomed me into his office. I was only twenty-five and I remember his magnetic gaze, his magnificent face, his splendid intelligence. But today, in a world that is falling to pieces, deconstruction is no longer enough. No longer can we respond to the global challenge of analytic philosophy with, or, rather, only with deconstruction. In order to meet this challenge, even by way of a productive confrontation with analytic philosophy, we must push Derrida beyond Derrida. We must push him to that radical outside that Foucault shows us.

Translated by Antonio Calcagno

Notes

1. Roberto Esposito, *Da fuori. Una filosofia per l'Europa* (Turin: Einaudi, 2016); translated into English as *A Philosophy for Europe*, trans. Zakiya Hanafi (London: Polity Books, 2018).

2. Jean-Luc Nancy, *Le differenze parallele. Deleuze e Derrida* (Verona: Ombre Corte, 2008).

3. Nancy, 13.

4. Jacques Derrida, "Cogito et histoire de la folie," *Revue de métaphysique et de morale* 3–4 (1963): 460–494.

5. Michel Foucault, "Mon corps, ce papier, ce feu," in *Histoire de la folie à l'âge classique* (Paris: Gallimard, 1972); Italian trans. "Il mio corpo, questo foglio, questo fuoco," in Michel Foucault, *Storia della follia nell'età classica* (Milan: Rizzoli, 1963), 665.

6. Jacques Derrida, *La bête et le souverain*, vol. 1 (2001–2002) (Paris: Galilée, 2008).

7. Derrida, *La bête et le souverain*, 131.

8. Jean-Luc Nancy, *La création du monde ou la mondialisation* (Paris: Galilée, 2002).

9. See Simone Regazzoni, *Biopolitica e democrazia* (Genoa: Il Melangolo, 2002).

10. Jacques Derrida, "Freud et la scène de l'écriture," *Tel Quel* 26 (1966); Italian translation: "Freud e la scena della scrittura," in Derrida, *La scrittura e la differenza*, 263.

11. Jacques Derrida, *Otobiographies. L'enseignement de Nietzsche et la politique du nom propre* (Paris: Galilée, 1084); Italian translation: *Otobiographies. L'insegnamento di Nietzsche e la politica del nome proprio* (Padua: Il Poligrafo, 1993), 43.

12. Jacques Derrida, "Spéculer—sur Freud," in Jacques Derrida, *La carte postale. De Socrate à Freud et au-de-là* (Paris: Aubier-Flammarion, 1980); Italian translation: *Speculare su Freud* (Milan: Cortina, 2000), 119–120.

13. Michel Foucault, "La vie, l'expérience et la science," *Revue de métaphysique et de morale* 1 (1985): 3–14.

14. Gilles Deleuze, "L'immanence: une vie," in *Philosophie* 47 (1995): 3–7.

15. Deleuze, "L'immanence: une vie," 5.

16. Jacques Derrida, *Apprendre à vivre enfin. Entretien avec Jean Birnbaum* (Paris: Galilée, 2005).

17. Jacques Derrida, *Spectres de Marx. L'état de la dette, le travail du deuil et la nouvelle Internationale* (Paris: Galilée, 1993); Italian translation: *Spettri di Marx. Stato del debito, lavoro del lutto e nuova Internazionale* (Milan: Cortina, 1994), 3–4.
18. Derrida, *Apprendre à vivre enfin*, 26.
19. Derrida, *Apprendre à vivre enfin*, 33.

Contributors

María del Rosario Acosta López is professor of Latin American studies in the Hispanic Studies Department at University of California Riverside, Riverside, California, USA. She obtained her PhD in philosophy from the Colombian National University and until recently was associate professor of philosophy at DePaul University, Chicago, Illinois, USA. She teaches and conducts research on Romanticism and German idealism, aesthetics and philosophy of art, and contemporary political European philosophy, and more recently her work has also moved into the areas of decolonial and Latin American studies, with an emphasis on questions of memory and trauma in the Americas. She has published extensively in English on the question of community in the work of Jean-Luc Nancy, Roberto Esposito, and Giorgio Agamben. She is the author of a book on silence and art in German Romanticism (2006) and a monograph on Friedrich Schiller and the political sublime (2008), and has edited or coedited volumes on Hegel (2008), Schiller (2008 and 2018), Paul Klee (2009), aesthetics and politics (2010), recognition theories (2010), contemporary political philosophy (2013), law and violence (2014), art and memory in Colombia (2016 and 2019), collective temporalities (2019), and philosophy in Colombia (2019). She is currently working on the manuscript of her next book, *Grammars of Listening: Philosophical Approaches to Trauma and Memory*.

Silvia Benso is professor of philosophy at Rochester Institute of Technology, Rochester, New York, USA. Among her areas of interest are ancient philosophy, contemporary European philosophy, the history of philosophy, ethics, and aesthetics. She is the author of *Pensare dopo Auschwitz. Etica filosofica e teodicea ebraica* (1992), *The Face of Things: A Different Side of Ethics* (2000), *Viva Voce: Conversations with Italian Philosophers* (2017), and coauthor (with Brian Schroeder) of the volume *Pensare ambientalista. Tra filosofia e ecologia* (2000). She has also coedited a number of volumes, including *Contemporary Italian Philosophy: Between Ethics, Politics and Religion* (2007), *Levinas and the Ancients* (2008), *Between Nihilism and Politics: The Hermeneutics of Gianni Vattimo* (2010), and *Thinking the Inexhaustible: Art, Interpretation, and Freedom in the Philosophy of Luigi Pareyson* (2018). During the past decade, she has devoted herself to the promotion of Italian philosophy; she is the general coeditor (with Brian Schroeder) of the SUNY Press series Contemporary Italian Philosophy and the codirector of the Society for Italian Philosophy (SIP).

Alexander U. Bertland is associate professor of philosophy at Niagara University, Lewiston, New York, USA. His research focuses primarily on Giambattista Vico's political philosophy and theory of myth. He is currently developing a project to place Vico's account of poetic wisdom and historical development in conversation with early modern social contract theory. He recently published an essay on Roberto Esposito's early interpretation of Vico and has written an essay on Vico's interpretation of Homer, which is forthcoming. He has also published on Ernst Cassirer, Jürgen Habermas, and business ethics.

Peg Birmingham is professor of philosophy at DePaul University, Chicago, Illinois, USA. She is the author of *Hannah Arendt and Human Rights: The Predicament of Common Responsibility* (2006), coeditor (with Philippe van Haute) of *Dissensus Communis: Between Ethics and Politics* (1996), and coeditor (with Anna Yeatman) of *Aporia of Rights: Citizenship in an Era of Human Rights* (2014). She is also the editor of *Philosophy Today*.

Maria Luisa Boccia is a feminist political philosopher who has taught at the University of Siena, Italy. She is the president of the Fondazione Crs-Archivio Pietro Ingrao. She is the author of *L'io in rivolta. Vissuto e pensiero di Carla Lonzi* (1990), with Grazia Zuffa, *L'eclissi della madre. La fecondazione artificiale. Tecniche, fantasie e norme* (1998), *La differenza politica. Donne e cittadinanza* (2002), "Faire autrement de la politique: Théorie et pratique dans le féminisme italien," in Christiane Veauvy, *Les femmes dans l'espace publique* (2004); "Parole di donne, discorsi sulle donne," in Alisa Del Re, ed., *Donne, Politica, Utopia* (2011); *Con Carla Lonzi* (2014); and *Le parole e i corpi. Scritti femministi* (2018). She also served as senator in the Fifteenth Legislature of Italy (2006–2008).

Antonio Calcagno is professor of philosophy at King's University College, London, Ontario, Canada. He is the author of *Giordano Bruno and the Logic* of Coincidence (1998), *Badiou and Derrida: Politics, Events and Their Time* (2007), *The Philosophy of Edith Stein* (2007), and *Lived Experience from the Inside Out: Social and Political Philosophy in Edith Stein* (2014). He is also the editor of the volume *Contemporary Italian Political Philosophy* (2015) and the collected work *Roberto Esposito: Biopolitics and Philosophy* (coedited with Inna Viriasova), both of which are part of the State University of New York Press series, Contemporary Italian Philosophy (edited by Silvia Benso and Brian Schroeder).

Alessandro Carrera is the John and Rebecca Moores Professor of Italian Studies and World Cultures and Literatures at the University of Houston, Houston, Texas, USA. He has published in the fields of Italian and continental philosophy, Italian and comparative literature, film studies, and classical and popular music. His recent books are *La distanza del cielo. Leopardi e lo spazio dell'ispirazione* (2011), *Il ricatto del godimento. Contributo a un'antropologia italiana* (2012), *Il corpo tra volontà e rappresentazione. Schopenhauer Nietzsche Bloch* (2015), *Benedetto Croce in Texas. Storie di filosofia italiana in America* (2017), *Filosofia del minimalismo. La musica e il piacere della ripetizione* (2018), *Fellini's Eternal Rome: Paganism and Christianity in the Films of Federico Fellini* (2019), *Il colore del buio. La Rothko Chapel a Houston* (2019), and *Fellini, o della vita eterna. Da Gelsomina a Mastorna* (2020). He has edited *Italian Critical Theory* (2011), Massimo Cacciari's *The Unpolitical* (2009), and Massimo Cacciari's *Europe and Empire* (2016) and has coedited (with Ines Testoni) Emanuele Severino's *The Essence of Nihilism* (2016). He has translated into Italian three novels by Graham Greene and all the songs and prose of Bob Dylan. Carrera has been the recipient of the Eugenio Montale Prize for poetry (1993), the Arturo Loria Prize for short fiction (1998), the Attilio Bertolucci Prize for literary criticism (2006), and the Flaiano Prize for Italian Studies (2019). His most recent collection of poems is *Songs of Purgatory* (2020). He is now editing Massimo Cacciari's *Dante: Mysticism and Politics* for the State University of New York Press.

Gaetano Chiurazzi is professor of theoretical philosophy at the University of Turin, Turin, Italy. He studied and worked as a research fellow at the Universities of Turin, Berlin, Heidelberg, Paris, and Oxford. His interests are especially concerned with French and German philosophy, notably Derrida, Kant, Hegel, Husserl, Heidegger, and Gadamer. His publications include *Scrittura e tecnica. Derrida e la metafisica* (1992), *Hegel, Heidegger e la grammatica dell'essere* (1996), *Teorie del giudizio* (2005; Spanish translation: *Teorías del juício*, 2008), *Modalità ed esistenza* (2001; German translation:

Modalität und Existenz, 2006), and *L'esperienza della verità* (2011; English translation: *The Experience of Truth*, 2017). He is also the coeditor (with Gianni Vattimo) of *Tropos. Rivista di ermeneutica e critica filosofica.*

Roberto Esposito teaches philosophy at the Scuola Normale Superiore, Pisa, Italy. He is the author of numerous works, which have been translated into many languages, including *Communitas: The Origin and Destiny of Community* (2004), *Bios: Biopolitics and Philosophy* (2008), *Immunitas: Protection and Negation of Life* (2011), *Third Person* (2012), *Living Thought: The Origins and Actuality of Italian Thought* (2012), *Two: The Machine of Political Theology and the Place of Thought* (2015), *A Philosophy for Europe: From the Outside* (2018), and *Politics and Negation: For an Affirmative Philosophy* (2019). His latest book is *Pensiero istituente. Tre paradigmi di ontologia politica* (2020).

Michael E. Gardiner is professor of sociology at the University of Western Ontario, London, Ontario, Canada, and has a joint appointment at the Centre for the Study of Theory and Criticism. His current research interests include the political economy of affective life, the everyday, and utopianism. He is the author of several books and numerous journal articles, and his latest major publications include *Weak Messianism: Essays in Everyday Utopianism* (2013) and (coedited with Julian Jason Haladyn) *Boredom Studies Reader: Frameworks and Perspectives* (2017).

Giulio Goria received his PhD in philosophy from the Scuola Normale Superiore, Pisa, Italy. Currently, he is a research fellow at the University Vita-Salute San Raffaele in Milan, Italy. He is the author of several journal articles on Kant, Hegel, and Italian Idealism. Among his book publications is a volume on Kant's transcendental philosophy, *Il fenomeno e il rimando. Il fondamento kantiano della finitezza della ragione umana* (2014). He is also a member of the editorial board for the Italian philosophical journal *Il Pensiero*.

Richard A. Lee Jr. is professor of philosophy at DePaul University, Chicago, Illinois, USA. He works in late medieval and early modern philosophy, Marxist philosophy (particularly the Frankfurt School and Antonio Gramsci), and twentieth-century European philosophy. He is the author, most recently, of *The Thought of Matter: Materialism, Conceptuality, and the Transcendence of Immanence* (2016).

Christian Lotz is professor of philosophy at Michigan State University, Lansing, Michigan, USA. His main research area is post-Kantian European philosophy. His most recent book publications are *The Capitalist Schema:*

Time, Money, and the Culture of Abstraction (2014), *Christian Lotz zu Marx, Das Maschinenfragment* (2014), *The Art of Gerhard Richter: Hermeneutics, Images, Meaning* (2015), and the edited volume, *Ding und Verdinglichung: Technik- und Sozialphilosophie nach Heidegger und der kritischen Theorie* (2012). His current research interests are in classical German phenomenology, critical theory, Marx, Marxism, aesthetics, and contemporary European political philosophy.

Pietro Pirani is assistant professor of Italian language and culture at University of Western Ontario, London, Ontario, Canada. He has also held appointments at Wilfrid Laurier University and McMaster University. He has coedited (with Maria Laura Mosco) the volume *The Concept of Resistance in Italy: Multidisciplinary Perspectives* (2017) and has published various essays in *Modern Italy*, *Journal of Multilingual and Multicultural Development*, and *Political Studies Review*.

Enrico Redaelli is professor of transformation of social ties at the Istituto di Ricerca di Psicoanalisi Applicata (IRPA), Milan, Italy. He obtained a PhD in philosophy at the Catholic University of Milan as well as a teaching certification for high school education. He then became a research fellow at the Centro Studi Diaforà in Albino and since 2006 has collaborated with the Department of Philosophy of the University of Milan in teaching and tutoring for graduation theses. His main research areas are contemporary philosophy, in particular Italian and French, and economic anthropology. He is the author of several books, chapters in collected volumes, and articles for specialized journals. Among his publications are *Il nodo dei nodi. L'esercizio del pensiero in Vattimo, Vitiello, Sini* (2008), *L'incanto del dispositivo. Foucault dalla microfisica alla semiotica del potere* (2011), and (with T. Di Dio, A. Bonfanti, and G. Spada and edited by Carlo Sini) *Prospettive della differenza. Economia, biologia, psicologia, estetica* (2014). He is the coauthor of the university textbook, *Filosofia teoretica*, edited by Rocco Ronchi (2009). He edited the books *Il filosofo e le pratiche* (2011) and *La lezione di Pasolini* (2020), and with F. Vandoni and P. Pitasi, he edited the book *Legge, desiderio, capitalismo. L'anti-Edipo tra Lacan e Deleuze* (2014). For ten years he wrote cultural articles for the daily paper *Il Manifesto*, and now he is a member of the scientific committee of Mechrí–Laboratorio di filosofia e cultura.

Elvira Roncalli is associate professor of philosophy at Carroll College, Helena, Montana, USA. She has studied philosophy in Italy, at the Università degli Studi di Milano, and received her PhD from the Université Catholique de Louvain-La-Neuve, Belgium, with a dissertation titled "Life of the Mind and Love of the World: The Crucial Role of Judging in Arendt's Thinking." Her research interests include the philosophy of Hannah Arendt, twentieth-century European thought, Italian philosophy, social and political philosophy, and feminist/gender theory.

Rita Šerpytytė is professor of philosophy and chair of the Department for Continental Philosophy and Religious Studies at Vilnius University, Vilnius, Lithuania. Her education includes a degree in law (1977) and a PhD in philosophy (1988) from the University of Vilnius. In 1993 and 1996, she was visiting fellow in the Department of Philosophy at the University of Rome "La Sapienza," Rome, Italy; in 2004, she was visiting researcher at the Center for Religious Studies in Trento, Italy. In 2020, she was Visiting Professor in the Department of Philosophy and Education at the University of Turin. Her research interests include Heidegger and Hegel studies, postmodern philosophy, contemporary Italian philosophy, and speculative and new realisms as well as the problem of nihilism and negativity in Western philosophy. Her published works include *Nihilism and Western Philosophy* (2007), *A Century with Levinas: On the Ruins of Totality* (2009), *Secularization and Contemporary Culture* (2013), *Transformations of Ontology: Media, Nihilism, Ethics* (2015), *Emmanuel Levinas: A Radical Thinker in the Time of Crisis* (2016), and *Specters of Reality: Western Nihilism between Diagnosis and Theory* (2019).

Erik M. Vogt is Gwendolyn Miles Smith Professor of Philosophy at Trinity College, Hartford, Connecticut, USA; he is also affiliated with the Department of Philosophy at the University of Vienna, Austria, where he teaches every year. His research focuses on twentieth-century and contemporary continental philosophy. He is the author, editor, or coeditor of twenty-three books, the author of more than sixty articles, and the translator of more than twenty books. His most recent published work includes *Jacques Rancière und die Literatur* (2020; edited with M. Manfé), *Zwischen Sensologie und aesthetischem Dissens* (2019), *Bruchlinien Europas* (2016; edited with G. Unterthurner), *Adorno and the Concept of Genocide* (2016; edited with R. Crawford), and *Aesthetisch-Politische Lektueren zum Fall "Wagner"* (2015). He is currently working on a book-length essay on Peter Handke.

Index

Action, 11, 13, 52, 70, 74, 100, 101, 104, 109, 118, 119, 124, 127, 128, 146, 148, 162, 179, 185, 186, 190–92, 194, 215, 217, 242, 244, 245, 247, 249n13, 251n57, 252n71, 256, 260, 261–65, 269–71, 292, 301–4, 306–8, 310–13, 316–19, 332, 347
Actuality, 1, 7, 16, 71, 72, 75, 90, 92, 99, 145, 156, 157, 204–6, 208, 212, 216n28, 332, 333, 339n15, 347
Adorno, Theodor W., 150, 156n15, 158n32, 234, 244
Aesthetics, 22, 32, 181, 189, 190, 191, 327, 343, 350, 365, 369
Affectivity, 88, 173, 179, 181, 189
Agamben, Giorgio, 3, 11, 12, 115n6, 126, 195n13, 199–218, 229n2, 356, 357
Althusser, Louis, 152, 158n37, 245
Arendt, Hannah, 14, 15, 111, 157n17, 215n21, 250n51, 280, 301–21
Aristotle, 48, 51, 58, 69, 89, 137, 138, 141, 146, 153, 200, 205–7, 325, 332, 333, 335, 354
Art, 6, 11, 15, 23, 32, 66, 68, 76, 77, 144, 177, 181, 184–86, 188, 215n26, 240, 269, 279, 325–27
Artist(ic), 6, 160, 182–84, 186, 248n1, 326
Artwork, 6, 188, 192
Atheism, 63n17

Augustine, 227, 306
Autonomy, 31, 171, 174, 191, 194n8, 256, 262, 304, 311, 333, 336
Autonomism, 159, 171

Badiou, Alan, 7, 12, 13, 58, 203, 209, 234–48
Barthes, Roland, 195n14
Bazzicalupo, Laura, 2
Benjamin, Walter, 53, 54, 87, 212, 339n22
Berardi, Franco "Bifo," 10, 12, 160
Bergson, Henri, 59, 60, 84, 86, 88, 91, 354
Biopolitics, 4, 11, 15–17, 214n8, 234, 239, 357–59
Bloch, Ernst, 212
Bobbio, Norberto, 2
Bodei, Remo, 1, 2, 4, 8, 9, 99–101, 103–5, 107–15
Borruti, Silvana, 2
Bruno, Giordano, 4
Butler, Judith, 233, 302, 314, 320n30

Cacciari, Massimo, 5, 12, 63, 219, 220, 224–28, 339n22
Capitalism, 12, 13, 46, 47, 56, 141, 159, 160–65, 168, 170, 171, 173, 174, 193, 234, 236–42, 251, 302, 316, 317
Catholic(ism), 47, 56, 58, 193, 222

Cavarero, Adriana, 5, 14, 15, 257, 276, 301–19
Christ, 219, 225, 227
Christianity, 38, 56, 58, 73, 74, 77, 112, 226, 333, 339
Communism, 47, 56, 101, 165, 171, 200, 234, 235, 237, 241–48, 251
Communist, 13, 140, 201, 233, 242, 243, 244, 247, 252
Community, 11, 12, 21, 99, 101–4, 107, 113, 199–214, 219, 221, 227, 238, 244, 258, 259, 261, 267, 275, 276, 288, 314, 315, 317
Croce, Benedetto, 2, 23

Debord, Guy, 10
Deconstruction(ist), 16, 17, 77, 118, 125, 190, 201, 202, 214, 327, 334, 336, 342, 344, 353, 357, 358, 361
Deleuze, Gilles, 9, 10, 117, 132n7, 138, 143–51, 153–55, 166, 354, 358–61
Democracy, 6, 12, 50, 113, 174, 231–33, 244–47
Derrida, Jacques, 16, 17, 100, 117, 133n16, 140, 141, 209, 217n66, 336, 343, 353–62
Descartes, René, 31, 89, 138, 139, 153, 155n2, 330, 355, 356
Dialectics, 2, 3, 5, 150, 211, 215n18, 237, 241, 334, 336
Dilthey, Wilhelm, 74, 75
Domination, 13, 48, 166, 167, 169, 170, 173, 236, 243, 257, 262, 268, 295n2, 346

Earth (the), 28, 50, 51, 67, 220, 228, 278, 287, 309, 334
Eco, Umberto, 21, 104
Economy, 10, 12, 13, 186, 190, 215, 234, 241, 245, 246, 279, 359
Embodiment, 11, 165, 308, 320n30
Enlightenment, 16, 71, 178, 221, 222, 341

Equality, 3, 182, 241, 247, 264–70, 273n39, 276, 284, 303
Esposito, Roberto, 1–4, 16, 17, 99, 114, 118, 213n8
Evil, 6, 23, 27–31, 36–39, 61, 124, 184, 207, 220, 224, 225, 228, 315
Existentialism, 23, 33, 71

Feminism, 3, 14, 257, 260, 262, 276, 277, 280, 283, 284, 289
Ferraris, Maurizio, 16, 68, 341–43, 345, 348–51
Foucault, Michel, 3, 9, 16, 17, 71, 72, 111, 117, 119, 120, 123–25, 128, 129, 131, 168, 169, 213–14n8, 233, 314, 343, 344, 353–62
Freedom, 3, 5, 6, 21, 23, 24, 29–39, 52, 63n8, 87, 106–9, 168, 169, 171, 174, 244, 245, 247, 250n51, 251n57, 256, 258, 276, 281, 282, 288, 290–93, 295, 336, 338
Freud, Sigmund, 10, 51, 59, 110, 159–61, 165, 168, 169, 344, 359

Gadamer, Hans-Georg, 7, 39, 49, 65, 66, 68–73, 76, 77, 79n17, 100, 336
Gender, 140, 235, 255, 256, 270, 285, 342
Genealogy, 14, 123, 127, 282, 285, 286, 288, 289, 291, 292, 294, 295, 307, 316–19, 327, 354, 355, 357
Globalization, 12, 108, 231, 245
God, 7, 38, 45, 47, 49, 51, 56, 58, 61, 72, 73, 89, 94, 96, 97, 112, 139, 150, 152, 219–21, 223, 224, 226, 277–81, 283, 284, 286, 287, 294, 295, 304
Gramsci, Antonio, 9, 10, 137, 138, 143–48, 151–55, 157n15, 158n32, 295n2, 368
Guattari, Félix, 132n7, 146, 147, 166

Habermas, Jürgen, 65, 74

Hegel, Georg Wilhelm Friedrich, 9, 10, 13, 16, 23, 25, 31, 32, 72–76, 140, 151–53, 165, 170–72, 200, 255–59, 261, 262, 264, 266, 325, 330, 333, 334, 339, 348–50, 351, 354
Heidegger, Martin, 5–9, 15, 16, 21, 23–34, 36–39, 46–49, 51, 52, 54, 55, 58, 65–69, 71, 72, 74, 76, 77, 83–85, 87–90, 93, 95, 96, 115n9, 120, 126, 156n15, 200, 235, 242, 301, 312, 326, 327, 331–36, 338n2, 346, 347, 351, 354–59
Hermeneutics, 2, 3, 22, 23, 27, 38, 39, 51, 52, 54, 65–69, 71, 73–76, 327, 329, 331, 334, 336
History, 22–24, 38, 46, 48, 49, 54, 58, 66, 68–74, 86, 99, 100, 103, 106, 107, 109, 114, 144, 145, 165, 166, 177, 178, 187, 189, 201, 203, 205, 213, 219, 221, 226, 227, 242, 248, 255–63, 289, 294–95, 307, 315, 328, 333, 355–57, 360
Hobbes, Thomas, 224, 307, 315–19
Honneth, Axel, 233
Horkheimer, Max, 169
Husserl, Edmund, 9, 66, 69, 84, 88, 89, 91–93, 119, 133n20, 327, 328, 338n2, 342, 354

Idealism, 67, 151, 178, 234, 242, 247, 341
Identity, 3, 10, 48, 59, 62, 70, 88, 95, 99, 100, 103–9, 142, 143, 146, 148, 149–51, 153, 157n22, 158n34, 182, 183, 189, 193, 201, 202, 204, 208, 209, 255, 256, 261, 263, 270, 286, 288, 304–6, 333, 334, 350, 355
Ideology, 11, 22, 48, 55, 140, 141, 180, 185, 190, 192, 193, 195n13, 316, 319
Individuality, 8, 13, 70, 106, 146, 147, 237, 243, 265
Interaction, 16, 68–70, 276, 304

Irigaray, Luce, 14, 277, 283, 284, 286–89, 291, 292, 294

Jaspers, Karl, 6, 23, 31, 315, 316
Judaism, 339n22
Justice, 50, 221, 226, 231, 264–66, 289, 294, 342

Kant, Immanuel, 15, 16, 23, 33, 56, 69, 70, 76, 77, 78n14, 151–53, 327, 329–31, 333, 334, 336, 347–49, 351, 354
Kierkegaard, Søren, 23, 31
Kristeva, Julia, 14

Labor, 13, 143–45, 155–57, 160–64, 166, 168, 171–73, 233–39, 241, 244, 26, 247, 249n21, 250n51, 308, 313
Lacan, Jacques, 59, 63n17, 117, 191
Laclau, Ernesto, 233
Law, 37, 56, 206, 207, 214n10, 222, 224, 242, 244, 245, 261, 263, 265, 266, 284, 287, 307, 309, 317
Leibniz, Gottfried Wilhelm, 25, 26
Levinas, Emmanuel, 24
Locke, John, 70, 103
Lonzi, Carla, 2, 3, 5, 13, 14, 255–66, 269–71, 276
Lyotard, Jean-François, 341–43

Machiavelli, Niccolò, 4, 99
Marcuse, Herbert, 10, 159–62, 164, 166–74
Marramao, Giacomo, 2
Marx, Karl, 10, 15, 133n20, 138, 140–42, 148, 155, 160, 168, 171, 180, 231, 232, 234, 236–38, 241, 244, 245, 248, 251n57, 251n68, 256, 344, 359, 361
Marxism, 12, 133n20, 159, 165, 178, 234, 235, 240, 241, 244, 256, 341
Materialism, 67, 151, 152, 236
Materiality, 141, 193, 320n30
Maternal, 286, 288, 293, 298n35

Media, 10, 11, 56, 100, 108, 182, 192, 195, 233, 251n57
Mediation, 72, 109–12, 114, 170, 179, 184, 186, 242, 262, 287–89, 291–93
Meillassoux, Quentin, 7, 58
Metaphysics, 3, 4, 7, 24–28, 34, 36, 46, 48, 51, 55, 58, 60, 67, 69, 72, 74, 75, 77, 151, 186, 187, 189, 199, 201, 203, 221, 222, 325, 331–33, 335, 346
Modernity, 2, 8, 15, 54, 58, 71, 118, 178, 220, 226, 242, 342, 348
Mother(hood), 14, 261, 269, 275, 280–83, 286–95, 296n6, 302–4, 307, 310, 312, 320n25
Mouffe, Chantal, 233
Multitude (the), 12, 173, 235, 237, 239, 244, 246, 248, 317
Muraro, Luisa, 2, 3, 5, 14, 275–84, 286–89, 291–95

Natality, 280, 302, 303, 306–8, 310, 312, 313, 317–19, 320n25
Natoli, Salvatore, 2
Nancy, Jean-Luc, 8, 9, 11, 100–114, 199–212, 301, 315, 354, 355, 357, 358
Negri, Antonio, 5, 10, 12, 13, 159, 173, 231, 234–40, 243, 244–48, 295n2
Neoliberal(ism), 12, 58, 163, 193, 233, 316
Nietzsche, Friedrich, 7, 16, 26, 39, 46, 50, 54, 55, 65, 66, 71–73, 75, 77, 114, 154, 327, 337, 342, 344–47, 350, 351, 354–56, 359
Nihilism, 6, 15, 27, 39, 45–49, 51, 52, 54, 55, 58, 61, 71, 73, 74, 351
Nothing(ness), 5, 6, 23–31, 33–39, 46–58, 60–62, 63n17, 69, 70, 75, 84, 85, 90, 91, 94, 102, 103, 128–30, 132, 139–42, 145, 146, 149, 153, 154, 155n2, 178, 187, 234, 277, 279, 307, 309, 333, 335

Objectivity, 72, 141, 148, 222, 263, 337, 342, 343, 346
Ontology, 5–7, 9, 11, 12, 14–16, 21, 23, 24, 27, 30, 32–37, 66–69, 71–76, 84, 85, 99–103, 107, 110, 147, 148, 199–204, 207, 211, 212, 236, 240, 241, 246, 247, 301, 302, 304–6, 310, 312, 313, 315–18, 333, 345, 346, 349, 351, 354, 355

Paci, Enzo, 9, 133n20
Pareyson, Luigi, 3, 5–8, 10, 21–39, 65, 71, 87
Parmenides, 7, 46, 49–51, 58–60, 67, 336
Particularity, 3, 22, 126, 129
Pascal, Blaise, 23, 32
Passion, 8, 50, 150, 186, 257, 275, 277
Peirce, Charles Sanders, 9, 119, 126
Performance, 8, 9, 117, 118, 130, 162, 182, 185, 252n76, 327
Performativity, 181, 182, 192
Perone, Ugo, 2, 8, 21, 83–85, 87–92, 95–97
Perniola, Mario, 2, 10, 11, 21, 177–89, 191–93
Pfaller, Robert, 10, 11, 177, 191, 192, 195n13
Phenomenology, 37, 66, 84, 88, 93, 94, 171, 181, 303, 327, 338n2, 348, 350, 354
Plato(nic), 46, 49–51, 58–61, 67, 68, 72, 74–76, 111, 118, 151, 153, 242, 279, 325, 330, 336, 354, 356, 361
Plotinus, 23, 32, 35
Plurality, 3, 4, 49, 103, 203, 211, 267, 301, 302–7, 309–13, 315, 317–19
Politics, 2, 3, 11–14, 106, 109, 115n6, 118, 166, 181, 185, 190, 199, 200, 204, 207, 211, 212, 215n26, 222, 234, 235, 238–41, 243, 245, 246, 251, 255, 256, 264, 265, 269–71, 283, 287–89, 302–4, 306, 315, 316, 318, 358

Postmodernism, 15, 16, 71, 74, 77, 341–43, 350, 351
Postmodernity, 16, 341–43, 345, 346, 348, 349
Potentiality, 6, 67, 90, 186, 200, 204–9, 211, 215, 239, 246, 247
Practice, 9, 14, 33, 34, 117–32, 166, 190, 193, 196n15, 233, 239, 242, 246, 255, 256, 271, 276, 277, 280, 281, 288–94, 295n2, 299n59, 315, 327, 334, 344
Pragmatism, 119
Proletariat, 140
Pulcini, Elena, 2

Realism, 4, 7, 15, 16, 58, 63n19, 67–69, 166, 183–85, 342–51, 357
Religion, 6, 11, 15, 45, 47, 51, 108, 188, 196n15, 227, 244, 326
Renaissance, 4, 65
Responsibility, 37, 87, 112, 180, 210, 225, 310, 311, 314, 315, 318
Revolution(ary), 8, 14, 53, 171, 178, 222, 223, 235, 238, 243, 255, 256, 263, 269, 280, 284, 288, 291
Ricoeur, Paul, 39n1
Romanticism, 167, 234, 244
Rousseau, Jean-Jacques, 33
Rovatti, Pier Aldo, 72, 357

Sartre, Jean-Paul, 31, 33, 235, 248n3
Schmitt, Carl, 12, 219–25, 228
Secularization, 8, 12, 58, 73, 221, 222, 224
Semiotic(s), 9, 104, 119, 165
Semantic(s), 188, 343, 355, 358
Severino, Emanuele, 3, 5–7, 24, 45–61, 335
Sexual difference, 5, 13, 14, 256–59, 261, 262, 264–68, 270, 271, 276, 277, 282–84, 286, 288–92, 294
Sexuality, 11, 169, 194n8
Singularity, 8, 103, 106, 139, 146, 182, 202–4, 208, 209, 267, 270, 314

Sini, Carlo, 3, 9, 24, 117–25, 127–32, 326, 339n22
Socialism, 167, 200
Spinoza, Baruch, 150, 157n28
Stein, Edith, 8, 83, 88–97
Struggle, 13, 123, 162, 189, 210, 220, 235–39, 241, 246, 248, 252n76, 256, 258–63, 276, 280, 285, 293, 294, 333
Subjectivity, 4, 12, 70, 86, 88, 161, 162, 167, 168, 189, 191, 193, 194n8, 234, 235, 239, 246–48, 252n76, 258, 265–68, 304, 317, 360

Technology, 2, 10, 30, 46, 48, 49, 74, 108, 146, 194n9, 221, 222, 235, 248, 251n68
Temporality, 8, 54, 56, 83–85, 89, 93, 98n7, 156n15, 173
Theology, 7, 8, 12, 49, 58, 221–25, 228, 242, 281
Totalitarianism, 15, 22, 164, 167, 201, 302, 306, 313–15
Tronti, Mario, 2, 5, 12, 295n2

Universality, 3, 22, 77, 166, 193, 247, 259, 266–68, 270
Utopia(n), 174, 311

Vattimo, Gianni, 3, 5, 7, 8, 15, 16, 21, 24, 65–68, 71–77, 339n22, 342, 343, 345–48, 350, 351, 357
Veca, Salvatore, 2
Vico, Giambattista, 4, 99, 156n10, 327
Virno, Paolo, 2, 160, 171
Vitiello, Vincenzo, 2, 3, 5, 15, 325–37
Vulnerability, 15, 301–3, 310–12, 314–19

Weak Thought, 5, 7, 15, 16, 65, 68, 72, 346, 347, 357
Weber, Max, 166, 221

Žižek, Slavoj, 10, 11, 177, 191, 195n13, 233, 238

www.ingramcontent.com/pod-product-compliance
Lightning Source LLC
Chambersburg PA
CBHW020120240426
43673CB00038B/543